AMERICANS AND FREE ENTERPRISE

Henry C. Dethloff
Texas A & M University

PRENTICE-HALL, INC., Englewood Cliffs, New Jersey 07632

Library of Congress Cataloging in Publication Data

DETHLOFF, HENRY C.
  Americans and free enterprise.

  Includes bibliographies and index.
  1. United States—Economic conditions.
2. Capitalism. I. Title.
HC103.Dr3   330.9'73   78-15515
ISBN 0-13-032490-6

We gratefully acknowledge:
Dictionary of American Portraits. Hayward Cirker and Blanche Cirker. Ed. by Dover
Editorial Staff. New York: Dover, 1967. For the portraits on the following pages: 15, 52,
62, 73, 80, 85, 89, 150, 151, 152, 159, 165, 169, 172, 188, 215, 219, 235, 248, 273,
287, 311.

Printed in the United States of America

10   9   8   7   6   5   4   3   2   1

Prentice-Hall International, Inc., *London*
Prentice-Hall of Australia Pty. Limited, *Sydney*
Prentice-Hall of Canada, Ltd., *Toronto*
Prentice-Hall of India Private Limited, *New Delhi*
Prentice-Hall of Japan, Inc., *Tokyo*
Prentice-Hall of Southeast Asia Pte. Ltd., *Singapore*
Whitehall Books Limited, *Wellington, New Zealand*

to
Myrtle Anne

CONTENTS

PREFACE

This text is a concise narrative history of the American experience with capitalism. Economic history is concerned not only with how we organized in times past for the production and distribution of goods and services, but why we do it the way we do today. The text incorporates an awareness of the cultural values and social forces that have affected the growth and development of American economic life. It reviews from the perspective of the average American in today's society those concepts and problems most pertinent to life today—the land and the environment, government's changing role in the economy, the "value" problem of authority versus liberty, the role of technology (knowledge at work), and the concepts of abundance, welfare, economic growth, and free enterprise. It considers historically such problems as inflation and depression and studies such areas of development as agriculture, industry, business, and labor by correlating today's experiences with those of the past. By this technique we better understand not only what happened in the past but what is happening today. Our past is but a prologue to the present, and we can best comprehend our present in the context of past experiences. The development of the American free-enterprise system is an intensely historical process that is, in part, an expression of the values, goals, aspirations, and culture of the American people.

Every adult American is involved in economics and economic history. How we make a living, and why we do it the way we do, is much on the national consciousness in this age when the American people have achieved an unparalleled level of material abundance. Our abundance has created both new opportunities and new problems. We are concerned with both the quantity and with the quality of life. We are concerned about population explosions in the non-Western world, underdeveloped nations, minority groups, personal liberties, monolithic government, energy and natural resources, and national security—all of which are pertinent to our economic life.

Inasmuch as this concern is very broad-based, and of particular moment to those who are or who will soon be entering the business of life in a variety of endeavors, this presentation is not highly specialized or technical. I hope it is clear, readable, and informative. The presentation includes tables, graphs, and illustrations that condense thousands of words into a comprehensive base for analysis and review. I hope that readers will seize the opportunity to supplement, enlarge upon, and evaluate special problems through the use of appropriate data and technical analysis, and that supplemental reading will be used profitably in conjunction with this study. Use of the readings listed at the end of each chapter is strongly encouraged.

Like the American economy, economic history has experienced a technological revolution in recent decades—the application of cliometrics, or the analysis of quantitative data, to historical problems. The traditional or "old economic history" examines the historical development of the economy through a narrative, qualitative analysis of change in a broad cultural and chronological context. The job of the historian is to discover the facts of "history as it happened" and to selectively relate this information to the contemporary reader in a meaningful way. Through sophisticated data analysis made possible by the computer, we can achieve a more definitive and accurate reconstruction of the past. Studies by the "new economic historians" have created both controversy and progress in economic history. Although some of the mathematical constructions used by cliometrics are highly technical, their purpose and intent and the product of their methodology is quite intelligible to the layman. This text notes some of the problems investigated and conclusions reached by the new economic historians and provides limited insight into their methodology, while retaining the framework of traditional economic history.

From a different perspective, Adam Smith, John Calvin, Charles Darwin, Herbert Spencer, Thorstein Veblen, and John Maynard Keynes are economists and philosophers whose ideas are as much a part of our present as they are of our past. We must know them better. Their ideas, and some correlation of their ideas with present circumstances, are briefly introduced in layman's terms. Because the economy is a broad cultural phenomenon, effort is made to draw upon the contributions of historians, geographers, sociologists, political scientists, and journalists who have helped promote an understanding of economic development. Economic *development* implies an increase in, or the capacity to increase, the quantity of goods and services produced by a society. It also implies structural alterations—changes in the mix of the factors of production, including natural resources, labor, and capital. The supply of and demand for resources and goods constantly changes, requiring a constant reproportioning of the factors of production. For example, as croplands or labor became more scarce, the application of greater capital (including technology and equipment) may be more cost-efficient. Economic *growth* or expansion requires an increase in the real value of goods and services on a per-capita basis. Neither economic growth nor economic development, as commonly used, measures the quality of life in terms of non-material social goals or aspirations, the quality of goods produced, or the equity resulting from the way in which goods are distributed within the society. Historians must not only identify the quantitative measurements of economic growth and development but evaluate historical change in the nonquantitative dimension of values and social goals. Ultimately, economic growth and economic development require value judgments. In presenting narrative history and in utilizing econometric data, historians evaluate the past from the context of the values of their own time and their personal conception of those values.

I am well aware of the limitations inherent in an abbreviated, essentially nontechnical study. The advantages of such a study is that it provides in a readable format the necessary broader historical dimensions within which more intensive and technical studies will gain greater significance. I hope this study offers insight into many of the questions of contemporary economic concern. Most important, I hope the book will prove as enlightening and enjoyable to the general reader as it was to the author in the writing of it.

I appreciate very much the assistance and encouragement given by David Schob, Keith Bryant, John Allen, and other friends and colleagues at Texas A&M University. The comment and direction provided by the many readers of the manuscript in its formative stages have been most helpful. I appreciate too the typing assistance provided by the College of Liberal Arts and the Department of History; I am very grateful to Rosa Richardson, Carole Knapp, Gloria West, and Vicki Ernst for their excellent typing skills and knowledgeable assistance. Brian Walker, my editor, has been a pillar of support. My special thanks to my family, who have been very understanding during my long and rather intensive preoccupation with this book.

Henry C. Dethloff

FREE ENTERPRISE

 chapter I

Americans are considered rich by most people of the world. Their wealth overshadows all their other attributes or liabilities. The American impact on the world since World War II cannot be measured in terms of democracy, humanitarianism, or charity; nor in terms of Christianity, godliness, or innate goodness; not even in terms of military power. More realistically, the American impact can be measured by the dollar. American money has rebuilt much of a world destroyed by war, fed millions of people who would otherwise have starved, armed millions who would otherwise have fought and likely been defeated without arms, and armed some who would never have fought at all. American money has in the twentieth century alienated much of the affection the world developed for Americans in earlier centuries. We have become Eugene Burdick's "Ugly Americans."

ABUNDANCE

Many people admired us more when we were poorer. For example, contemporary Philippine historians are critical of the American impact on the lives of the Filipinos and point an accusing finger at the American cult of materialism.

> The "movies" have been the purveyor of American materialism; for they show the advantages of having flashy cars, mink coats, large and well-appointed houses, refrigerators, television and radio sets, and such other appurtenances as would make for "success." Success is measured in terms of material possessions. He is successful who earns a "fast buck," he is successful who has made millions out of nothing; he is successful if, in spite of his illiteracy, he wins a congressional or municipal seat. The people as a rule have lost their sense of values. Values to them are those that can be turned into hard cash; if they are not or cannot, they are valueless.

1

But, conclude the authors of this quotation, "the Filipinos continue thinking of America and the Americans with something akin to awe."[1] What Americans have done is awesome.

United States foreign aid from September 2, 1945 through December 31, 1970 totaled $123 billion. At the close of World War II, Congress appropriated $3.4 billion to aid the needy in war-torn areas. The Marshall Plan, designed to provide relief, enhance economic recovery, and promote political stability in Europe, was approved by Congress in 1948. By mid 1952, this program had delivered $9 billion in economic aid and $2 billion in loans to Europe. Point IV technical-aid programs (1949), the Alliance for Progress (1961), the Peace Corps (1961), the International Monetary Fund (1944), and various United Nations agencies have absorbed billions of American dollars. Of the $123 billion of American foreign aid from 1945 through 1970, approximately one third took the form of military assistance, a large portion of this going to Korea and South Vietnam. The United States had, in fact, emerged from the war with most of the world's money, and its people enjoyed the highest standard of living.

The American people constitute about 5 percent of the world's population. They consume about one third of the world's energy. American imports and exports accounted for 28 percent of world trade in 1973, down slightly from their high of 33 percent in 1948. In 1970, the median income of American families was nearly $10,000. Per capita production is greater in the United States than in any other country, as are per capita expenditures. The American national income exceeded $1 trillion in 1973. The American people own and operate about half of the world's motor vehicles. In 1970 alone, Americans bought over 4 million

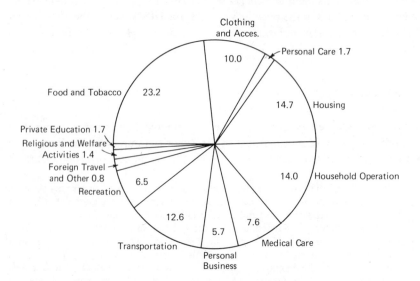

FIGURE 1.1 How Americans spend their dollar (1970).

Source: Historical Statistics of the U.S. Colonial Times to 1970, Series G. 416–469.

electric ranges (at an average cost of $229), 7,382,000 electric vacuum cleaners ($68), 5,286,000 electric refrigerators ($274), and 9,483,000 television sets ($400). The proportion of Americans who can afford a college education and a nutritional diet during "hard times" is larger than that of most peoples of the world during "good times."

Table 1.1 lists the value of goods and services produced per capita by the United States and ten representative nations in 1976. In that year the gross national product (GNP) of the United States was estimated by the Union Bank of Switzerland to be $1,692 trillion, almost three times the GNP of the Soviet Union. Of 160 nations surveyed by the Union Bank, only 49 had a per capita GNP of over $1,000. Figure 1.1 illustrates how Americans spend their wealth, and Tables 1.2–1.4 profile their consumption of food, automobiles, and energy.

TABLE 1.1

Per Capita Wealth of the United States and Selected Nations (1976).

Kuwait	$12,565
Switzerland	9,320
Sweden	8,995
Canada	8,090
United States	7,865
Japan	4,920
Saudi Arabia	4,665
Britain	3,940
Israel	3,565
Soviet Union	2,620

Source: Union Bank of Switzerland

TABLE 1.2

The Foods Americans Eat (Pounds per Capita), 1970.

Red meat	186.2
Poultry	50.4
Fish	14.8
Eggs (number)	319.0
Milk and cream	264.0
Cheese	11.5
Butter	5.3
Margarine	11.0
Fats and oils	40.0
Fresh fruits	82.0
Potatoes, sweet potatoes	123.8
Sugar	102.5
Corn products	28.1
Wheat flour	110.0
Coffee	13.8
Cocoa	3.9

Source: U.S. Department of Agriculture.

TABLE 1.3

Automobile Factory Sales (Passenger Cars), 1900–1975.

1900	4,192	1940	3,717,385
1905	24,250	1945	69,532
1910	181,000	1950	6,665,863
1915	895,530	1955	7,920,186
1920	1,905,560	1960	6,674,796
1925	3,735,171	1965	9,305,561
1930	2,787,456	1970	6,546,817
1935	3,273,874	1975	6,713,000

Source: Motor Vehicle Manufacturers Association, Detroit, Michigan.

TABLE 1.4

U.S. Energy Consumption

SOURCES OF ENERGY PRODUCTION AND CONSUMPTION

| | Production | | | | Consumption | | | |
| | Total (quad. Btu) | Coal | Percent Petro-leum[1] | Natural gas[2] | Total (quad. Btu) | Coal | Percent Petro-leum[1] | Natural gas[2] |
Year								
1850	.2	100.0	na	na	.2	100.0	na	na
1875	1.5	96.6	3.4	na	1.5	99.2	.8	na
1900	7.9	88.9	4.7	3.2	7.6	90.3	3.0	3.3
1910	15.4	85.0	7.9	3.6	14.8	85.9	6.8	3.6
1920	21.4	80.4	12.0	4.1	19.8	78.4	13.3	4.4
1930	22.1	63.3	23.5	9.7	22.3	61.2	25.4	9.9
1940	25.1	53.3	31.3	11.9	23.9	52.4	31.3	12.4
1950	34.5	42.4	33.2	19.8	34.2	37.8	37.2	20.3
1960	41.6	26.8	35.3	34.0	44.6	22.8	41.8	31.7
1970	62.5	24.1	32.6	38.7	67.1	18.9	40.3	36.5
1975[3]	60.1	25.8	29.5	36.9	71.1	18.8	42.6	31.8

na   Not available. [1]Includes petroleum products. [2]Marketed production of natural gas, wet consumption includes dry and liquid gas. [3]Preliminary.

ELECTRIC ENERGY PRODUCTION AND CAPACITY

(Includes industrial establishments)

Item		1902	1920	1940	1960	1970	1975
Net production	bil. kWh	6	57	180	842	1,602	2,000
Percent steam generated		64	64	69	81	82	83
Installed capacity	mil. kW	3	19	51	186	361	525
Percent private utilities		37	62	67	69	73	76
Production per kW	1,000 kWh	2.1	3.1	3.6	4.5	4.4	3.8

U.S. Bureau of the Census, *Bicentennial Statistics.* Reprinted from Pocket Data Book, USA 1976.

Btu = British thermal unit. Quad. = Quadrillion.

"It approaches the commonplace, then, to observe that . . . relative abundance is . . . a basic condition of American life," notes David Potter in his intriguing study of the impact of abundance on the American character. "We have not sufficiently considered," he says, "the pervasive influence of abundance upon many aspects of our lives which have no obvious relation to the standard of living. For certainly it is an influence that impinges upon all American social conditions and contributes in the most fundamental way to the shaping of the American culture and the American character."[2]

If a measure of human success is the procurement of the food, clothing, and shelter necessary for survival, then Americans individually have enjoyed remarkable success. If the measure of a governing system's success is the procurement of the best possible sustenance for the largest possible number of people, then the American government has largely succeeded. Indeed, the material welfare of the American people has been second to none. This is not to say that there are no problems, no poverty, no unemployment, no starvation. But it is to say that in all of human experience there have been few occasions where so many people could live as well as they do in America and in the world at large.

Have Americans become so entranced by the cult of materialism that their entire existence has become a quest for the almighty dollar? Critics of modern society argue that this is in fact the case. But it can also be suggested that only with the satisfaction of humanity's animal needs can the person become wholly human. The modern economy is concerned not solely with group survival but with human, as opposed to merely animal, existence. The American economy is in part an expression of American humanity, of the values, goals, and religious and political aspirations of the American people. An economy is a reflection of a people's culture. It is, of course, concerned preeminently with the production and distribution of goods and services.

CAPITALISM

From the earliest days of civilization, a national economy has been an intrinsic and key mechanism in the struggle for survival. A national economy is the group response—be it through a monarchy, constitution, congress, or junta—to the need for cooperation in order to best promote the interests and survival of the individuals within the group. The "group," of course, need not always reflect the best interests of the majority. "The greatest good for the greatest number" does not reflect the purposes of most of the world's socioeconomic systems over the past six or eight thousand years. The few have been known to sacrifice the interests of the many in order to promote their own fortunes. Similarly, the many have been known to destroy the few in order to obtain a greater share of the available resources. The patrician order in the Roman Empire excluded the far more populous plebeian order. The European aristocratic societies controlled the wealth of the nations. Historian Henri Pirenne, seeing the historic persistence of oligarchic control of wealth, argues that social progress necessarily springs from below. Each new phase of economic development comes from classes that rise from humble origins.[3] Through most of its civilized existence, then, humankind has tread the precarious line between absolute monarchy or dictatorship on the one hand and democracy shadowing on anarchy on the other hand. An economic order constantly changes. The prime purpose of all this change is to determine how people should organize in order to be productive and, once productive, to provide the basis for orderly allocation among the members of the group.

This is what capitalism is all about. It prescribes a way of organizing in order to produce and establishes rules for the distribution of the fruits of people's labor. First, modern capitalism prescribes that property, real and personal, be autonomous and private. It is to be owned by the individual within the society, and it should be transferable. Second, there must be a free market that facilitates the transfer of property in response to supply and demand. Third, there must be a technology or kowledge that supports innovation, mechanization, and trade. Fourth, the institutional framework of capitalism, prominently the law and political structure, must be stable, rational, equitable, and reasonably dependable. The law is the bulwark of rights in the area of private property. Fifth, there must be free labor. A labor supply must exist, and labor must have the incentive to produce. Finally, there must be a commercialization of economic life. This requires the existence of the instruments that represent a share in capitalistic enterprise—money, corporate stocks, bonds, leases, titles, contracts, and the general paraphernalia of business.

The *marketplace* in a capitalist society is the point or place at which an exchange of goods or services occurs. An autonomous economic unit, such as a household, firm, or individual, indicates a desire for certain goods or services, thereby creating a *demand*, and may simultaneously offer or *supply* other goods or services in exchange. A unit, or individual, that can supply the goods wanted and is satisfied in its own needs or demands with the goods being offered may accept the exchanges. If the exchange of goods and services is negotiated on the basis of money, as it almost necessarily is in a sophisticated and complex society, the rate of exchange sets the monetary *price* or value of each good or service being transferred. The market, then, coordinates the activities of each economic unit in an economy and guides resources into their most efficient or "valuable" use.

In theory, free enterprise assumes the absence of external direction or controls on individuals in their negotiations at the marketplace. In this sense there is no "pure" free-enterprise or capitalist system, for any government imposes legal constraints on the individual's production and consumption of goods and services, as well as providing nonmarket stimulants. Such constraints or incentives, at least in democratic societies, are voluntary. Nonetheless, to the extent that governments impose an external control on the exchange of goods and services in the marketplace, they create a mixed economy rather than a pure free-enterprise system. When the exchange of goods and services is controlled or *directed* predominantly by a government or central authority rather than determined by the independent, or individual units, the free-enterprise system has been supplanted by a *command system*. Americans generally believe that self-interest, private ownership and control of property, competition, and a free market result in a more efficient, productive, expansive, and mutually beneficial economic order. Free enterprise best answers the questions of *what* to produce, *how* to produce, and *to whom* the fruits of production are to be distributed.

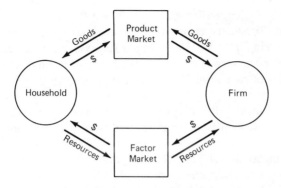

FIGURE 1.2. Circular-Flow diagram.

No economic unit can continue to buy or consume without also supplying something. In a free-enterprise system, each unit should be able to consume as much as it can afford. In other words, according to ability. The economy, through the instrument of the marketplace, develops a circular flow (Figure 1.2) wherein each household buys in the *product market* from a firm and sells in the *factor market* to a firm. The product market distributes goods and services according to need and the ability to pay for them, and the factor market absorbs resources, labor, and capital in order to produce the goods and services demanded. Thus, laborers will sell their skills and time at the best price they can command, and they will absorb those goods or services commensurate with their wages. Both the household and the firm seek to maximize the return on their activity, either through more profit or higher wages.

The value of all goods and services exchanged in an economy constitutes the total wealth or activity of that economy. It provides an index of a society's well-being, or gross national product—the value of all goods and services produced. Economic growth requires a per capita increase in the output of a society. If a society's production expands less rapidly than its population, the welfare of many of the individuals within the society declines.

STAGES OF CAPITALIST DEVELOPMENT

It is convenient to speak of capitalism with a modifying adjective, for there are different kinds or degrees of capitalism. Capitalism is not a static or eternal state of humankind's socioeconomic organization. It changes with the times, with technology, with necessity, and with changing human values and aspirations. Successes and failures effect changes in the concept of capitalism—that is, in what people believe capitalism to be.

N. S. B. Gras traces capitalist development through five major stages: (1)

7

petty capitalism, (2) mercantile capitalism, (3) industrial capitalism, (4) financial capitalism, and (5) national capitalism.[4] These stages can be conveniently diagramed as shown in Figure 1.3. Each of these stages is delineated from the others by some unique phenomenon or characteristic, yet all retain to some extent the basic ingredients of capitalism. The stages can be identified as follows:

1. *Petty Capitalism.*   Private property, free labor, craft skills (or technology), and a supportive institutional framework, such as indulgent feudal lords, are in evidence. Trade, the commercial instruments—such as notes, stocks, and bonds—and the free market are primitive or nonexistent. The feudal town marketplace where food, vendors, tailors, cobblers, and goldsmiths deal on a one-to-one basis with their customers exemplify petty capitalism.

2. *Mercantile Capitalism.*   The scale of operations has expanded markedly. Commercial instruments, a more adequate money supply—made possible by the rise of private bankers—and an advanced technology devoted largely to the movement of goods to more distant points—such as the compass and cartography, the astrolabe and navigation, and improved ship design—exist. The law is applied more equitably and uniformly to more and more people, consequent with the rise of the nation-state. A free market is developing. Government begins to play an active role in directing economic activity. For example, Spain finances part of Christopher Columbus's voyage in order to find new opportunities for trade.

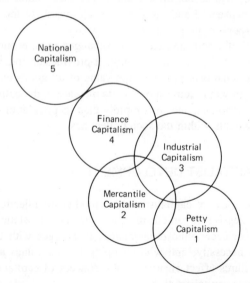

FIGURE 1.3. The development of capitalist systems.

3. *Industrial Capitalism.* New technology—that is, knowledge at work and inventions—is harnessed more to the production than to the distribution of goods. There is a marriage of the mercantile capitalist with technology. The corporate structure emerges. The national bank (such as the Bank of England, the Bank of the United States, and the Bank of France) emerges, and is increasingly responsive to commercial and industrial interests. The law is more rational and universal. The absolute monarchy declines or ceases altogether, and the uncertainty and whims of a single ruler who might do injury to laws affecting rights in property are thereby eliminated. The domestic market is relatively free and well developed.

4. *Financial Capitalism.* The instruments of modern capitalism are full-blown. The managers of industry, such as Jay Cooke, Andrew Carnegie, and J. P. Morgan in the United States, increasingly become the absentee bankers and brokers. The economy has become distinctly national, interrelated, and highly sophisticated. The government and law are responsive to the dictates and ideology of the business elite. Mass production and mass consumption are the rule, but the masses fail to share equitably in the distribution of goods. Large segments of the society question the socioeconomic order and seek to improve, alter, or, on occasion, destroy it. Capitalism and democracy have a day of reckoning.

5. *National (or State) Capitalism.* Where capitalism has survived this day of reckoning, its form is sufficiently altered for it to appear detached from the evolutionary processes of capitalism (see Figure 1.3). Its outstanding characteristic is that *property remains private, but control over that property is largely public.* Democracy has dictated a more equitable distribution of goods than previously allowed by the free market. Counter-depression public expenditures, including high taxation, have occurred, as has labor legislation regulating hours and wages, price controls, and on occasion some nationalization of service industries. Some economic historians believe the United States is now entering the phase of national capitalism.

Joseph Schumpeter, an American economic historian, believes that in this fifth stage capitalism is being kept alive in an oxygen tent. This stage of capitalism occurs not because of a defused Marxian revolution, but because capitalist enterprise tends to make itself superfluous by its very achievements. The continuing consolidation of business, the automation of "progress," "invention," and the entrepreneurial functions, and the depersonalized and "absentee" ownership achieved by welfare economics undermines the support for the primacy of private property and free enterprise. In other words, the relatively fewer farmers and landowners, the larger the proportion of retired persons drawing social security and no longer dependent on the wage market, the greater the number of public employees, the fewer there are who really care about private property, a free market, and profits.[5] Despite the changes, the folklore of capitalism is so well entrenched that there is really little or no overt opposition to capitalism. Indeed, ''progressive'' changes in the capitalist system in America have almost invariably been justified in the name of preserving or purifying capitalism.

President Wilson's inaugural address in 1913 illustrates the pressures for changes in the older capitalist order, pressures that have not abated since that time:

> We have built up . . . a great system of government, which has stood through a long age as in many respects a model for those who seek to set liberty upon foundations that will endure against . . . storm and accident. Our life contains every great thing, and contains it in rich abundance.
>
> But the evil has come with the good. . . . With riches has come inexcusable waste. We have squandered a great part of what we might have used and have not stopped to conserve the exceeding bounty of nature. . . . We have been proud of our industrial achievements, but we have not hitherto stopped thoughtfully enough to count the human cost, the cost of lives snuffed out, or energies overtaxed and broken. . . . The great government we loved has too often been made use of for private and selfish purposes, and those who used it had forgotten the people.
>
> . . . Our duty is to cleanse, to reconsider, to restore, to correct the evil without impairing the good, to purify and humanize every process of our common life. . . . There has been something crude and heartless and unfeeling in our haste to succeed and be great.[6]

Sixty years later, Wilson's observations are no less pertinent.

Whatever form it has assumed, capitalism has been synonymous with ''Americanism'' for the past two hundred years. American support for free enterprise derives from a European heritage, but one untrammeled by Europe's more ancient feudal and Catholic heritage, its monarchical institutions, and its relatively more limited resources. Because it was not enmeshed in the trappings of a preexisting feudal order, capitalism found a more fertile ideological ground in America than in Europe and became more than a rote economic routine or structure. More accurately, it became a way of life—free enterprise.

One of the reasons for the instant appeal of free enterprise in America was simply that there was enough to go around. The natural wealth of America was conducive to a system of distribution based upon individual effort, acquisition, and ownership. Abundance has been the key ingredient in the working and survival of capitalism in the United States. As David Potter and even the earliest commentators on American life, such as Hector St. John de Crevecoeur, observed, the abundance of Americans has been endemic to American-style capitalism. Capitalism, if it had meant sustained exploitation of the masses, the deprivation of personal liberty, or the destruction of democratic processes, could not have survived even in America. But it did not mean that. On the contrary, capitalism, liberty, and democracy have for most Americans been synonymous. The American socioeconomic system is best styled the free-enterprise system, which, though distinctly capitalistic, invokes liberty, freedom of choice, equality of opportunity, and a degree of humanity that may escape the more narrow concept of capitalism. Capitalism suggests economics (the marketplace, profits, supply and demand); free enterprise argues a broader social organization, one in which individuals operate as independent decision makers and tradition and central authority exert a lesser influence than is true in other societies. Americans have perhaps been more free-enterprising than capitalistic. Although it may be redundant to say so, Americans *care* about free enterprise; their ideas of capitalism are frankly confused. Thomas Jefferson, for example, equated liberty and democracy with economic self-sufficiency, not with survival of the fittest, profits, or exploitation. So have most Americans considered free enterprise a way of life rather than an economic system. Being a "way of life," free enterprise is much more tolerant of diversity, inconsistency, and change than capitalism might be.

American ideological support for free enterprise stems from very strong *political*, *economic*, *religious*, and *environmental* roots, each conveniently identified by representative spokesmen. The political persuasion, for example, follows the Enlightenment precepts of such men as Voltaire and Rousseau, who rejected the *ancien régime* with the notion of a great natural law applicable to society everywhere and critical of injustice and inefficiency in government. Interestingly, these French thinkers were in turn influenced by reports from America of primitive tribes in which the "Noble Savage" lived in a state of nature, without poverty, wealth, or class distinction. A belief in a natural law, in the basic equality of humans, and in just and equitable laws, and a concern for rationality and efficiency that derives largely from the Enlightenment, provided the fabric from which the American free-enterprise system would be woven.

CALVINISM

The religious sentiments of the English settlers in America strongly accorded with the precepts of the Enlightenment. Humans were equal under God, to be blessed or damned by God. Their understanding of God's will could be achieved through individual study of God's word, and through prayer. According to the Calvinistic doctrine, which undergirded Presbyterian, Puritan, and Anglican beliefs, salvation or damnation was preordained. And if humanity was damned or saved from the beginning, no church hierarchy could alter that condition. But rather than holding merely a dismal doctrine of predestination, the Calvinist believed that the "elect" were blessed and favored by God. Their election, the individuals of the lay congregation came to believe, could be determined by their adherence to religious observances that had been prescribed quite literally by John Calvin. Thus, church attendance, tithing, abstinence, and religious decorum reflected one's state of grace. Moreover, God obviously blessed those who were among the elect. God "called" one to perform tasks or to enter business. American Puritanism increasingly came to hold, although it constituted an aberration of Calvinism, that God's blessings included the earthly comforts. Thus, a good indicator of one's state of grace came to be one's material welfare. God would not favor the damned with material comforts. It was an easy if not inevitable step to the superficial conclusion that if one wants to attain salvation (or know that one is saved), he or she must become rich. The "Protestant ethic" in America thus became a powerful stimulus to the free-enterprise system. Go out, get rich, and be saved. Even so, extravagance, sloth, and idleness had no place in the Protestant ethic. The American Puritan and contemporary American Protestants held an ambivalent attitude toward wealth. God forbade indolence and a lack of industry by either the rich or the poor. Wealth, then, led to temptation, and the wealthy were properly objects of suspicion.

Nonetheless, the Protestant ethic has strongly supported the American's acquisitive instincts. Benjamin Franklin's homilies, for example, presented a morality based on hard work and thrift. "Early to bed, and early to rise, makes a man healthy, wealthy and wise" is advice "Poor Richard" has given Americans for two hundred years. "Poor Richard" also suggested that "he that hath a trade hath an estate, and he that hath a calling, hath an office of profit and honor."[7] Max Weber observed in 1930 that Calvinism "released the businessman from the clutches of the priest, and sprinkled holy water on economic success." In the 1920s, Calvin Coolidge attached a definite religious ethic to modern industrialism with the observation that "he who builds a factory, builds a temple" and "he who works there, worships there." Andrew Carnegie's "Gospel of Wealth" holds that the wealthy or successful businessmen are anointed by God as trustees or custodians of his resources. Hard work, thrift, and virtue are very much alive in the American conception of free enterprise.

LAISSEZ FAIRE

Adam Smith's economic theory of *laissez faire* complemented the Enlightenment concept of personal liberty as well as the Protestant notion of individual salvation. Smith's *Inquiry into the Nature and Causes of the Wealth of Nations* and the Declaration of Independence are the two documents that have had the greatest impact upon American historical development. Both were written in 1776. Both stressed the role of the individual, the one in government, the other in the national economy. Read the Declaration of Independence with care. In the phrase "We hold these truths to be self-evident, that all men are created equal, that they are endowed by their Creator with certain unalienable Rights, that among these are Life, Liberty and the pursuit of Happiness," substitute for the last word, "property." The word "property" appeared in one of the preliminary drafts of the Declaration. The substitution of "happiness" changed the meaning of the document not one whit, for in modern America perhaps no words are as synonymous as "happiness," "property," and "money." What is significant is that the Declaration perfectly embodied the Enlightenment concept of personal liberty, the Reformation conception of individual salvation, and the capitalistic ideas of Adam Smith—among them, the right to accumulate and enjoy private property. Smith regarded the end product of a national economy as the strengthening of the realm, as did the merchantilist economists, such as Jean Colbert.

NATIONALISM

A national economy was the concomitant of the rising nation-state. Certainly, one of the motives for the creation of a nation—which may essentially be defined as a group consciousness seeking territorial identification—was the desire to create a political climate conducive to the development and protection of wealth. Conversely, the nation sought to encourage the enrichment of the realm in order to perpetuate its existence. The existence of the new nation-states depended in good measure upon their ability to successfully wage war. The more successful the wars, the bigger the realm and the more urgent the need for larger armies to wage the inevitably bigger wars. The bigger the war, the higher the cost of national defense and the more urgent the need to accumulate money (gold) within the realm. Thus, the mercantilist used the offices of the nation to encourage and assist certain citizens in their personal enrichment so that the nation could raise money through taxes for the waging of war. The individual, group, or class blessed with wealth desired to protect that wealth and therefore acquiesced (after negotiation through political processes) in the taxes used to raise armies and enforce the laws protecting property.

For example, Christopher Columbus was assisted by Spain through titles, patents, and cash grants (which paid for seven eighths of the cost of the voyage) in his efforts to find a new, more direct trade route to India. In return, the realm was to receive ninety percent of the profits arising from the voyage; Columbus would enjoy the remaining ten percent. The difference between mercantile capitalism and Adam Smith's laissez-faire capitalism was more a matter of technique than a change in purpose. Smith believed that the best way a nation could accumulate gold was to leave individuals to their own natural inclination and their instinct for survival:

> As every individual, therefore, endeavors as much as he can to employ his capital in the support of domestic industry, and so to direct that industry, that its produce may be of the greatest value, every individual necessarily labors to render the annual revenue of the society as great as he can. . . . the obvious and simple system of natural liberty establishes itself of its own accord. Every man, as long as he does not violate the laws of justice, is left perfectly free to pursue his own

interests in his own way, and to bring both his industry and capital into competition with those of any other man or order of men.[8]

Smith believed that like an "invisible hand" the self-interests of the individual served the broader interests of the community. Again, the idea of laissez faire accorded with the ideas of personal liberty and democracy written by Thomas Jefferson in the Declaration of Independence.

SOCIAL DARWINISM AND CAPITALISM

Social Darwinism also complemented the concepts of individual salvation, personal liberty, and laissez faire. Charles Darwin published his *Origin of Species* in 1859. This provocative work argued that organic life evolved from a lower state to a higher state through a process of natural selection. Darwin was completely innocent of any attempt to reshape economic thought. Herbert Spencer, however, a fellow English scholar, applied Darwin's theories of evolution to society. Social institutions, like organic life, evolve from a lower state to a higher state through a process of natural selection. In other words, the fit survive and the feeble fail, and that is good. Through survival of the fittest, society necessarily progresses. There must be no artificial or governmental impediment to the process of natural selection. There must be complete laissez faire and individual competition.

William Graham Sumner, an ordained Episcopal minister and professor of political science and social science at Yale in the 1880s, explained Social Darwinism as follows:

> Private property . . . is aimed against nature. It is from her niggardly hand that we have to wrest the satisfactions for our needs, but our fellow men are our competitors for the meager supply. Competition, therefore, is a law of nature. Nature is entirely neutral; she submits to him who most energetically and resolutely assails her. She grants her rewards to the fittest. . . . If, then, there be liberty, men get from her just in proportion to their works, and their having and enjoying are just in proportion to their being and their doing. Such is the system of nature.[9]

A popular statement of "survival of the fittest" is simply, "To each according to ability."

The idea that each person must earn or achieve according to his or her ability is at heart a democratic idea, one that derives in part from the American environmental experience. Once the American colonists learned to tap the abundance of the American wilderness, they obtained the key to the continent. Food, clothing, and shelter lay within the grasp of each settler. The fusion of European technology, prominently the ax and the plow, with the natural environment provided an abundance almost unparalleled in human experience. The delight of it was that nature's plenty seemed to be in unlimited supply, there for the taking according to the individual's desires, capabilities, and efforts. American expansion, a wholly democratic and individualistic effort, almost necessarily bred inequality and tended to constantly reduce the opportunities of the individual. Although on the one hand the American free-enterprise system promised something to nearly everyone, on the other hand it delivered that something in unequal portions. But although the free-enterprise system carried the potential seeds of its own destruction, in the form of the concentration of wealth in the hands of the few, it also contained the seedbed for the growth of a human productivity that could create a yet greater abundance for all.

THE PRIMARY AND SECONDARY ENVIRONMENTS

Abundance derives from a *primary environment*—society's natural resources— and a *secondary environment*—human technological and cultural resources. Frederick Jackson Turner's evaluation of the historical significance of the American frontier concludes:

> Thus American development has exhibited not merely advance along a single line, but a return to primitive conditions on a continually advancing frontier line, and a new development for that area. American social development has been continually beginning over again on the frontier. This perennial rebirth, this fluidity of Ameri-

FREDERICK JACKSON TURNER *(1861–1932)*
Historian, educator.
Courtesy University of Wisconsin.

can life, this expansion westward with its new opportunities, its continuous touch
with the simplicity of primitive society, furnish the forces dominating the American
character.[10]

The frontier, which Turner describes as "the meeting point between savagery
and civilization," continually re-creates the environment in which persons may
compete equitably and earn according to their ability. But the frontier had offi-
cially disappeared by the time Turner made his presentation before the American
Historical Association. As long as the frontier existed, the promise of American
life—the right to both equality and opportunity—appeared to exist. Once the
frontier was gone, Americans became poised between the horns of a dilemma—
can free enterprise preserve both democracy and the right to an unequal distribution of goods?

This dilemma has continued to stir intellectual argument and debate and
change the political dogma. John F. Kennedy's "New Frontier" slogan was no
accident, but reflected a genuine interest in reasserting the idea that all Americans must have an equal opportunity to earn according to ability. President
Kennedy enhanced this idea with the vision of a frontier in space and technology
in which one's "having and enjoying" would once again be in proportion to
one's "being and . . . doing." The promise, as in former times, was that human
science, technology, and faith could achieve a world of relative abundance. The
American dream had been reaffirmed. As an article of faith or as abstract theory,
the step from the old frontier of Frederick Jackson Turner to the New Frontier of
John F. Kennedy was a relatively short one.

Yet the two frontiers were two different worlds. Turner's frontier was
essentially land and the natural resources that until the twentieth century appeared to be limitless. This was America's primary environment. The New
Frontier concerned a sophisticated, secondary, human-made environment. "A
vital distinction separates mere potential abundance—the copious supply of
natural resources—and actual abundance—the availability to society of a generous quota of goods ready for use," observed David Potter. "Social wealth, as
contrasted with natural wealth, results not only from the supply of resources but
also from a nation's system of production and distribution." "The social value of
natural resources," he wrote, "depends entirely upon the aptitude of society for
using them." Thus, this secondary environment, which might be equated to the
economists' "social capital," comprises the technology of know-how, the education, and the motivation to do a thing. It is this second environment that can
and does change and that intrigues modern Americans with its seemingly unlimited capacities. The impact of the two frontiers on Americans has been much
the same: each created an optimism, an equalitarianism, and perhaps a democratic spirit, but more important, each reaffirmed America's faith in free enterprise.[11]

Since the 1970s especially, Americans have become increasingly aware
that the primary and secondary environments are in fact interdependent. During

FIGURE 1.4. The man on the moon is a result of the enormous resources and technology of the American free-enterprise system.
Courtesy NASA.

the past hundred years, it appeared that the human-made environment had unlimited capacity for growth. There could always be more railroads, more food products, more factories, more automobiles, more television sets, more computers, more of whatever Americans set as their priorities. And for a hundred years, American industry and agriculture turned out a constantly increasing abundance of goods, without overtaxing the capacity of the primary environment. But since World War II, and especially with the advent of the energy shortages of the 1970s, we have come to realize that a human-made environment does have limited capacities, and is ultimately responsive to the primary environment. There is only so much oil, coal, iron ore, and topsoil. Resources are limited, but the methods of using them may not be. When resources become scarce there is a need to apply capital (or technology) more intensively. In the past, our "technology" has been geared exclusively to production; there has been relatively little regard for conservation. For example, in the nineteenth century the American lumber industry concentrated its technology almost wholly on the harvesting of timber. But today, it emphasizes production and "selective harvesting." There is now a technology of conservation. There are more efficient engines, more efficient sources of energy, better farming techniques, seemingly always that "better mousetrap." We can also learn to live better with less, to control the population explosion, and to better harmonize the structure of our human-made urban-industrial world with the capacities of our natural environment. An awareness of ecology must become part of that "know-how" of our secondary environment.

The ecology has always been there. America's economic pursuits during its first one hundred years as a nation, 1776–1876, were very distinctly conditioned by the natural environment. In its second one hundred years, its economic development was conditioned largely by the secondary environment—science, technology, and machines. It is anticipated that American economic development in the third one hundred years will be conditioned by both the primary and secondary environments acting in greater concert or equilibrium upon people. Should this be true, we can expect a revision of the technological "know-how," the organizational structure, and the values and motivations loosely characteristic of the free-enterprise American. Both the abundance of the frontier and the abundance of the industrial society contributed to making Americans a "People of Plenty." The "new" and the "old" frontiers, both already a part of the past, reaffirmed the American belief in free enterprise.

Notes

[1]Theodore A. Agoncillo and Oscar M. Alfonso, *Hisotry of the Filipino People*, 2nd ed. (Manila: University of the Philippines, 1960), pp. 442–443.

[2]David Potter, *People of Plenty: Economic Abundance and the American Character* (Chicago: University of Chicago Press, 1954), p. 84.

[3]See Pirenne's "The Stages in the Social History of Capitalism," *American Historical Review*, 19 (April 1914), 494–515.

[4]See N. S. B. Gras, *Business and Capitalism: An Introduction to Business History* (New York: Crofts, 1947).

[5]See Joseph Schumpeter, *Capitalism, Socialism and Democracy*, 2nd ed. (New York: Harper & Brothers, 1950). For a critical evaluation of Schumpeter, see Sumner H. Slichter, *Economic Growth in the United States: Its History, Problems and Prospects* (New York: Free Press, 1966).

[6]Woodrow Wilson, First Inaugural Address, March 4, 1913, 63rd Congress, Special Session, Senate Document No. 3.

[7]See Max Weber, *The Protestant Ethic and the Spirit of Capitalism* (New York: Scribner, 1930); and commentary by Samuel Eliot Morison, *Builders of the Massachusetts Bay Colony*, 2nd ed. (Boston, Houghton Mifflin, 1958), p. 160.

[8]See the material by Smith in *Government and the Economy: Some Nineteenth-Century Views*, ed. E. David Cronon (New York: Henry Holt, 1960) pp. 19–22.

[9]See the material by Sumner in *Government and the Economy: Some Nineteenth Century Views*, ed. E. David Cronon (New York: Henry Holt, 1960), p. 20.

[10]Frederick Jackson Turner, "Significance of the Frontier in American History," Annual Report of the American Historical Association, 1893 (Washington, D.C.: Government Printing Office, 1894), pp. 199–227.

[11]Potter, *People of Plenty*, pp. 142–165.

SUGGESTED READINGS

BRUCHEY, STUART, *The Roots of American Economic Growth, 1607–1861*. New York: Harper & Row, 1965.

GRAS, N. S. B., *Business and Capitalism: An Introduction to Business History*. New York: Crofts, 1947.

HEILBRONER, ROBERT, *The Limits of American Capitalism*. New York: Harper & Row. 1965.

HEILBRONER, ROBERT L., *The Worldly Philosophers*. New York: Simon & Schuster, 1972.

MCCLELLAND, DAVID C., *The Achieving Society*. Princeton: N.J.: Van Nostrand, 1961.

NORTH, DOUGLASS C., *Growth and Welfare in the American Past*, 2nd ed. Englewood Cliffs, N.J.: Prentice-Hall, 1974.

POTTER, DAVID, *People of Plenty: Economic Abundance and the American Character*. Chicago: University of Chicago Press, 1954.

RIESMAN, DAVID, *The Lonely Crowd: A Study of the Changing American Character*. New Haven: Yale University Press, 1950.

RISCHIN, MOSES, ed., *The American Gospel of Success*. Chicago: Quadrangle, 1965.

WEBER, MAX, *The Protestant Ethic and the Spirit of Capitalism*. New York: Scribner, 1930.

THE ECONOMICS OF GEOGRAPHY

_____ chapter II __

For all their civilization and technology, humans are as much conditioned by their environment as they are masters of that environment. The history of the United States and its economic development is strongly influenced by physiographic features. The excellent harbors, the fine fisheries, and the timbered coasts of the eastern seaboard helped develop the American colonists as a maritime people. The Appalachian Mountains, as well as the French and the Indians on the other side of those mountains, encouraged colonial settlers to concentrate along the seaboard and to depend on the sea during the first two hundred years of American economic development.

Once the mountains were penetrated, the great Mississippi River and its tributaries provided the vital arteries for settlement, and agriculture and commerce expanded throughout the Mississippi Valley and into the Great Plains. Between the Rocky Mountains and the coastal ranges of California lay the great American desert, largely unsuited for farming but rich in minerals. The western coast, although lacking the numerous harbors of the east, offered rich soil, a temperate climate, the nation's finest forests, and gold. The natural environment in which the American nation developed offered an abundance and a variety almost unexcelled in human experience.

This primary environment was the major influence on American economic development until at least the mid nineteenth century. Although the secondary environment—the technology, the know-how, and the skill provided by civilization—has since become preeminent, the natural environment remains a conditioning factor. It is with the fuller realization of the interdependence of man and nature that the modern concept of ecology has become popular and significant. Americans, however, generally have a very hazy idea about American geography and their natural environment.

THE PHYSIOGRAPHY OF THE UNITED STATES

The United States, excluding Alaska, lies between the twenty-fifth and the forty-ninth parallels. Part of Alaska lies within the Arctic Circle. Point Barrow, Alaska is the northernmost point in the United States; Ka Lae (South Cape), Hawaii is the southernmost point. West Quoddy Head, Maine is the easternmost point, and Cape Wrangell, Alaska is the westernmost point. The United States comprises 3,615,122 square miles—approximately 6.9 percent of the earth's land area—and may be divided into eight generally distinct geographic regions.

Although the *eastern lowlands* are not as rich and fertile as the regions to the west, their soils are suitable for the successful cultivation of vegetables, wheat, corn, tobacco, and rice—the major colonial crops. The coastal harbors and the fall line were likely the most influential physiographic features in the colonies. The harbors were a major maritime resource, and the fall line—the area where the rivers shallowed or became rapids—marked a transition point in inland transportation and, more important, a site for water power.

Two strings of cities are evident on the coastal plain. The first, extending southward from Boston, includes New York, Philadelphia, Baltimore, Norfolk, Charleston, and Savannah. These are the seaport towns. The second, extending southward approximately from Hartford, Connecticut, includes Trenton, Richmond, Raleigh, Columbia, Augusta, and Macon. These are the fall-line cities. When coastal trade was transferred to inland barges or wagons, and where water power could easily be harnessed by mills, lathes, and saws, these cities soon became manufacturing and transportation centers.

The *Appalachian region* is marked by two parallel ridges, the Alleghenies and the Blue Ridge Mountains, extending from Newfoundland to Alabama. Fertile valleys intersperse these ranges, which rise to 6,000 feet in New Hampshire and North Carolina. Water power, fertile soils, minerals, and coal and iron deposits make this region a natural habitat for humans. The great coal and iron industries began developing here very early in the American experience. Pittsburgh and Birmingham mark the approximate terminals of a chain of cities and towns along the Appalachians that could exist because coal, iron ore, water power, and food supplies were nearby.

The semitropical climate and the rich, predominantly alluvial soils of the Gulf Coast, plus easy access by water, have made the *Gulf States lowlands* a great source of soybeans, rice, other vegetables, cotton, and livestock. The first-generation cities and towns of the South were concerned primarily with the gathering and distribution of farm produce. A second-generation urban development has been stimulated by the extraction of oil, natural gas, and chemicals. These second-generation southern cities include Houston, Lake Charles, Baton Rouge, New Orleans, Atlanta, and Jacksonville, several of which had first-generation origins.

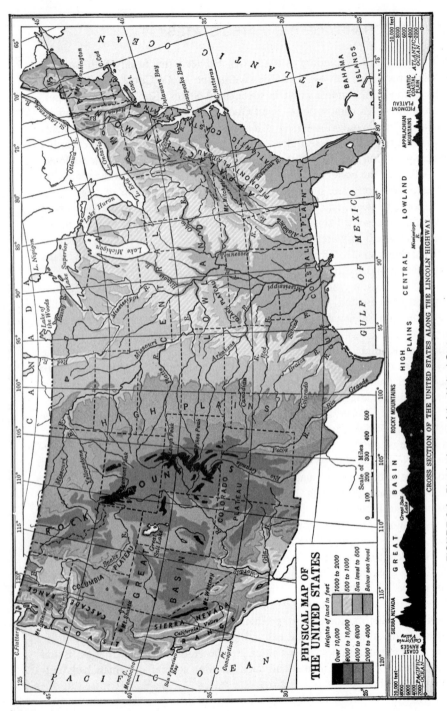

FIGURE 2.1. Physical map of the United States.

Source: Harold Underwood Faulkner, *American Economic History*, 8th Edition. (New York: Harper & Brothers), 1960. p. 47.

The midwestern and northern plains of the *Mississippi Valley* are distinct from the southern alluvial basin of the valley, which is much like the Gulf Coast lowlands. Its fertile prairies and river valleys have made the Mississippi basin the agricultural heartland of America. Wheat, corn-hogs, and dairying predominate in the northern portions of the basin; cotton, rice, soybeans, lumbering, and fruit predominate in the southern regions. Rainfall is abundant to adequate in all sectors. Many of the towns and cities in this region began as French frontier fortresses and later became thriving commercial centers. Senator Thomas Hart Benton, for example, viewed St. Louis in the 1840s as the American corridor (or Constantinople) for trade with the Orient.

Extending from the Rocky Mountains in the east to the Sierra Nevada in the west, the *Cordillera region* is generally arid and without navigable waterways. Its soils do not support substantial crop production, and potable water supplies are relatively scarce. Population has remained sparse. The development of the

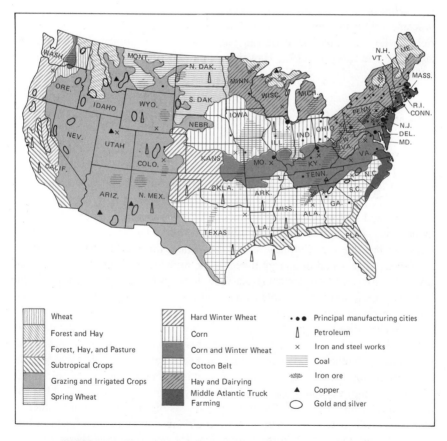

FIGURE 2.2 Economic regions and resources of the United States.

region has been geared largely to the extraction of copper, iron, silver, and gold, and to cattle raising. Twentieth-century hydroelectric-power and irrigation projects have made parts of the region more hospitable and productive.

Relatively low mountain ranges interspersed with fertile valleys made arable by the run-off from the higher mountain ridges, several natural harbors in Puget Sound and San Francisco (plus a man-made one in Los Angeles), and a generally temperate climate have made the *Pacific Coast* a very habitable and productive region. Gold brought Americans there, but the production of fruits, vegetables, cereals, and timber sustained them.

Alaska, purchased by the United States from Russia in 1867, is rich in oil, minerals, fish, fur, and timber. But the capability of developing these resources has been severely limited by an intemperate climate. And even with modern technology, access to the interior of Alaska is hazardous and inconvenient. Difficulties in tapping the oil resources of Alaska's northern slope reflect the climatic barriers to the economic development of the Alaskan wilderness.

Hawaii is a 1,600-mile chain of numerous islets and eight main islands of volcanic origin that enjoy a tropical to semitropical climate. Easy access and rich, fertile soils have made Hawaii most hospitable to human population. Obtained as a territory in 1898, Hawaii became the fiftieth state of the Union in 1959.

THE NATURAL ENVIRONMENT

Wherever they live, people must have a supply of food, water, and energy for survival. Within these general parameters, humans are highly flexible and resourceful. There is relatively little organic material they cannot eat. There are certainly foods they prefer, but these preferences are often culturally conditioned, and that conditioning is most often a product of the natural environment. Thus, fish is often preferred by those who live by the water, and meat by those on the interior. Culinary skills also reflect the locale and habits of the consumer. A sea-food dinner prepared in the midwestern United States is often markedly different from the same sea-food dinner prepared on the coasts. In the last analysis, food is inseparable from human history, and geography is a determining factor in dietary habits.

For thousands of years, the search for food has helped shape the development of society. It has dictated population growth and urban expansion, and has profoundly influenced economic, social, and political theory. It has widened the horizons of commerce, inspired wars of dominion, played no small role in the creation of empires, and precipitated the discovery of new worlds. Food has had a part in religion, helping define the separateness of one creed from another by means of dietary taboos. The prehistoric cook's discovery of the effects of heat applied to raw materials laid the foundations for much of early chemistry. The water wheel, first used in milling grain, promoted many technological developments. Medicine was based largely on dietary principles until well into the eighteenth century. During wartime, battles were postponed until the harvest had been gathered. Well-fed armies usually defeated hungry ones. Even in social relations, there has been a steady undercurrent of antagonism for twelve thousand years between those whose diet consists mainly of grain and those who depend on animal foods.[1]

Humankind has been highly adaptable in its search for and use of foods. People have also adapted their shelter to the environment. In the woodlands houses are of logs and timber; stone is used in the mountains; along the waterways wood and brick are used; in the prairies home builders used sod; and in the Arctic they used ice. The pioneer homestead was located almost invariably on rising ground, which provided adequate drainage and run-off, it had easy access to water, and it was on or adjacent to a cultivable plot of land. Fuel—most often wood (or perhaps buffalo chips in the West) had to be close at hand. Streams, rivers, and lakes were preferred locations because of their potable water, fish, and opportunity for transportation. Wildlife usually had similar environmental preferences, which made the homesteader's chosen locale doubly attractive. Moreover, it is no coincidence that pioneer homesteads can be found on the sites of Indian encampments, and modern cities on the ruins of more ancient cities. The needs of humans are basic, but their methods of adapting the materials in their environment to fulfill those needs have changed as they have gained more knowledge of their environment.

As rich and as bountiful as the United States was, natural abundance alone would not sustain the American people. Americans had to have the aptitude, the knowledge, and the technology to use that environment to their best advantage. The more advanced their technology, the greater the advantage they could derive from their natural environment. Thus, the *secondary*, human-made environment—basically, the individual's knowledge, which was constantly changing and growing—became in effect a new frontier, one that was something of an alter ego to the older, environmental frontier. The American Indian, in other words, enjoyed the same environmental advantages as the American pioneer, but after thousands of years his way of life, his material welfare, had changed little. Yet once he began to absorb Western technology, his life also changed dramatically. Within two centuries, iron, steel, gunpowder, and the horse revolutionized Indian society in America.[2] Had it not been for Western diseases that came with the new technology, the Indian may have been a far more formidable contestant for control of the continent.

When Europeans first arrived in the New World, many of them starved, although they lived amidst abundance. Their superior technology at first seemed of no avail. Of the first 500 settlers at Jamestown, 50 survived the dreadful starvation of 1609; of the 100 Pilgrims settling at Plymouth in 1620, 50 survived the first winter. We still wonder about the fate of the colonists at Roanoke in

1588. The great sixteenth-century exploring expeditions of the Spanish, although often far better equipped than the English colonizing expeditions, sometimes fared even worse. There were, of course, many reasons for the fearful loss of life. One of those reasons was starvation. It was difficult for the early settlers to revert to a different stage of civilization. It was even difficult for proficient Old World farmers to adjust their agricultural know-how to New World conditions. The experience of the early settlers would not be unlike that of a modern Bostonian fleeing the city to settle in the Alaskan wilderness. It would not be an easy transition.

A successful transition, as from Boston to Alaska or from London to Jamestown, required the absorption of a new kind of knowledge. For example, new techniques of house construction though similar to the old in general principle, would be distinctively different in technique. There would be new kinds of food for the old kinds. English barley seemed less acclimated to New England than to the Mother country. Beans and squash were foods the colonists had never eaten; corn (or maize) was a crop they had never grown. It was not "until the English settlers adopted the American Indians' agricultural plants, cultivation, and harvesting methods, and processes of food preparation that they were assured of adequate food supplies. . . . The union of American Indian and European farming produced the beginnings of American agriculture and provided the essential basis for its ultimate development."[3] In order to survive, the Europeans very clearly had to adopt a New World technology conditioned by a New World environment.

COLONIAL AGRICULTURE

Plants domesticated by the Indian and cultivated by the settler constitute a large part of the American farm product today. Maize (or corn), cotton (the New World variety found by Coronado in New Mexico in 1540), peanuts, pumpkins, squash, beans, "Irish" potatoes (brought to Europe from America), sweet potatoes, tobacco, and tomatoes were all indigenous to America. They were alien to the first colonists. Without knowing what these things were, and how to use them, the strangers in a strange land could, and did, easily starve. The primary environment offered abundance, but only if the settlers knew how to tap that abundance. Fortunately, they learned very quickly, and the fusion of European and American agricultural technology proved advantageous. Tobacco, rice, indigo, and cotton had become well-established commercial crops by the time of the American Revolution.

The earliest success came with tobacco. Christopher Columbus found tobacco being cultivated by the Indians in the West Indies in 1492. By the mid 1500s, tobacco had become a popular but expensive luxury in England. The early settlers at Jamestown experimented with tobacco cultivation, but the results were judged "weak and biting." Credit for the successful cultivation and curing of tobacco is given John Rolfe, who most likely introduced a West Indian variety. Rolfe's first commercial shipment of tobacco to England seems to have occurred in 1613. The crop attracted such excellent prices that the Virginia farmers appeared inclined to put all of their land and labor into tobacco, at the expense of food production. To forestall this, Sir Thomas Dale, governor of the colony, directed that each Virginia farmer plant two acres of corn as a prerequisite for planting tobacco.

Virginia's exports of tobacco soared from 20,000 pounds in 1618 to over 500,000 pounds in 1627. But by the latter date, tobacco prices in England had declined markedly. Once a luxury item, tobacco became a basic commodity. From 1630 until the American Revolution, colonial governors and legislatures attempted, largely without success, to limit tobacco production in order to maintain adequate prices. Programs for the destruction of inferior grades of tobacco, and tax subsidies provided tobacco growers by colonial legislatures, are reminiscent of contemporary efforts to reduce farm production and provide price subsidies.

Indigo, a vegetable dye that had been grown with some success in the West Indies, was first cultivated successfully in the Carolinas by Eliza Lucas about 1739. The British Parliament exempted indigo from import duties in 1734, and in 1748 approved a price subsidy that remained in effect until 1777. Indigo was planted in rows, by hand, and cut with a sickle. The plant was then boiled into a paste, which was allowed to harden, and then cut into cubes for shipment. The loss of the British subsidy after American independence, plus the almost contemporaneous development of chemical dyes, were twin blows from which the indigo industry never recovered.

Although a wild relative of rice (*Oryza sativa*) existed in the Americas, commercial rice production began with the importation of a variety of rice from Madagascar about 1694. Rice was first planted in the tidal marshes of South Carolina, but within a few decades rice cultivation had moved to the inland river marshes. Irrigation (or cultivation by flooding) developed about 1724, and various refinements continued until the Revolution. The world's demand for rice proved insatiable even in the colonial era. Traders in Charleston reported in 1724 that there were more ships in port to haul the rice away than there was rice to ship. The Carolinas exported 128 million pounds of rice to England in 1738, and 577 million pounds in 1775. Despite improvements over the old flail and hand-pounding milling processes, rice-milling procedures remained fairly primitive and inefficient well into the nineteenth century.

Francisco Coronado found cotton being cultivated by the Indians of the Southwest in the 1540s. Virginia planters experimented with cotton growing in the 1690s. Cotton was grown extensively by the colonists for home consumption, but large-scale commercial production was limited by the need to hand-pick the seed from the lint. A roller gin produced 60 or 70 pounds of cotton a day in the early 1700s. But by the end of the eighteenth century, Eli Whitney's gin had magnified ginning capacities tenfold. The first record of cotton exported to England was for a 1,000-pound shipment made in 1789. Although the development of a "cotton economy" came after the American Revolution, the technology of cotton production was widely established in the southern colonies at an early period. Tobacco, rice, indigo, and cotton, in the order of their importance, became staple products of the middle and southern colonies upon which the development of the entire colonial economy depended. Table 2.1 provides a brief résumé of colonial agricultural, extractive, and manufacturing industries.

The cattle and livestock industries flourished along the eastern seaboard by the mid seventeenth century. Cattle and hogs were not native to the Americas, but by the time the English settlers arrived, wild horses, cattle, and hogs roamed much of North America. These animals sprang from stock brought by the Spanish in the 1500s. By the early 1600s, the descendants of European cattle and swine had been redomesticated by the Indians in the Carolinas. By the mid 1600s, settlers in Virginia and Maryland had declared wild horses a public nuisance. The colonial "cattle frontier" brought with it all of the nomenclature usually attributed to the later American West, including the cowboy, the cow pen, branding, the roundup, rustlers, and horse thieves. A 1786 act of North Carolina provided that horse thieves "should stand in the pillory one hour, be publicly whipped with thirty-nine lashes, nailed to the pillory by the ears, which were afterwards to be cut off, and branded on the right cheek with the letter H and on the left cheek with the letter T."

Although little beef or pork was exported from America in colonial times, the livestock industry provided a substantial part of the meat on American tables from a very early time, and constituted an important part of a ship's provisions. Excepting rice, tobacco, indigo, and cotton, crops cultivated in America prior to 1815 were largely for home consumption. The development of commercial agriculture correlated closely with the rise of the city and the development of adequate transportation facilities. The turnpikes and national roads, steam navigation, and the railroad involved a critical application of technology to the primary environment.

THE "WORLD CITY"

The interaction of the city and transportation in the development of the American frontier are evident in the spatial concepts of Johann Heinrich von Thünen. Von Thünen has identified the huge, noncontiguous urban-industrial complex in northwestern Europe and northeastern Anglo-America as a global economic core region that arose about 1750 and has since shaped world economic development. Commercial agricultural production, keyed to the demands of the "Von Thünen World City," has created a series of agricultural zones or belts at different

TABLE 2.1

The Colonial Economy.

AREA	AGRICULTURE	EXTRACTION	MANUFACTURING

New England	Individual farmer
	50 acres typical
	Subsistence crops:
	  wheat, corn, beans,
	  vegetables, fruits,
	  wool, flax
	Commercial crops: none
		Fish
		Lumber
		  (masts, ribs
		Fur
		Potash
		Naval stores
			Rum
			Shipbuilding

Middle Colonies	Individual farmers and
	indentured servants,
	100 acres typical
	Subsistence crops:
	  fruits, vegetables,
	  beans, rye, corn,
	  oats, barley,
	  hay, wool
	Commercial crops:
	  wheat (flour),
	  beef, pork
		Lumber
		Potash
		Iron
		Furs
		Naval stores
			Iron products
			Shipbuilding

South	Individual farmers and
	slaves
	Plantations (1000+ acres)
	Small farms (50 acres)
	Subsistence crops:
	  corn, vegetables,
	  beans, livestock,
	  hay
	Commercial crops:
	  tobacco, rice,
	  indigo, hemp
		Lumber
		Naval stores
		Iron (Virginia
		  and Maryland)
			Few

Frontier	Individual farmers
	Small farm (50–100 acres)
	Subsistence crops:
	  corn, wheat, vegetables,
	  fruits, beans, livestock,
	  hay, wool
		Lumber
		Furs
			Alcoholic
			beverages

distances from this core. Geographer Terry Jordan explains the concept as follows:

> Each of these agricultural zones produces the commodity which it is ''best fitted to export by virtue of location relative to the markets'' of the great urban-industrial

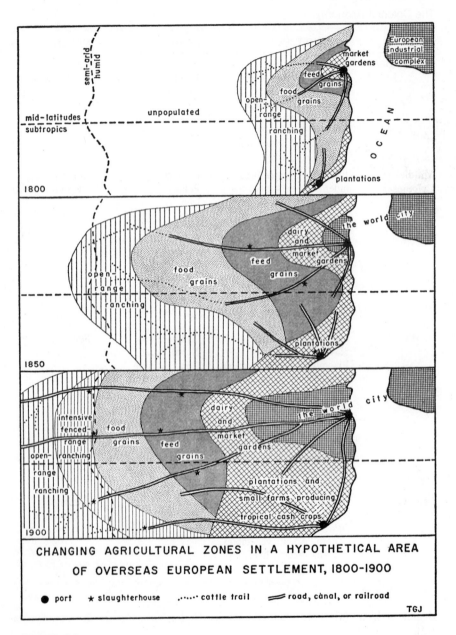

FIGURE 2.3.

Source: Terry G. Jordan, "The Origin and Distribution of Open-Range Cattle Ranching." *Social Science Quarterly* (June 1972), p. 120.

complex. Nearest the "World City" are zones of dairying and market gardening, intensive forms of agriculture which must have quick access to market. Nearness to market provides the farmer with greater profits, enabling a greater investment in capital and labor or, in other words, greater intensity. Moreover, greater yields per acre are necessary in these inner zones in order to offset the high costs of labor and land, in addition to high taxes. Following, at increasing distances from the "World City" are (1) a region producing feed grains and fattened meat animals, (2) a commercial food grain zone, and on the outermost periphery, (3) the ranching region producing lean animals, hides, tallow, and other herd animal products. The intensity of land use decreases steadily with increasing distance from the urban-industrial core, reaching its lowest level in the ranching zone, where, in the open-range era, "only by concentrating the feed from many acres into a few valuable pounds of commodity" could the inhabitants join the international economy.[4] Jordan has produced a hypothetical schematic of the changes in agricultural zones resulting from growth in the world city (Figure 2.3).

Spatial economic pressures affected the distribution of land in America, as did cultural preferences and political pressures.

LAND USE

The problem of distributing nature's largesse, the land, was never adequately solved during the colonial and early national periods. The colonial land-distribution systems were basically three: (1) the manorial system, (2) the New England system, and (3) the headright system. The latter two, which were more successful, adapted European law and land patterns to the unique American environment.

The manorial system, a survivor of feudalism, sought to apportion lands into feudal estates tenanted by farmers or peasants who paid for the use of the land in quitrents, payments in kind or in cash. The physical impossibility of collecting rents, supervising tenants, and attracting settlers doomed the manorial system before it got started, but such a system was attempted in Pennsylvania, the Carolinas, and elsewhere in the New World.

The New England, or township, system developed from the granting of territory by the Crown to a corporate body or group of settlers rather than to a single proprietor. The corporate body, such as the Massachusetts Bay Company, in turn established a town and distributed land by lot to settlers in portions radiating out from the town or public square. This system provided for independence but stressed cooperation.

The headright system, used extensively in Virginia, derived from the granting of land by a company to a settler. Additional apportionments, or "headrights," were given for each member of his family, and sometimes for each of his slaves or indentured servants. The headright, usually fifty acres, could be located by the settler on any part of the unappropriated public domain, and would be surveyed after settlement. This system very clearly stressed individual initiative, and it encouraged rapid, if not legal, settlement of the western lands.

Colonial land-distribution policies and practice reflected environmental conditions. The New England geographic and climatic conditions encouraged community, cooperation, and intensive agriculture. Concentrations of population, in turn, facilitated specialization and industrialization. In the southern regions, populations were more scattered, the people tended to be more independent, and technology tended to remain more primitive. Self-sufficiency, rather than cooperation, characterized the Southern and Middle Atlantic colonies and most of interior New England as well.

In summary, the settlement of America involved the interaction of both the primary and secondary environments with the settlers and their society. In the colonial era the primary, or natural, environment was a preponderant, but not exclusive, conditioner of human habitation of the New World. The most important aspect of the natural environment in America was the great variety and abundance of resources it offered—water, good soil, timber, wildlife, and minerals. Yet this abundance could not be used until Americans had the technology or know-how for using nature's storehouse. An adaptation or amalgamation of European and Indian technology made possible the successful commercial production of tobacco, indigo, cotton, and rice, crops that became the basic commodities of the colonial economy. The township system, which stressed cooperation but allowed land distribution among individuals, was dominant in New England; the headright system, which stressed individualism and ignored community, was dominant in the south and west. Throughout their colonial experience, Americans were far more conditioned by their environment than they were masters of it. Too little analysis has been given by the economic historian to the relationship between the natural environment and the technology that makes that environment useful.

ASTRONOMICAL DIARY (1758)

Nathaniel Ames

The following lines by Nathaniel Ames express the hope and optimism that Americans derived from the realization of the great natural abundance awaiting exploitation and development. The frontier long remained a part of the national consciousness, although most Americans would never experience it as a reality.

So Arts and Sciences will change the Face of Nature in their Tour from Hence over the Appalachian Mountains to the Western Ocean; and as they march thro' the vast Desert, the Residence of wild Beasts will be broken up, and their obscene Howl cease for ever;—Instead of which, the Stones and Trees will dance together at the

Music of *Orpheus*,—The Rocks will disclose their hidden Gems,—and the inestimable Treasures of Gold & Silver be broken up. Huge Mountains of Iron Ore are reserved for future Generations: This Metal more useful than Gold and Silver, will employ millions of Hands, not only to form the martial Sword, and peaceful Share, alternately; but an Infinity of Utensils improved in the Exercise of Art, and Handicraft among Men. Nature thro' all her works has stamp'd Authority on this Law, namely, "That all fit Matter shall be improved to its best Purposes."—Shall not then those vast Quarries, that team with mechanic Stone,—those for Structure be piled into great Cities,—and those for sculpture into Statues to perpetuate the Honor of renowned Heroes: even those who shall now save their Country,—*O! Ye unborn Inhabitants of America! Should this Page escape its destin'd Conflagration at Year's End, and these Alphabetical Letters remain legible;—when your Eyes behold the Sun after he has rolled the Seasons round for two or three Centuries more, you will know that in ANNO DOMINI 1758, we dream'd of your Times.*

POEM ON THE RISING GLORY OF AMERICA (1771)

Philip Freneau and Hugh H. Brackenridge

The emphasis in this poem is on the wondrous abundance of American life and the application of science to the development of the "luxuries of life."

This is thy praise America thy pow'r
The seat of empire the abode of kings
The final stage where time shall introduce
Renowned characters, and glorious works
Of high invention and of wond'rous art,
While not the ravages of time shall waste
Till he himself has run his long career;
Till all those glorious orbs of light on high
The rolling wonders that surround the ball,
Drop from their spheres extinguish'd and consum'd,
When final ruin with her fiery car
Rides o'er creation, and all natures works
Are lost in chaos and the womb of night.

Notes

[1] Reay Tannahill, *Food in History* (New York: Stein & Day, 1973), p. 388.

[2] See Elizabeth A. H. John, *Storms Brewed in Other Men's World's: The Confrontation of Indians, Spanish and French in the Southwest, 1540–1795* (College Station, Tex.: Texas A&M University Press, 1976).

[3] Everett E. Edwards, "American Agriculture—The First 300 Years," *Yearbook of Agriculture* (1940), 174.

⁴Terry G. Jordan, "The Origin and Distinction of Open-Range Cattle Ranching," *Social Science Quarterly*, June, 1972, pp. 118–19. See also Johann Heinrich von Thünen, *Von Thünen's Isolated State*, trans. Carla M. Wartenberg (Oxford: Pergamon Press, 1966).

SUGGESTED READING

BIDWELL, PERCY W., AND JOHN I. FALCONER, *History of Agriculture in the Northern United States, 1620–1860*. Washington, D.C.: Carnegie Institution, 1925. Reprint ed., Gloucester, Mass.: Peter Smith, 1941.

BOORSTIN, DANIEL J., *The Americans: The Colonial Experience*. New York: Random House, 1958.

CLAWSON, MARION, *Man and Land in the United States*. Lincoln, Nebr.: University of Nebraska Press, 1964.

GRAY, LEWIS CECIL, *History of Agriculture in the Southern United States*, Vol. I. Washington, D.C.: Carnegie Institution, 1932. Reprint ed., Gloucester, Mass.: Peter Smith, 1958.

HAYSTEAD, TODD, AND GILBERT C. FITE, *Agricultural Regions of the United States*. Norman, Okla.: University of Oklahoma Press, 1955.

VER STEEG, CLARENCE, *The Formative Years, 1607–1763*. New York: Hill & Wang, 1964.

WARNTZ, WILLIAM, *Toward a Geography of Price: A Study of Geoeconometrics*. Philadelphia: University of Pennsylvania Press, 1959.

WEBB, WALTER PRESCOTT, *The Great Plains*. Boston: Ginn, 1931.

THE ROAD TO
REVOLUTION

<hr>chapter III

During the 170 years of British governance, remarkable changes occurred within the colonies as well as the mother country. The British colonial experiment in America began over 100 years after Columbus sailed, and lasted almost as long as the government under the Constitution has lasted. The relationship between the colonies and the mother country changed as the colonial economy matured, and the relationship of England to the world altered greatly between 1607 and 1776. The American Revolution marked a climax in the accumulating changes within the colonies, which were accelerated by the French and Indian War.

One difference between Britain and her American colonies lay in their views of the capitalist system, both in its manifestation and in its idea. It is no coincidence that Adam Smith's treatise on laissez-faire capitalism appeared the same year as the Declaration of Independence, itself in many ways a proclamation of free enterprise. By 1775, capitalism had a different meaning in America than in England.

2033750

COLONIAL ECONOMIC GROWTH

During the 170 years of British rule, substantial demographic and institutional changes occurred in America. The English colonies grew from a few hundred hardy souls to almost three million people, most of them young, energetic, and highly fertile and productive. The "American multiplication table" alone altered the colonial status of the Americans.

The settled territory comprising the American colonies expanded rapidly, almost doubling in the decade before the Revolution. By 1775, Americans operated the world's third largest merchant marine, inhabited a region larger and richer in natural resources than any western European power, and provided a

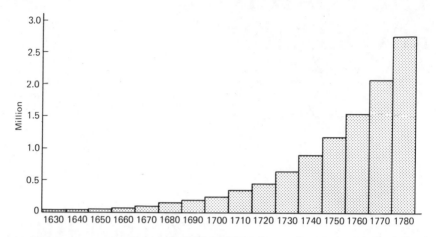

FIGURE 3.1. Estimated population of the colonies (in millions), 1630–1780.

Source: Data taken from *Historical Statistics of the United States Colonial Times to 1970,* Series 2 1–19, p. 1168.

large portion of the timber, staves, pitch, tar, ships, tobacco, furs, rice, rum, pig iron, indigo, beef, and wheat consumed by the British Empire.

The American colonies experienced substantial economic and physical growth during the period of British stewardship. The best data-analysis of the era, by James F. Shepherd and Gary M. Walton,[1] reveals a significant growth of capital derived from domestic savings rather than from foreign investment. Shepherd and Walton conclude that colonial economic growth did occur, and that it was prompted largely by improvements in colonial economic organization.

An evaluation of economic growth requires examination of the traditional

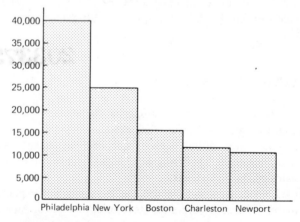

FIGURE 3.2. Estimated population of major port cities, 1775.

Source: Data taken from Bureau of the Census, *A Century of Population Growth in the United States, 1790–1900,* p.11.

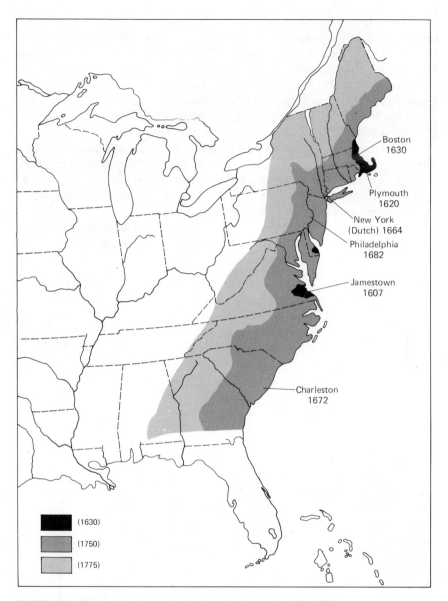

FIGURE 3.3 Westward movement of colonial settlement, 1630–1775.

Legend:
- (1630)
- (1750)
- (1775)

Map labels:
- Boston 1630
- Plymouth 1620
- New York (Dutch) 1664
- Philadelphia 1682
- Jamestown 1607
- Charleston 1672

factors of production—including land (resources), labor, and capital—plus a number of other considerations, which economists have had some difficulty in defining. Labor, for example, is rather difficult to quantify. It can be evaluated by a simple population count, or the census can be refined to provide certain age or sex parameters. Labor could also be evaluated in terms of kilowatt hours or horsepower, which are indexes of capital investment in tools and machinery. Labor can be skilled or unskilled, it can be willing or unwilling, and laborers can have goals different from earning a living or making profits.

Economists apply concepts such as social capital, the entrepreneurial function, and government to these and similar contingencies. In its broadest construction, social capital is an accumulated social resource that has no physical measurement. It consists of the will or incentive to work, education, and the institutional arrangements that make a system work. The corporate structure, patents, stocks, bonds, contracts, colleges, police, pollution controls, medical facilities, and the institutional devices that enable a people to survive and function in a

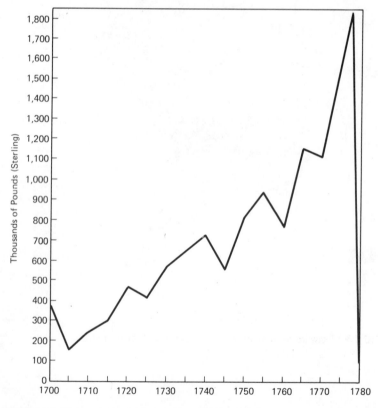

FIGURE 3.4. Value of exports in pounds sterling, 1700–1775.

Source: Data taken from *Historical Statistics of the United States Colonial Times to 1970,* Series Z 213–226, p. 1176.

society could be considered forms of social capital. In a more narrow sense, a social rate of return applies to earnings or benefits beyond the private rate of return. A railroad or airline, for example, provides a community with secondary profits or benefits, which are beyond the income or profits earned by the private enterprise.

The *entrepreneurial function* concerns individual expertise or ingenuity. The entrepreneur provides the innovative function of bringing resources, labor, and capital together to provide a unique service or product. Business and entrepreneurial history may be distinguished from economic history in that they are the study of the management or the administration of the household or firm which is a single economic unit within the economy.

Government and the economy may be considered alternative ways of organizing society for the allocation of scarce resources. The market economy establishes a pattern of regular, recurrent exchange between economic units, using a medium of exchange expressed as *price*. Price is the ratio at which money and resources are exchanged. It establishes a value for which anything is bought, sold, or offered for sale. When the market fails to effect a "desirable" exchange of goods or services, government may intervene in, supplement, or supplant the market. The larger the impact of nonmarket decisions on the distribution of goods and services, the less capitalistic the economy. The American economy, during colonial and subsequent times, has been a *mixed* economy. That is, government and the economy have acted interdependently in providing for the allocation of scarce resources.

The empirical measurements of economic growth, including the now popular gross national product (GNP)—the total value of the goods and services produced by an economy in any one year—can be deceptive. GNP does not show currency depreciation. Moreover, it is an *extensive* rather than an *intensive* measurement. That is, it measures total output rather than production per capita; intensive growth measures per-unit production. It is possible to have an expanding GNP but declining individual well-being. Resources, labor, capital, social capital, the entrepreneurial function, and government must all be evaluated in the measurement of a developing economy, such as the American colonial economy.

MERCANTILISM

The British government, following the dictates of mercantilism, played a major role in the development of the American colonial economy. British mercantile economists desired to achieve national security and profits for the realm. These two goals were regarded as intertwined. National security, mercantile economists believed, is preserved by war, or by the ability to wage war. Wars are costly affairs requiring large expenditures of specie—gold and silver. The nation that accumulated the largest supply of gold was expected to wage the most successful wars.

The accumulation of gold in the realm could best be achieved in two ways: (1) by establishing a favorable balance of trade, which entailed selling more goods and services than were bought, and (2) by plunder and conquest. England and most other European powers of the seventeenth and eighteenth centuries used both techniques, although the former, it was usually discovered, was less hazardous.

War and wealth are equated today, as they were several hundred (or thousand?) years ago. Wealth, we say, is power. But it is clearly not an invincible power, as the war in Vietnam demonstrated to the United States and, indeed, as the American Revolution demonstrated to England. We are also aware today, as people were yesterday, that war drastically affects the production and distribution of resources.

Mercantilists, who elected the more peaceful means of enhancing national fortunes, discovered that colonies were useful in establishing a favorable balance of trade. Colonies could enlarge the supply of natural resources, particularly the raw materials used in manufacturing. Colonies could serve as a market for the goods manufactured by the mother country. Yet the colonial relationship involved exploitation of natural resources in the colonies.

For example, let us assume that a hat made in England of two beaver pelts sold to an American for $10. The pelts were bought from American trappers for $1 each, including shipping costs. Thus, the cost of the raw material was $2. The British merchant had gross receipts of $8 on the transaction. Part of this was labor costs, part was profit, and part was taxes for the realm, but all of it made England $8 wealthier than before. The colonies suffered an $8 trade deficit, which had to be covered. This could be done most readily by trapping at least eight more beaver. Thus, it would take ten beaver skins for the colonial to buy a hat. To take another instance, when a colonist bought a 10-pound iron plow, he had to export 100 pounds of pig iron to pay for it.

Why didn't colonists make their own hats or plows? There were a number of reasons. One was that colonial technology was not adequately developed. Where it did exist, colonial manufacturing was often less efficient than established British plants. In addition, the scarce and largely unskilled American labor supply could be applied most efficiently to mining or to the extensive (as opposed to intensive) harvesting of crops and natural resources. A third reason was that British laws of 1732 and 1750 specifically discouraged colonial hat and plow manufacture, respectively. The colonial economic relationship generally encouraged colonists to expand their production of raw materials and discouraged them from manufacturing finished products.

In the United States today, the areas that produce raw materials are under constant pressure to expand production and exploit the natural resources. Coal, timber, and petroleum, for example, are subject to a seemingly inexhaustible demand. It takes many barrels of raw petroleum for a Texan to earn enough money to buy an automobile. It requires the harvesting and sale of a large quantity of lumber for an Oregon man to earn enough to pay for his television set. The colonial relationship, however, was not as one-sided as it may at first appear. The alternative is to not pump oil (or buy an automobile), not cut timber (or buy a television set), not trap beaver (or buy a hat). Conservation, whether practiced by the individual or by the society, requires self-denial. For most of their existence, the American colonies had the natural resources, but not the labor or capital, to achieve an adequate degree of national self-sufficiency. Independence did not, in fact, alleviate America's dependency, if balance of payments may be taken as an indicator (see Table 3.1).

TABLE 3.1

American Balance of Payments, 1790–1850 (Millions of Dollars).

YEAR	BALANCE ON GOODS AND SERVICES	YEAR	BALANCE ON GOODS AND SERVICES
1790	−1	1821	4
1791	−8	1822	−9
1792	−8	1823	2
1793	2	1824	0
1794	10	1825	6
1795	−12	1826	−4
1796	−3	1827	8
1797	−11	1828	−14
1798	−2	1829	0
1799	15	1830	6
1800	−2	1831	−15
1801	2	1832	−12
1802	7	1833	−19
1803	8	1834	−24
1804	12	1835	−33
1805	−10	1836	−68
1806	−7	1837	−28
1807	−5	1838	−7
1808	−17	1839	−53
1809	12	1840	26
1810	7	1841	−12
1811	35	1842	1
1812	−21	1843	20
1813	15	1844	0
1814	−9	1845	−2
1815	−15	1846	−10
1816	−58	1847	3
1817	−11	1848	−15
1818	−25	1849	−8
1819	−15	1850	−44
1820	1		

Source: *Historical Statistics of the United States Colonial Times to 1970*, Series U 1–25, p. 866.

In 1731, James Peele described the variety of products coming from the colonies. Prominent among them were rice, tobacco, iron, deerskins, pitch, tar, turpentine, beef, pork, tanned leather, cedar, staves, timber masts, and yards. "Peoples and Riches," said Peele, "are the true strength of a Country; the first will increase by Liberty and the other by Trade."[2] American colonials enjoyed a considerable portion of both liberty and trade.

Trade between the colonies and the mother country sprang from the abundance of natural resources in America and the demand for them in Europe. This trade soon developed a pattern that was given legal form by British Navigation Acts. The development of trade and commerce between England and the colonies provides a vital key to understanding the American Revolution. "A study of colonial commerce carries us at once," said historian Charles Andrews, "into the very heart of that most fundamental of all colonial questions, the relation of the colonies to the sovereign power across the sea."[3]

THE NAVIGATION ACTS

By the mid seventeenth century, England found herself in a fierce worldwide commercial rivalry with the Dutch, Portuguese, French, and Spanish. By 1650 the Dutch, by virtue of the East India Company (1602), the West India Company (1621), and a larger, more efficient merchant marine, were threatening the economic survival of England. In defense of British trade, Parliament authorized in 1651 "An Act for Increase of Shipping and Encouragement of the Navigation of the Nation." The act prohibited the importation of goods into any part of the British Empire other than in English or colonial vessels. The act, which intended to eliminate the Dutch from the carrying trade and to preserve profits in English pockets, did more than that. It almost wrecked the British economy. In 1650, the Commonwealth simply lacked the necessary ship tonnage to carry the continually rising cargoes.

An act of 1660 revised the law of 1651, and accomplished much the same purpose as the earlier law without creating its severe repercussions. This act, which is generally regarded as the first Navigation Act, remained in effect, with minor revisions, throughout the colonial period. The Act of 1660 specified that imports into the Commonwealth had to be transported in English or colonial ships, or in ships of the country of origin. Dutch ships, in other words, could sail into British ports only if they carried cargo directly from Holland. They could not transship cargo from Commonwealth or foreign ports to England. The Act of 1660 was supplemented by a clause "enumerating" sugar, tobacco, indigo, and cotton as goods that could be sold only to England or other English colonies. The purpose of this clause was to confine shipping earnings to the empire. Rice, molasses, beaver skins, fur, and copper were later added to the list.

The Act of 1663 required all European goods headed for the colonies to pass through England. An act of 1673 called for the levying of duties on cargo at the port of clearance, rather than at the port of arrival. As Thomas C. Barrow indicates, prior to 1763 this act functioned to regulate trade rather than to raise revenues.[4]

By these acts, Parliament established very strong guidelines affecting colonial-British commerce. Lawrence A. Harper, who conducted a scholarly study of the Navigation Acts, regarded them as an experiment in social engineering. The acts were the administrative devices used to eliminate Dutch competition, build a strong merchant marine, train seamen for war, promote shipbuilding, and help establish a favorable balance of trade. Although the acts, according to Harper, accomplished the purposes of the mother country, their overall impact upon the American colonies was adverse.[5]

More recent studies hold that the negative impact of British controls on colonial trade was relatively small. There is renewed interest in the question of how much control or restraint on trade the British actually imposed. Was "salutary neglect" a *modus operandi* that avoided most of the abuses that could have followed from an absolute enforcement of the law? Salutary neglect, or nonenforcement of the laws, appears to have had roots in both policy and practice. On the one hand, it involved inattention to administrative details by colonial officials and customs inspectors. On the other hand, it included practices of patronage and the lack of parliamentary and court enforcement of the laws.[6]

What did the Navigation Acts propose to do, and what did they actually accomplish? The acts proposed to, and did, virtually eliminate foreign competition in the American carrying trade. American goods were carried almost exclusively in British or colonial bottoms by 1700. As American exports, which were negligible in the seventeenth century, expanded rapidly in the eighteenth century, the demand for ships rose proportionately and the American shipbuilding industry expanded more than proportionately. British shipyards, already highly productive, did not have the capacity for further expansion.

Although shipbuilding in the colonial era has never been adequately quantified, it is clear that it had become a major industry by the mid 1700s. Though centered in New England colonial ship construction extended south to North Carolina. Philadelphia was the chief shipbuilding city in America between 1727 and 1766, and there was substantial shipbuilding in Maryland, Virginia, and North Carolina during these years. During the last half of the eighteenth century, shipbuilding declined in the Southern colonies and became confined more to New England. New England–built vessels ranged from 250 to 20 tons, although most were nearer in weight to the smaller figure.[7]

The enumeration clauses of the Navigation Acts required that the major items of colonial export go only to England, where they might then be reexported. English, rather than colonial merchants might then skim the cream from the profits. Conversely, colonists could buy certain commodities, such as lead, paper, tea, iron products, and later molasses, only from England or British possessions. These laws eliminated competition, often to the detriment of the colonists. With only one market for tobacco, for example, colonists had little choice but to accept the prevailing market price. Tobacco, which had sold as a luxury item before 1640, thereafter became so overproduced that prices collapsed, despite the Virginia legislature's efforts to control acreage and to institute price-support programs reminiscent of modern federal agricultural programs. Nevertheless, the total volume, and the total value, of colonial tobacco exports generally increased over the next hundred years. Having a closed market also meant having a guaranteed market and a protected market. England not only prevented the sale of certain goods to non-English markets, she invariably absorbed all the enumerated commodities the colonies could ship, on occasion paying prices higher than those of the world market, as in the case of indigo.

Although the Iron Act of 1750 prohibited the colonial manufacture of finished iron products, it also allowed the importation of bar and pig iron into England duty-free. Since there had been little manufacture of finished iron products in the colonies during the preceding 100 years, the few American iron manufacturers would have been unable to compete in an open market with the British. Ironically, the Iron Act of 1750, ostensibly designed to restrain colonial commerce, had the effect of enticing the colonies to export crude iron in ever greater quantities.

Until at least 1763, England was negligent in enforcing many of the trade restrictions and duties it had enacted. A petition to the king in 1732 from the Council and Burgesses of Virginia observed that because of onerous new regulations ''there arose a sufficient temptation to defraud the Customs, and the Running of Tobacco became soon a great Abuse.'' But in other respects the course of trade was little altered. The stratagems resorted to by New England shippers such as Thomas Hancock in circumventing the Molasses Act, which prohibited the purchase of non-British molasses, and the various Navigation Acts that prohibited the direct importation of European goods into the colonies must have been notoriously flagrant, but in general they were overlooked.

An act of Parliament ''made in the Third and Fourth Years of the Reign of her late Majesty Queen Anne'' required that all colonial rice go directly to England. But in 1731, Parliament reversed itself and made a special exception of rice:

> Whereas his Majesty's Province of Carolina in America has, by Experience, been found to be a proper Soil for producing Rice to very great Perfection, and for many years last past the Produce thereof has increased; and it is reasonable to expect, that not only the Produce thereof in those Parts, but also the Exportation thereof would be greatly increased, for the mutual Benefit of this Kingdom and the said Province if (notwithstanding the Laws relating to Navigation and Trade to and from the Plantations) Liberty or License were granted to Ships built in, and sailing from Great Britain, to load Rice in the said Province, and to carry the same directly to any ports of Europe lying Southward of Cape Finisterre. . . .[8]

Although as a matter of policy English merchants would have preferred to reexport rice to the markets in Italy and Spain, as a matter of practice anything that prolonged the delivery of rice to its final market increased the losses from spoilage more than proportionately. If the British wanted to make money out of rice, they had better sell it directly. They did. The act of 1731 exempting rice was renewed periodically, on the last occasion by an act of January 13, 1774.

Although the British trade regulations may at first appear to have been onerous, a closer examination suggests other possible conclusions. The primary purpose of the Navigation Laws was to protect British and American markets. When the laws were repugnant or injurious because overzealously enforced, Britain provided wide latitude in their enforcement or, when warranted, changed them. Some of the laws, such as the Iron Act, are perhaps incorrectly regarded as exercising restraints when in fact they offered a trade advantage—lower taxes or none at all.

ECONOMICS AND INDEPENDENCE

Traditionally presented in textbooks as triangular in nature, Colonial trade seems to have been conducted more often on a shuttle basis between many different points. Ships did sail triangular routes from Boston to the African coast, where rum was bartered for slaves, and then to the West Indies, where the slaves were traded to planters for molasses and sugar. And profits did develop at each leg of the voyage. Trade, however, particularly in colonial ships, seems to have occurred prominently with other colonies and the West Indies. The "Yankee merchant" began as a sailing, "rolling-store" operator, buying and selling whatever was worth buying and selling at the moment in one of the hundreds of ports he might visit. Trade in the staple items—for example, those items enumerated in the Navigation Acts—was conducted by larger firms, most of them British, who operated their own ships. Occasionally, such trade was undertaken by British-American firms: the American firm arranged for the buying, warehousing, and trading, and the British firm provided the ships, capital, and marketing in England. Most British imports from the Commonwealth originated in the southern colonies and the West Indies. Rice, sugar, tobacco, indigo, and cotton were the great money crops of the eighteenth century. The northern colonies produced relatively few commodities for direct sale (among these few items were furs, ships, and whale oil), but they reexported considerable quantities of staple goods acquired in the peddling expeditions up and down the coast. By the time of the Revolution, some American shippers had developed large shipping operations and accumulated sizable fortunes.

Integral to trade between the colonies, and between the colonies and England, was an elaborate but chaotic system of business agents. The agent was variously the buyer or seller, commission merchant, consignor or consignee, creditor or debtor, or whatever was appropriate. He could be an employer of a large firm, or an independent. In eighteenth-century South Carolina, many agents functioned much like the cotton factors of the nineteenth century: they served as the business manager of one or several plantations, as a shipping agent, and as a branch banker of a firm in London, England or Bristol, Connecticut. Such an agent was Richard Splatt of Charleston, South Carolina, who in 1721 recorded "thirty seven barrels of Rice and Two chest of Deare skin shipt by me Richard Splatt on board the Lovely Polly Michael Bath Master bound for London on my proper account and . . . Consigned to Mr. William Crisp." Tobacco men in the middle colonies appear to have functioned as buyers and bankers, but less frequently as estate managers. Agents specialized in various functions or services. Some dealt only in books or paper, some only in grain, and some just in precious metals. Thomas Hancock began his massive trading ventures with consignments of books from an agent in England.[9] These agents, in whatever capacity, kept the wheels of commerce moving and the account books straight.

Although there remains considerable controversy as to the impact of British commercial regulations on the development of the colonial economy, more credence is given the idea that British regulations were not that bad. No one has gone as far as to credit the British colonial system with having been a positive good. But it is safe to suggest that on the balance, and at least until the close of the French and Indian Wars in 1763, British mercantile regulations were not detrimental to colonial development. The British navy provided the necessary security for world commerce. British bankers, until the Revolution, provided the main source of credit. British law provided the financial and institutional organization necessary for hemispheric trade. If one looks at the colonial-British trade relationship and then at the alternatives, the Colonial-British system commands considerable respect.

The Navigation Acts were supplemented and amended as the need arose, but the overall mercantile policy remained consistent—to do those things necessary to maintain a favorable balance of trade. The Wool Act of 1699 prohibited the exportation of raw wool or finished woolen products by any colony to England or another colony. Because sheep raising and woolen-textile manufacturing were primary sources of British profit, competition from the colonies could not be tolerated. The Hat Act (1732) banned the sale of hats by any colony to England or another colony, so preventing the development of colonial hat manufacture and protecting English domestic trade. The Molasses Act of 1733 provided for a hefty tax on foreign (i.e., French) molasses coming into the colonies in order to force American shippers to buy from British planters in the West Indies rather than from the French, who often undersold the British. There is little doubt that such legislation had an adverse impact upon colonial economic growth. It is useful to consider, however, that legislation such as the Hat, Molasses, Wool, and Iron Acts were less the product of economic planning and policy than the result of special-interest lobbying. Sir Lewis Namier, a British scholar, argues that British economic legislation in the seventeenth and eighteenth centuries evolved from no grandiose master plan or policy, but from a hodgepodge of special-interest legislation—legislation, nonetheless, that was consistent with British imperial mercantilistic policy. It is no less erroneous to label acts of Congress today as part of an overall plan than to attribute the acts of Parliament in the eighteenth century to a master plan for the development of the British Empire.

"Empire" is a misnomer for the British economic and political system before 1750. "Struggling Island" might be more appropriate. The struggles, to be sure, occurred on a global scale. Each of the colonial wars that occurred between 1689 and 1763 was an extension of conflict between the major western European powers. These wars may best be understood in the context of the modern cold war, which as to style and technique is actually not so modern at all. In seventeenth and eighteenth-century western Europe unceasing economic and political rivalry and numerous military skirmishes occasionally erupted in hot wars. Some effort had been made by European powers to make their American colonies "neutral territories" in the event of war in Europe. In 1686, James II of England and Louis XIV of France agreed to refrain from hostilities in the New World, even if France and England should become engaged in war in Europe. The Glorious Revolution of 1688 ended James's part in the pact, and when William of Orange (William III) succeeded James to the throne of England, a hot war broke out between England and France that immediately involved the colonials. Queen Anne's War followed upon the heels of King William's War, lasting from 1701 to 1713. Both wars involved fighting in America between English and French colonists and their Indian allies.

Hostilities between England and Spain renewed (if they had ever ceased) around 1740 over the continuing issue of English trading rights in the Caribbean. The ensuing War of Jenkins' Ear soon assumed global proportions, when Frederick the Great of Prussia seized Austrian territories. France joined Prussia, hoping to acquire Austria's Belgian provinces. England gave aid to Austria, and Spain joined Prussia and France. In the colonies, French and English settlers and their Indian allies fought King George's War (1744–1748). During this war the American colonists captured the French fortress of Louisbourg, which blocked access to the St. Lawrence seaway and had impeded American colonial fishing and fur trading. England, however, did less well in Europe, and the fortress reverted to France with the signing of the treaty of peace.

Unlike modern cold-war contestants, colonial powers were not divided by different political and economic philosophies. Their wars were those of similar governments that had similar but competing economic aspirations. American colonists, however, were not entirely the innocent pawns of empire that they are sometimes characterized as being. French, Spanish, and English colonists had competing domestic economic interests. This competition shows up in marginal but interesting ways. New England, French, and English fishermen competed vigorously and sometimes violently for fishing and drying rights around Nova Scotia and Newfoundland. John Winthrop launched Massachusetts' first fishing boat in 1631; in 1700, the colony exported fish valued at an estimated $300,000 in gold. By 1750, some 400 New England–owned fishing vessels operated in the offshore cod fisheries, and 200 more fished the coastal waters. Whaling was a flourishing industry by 1750. Massachusetts alone sent out some 300 whalers in 1771, and these often competed with British vessels. Rivalry between French and English traders was intense around the Great Lakes, Hudson's Bay, and the lower Mississippi throughout the eighteenth century. The curious territorial settlement made by the Treaty of Utrecht, which gave England the shores of Hudson's Bay, derived from competing English and French interests. Interestingly, French traders in the region preferred doing business with the English, who paid better prices on pelts than did the French merchants. The Indians, properly characterized as the scapegoats of imperialism, nevertheless became proficient at playing off English and French traders against each other—and the English and French returned the favor. English traders were penetrating deeply into the lower Mississippi Valley by 1700. In 1713, a trader named Price Hughes instigated an Indian massacre of French traders at Natchez.

Despite royal prohibitions, considerable illicit trade occurred among French, English, and Spanish colonies. One Yankee captain, for example, sailed into Mobile Bay in 1735 to collect a personal debt. While in this French port illegally, his ship was unloaded of its cargo and another cargo was loaded aboard. Charleston, South Carolina, was visited not infrequently by French ships driven into port by providential storms. They used the occasion to load rice aboard in exchange for cloth or spices. Despite the grand imperial notions of the day, commerce was a highly individualistic, enterprising business. Rules, when they existed, had to be interpreted and enforced locally. Despite the best intentions of their majesties' governments, trade in the New World early reflected salutary neglect and laissez faire.

THE NEW IMPERIAL SYSTEM

The conclusion of the French and Indian War in 1763 threatened to end the individualistic, free-enterprising economy that had been developing in America for well over one hundred years. In part, this war had begun as a result of competing claims for land and trade rights in the Ohio and Mississippi valleys. These claims derived somewhat less from imperial considerations than from domestic speculative interests. By 1750, colonial land companies had claimed tracts in the Mississippi Valley ranging from Pennsylvania to Georgia. American settlers, land speculators, trappers, and traders began moving into the Ohio Valley in the 1740s. The Ohio Land Company, formed by Virginia investors, planned to derive profits from the Indian trade and from land sales in the Ohio

Valley. In 1750, the company sent Christopher Gist to the upper Potomac to build a post. Pennsylvania investors, headed by George Groghan, opposed Virginia's penetration, as did the French. The Americans soon buried their differences for a time and united in opposition to the French. American speculators also anticipated British financial interests in the west:

> In America, colony was already pitted against colony in the race for the speculative profits of the west; English speculators were just beginning to be interested. When the time should come when the great British speculators would discover the possibilities of the American west—as come it did soon after the war then starting—the competition between colonial speculators and British speculators would have a profound effect upon the formation of British policy toward the west, and would pit the colonies against the mother country.[10]

The Treaty of Paris (1763) which ended the French and Indian War, awarded Canada, Florida, and the Mississippi Valley west of the river, excluding the Isle of Orleans, to England. The treaty had several results. The colonial appetite for western land rose precipitously, British financial interests in the west quickened, and Indians arose in a desperate and bloody attempt to halt the white tide in a series of wars known as Pontiac's Conspiracy. The French and Indian War also removed the French threat to colonial expansion and security and the dependence of the colonists on British military power.

The French and Indian War and the expansion of an empire that now stretched from India to the Mississippi River forced England, already drained financially, to maintain an elaborate and expensive system of frontier defense, a system that would require greater financial support from the colonies. At a time when the American colonies needed her less—the one great threat to American frontier security (France) being gone—England was compelled to impose higher taxes and stronger trade regulations, to enforce more rigidly those in existence, and to station troops within the colonies. Furthermore, British investor and speculator interests used Parliament as a weapon to undermine competing American commercial interests. The Proclamation of 1763, which prohibited settlement west of the Appalachian Mountains, denied American settlers and business interests the opportunity of acquiring land within the Ohio and Mississippi valleys. This act robbed Americans of what they considered their rightful property, acquired by grant, war, and possession.

In effect, Parliament had supplanted the colonial legislature as the constitutional source of property rights in the western territories. The apparent extinction of colonial rights to the western lands led to the creation of numerous new land ventures in England. The most prominent of these was the Vandalia project, which would establish a new proprietary colony across the mountains. The scheme involved intensive political maneuvering in Parliament and within the colonial legislatures, but was aborted by war. The colonial reaction to the Quebec Act of 1774, which recognized the Roman Catholic religion in that

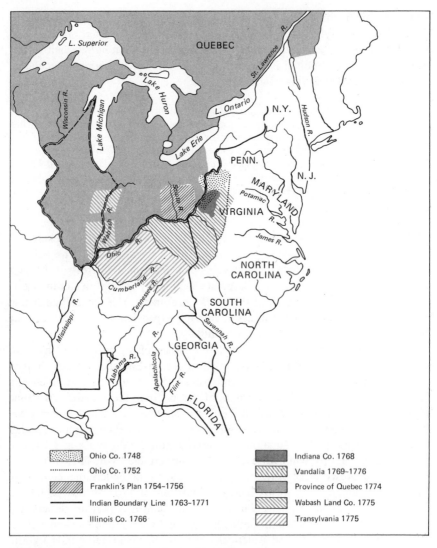

FIGURE 3.5. Claims by colonial land companies.

Source: Savelle & Middlekauf, *A History of Colonial America* (Holt, Rinehart & Winston), 1964, p. 520.

Legend:

- Ohio Co. 1748
- Ohio Co. 1752
- Franklin's Plan 1754–1756
- Indian Boundary Line 1763–1771
- Illinois Co. 1766
- Indiana Co. 1768
- Vandalia 1769–1776
- Province of Quebec 1774
- Wabash Land Co. 1775
- Transylvania 1775

province, was based less on religious intolerance than on the fact that the act defined Quebec's boundaries so as to include the Ohio Valley and thus again eliminated colonial land claims to that region.

The Currency Act of 1764 delivered another economic blow to the American colonies. British merchants protested the payment of American debts in cheap, legal-tender paper money, such as that issued by the Virginia Assembly during the French and Indian War. Parliament responded by prohibiting the issuance of legal tender and by retiring circulating paper. The act forced financial retrenchment and recession throughout the middle and New England colonies. The Revenue Act (Sugar Act) of 1764 compounded colonial difficulties by imposing high duties on foreign imported goods, including sugar. The Quartering Act of 1765 required colonial housing and provisioning of troops stationed within the colony. The Stamp Act of 1765 sought to aid the British government in the collection of at least £100,000 annually, which was only a portion of the £350,000 needed to support British civil and military establishments in the American colonies. The act imposed a tax on all printed materials and legal documents, provoked an outcry from the most vocal elements of society (the lawyers, merchants, and journalists), and prompted the calling of the Stamp Act Congress in 1765, which marked the first unified colonial resistance to British postwar policy. Parliament repealed the Stamp Act, but refused to relinquish any constitutional authority over the colonies.

The Townshend Duties of 1767 imposed import duties on glass, lead, paint, paper, and tea, primary items imported and used by most colonies. The impact and revenue potential of this act could be compared to those of the modern gasoline tax. Public indignation, fanned by expert publicists such as John Dickinson, Patrick Henry, and Samuel Adams, brought rioting, violence, and a nonimportation agreement. Parliament again relented to the commercial pressure by repealing the Townshend Duties, retaining only the tax on tea. The Tea Act of 1773 gave the British East India Company a monopoly on the sale of tea in the American colonies, and represented to the colonies a further usurpation of colonial property rights. The Boston Tea Party, which symbolized American defiance of British property rights, led to the Coercive Acts, which involved both economic and political retribution.

By the time the First Continental Congress assembled in Philadelphia in 1774, the conflict over authority regarding land distribution, trade regulation, taxes, and currency had reached an impasse. Emotions were inflamed. War had become inevitable. The American Revolution was kindled in the aftermath of the French and Indian War. The fuel, however, had been gathered earlier, in the American wilderness. The physical growth of the American economy made the colonies increasingly attractive to British business interests. This same growth generated the capital and the institutions that made the colonies less dependent on and more competitive with the British. The development of the American economy before 1763 may also be characterized by an absence of authority and

CHARLES TOWNSHEND *(1725–1767)*
English statesman;
author of Townshend Duties, Tea Act.
Courtesy British Museum.

regulation. The Navigation Acts provided a protective shield rather than fetters. The imposition of authority and regulation after 1763 constituted a genuine economic jolt, but an even more acute psychological one, to the colonies. The colonists, who had known little government and enjoyed a low rate of taxation, became aware of what government could do to them rather than for them. Americans desired political as well as economic freedom.

The French and Indian War marked a distinct change in American-English relationships. Expanded British interests in the colonies after 1763 derived from several factors. The removal of the French created new investment opportunities and made old investments more attractive and secure. Furthermore, by 1763 the American colonies had clearly developed the institutional framework, the laws, the business agents, and the sheer number of people to make business in America more attractive. Yet the very features that attracted the British made them less welcome to Americans. With the French gone there was less need for the British, especially if they intended to preempt the former French territories and exclude the colonies from their possession or from their right to profits in the west. As investment opportunities became more attractive, long-established American-British trade rivalries became critical. Americans ultimately had no recourse short of war against what they believed to be Parliament's self-interested and commercially inspired tinkering.

Notes

[1] See James F. Shepherd and Gary M. Walton, *Shipping, Maritime Trade, and the Economic Development of Colonial North America* (Cambridge: The University Press, 1972).

[2] James Peele, *The Importance of the British Plantations in America to the Kingdom with the State of their Trade, and Methods for Improving It* (London, 1731) 18–19.

[3] Charles M. Andrews, "Colonial Commerce," *American Historical Review*, 20 (October 1914) 48.

[4] See Thomas C. Barrow, *Trade and Empire: The British Customs Service in Colonial Americal 1660–1775.* (Cambridge, Mass.: Harvard University Press, 1967).

[5] See Lawrence A. Harper, *The English Navigation Laws: A Seventeenth Century Experiment in Social Engineering* (New York: Columbia University Press, 1939).

[6] See Barrow, *Trade and Empire.*

[7] See Andrews, "Colonial Commerce," 43–51.

[8] *Acts of Parliament: Anno Tertio Georgii II*, Regis, 559–64 (1731).

[9] See Edward Edelman, "Thomas Hancock, Colonial Merchant," *Journal of Economic and Business History*, 1 (1928–29), 77–104.

[10] Max Savelle, *A History of Colonial America*, rev. Robert Middlekauff (New York: Holt, Rinehart & Winston, 1964), pp. 521–22.

SUGGESTED READINGS:

BAILYN, BERNARD, *The New England Merchants in the Seventeenth Century.* Cambridge, Mass.: Harvard University Press, 1955. Reprint ed., New York: Harper & Row, 1964.

BARROW, THOMAS C., *Trade and Empire: The British Customs Service in Colonial America, 1660–1775.* Cambridge, Mass.: Harvard University Press, 1967.

BRUCHEY, STUART, ed., *The Colonial Merchant: Sources and Readings.* New York: Harcourt, Brace & World, 1966.

DICKERSON, OLIVER M., *The Navigation Acts and the American Revolution.* Philadelphia: University of Pennsylvania Press, 1951, Reprint ed., New York: A.S. Barnes, 1963.

HARPER, LAWRENCE A., *The English Navigation Laws: A Seventeenth Century Experiment in Social Engineering.* New York: Columbia University Press, 1939.

MAIN, JACKSON T., *The Social Structure of Revolutionary America.* Princeton, N.J.: Princeton University Press, 1965.

SHEPHERD, JAMES F., AND GARY M. WALTON, *Shipping, Maritime Trade, and the Economic Development of Colonial North America.* Cambridge: The University Press, 1972.

SOSIN, JACK, *The Revolutionary Frontier, 1763–1783.* New York: Holt, Rinehart & Winston, 1967.

TOLLES, FREDERICK B., *Meeting House and Counting House: The Quaker Merchants of Colonial Philadelphia, 1682–1763.* Chapel Hill, N.C.: University of North Carolina Press, 1948.

VAN ALSTYNE, RICHARD W., *Empire and Independence: The International History of the American Revolution.* New York: John Wiley, 1965.

CREATING A
NATIONAL ECONOMY:
THE CONSTITUTION AND
THE SUPREME COURT

————————————— chapter IV——

The Articles of Confederation did little more than give legal sanction to the mode of government that had been in effect since the Second Continental Congress convened in 1775. That government was at best a "firm league of friendship" entered into by sovereign states. Serious search for a plan of union did not begin until 1776, one year after the war had commenced. That plan, finally approved in 1781, established the United States of America under the authority of the Articles of Confederation.

THE ARTICLES OF CONFEDERATION

The deficiencies and inadequacies of the new government created by the Articles of Confederation have been described perhaps too generously by historians, and indeed by contemporary critics of that government. The new nation, it is argued, became mired in debt and paper money. Soldiers fought without pay, clothing, and provisions. Desertions were high. A general turned traitor. Trade was idled. Taxes, when levied, went uncollected. The prices of all goods soared to unbelievable heights, which led to profiteering and speculation. The frontier was unprotected. Farmers and debtors openly revolted. Veterans plotted a military coup. The government was paralyzed. "By the end of the Confederation period," wrote John D. Hicks in his classic text *The Federal Union*,

> the line of cleavage in the new nation between the possessors of considerable property and the common people was clearly drawn. The merchants and importers, the shipbuilders and shipowners, the possessors of landed estates, the speculators and money-lenders were set apart by their economic interests from the small farmers, the artisans, and the non-propertied classes generally. Among men of property the fear had grown almost to the proportions of panic that the lower classes

would eventually secure control of the state governments, and that as a result property interests everywhere would suffer perhaps even to the point of confiscation.[1]

It is likely that *war*, rather than government, fostered inflation, the disruption of trade, dissension, and social instability. Such has certainly been true of modern wars. The American Revolution would have been no exception.

The loose union of states under the Articles is not to be lightly dismissed as a failure. In its mechanics and functions it had serious defects, yet the Confederation must be credited with some remarkable accomplishments. In their basic precepts and theories the Articles were true to the spirit and purposes of the Revolution. In addition, the Articles provided the intellectual and some of the institutional footing for the creation of the Constitutional government.

The government created by the Articles had a unicameral legislative assembly in which each state had one vote. Each state had to have at least two delegates, but no more than seven. A Committee of the States, comprising one delegate from each state, sat as the governmental authority during the absence of Congress. Congress and the Committee selected its own presiding officer. No action on matters of war, treaties, money, or appointment of military commanders could be taken without the support of nine states. The government had no executive or judicial branch. Amendments to the Articles were to be approved unanimously by the states.

The national assembly reserved the exclusive right to coin money, accept ambassadors, institute a postal service, pay and enter into debts, fix the standards of weights and measures, manage trade and Indian affairs, and wage war. It could appoint a board or commission to negotiate interstate problems and disputes.

The national government, however, was denied two basic powers of a sovereign government: it could not levy taxes or raise troops. Government finances were to be provided by a tax levy made by each state legislature. These levies were based on the value of land within the states. Troops, when ''requisitioned by Congress, must be raised by authority of the state.'' The national government depended upon the good will of the states for money and national defense.

The physical accomplishments of the Confederation can be documented easily. It concluded the war successfully and negotiated an unusually generous treaty of peace. Various departments of government were organized, such as the offices of Secretary of War, Secretary of Foreign Affairs (State), and Treasurer, all of which provided the experience and institutional framework needed in the Constitutional period. Robert Morris organized a prototype of a national bank and initiated a system of currency. The government survived an inflationary boom and a postwar bust. Even the most outspoken critic of the Confederation government reported that during the Confederation period several important branches [of manufacturing] have grown up and flourished with a rapidity which surprises.

. . . Of these it may not be improper to enumerate the most considerable—

    I. Tanned and tarred leather dress skins, shoes, boots and slippers, harness and saddlery of all kinds, Portmanteaux and trunks, leather breeches, gloves, muffs and tippets, Parchment and Glue.

    II. Bar and Sheet Iron, Steel, Nail-rods & Nails, implements of husbandry, Stoves, Pots and other utensils, the steel and Iron work of carriages and for Shipbuilding, Anchors, scale beams and Weights and Various tools of Artificers, arms of different kinds, though the manufacture of these last has of late diminished for want of demand.

    III. Ships, Cabinet Wares and Turnery, Wool and Cotton cards, and other machinery for manufacture and husbandry, Mathematical instruments, Coopers wares of every kind.

    IV. of flax and Hemp. Cables, sail-cloth, Cordage, twine and Packthread.

    V. Bricks and coarse tiles & Potters Wares.

    VI. Ardent Spirits and malt liquors.

    VII. Writing and printing paper, sheathing and wrapping Papers, pasteboards, fullers or press papers, paper hangings.

    VIII. Hats of fur and Wool and mixtures of both. Women's Stuff and Silk Shoes.

    IX. Refined Sugars.

    X. Oils of animals and seeds, Soap, Spermaceti and Tallow Candles.

    XI. Copper and brass wares particularly utensils for distillers, Sugar refiners, and brewers, and Tuns and other Articles for household Use Philosophical apparatus.

    XII. Tin Wares for most purposes and Ordinary use.

    XIII. Carriages of all kinds.

    XIV. Snuff, chewing & smoking Tobacco.

    XV. Starch and Hairpowder.

    XVI. Lampblack, and other Painters colours.

    XVII. Gunpowder.[2]

George Washington reported in 1784 that there existed a "Spirit of enterprise [that] may achieve almost anything." There was cause for optimism. The American-built *Empress of China* opened the China trade in 1785. John Fitch began experimenting with a steam-operated mechanical-oared boat the same year. The first cotton factory in America was built at Beverly, Massachusetts in 1787, and a woolen factory at Hartford, Connecticut in the same year. Data for the Confederation period is woefully sparse, but there are strong indications that agricultural production and industrial output increased markedly during that time. Despite British blockades, exports remained rather high, increasing substantially, of course, to the Dutch and French. There is evidence that some trade continued even with England—through transshipment from the West Indies, and sometimes directly from American ports—and with English army-procurement officers. During the British occupation of Charleston considerable rice found its way into English markets, and in August 1783, shipping agents were anticipating unusually large crops of rice and indigo. Colonial factors and merchants, however patriotic, desperately needed to sell for specie rather than for failing colonial currency.

TABLE 4.1

Value of Exports From the Southern Colonies to England and Scotland From Christmas, 1769 to Christmas, 1782.

	Virginia and Maryland	The Carolinas	Georgia
Annual Average, 1769–1774	548,636	402,792	67,693
1775	758,357	579,550	103,477
1776	73,225	13,668	12,570
1777	58	2,234	—
1778	—	1,074	—
1779	—	3,732	607
1780	—	708	2,251
1781	—	94,368	506
1782	—	14,182	6,804

Source: L. C. Gray, *History of Agriculture in the Southern United States to 1860* (1932; reprint ed., Gloucester, Mass.: Peter Smith, 1958, Vol. II, p. 577.)

Although Table 4.1 suggests a tremendous curtailment in American exports, it must be remembered that these figures show sales to England, which in theory ended in 1776. The absence of recorded exports to England from Virginia and Maryland in this table cannot be taken as evidence that such exports ceased entirely. The amount of tobacco imported into England from the West Indies seems to have increased in inverse proportion to the decline in tobacco imports from North America after 1776. But although greater tobacco production in the West Indies could explain some of this increase, there is evidence that American shippers nursed traditional English outlets for cargoes by indirect shipments through the West Indies.

Rapid recovery in major-export trade seems to have occurred with the return of peace after 1783. Within three years of the close of hostilities, Virginia tobacco exports had returned to prewar levels (Table 4.2).

TABLE 4.2

Virginia Tobacco Exports, 1783–1789.

1783–1784	49,497 hogsheads
1784–1785	55,624 hogsheads
1785–1786	60,380 hogsheads
1786–1787	60,041 hogsheads
1787–1788	58,544 hogsheads
1788–1789	58,673 hogsheads

Source: L. C. Gray, *History of Agriculture in the Southern United States to 1860* (1932; reprint ed., Gloucester, Mass.: Peter Smith, 1958, Vol. II, p. 605.)

Rice exports recovered less rapidly, averaging only half the prewar level between 1783 and 1788. By the 1790s, though, rice prices and shipments had exceeded prewar levels. The indigo industry, despite the loss of the English subsidy, rebounded from the war to achieve new heights in prices and quantities exported, only to expire by 1800. Revolution, the loss of subsidy, and the introduction of chemical dyes appear to have had less to do with the end of indigo production than the lure of very high prices for cotton. Generally, the cessation of hostilities produced a spontaneous and surprising renewal of commercial relations between England and her former colonies.

The Articles of Confederation created a commercial framework for the states that was superior to the one provided by England during the colonial period. The Articles have too often been criticized, when in fact they created a positive environment for economic growth and expansion. Article IV and provisos of other Articles created a free-trade zone in North America that was larger than any then existing in Europe. In their impact and conceptual framework, in fact, the Articles might be compared to the European Common Market, where despite the retention of absolute sovereignty by the member countries, a far greater and freer marketplace exists than ever before. The Common Market, of course, has not reached the degree of economic integration provided by the Articles.

Under the Articles, citizens of the United States had "free ingress and regress to and from any other state," and enjoyed therein "all the privileges of trade and commerce, subject to the same duties, impositions and restrictions as the inhabitants thereof respectively . . ." The national government had the exclusive power to regulate the alloy content and value of coinage struck by the government or by the states. Congress had the sole authority to fix the standards of weights and measures, to regulate the Indian trade, to establish and regulate post offices throughout the states, and to settle conflicting land grants or questions of territorial jurisdiction arising between states. Free trade, private enterprise, and laissez faire were very much a part of Confederation policy. Unfortunately, although the Articles created a free-trade region, they failed to create the "protective umbrella" formerly provided by Parliament.

SETTLEMENT OF THE WEST

Conflict over the proprietorship and distribution of land had helped precipitate the American Revolution. Each state claimed jurisdiction over the "public lands" within its dominions. What were the boundaries of each state? Did Virginia's western territories embrace the Ohio Valley, as Virginia claimed, or possibly all of the land between the thirty-fourth and thirty-eighth parallels, as established in Virginia's original charter? The Proclamation of 1763, the Quebec Act, and other legislation drafted by Parliament after the French and Indian War appeared to replace colonial authority over the western territories with Parliamentary authority. Perhaps one of the greatest successes of the Confederation was to counteract this development by expropriating the authority over the western territories that Parliament had attempted to reserve for itself since 1763.

The American Revolution temporarily removed British competition for the western lands, but failed to stem American expansion and land fever. On the contrary, settlers and speculators took advantage of the war to push their special interests. In 1779 John Donelson led a party from western Virginia through hostile Indians to Nashville. His party settled there, joining a group led by James Robertson, who with John Sevier and Daniel Boone had developed the Watauga settlements in eastern Tennessee some years earlier. Of the twenty-two persons in Colonel Donelson's expedition who died during the first year of settlement only one died of natural causes. The Creek Indians created havoc and bloodshed along the western frontier. Colonizing and speculation was not an easy business. John Donelson died in 1785, and leadership of the large Donelson clan soon fell on the shoulders of a strong and aggressive son-in-law, Andrew Jackson.[3] Jackson skillfully parlayed his small capital into a fortune by speculating in land, buying slaves, and raising cotton.

For a time, Sevier, who was left in control of the eastern settlements of the Watauga colony, moved with local sentiment to create an independent state. In 1784, North Carolina ceded the Watauga territory to Congress. Frontiersmen seized the occasion to proclaim the Watauga country the independent state of Franklin. Franklin returned to the fold with the establishment of the new government under the Constitution, and became a part of the state of Tennessee.

Richard Henderson, who had been a financial backer of Robertson, Sevier, and Boone, organized the Transylvania Company in 1775. Over the next decade, this company promoted the settlement of thousands of pioneer families within the approximate boundaries of present-day Kentucky. During these years Kentucky vacillated between independence, statehood, and annexation by Spain. Seeking to secure her trans-Mississippi dominions, Spain invited the western regions of the United States to annex themselves to her in return for trade privileges, particularly the right of free and unrestricted navigation of the Mississippi River. This "Spanish Conspiracy" and the problem of opening the Mississippi River to American commerce created tremendous difficulties for the new government, difficulties that did not stop with the adoption of the Constitution.

In 1786, several army officers organized the Ohio Company. This company proposed to buy one million acres of land, to be paid for by land warrants received by Revolutionary War veterans in lieu of pay. The speculative aspects of the enterprise derived not only from the profits anticipated from the sale of land, but also from the acquisition of the land warrants at the depreciated price of nine cents on the dollar. Congress was expected to redeem the warrants at face value, but it resolutely abstained from doing so.

After unsuccessful efforts by Reverend Manassah Cutler to persuade Congress to sell land to the Ohio Company, William Duer succeeded with a clever stratagem. Duer organized the Scioto Company, whose major stockholders were himself and members of Congress. The Ohio Company was sold 1.5 million acres of land, and was granted an option by Congress on an additional 5 million acres. The option was transferred to the Scioto Company, an arrangement that gave members of Congress a discreet but vested interest. The Scioto Company failed to realize any profits, but the Ohio Company did better.

The exigencies of war, conflicting state claims, private competition, and popular demand urged the cession of western land claims by New York, Virginia, Massachusetts, and Connecticut to the national government. Upon the cession of the western land claims and the adoption of the Articles, Congress proceeded to provide an orderly basis for the distribution of the western lands. Pressure from the Ohio Company in particular and from land developers in general had contributed to the passage of the Land Ordinance of 1785 and the Northwest Ordinance of 1787. The Land Ordinance of 1785 provided for the rectangular survey of the public lands into townships six miles square by means of lines running due north and south crossed by lines running due east and west. The townships were divided into 36 sections or lots of one square mile (640 acres) each. Four sections of land were reserved for the national government, one section was reserved for public schools, and the remainder was sold at public auction at a minimum of $1.00 per acre. This was an orderly and durable system for the survey and settlement of the western lands. (See Figure 4.1.)

The Northwest Ordinance of 1787 provided for the organization of the Northwest Territory into states that had an "equal footing" with the original states. This measure has justifiably been called the crowning achievement of the Confederation, not only because it established the principle of equality among the states, but also because it prescribed many of the personal and political rights

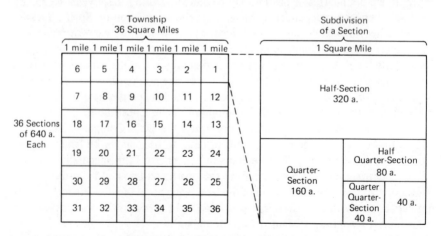

FIGURE 4.1. Rectangular survey system.

later incorporated in the Bill of Rights. Moreover, it abolished the institution of slavery within the Northwest Territory. Of equal significance, Congress clearly intended the ordinance to perpetuate the idea of a free-trade zone throughout the United States and to guarantee the protection of property rights throughout the republic. "No man," reads Article II of the Northwest Ordinance, "shall be deprived of his liberty or property, but by the judgment of his peers" (due process of law). "In the just preservation of rights and property . . . no law ought ever to be made or have force in the said territory, that shall in any manner whatever, interfere with or affect private contracts, or engagements, bona fide. . . ." Article IV specified that the legislatures of the new states could not interfere with the primary disposal of the soil by the United States, nor with any regulations made for the securing of title in the soil by the bona fide purchasers. The navigable waters and "the carrying places between the same shall be common highways, and forever free" to all. Free trade, private property, and the sanctity of contracts had become an inalienable right in the American free-enterprise system.

In terms of support for free enterprise, much was right with the Articles of Confederation and the government it created. The political framework for free enterprise created by the Articles was essentially perpetuated by the Constitution. The wrongs of the Confederation were sins of omission. Although the Articles presented a social and economic climate that was highly compatible with the purposes of the Revolution, the new government could not provide the protective umbrella that could guarantee property, contract, and trade rights. The Constitution continued to build upon the foundations laid by the Articles in that it sought to preserve the same free-enterprise system fostered by the Articles. The Constitution gave greater powers of enforcement and protection of property rights to the national government in order to overcome the weaknesses of the Articles. But in allowing the national government to enforce or protect property rights, the Constitution also created the potential for that government to direct and regulate the use of property. A new dilemma thus arose: How does one protect free enterprise without directing the enterprise? How does government, the force of collectivism, sustain individualism? The dialogue over that thorny proposition has not ceased since the publication of *The Federalist Papers,* a series of pamphlets written to gain support for the proposed Constitution.

LIBERTY AND PROPERTY

James Madison addressed the problem of public power and private rights in *The Federalist*, Number 10. Madison argued that a well-constructed Union should guard against the "violence of factions." Rights in property, he said, originate from the diversity in the faculties of men. This diversity, in turn, led to the unequal distribution of property. The possession of different quantities and kinds

ALEXANDER HAMILTON *(1757–1804)*
First U.S. Secretary of the Treasury (1789–1795)

of property divided society into different interests and parties. The great dilemma of the American governing system was that although its first object was to protect the individual's rights to diversity, it also had to prevent the destruction of society by factional violence deriving from that diversity.

Madison did mention two methods of removing the causes of faction: (1) "destroying the liberty which is essential to its existence" and (2) giving to every citizen the same opinions, passions, interests, and quantity and kind of property. Since the causes of faction obviously could not be removed, Madison believed, government must concern itself with controlling the adverse effects of faction.

Alexander Hamilton argued strongly in his *Federalist Papers* that an energetic national government having the power to exact obedience to its resolutions would provide the additional security necessary to the preservation of republican government, liberty, and property. *The Federalist Papers*, written by Hamilton, John Jay, and James Madison, constitute the most knowledgeable and informative statement of American political philosophy ever written. They are worthy of being read in their entirety by those seeking to understand the American past and present. Hamilton noted, incidentally, in *The Federalist*, Number 21, that

> the wealth of nations depends upon an infinite variety of causes. Situation, soil, climate, the nature of the productions, the nature of the government, the genius of the citizens, the degree of information they possess, the state of commerce, of arts, of industry—these circumstances and many more, too complex, minute, or adventitious to admit of a particular specification, occasion differences hardly conceivable in the relative opulence and riches of different countries.

Hamilton, as did Madison, worried about the problem of factions within the Union, but he saw the threat as existing within the state government. The Confederation had no control at this level, and therefore could offer no guarantee to life, liberty, and property. The Constitution proposed that the national government assume the power to institute those guarantees within the states.

The first steps in the formation of the new government were taken by George Washington, Alexander Hamilton, and others at Mount Vernon. There, discussions concerning the problem of improving navigation on the Potomac River drew representatives from several states. The Annapolis meeting that followed involved a broader representation from five states. These delegates discussed ways of improving commerce among the states. This conference, inspired by Hamilton's careful report on the sad financial state of the Union, and by the unnerving rebellion led by Daniel Shays in Massachusetts, precipitated the call for a nationwide convention to consider amending the Articles of Confederation. The Philadelphia Convention subsequently drafted a new Constitution.

Some historians have concluded that the Constitution derived from the self-interested actions of a relatively small faction. In his landmark work *An Economic Interpretation of the Constitution* Charles Beard suggested that the Constitution represented a successful effort by a minority faction (as had been warned against by Madison) to wrest power from the people for its own special interests. "The movement for the Constitution of the United States," wrote Beard, "was originated and carried through principally by four groups of personality interests which had been adversely affected under the Articles of Confederation: money, public securities, manufactures, and trade and shipping."[4] No popular vote was taken on the question of calling a Constitutional Convention. A large mass of the population, Beard indicated, was excluded from participating in the framing of the Constitution because they were disfranchised by existing suffrage qualifications, which included property ownership. Three fourths of the adult males never voted on the questions of ratification, because they were either disqualified or indifferent. The major portion of the members of the Convention, said Beard, were on record as "recognizing the claim of property to a special and defensive position in the Constitution." With few exceptions, he argued, the delegates derived personal economic advantages from the establishment of the new system. Beard concluded, "The Constitution was essentially an economic document based upon the concept that the fundamental private rights of property are anterior to government and morally beyond the reach of popular majorities."[5]

Beard's work has stimulated considerable investigation and an intensive dialogue on the proposition that the American Constitution was the product of a conspiracy in an undemocratic society on behalf of personal, propertied interests. Thus far, the resolution of the great debate seems to be that the Constitution may have favored propertied interests, but if so, those interests reflected the interests of a democratic majority. Robert E. Brown found evidence that most men within the states were qualified voters, and that the Constitution was adopted in a fundamentally democratic society comprising middle-class owners of real and personal property. Almost all Americans owned or aspired to own property. The Constitution was in accord with the revolutionary principles of life, liberty, and property. Finally, Brown argues, the Constitution sought to secure those principles that the Articles of the Confederation pursued but could not secure.[6]

The adoption of the Constitution did not settle the constitutional questions involving national, state, and/or property rights. Nor are those questions permanently resolved today. However, through congressional legislation, court decisions, and executive action the authority of the national government over states, civil liberties, and private property has generally expanded. Today, the national government can exercise enormous control over almost every kind of private property. This control, however, is the product of two hundred years of political and economic development. The great universal conflict between liberty and authority is as unresolved today as it was two hundred years ago—or two thousand years ago. "What belongs to the nation, and what to the states? . . . What is Caesar's due, and from what must Caesar abstain?"

THE SUPREME COURT AND PROPERTY RIGHTS

During the first half of the nineteenth century, the Federalist Party, Congress, and the Supreme Court generally followed William Blackstone's "Old World rule" that "so great . . . is the regard of the law for private property . . . it will not authorize the least violation of it, no, not even for the general good of the whole community." In Europe and America, rights in property were regarded as superior to all other rights and interests. Upon assuming authority to review and rule upon the constitutionality of legislation in *Marbury* v. *Madison*, the Supreme Court under John Marshall tended to have an exaggerated regard for private property, at the expense of public interests.

One of the first tests of public versus private interests concerned the sale in 1795 by a Georgia legislature of the Yazoo territory, located in what is now Mississippi and Alabama, and the revocation of the sale by a subsequent legislature. When Georgia ceded her western lands to the United States in 1802, the Yazoo claimants were to be reimbursed by the federal government. Congressman John Randolph, among others, opposed the compensation and attempted to delay any settlement by Congress. Yazoo stockholders took their case to the Supreme Court, where John Marshall ruled, in *Fletcher* v. *Peck* (1810), that the Georgia sale of 1795 was a legitimate contract and that the next legislature (representing public interests) could not break or rescind the contract with the private interests. In 1814, after John Randolph retired from Congress, Congress appropriated $48,000 for a settlement of the Yazoo claims.

The contractual rights of private property were strengthened further in the Dartmouth College case. Dartmouth College was established as a private institution by royal charter in 1769. After the Revolution, the state of New Hampshire approved legislation converting the college into a public institution. The trustees brought suit, and in *Dartmouth College* v. *Woodward* (1819) the Supreme Court held that the royal charter was an inviolable contract; the legislature could not set it aside. In *Sturges* v. *Crownmshield* (1819), Marshall ruled that a state could not use legislation to relieve a debtor of his debts, for that constituted an impairment of contractual obligations.

Although the Marshall Court persistently ruled in behalf of rights in property, it ruled as consistently that in any contest of authority between state and national government over regulation of property, the national government had primacy. The extent to which the national government rather than the state governments have the power to regulate commerce has been one of the most controversial and prolific areas of litigation since the ratification of the Constitution. Beginning with *Gibbons* v. *Ogden* (1824), the Supreme Court moved in the direction of the advice given by James Madison at the Constitutional Convention that "the regulation of commerce was in its nature indivisible and ought to be wholly under one authority." *Gibbons* v. *Ogden* involved a grant by the state of New York of an exclusive license to operate steamboats on the Hudson River for a limited term of years to Robert Fulton, the inventor of the steamboat. Ogden operated a steamboat under the Fulton license, and complained when Gibbons operated a competing boat under a federal license in violation of the New York patent. The Marshall Court rejected the New York monopoly, interpreted the term "commerce" to include all navigation within a state, and excluded a state from acting in areas affecting interstate commerce when such acts conflicted with acts of Congress. That over three decades passed without the Supreme Court's making any ruling on the commerce clause of the Constitution, which delegates to Congress power to regulate commerce among the states, suggests one of two things: (1) the Constitution was unusually effective in alleviating commercial barriers existing under the Confederation; (2) few such prohibitive trade restraints had ever existed among the states.

A case of considerable economic importance, and one often regarded as marking the democratic era of court interpretation and representing an attack against property's privileged position, is *Charles River Bridge* v. *Warren Bridge* (1837). Acting under a charter issued by the state of Massachusetts in 1785, the Charles River Bridge Company erected a toll bridge across the Charles River. Later, the Massachusetts legislature authorized the construction of a second (and badly needed) toll bridge near the site of the first bridge. The Charles River people argued that the second grant was an unconstitutional invalidation of their contract. Under Chief Justice Roger Taney, the Supreme Court held that a franchise or grant is not by implication exclusive. This ruling created fears among some that the Court was attacking the sanctity of rights in property. However, it marked no new departure on the question of public versus private rights. In earlier cases, John Marshall had already established the rule of strict construction of public grants.

Marshall seems to have advocated the absolute authority of the national government on all questions involving interstate commerce. After 1851, however, the Court moderated the idea of exclusive federal authority, by holding that states have some power to regulate interstate commerce unless and until Congress acts. If Marshall held that the power to regulate interstate commerce represented an exclusive grant to Congress by the Constitution, by 1860 a formula of "selective exclusiveness" had gained preference. It is doubtful, however, that Marshall would have opposed such a formula. Marshall never declared state regulation of commerce unconstitutional unless it conflicted with an act of Congress.

Although the membership of the Supreme Court changed from Federalist to Republican to Democrat between 1789 and 1865, the striking aspect of Court activity is the basic continuity of the decisions. The expansion of federal power and authority was slow but steady. In this period, the Supreme Court ruled on sixty-two cases relating to constitutionality. In two of these, the Court ruled against the constitutionality of the acts of Congress; in the other sixty, it ruled against state legislatures. Only one of these cases concerned civil rights. Twenty-six of the cases protected an impairment of contract. Most of the remaining cases involved federal treaties of questions of jurisdiction.[7] The decisions of the Court in the few cases involving the commerce clause were generally in harmony with the intentions of the founding fathers and seemingly consistent with the purposes of the Articles of Confederation and the Ordinance of 1787.

Indeed, there are those who agree with Charles Beard that in terms of the primacy of private property over public interests "in 1860 the country stood in fundamental respect just where it did in 1787 under the Articles of Confederation."[8] The protection of rights in property did remain reasonably consistent, but as a result of court decisions and legislative action that protection increasingly devolved upon the federal government. The Supreme Court made it clear in the Dred Scott case (1857) that federal authority, not that of the states, guaranteed rights in property. Ironically, the Court's decision in the Dred Scott case and other cases involving slavery, decisions that recognized the constitutional right of property in slaves, implicitly rejected Southern theories of states' rights. Here the Court clearly seems to have had an exaggerated regard for private property as opposed to public interests. Although the Civil War changed the constitutional provision for rights in slave property, in other respects it strengthened federal guarantees of and authority over rights in property.

Overall, American constitutional development, particularly as it affected commerce and property, was from the days of the Articles of Confederation remarkably consistent. Free enterprise, private property, and personal liberty were the essential objectives of the Revolution that the Articles, the Constitution, and the Supreme Court sought to preserve. But the American free-enterprise system was built upon a great dilemma: how to balance liberty with authority, how to protect individualism through collective effort, how to defend the diversity that ultimately divides society into potentially violent factions, how to sustain private property without violating democratic prerogatives. Within this conceptual framework of free enterprise, American constitutional development provided the organizational framework that facilitated the unparalleled economic growth and development of the new American republic.

Notes

[1]John D. Hicks, *The Federal Union* (Cambridge, Mass.: Harper & Row, 1948), p. 184.

[2]Alexander Hamilton, "Report on Manufactures," (December 5, 1791) in *The Reports of Alexander Hamilton*, ed. Jacob E. Cooke (New York: Harper & Row, 1964), pp. 155–56.

[3]For a fascinating early account of this migration, see John Haywood, *The Civil and Political History of the State of Tennessee from its Earliest Settlement up to the Year 1796* (Knoxville: Heiskell & Brown, 1823).

[4]Charles Beard, *An Economic Interpretation of the Constitution of the United States* (1913; reprint ed., New York: Free Press, 1965), p. 324.

[5]*Ibid.*, pp. 324–25.

[6]See Robert E. Brown, *Charles Beard and the Constitution: A Critical Analysis of "An Economic Interpretation of the Constitution"* (1956; reprint ed., New York: Norton, 1965).

[7]For an excellent review of Supreme Court decisions, see Benjamin F. Wright, *The Growth of American Constitutional Law* (Chicago: University of Chicago Press, 1967), pp, 1–79.

[8]Charles A. and Mary Beard, *The Rise of American Civilization* (New York: Macmillan, 1934), I, p. 689.

SUGGESTED READING

BEARD, CHARLES, *An Economic Interpretation of the Constitution of the United States.* New York: Macmillan, 1913. Reprint ed., New York: Free Press, 1965.

BROWN, ROBERT E., *Charles Beard and the Constitution: A Critical Analysis of "An Economic Interpretation of the Constitution."* Princeton, N.J.: Princeton University Press, 1956. Reprint ed., New York: Norton, 1965.

CALHOON, ROBERT MCCLUER, *Revolutionary America: An Interpretative Overview.* New York: Harcourt, Brace & Jovanovich, 1976.

COOKE, JACOB E., ed., *The Reports of Alexander Hamilton.* New York: Harper & Row, 1964.

CUNLIFFE, MARCUS, *The Nation Takes Shape: 1789–1837.* Chicago: University of Chicago Press, 1959.

GOODMAN, PAUL, ed., *The American Constitution*. New York: John Wiley, 1970.

JAMESON, J. FRANKLIN, *The American Revolution Considered as a Social Movement*. Princeton, N.J.: Princeton University Press, 1926.

MORGAN, EDMUND S., *The Birth of the Republic, 1763–1789*. Chicago: University of Chicago Press, 1956.

WRIGHT, BENJAMIN F., *The Growth of American Constitutional Law*. Chicago: University of Chicago Press, 1967.

TECHNOLOGY AND THE NATIONAL BANKS: 1790–1850

_____chapter V__

The emerging national economy of 1800 operated in the face of critical shortages of labor, both skilled and unskilled, and a lack of capital for investment. Technological innovation (labor-saving devices) and capital formation became vital to the developing economy. Although labor and capital were scarce, America enjoyed immense, diversified, and essentially undeveloped natural resources. Those resources, however, were more _potential_ than _actual_. Actual resources are those that can be utilized immediately by society. Most American resources in 1800 were _potential_ in that they could not be tapped because of inadequate transportation facilities. Utilization of the resources was limited further by the deficiency of technical knowledge necessary to make them useful. Resources are limited less by geography and quantity than by the state of the technology employing those resources. As Abbot Payson Usher explained, "The limitations of resources are relative to the position of our knowledge and of our technique. The limits of both actual resources and potential resources recede as we advance, at rates that are proportionate to the advance in our knowledge."[1] Thus, water power, coal, petroleum, and nuclear fission have evolved, each in their turn, from being potential and even unrealized resources into being actual resources available for human consumption. Even so, the "supply" of these fuels has continually been redefined according to the efficiency and availability of the _technology_ for converting the raw material to a usable power source. Technology, or "knowledge at work," has perhaps been as important as the classic ingredients of an economic system—land, labor, and capital—in the growth and development of the American free-enterprise system. Technology is a vital form of human capital.

THE ROLE OF TECHNOLOGY

The American farmer and the American manufacturer were constrained to substitute units of abundant input (land and natural resources) for the scarcer units, labor and capital. For example, the costs of doubling yields per acre were greater to the farmer than the costs of doubling the acreage under cultivation. The manufacturer enjoyed greater profits by exploiting the land and natural resources and by conserving labor and capital when possible. It was more profitable to standardize the production of firearms than to fit each weapon to its user in the traditional European manner, a method that was costly in its intensive application of skilled labor. To be sure, neither the farmer nor the arms manufacturer had a free choice: the farmer did not possess the sophisticated scientific knowledge necessary to double his yields, nor did the manufacturer have access to the skilled labor required to perfect or fit a firearm. Mass-production techniques, which developed in both the agricultural and manufacturing industries in the nineteenth century, generally exploited the more abundant natural resources and conserved labor by using "labor-saving devices." These devices were generally organizational and mechanical rather than scientific or conceptual.

Because of technology, American economic development—and even the availability of resources and the nature or degree of consumer demand—was a far more fluid and uncertain course than "growth" and "development" denote. Because of technology, the building blocks of economic development on both the supply and demand sides could be transformed or dismantled. New knowledge and inventions tend to enlarge the environment, increase the availability of natural resources, and create knowledge and skills, which in turn create new demands. The computer, for example, is opening up vast capabilities while creating new demands and patterns of consumption. The automobile has created a whole life-style for Americans: suburbs, fast-service food chains, drive-in "everythings," highways, expressways, air pollution, and fuel shortages. Each industry or area of impact generates new demand and consumption patterns. The derivatives, or "spin-off," of technological changes are often unpredictable as to the nature or time of their occurrence. An economy that might be relatively static or predictable becomes a vibrant force under the influence of technology.

Alexander Hamilton's "Report on Manufactures," presented to the First Congress of the United States in 1791, suggested that the expediting of manufacturing enterprises in the nation might require the "incitement and patronage of government." Old customs and habits, the apprehension of failure, and competition from established industrial nations whose products are superior in both quality and price discourage the development of new manufacturing enterprises, Hamilton said. In this economic climate, the confidence of "cautious, sagacious capitalists" must be excited by the "extraordinary aid and protection of government." Hamilton outlined a number of aids and encouragements that government might extend, such as duties, bounties, premiums, exemptions, and a prohibition on exports. Three of these aids affect technological innovation.

The "most useful and unexceptionable" aid that government can give manufacturers, said Hamilton, is "the encouragement of new inventions and discoveries at home, and of the introduction into the United States of such as may have been made in other countries; particularly those which relate to machinery." Patents, privileges, and awards, he said, should be given authors, inventors, and "introducers" of new ideas. In granting authority to Congress "to promote the Progress and Science and useful Arts, by securing for limited Times to Authors and Inventors the exclusive Rights to their respective Writings and Discoveries," Article I, Section 7 of the Constitution provided a climate that supported innovation. In granting awards and privileges, the states rewarded innovation. New York's funding of canals, roads, and railroad construction and its attempt to grant an exclusive license to Robert Fulton and Robert Livingston's steamboat company to operate on the Hudson River as far as New York City are examples. The Fulton-Livingston franchise, according to John Marshall, overstepped the bounds of a reward: in constituting a monopoly, it discouraged rather than encouraged innovation and competition. Thus, the national government sought to support a broad policy of free enterprise. During the first half of the nineteenth century the political and public climate supported innovation at almost every level, but not without confusion and conflict in state and national laws.

A public atmosphere conducive to innovation was not unique to America; it was an inheritance of the British industrial revolution. But innovation seemed to be a more urgent priority in America than in England and the rest of Europe, where labor—especially skilled labor—was more abundant. Public policy early recognized the "necessity of invention." For example, an act of the General Assembly of South Carolina on September 26, 1691 directed that Peter Jacob Guerard, who "hath at his proper cost and expence of time, lately invented and brought to perfection, a Pendulum Engine, which doth much better, and in lesse time and labour, huske rice, than any other heretofore hath been used in this Province," be given a royalty of forty shillings by anyone who employed or constructed such an engine during the next two years. Similar incentives to invent are evident throughout the colonies. The American imperative to save time and labor emerged very early.

TRANSPORTATION

Hamilton also urged the improvement of transportation facilities, noting especially the importance of public roads and canals to commerce and manufacturing. In his excellent study *The Transportation Revolution, 1815–1860*, George Rogers Taylor argues that "transportation developments were so revolutionary and so fundamental to the economic growth of the country'' that they are central to an understanding of American economic life.[2] Expanding transportation facilities removed some of the limits that geography imposed on resources. The railroad alone, Abbot P. Usher indicated, profoundly transformed life in North America and Europe, reversed the traditional rural domination over the urban centers, and created new forms of economic structure.[3] What the railroad did not do the automobile completed in the twentieth century. Industrial production, the development of suburbs and shopping centers, and even dietary habits and courtship have been profoundly affected by the technological innovations generated by the automobile. The transportation revolution contributed to the regional specialization that some historians incorrectly confuse with sectionalism, to the economies of scale that make mass production cost-efficient, and in effect to the industrialization and specialization of the national economy.

Roads and Turnpikes

The story of domestic transportation in the new American nation properly begins with the public roads and private turnpikes. Colonial transportation needs had been adequately served by the sea and by tributary rivers. Land transportation was so unimportant that a map of American roads was not published until 1729. There was no regular stage service between New York and Philadelphia until 1756. By the time the first American Congress convened in Philadelphia in March, 1789, it had become painfully obvious that the United States had an inadequate system of roads. A full month passed before a congressional quorum was present to carry on the nation's business. George Washington's trip from Mount Vernon to the temporary capital of New York City occupied several weeks of difficult travel.

In 1789 Christopher Colles, who had emigrated to America from Ireland in 1771, began publishing an annotated ''Survey of the Roads of the United States of America.'' He sought a congressional contract that would enable him to extend his work, but obtained only favorable recommendations and good wishes from the postmaster general and various congressmen. That is about as much as he ever received for his various inventive enterprises, which included a steam engine and pump system for cooling a distillery, a plan for the development of a public water-works system in New York City, an inland waterway of above-the-ground canals, a solar microscope, and a semaphoric telegraph. Colles was representative of the visionary, indefatigable inventor and ''engineer'' who seemed to be so much a part of the American scene at the close of the eighteenth century.

As economic conditions improved, road construction expanded. In 1808, Secretary of the Treasury Albert Gallatin presented Congress with a comprehensive plan for the improvement of roads and navigation. Although Congress took

CHRISTOPHER COLLES *(1739–1816)*
Engineer, Inventor.

no general action on the plan, a number of roads were built for postal and military purposes. One of these roads followed the Natchez Trace and connected Georgia and Tennessee with Natchez. The more famous Cumberland (or National) Road extended from Cumberland, Maryland to Wheeling, Virginia and thence, by 1850, to Vandalia, Illinois. The National Road and many state roads were public projects designed to enhance opportunities for private investment. Little real progress in federal road construction occurred in the early nineteenth century because of a widely held belief that federally sponsored internal improvements were unconstitutional. Presidents Madison (1817), Monroe (1822), and Jackson (1830) vetoed such legislation because of state and sectional jealousies and because the more densely populated areas of the eastern seaboard and the Gulf States were accessible by water. However, state governments and private companies, particularly in New York, Pennsylvania, New Jersey, Virginia, and South Carolina, built extensive turnpike systems between 1815 and 1838. George Rogers Taylor estimates that in New England alone, $6.5 million had been invested in private roads by 1840. Many states followed Pennsylvania in investing state funds in private turnpike companies. Roads in South Carolina and Indiana were financed and owned almost exclusively by the state. State governments, and on occasion the federal government, regularly supplemented private capital and played a vital role in capital accumulation in antebellum and later days. Plank roads, stone and iron bridges, and by 1855 even a sophisticated, 821-foot suspension bridge carrying rail and highway traffic across the Niagara River reflected the strides that had been taken in construction techniques.[4]

Canals

The opening of a major segment of the Erie Canal in 1819 and the completion of the canal from Albany to Buffalo in 1825, initiated a boom in canal construction throughout the Northeast. By 1840, this region had produced 3,326 miles of canals at an estimated cost of $125 million. The Erie was the greatest financial success. Poor construction, bad planning, sorry management, and speculation doomed many of the canal companies to failure and nearly bankrupted several states that had overinvested in them. The advent of the railroads and the Panic of 1837 effectually ended the canal craze.

The Steam Engine and Usher's Theory of Mechanical Invention

The steam engine revolutionized land and water transportation in America and transformed American life in a brief span of years. Abbot Payson Usher provided a useful schematic for understanding the development of the steam engine and other mechanical inventions. Usher proposed that a distinctive set of mechanical problems and principles underlies each invention. The reciprocating steam engine and the turbine engine involve distinct principles and problems, and their development was independent. Parallel development can occur, as in the case of weaving, where patterns of development in Syria were distinct from those in Egypt and Greece. Invention occurs when novelty in thought is realized by action. Invention involves, first, a synthesis of familiar ideas and knowledge, and the perception of an incomplete pattern or need; second, a fortuitous configuration of thought or events that offers a solution· third, the act of insight or invention (seeing the solution); and finally, critical revision and mastery of the new pattern.

Applying this scheme in abbreviated fashion to the development of the steam engine suggests that the first stage involved acquiring existing knowledge about power production, metallurgy, and steam. Such knowledge was quite extensive by the sixteenth and seventeenth centuries. In the seventeenth century, the expansion of public water works, the development of pumps and a piston-type apparatus, and studies of air pressure set the stage for the development of primitive "water-commanding" engines, perhaps first devised by Solomon De Caus in 1615 and improved by the Marquis of Worcester about 1630.[5] The need for such engines became imperative as water began to flood British mines at the turn of the eighteenth century. The water-commanding engines, however, used a vacuum but no pistons. The successful invention of the prototype of the modern steam engine, which uses a piston and a vacuum principle, is attributed to Thomas Newcomen of England about 1712. This engine had a cylinder 21 inches in diameter and 7 feet 10 inches long that made 12 strokes a minute and developed approximately 7 horsepower. While repairing a Newcomen engine,

James Watt devised a condenser that enabled live steam to be injected at either end of a piston, and allowed the rapid ejection of depleted steam, and created a generally more efficient engine. Usher assigned Watt's work to the "critical revision" stage of invention. With the backing of Mathew Boulton, Watt obtained patents and began the commercial manufacture of steam engines about 1769. The higher pressures developed by the Watt engines and subsequent engines required new advancements in metallurgy and machine-tool manufacture, which occurred over the next half-century. Meanwhile, the steam engine literally exploded human progress. For example, in 1848 the commissioner of patents estimated that in the previous 32 years a total of 233 steamboat explosions had killed over 2,500 persons in the United States, injured another 2,000, and caused property losses in excess of $3 million.[6]

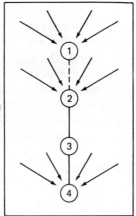

A.

The emergence of novelty in the act of insight: synthesis of familiar items: (1) perception of an incomplete pattern; (2) the setting of the stage; (3) the act of insight; (4) critical revision and full mastery of the new pattern.

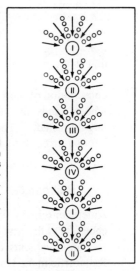

B.

The process of cumulative synthesis. A full cycle of strategic invention, and part of a second cycle. Large figures I - IV represents steps in the development of a strategic invention. Small figures represent individual elements of novelty. Arrows represent familiar elements included in the new synthesis.

FIGURE 5.1. Usher's theory of mechanical invention.

Source: Abbot Payson Usher, *A History of Mechanical Inventions*, rev. ed. (Cambridge, Mass.: Harvard University Press), 1970 pp. 66, 69.

Steamboats

By 1800, steam technology had become "public knowledge" in Europe and America. During the early decades of the nineteenth century a myriad of inventors and mechanical innovators in America experimented with steam-powered boats. Credit for inventing the steamboat is often given to Robert Fulton for his work with the *Claremont* on the Hudson River. In 1811 Fulton and his associates built the *New Orleans*, which traveled to that city from Pittsburgh in 1812 but was unable to make the return trip beyond Natchez. Despite the fact that she soon sank from a boiler explosion, the *New Orleans* earned her owners $20,000 above costs during the few years she was in service. John Stevens, John Fitch, Oliver Evans, and Henry Miller Shreve should perhaps receive equal credit as "inventors" of the steamboat. Shreve and his associates, using engines built by Daniel French in Brownsville, Pennsylvania, constructed three river steamers between 1813 and 1815, the *Comet* (25 tons), the *Despatch* (25 tons), and the *Enterprise* (75 tons). In 1815 the *Enterprise* made the first successful voyage by a steamboat up the Mississippi to Louisville and then proceeded to Pittsburgh and Brownsville on the Monongahela. The *Aetna*, a Fulton boat, also reached Louisville in 1815. The *Washington*, designed by Shreve and constructed in 1816, incorporated several important innovations, including raising *part of* the engine above the main deck and raising the superstructure. However, the *Washington* probably did *not* have a shallow-draft hull, as is often alleged.[7]

Louis C. Hunter credited Oliver Evans, rather than Shreve, with the development of the high-pressure steam engine that became universally adopted on the western waters. In effect, Hunter and Usher argued that the successful development of the steamboat was a cumulative process involving technological innovations in many related areas. As Hunter states, "There is reason to believe that if the returns were all in, the accomplishments of a Fulton, a Shreve, an Evans or a French would assume a quite modest position beside the collective contribution of scores of master mechanics, ship carpenters, and shop foremen in whose hands the detailed work of construction, adaptation, and innovation largely rested."[8] The heroic theory of invention, though it makes a better story, is quite difficult to substantiate.

Railroads

American railway development drew heavily upon British and European experiences.[9] Yet the first decade of American railroad building witnessed innovations and improvements that made American railroads superior to those in Europe. Rail traffic in the United States began with horses, mules, stationary engines, and even sails as the source of power. The first American tramway, the Granite Railroad at Quincy, Massachusetts, began service in 1826. It moved granite from a quarry in horse-drawn cars on two miles of wooden rails. The Baltimore and Ohio Railroad, which began service in May, 1830 with a horse-drawn car on

FIGURE 5.2. The top figure shows an eight-wheel-coal car in use on the Pennsylvania Railroad about 1863. The bottom figure is an early roofless stock car.

Credit: Pennsylvania Railroad and Assocation of American Railroads

thirteen miles of track, experimented with a steam locomotive, the *Tom Thumb*, built by Peter Cooper in Maryland. But it relied primarily on horse power until a new engine, the *York*, began operation in 1831. Charleston, South Carolina businessmen inaugurated the *Best Friend of Charleston* on Christmas day, 1830, and this train maintained continual service until the Civil War.

By 1840, the United States boasted 3,000 miles of track, compared with Europe's 1,818 miles. Over the next two decades, American rail mileage increased tenfold. It continued to increase until 1916 (which, by coincidence, was the year the Federal Highways Act was passed), but has declined each subsequent decade. (See Table 5.1.)

TABLE 5.1

Railway Mileage in the United States.

1830	23	1880	93,267	1930	249,052
1840	2,808	1890	163,597	1940	233,670
1850	9,021	1900	193,346	1950	223,779
1860	30,626	1910	240,439	1960	217,552
1870	52,922	1920	252,845	1970	205,782

Source: Interstate Commerce Commission

The rapid expansion of railroad construction in the United States after 1830 derived from numerous factors. Most important, there was a clear need for faster and more efficient transportation. Land costs for right-of-ways and, after mid-century, costs for labor and rails, and hence construction costs, were lower in America than in England and the rest of Europe. The cost of constructing one mile of track was, of course, considerably lower than the cost of building one mile of canal. Railroads also offered an obvious advantage over river traffic by providing access to interior areas away from rivers. Moreover, few rivers inland from the eastern seaboard run east and west. Opening the western regions to settlement and commerce became an urgent priority early in the 1800s. In addition, state and local funds heavily subsidized rail construction throughout the nineteenth century. Robert Fogel, who has conducted quantitative studies of the rates charged for shipping produce by rail and by water, rejects the notion that railroads were a prerequisite for economic growth.[10] Nonetheless, the commitment to rail transportation rapidly surpassed the commitment to alternative systems. Finally, American expansion in railroading was substantially aided by a number of important inventions and adaptations.

Perhaps the most important of these innovations was the T-rail. The first tracks were made of either logs or strap iron fastened to wooden rails secured to blocks of stone. The logs splintered or wore out. The iron buckled and curled, frequently ripping the bottom out of cars or derailing the train. Even while these materials lasted they provided a hard, jolting ride. Robert L. Stevens, president of the Camden and Amboy Railroad, designed the T-rail, carving his first model of it out of wood. He had the rails manufactured in Wales and began installing them in 1831. T-rails were installed more easily than strapped rails and could be spiked directly to a wooden crosstie. Wooden crossties imbedded in gravel were found to provide a more durable and softer roadbed than crossties imbedded in stone.

The diversity in track gauges, which ranged from the narrow 3-foot gauge to the wide 6-foot gauge, proved to be an impediment to rail traffic throughout the first half-century of railroading. By 1886, most rail lines in America had shifted to the standard 4-foot-8½-inch gauge (the wheelbase of the Roman chariot). John B. Jervis designed the first swivel (or "bogie") wheels about 1832. These made engines more stable on curves. The equalizing beam, invented by Joseph Harrison in 1839, allowed equal pressure to be maintained on drive wheels. Cowcatchers, whistles, lights (fueled at first by kerosene), cabs, sandboxes (for traction), and a variety of engine improvements were American innovations adopted during the first *decade* of American railroading.

The United States passed quickly through an economically stimulating revolution in transportation. As John Stover relates,

> Perhaps the really significant theme in the early transportation history of this country was the tendency of each new type or phase of transportation to be so

quickly challenged and largely supplanted by the next succeeding type or phase that no single form of transportation had a decent opportunity to grow. Fortunately for the railroad, this trend was halted by the middle of the nineteenth century. By then the railroad had achieved a position of dominance that it was to retain until early in the twentieth century.[11]

The railroad and the transportation revolution made possible the rapid settlement of the West and the swift rise of the factory system in the United States. They opened vast new resources and markets and provided for the rapid (and hence labor-saving) transfer of raw materials to industrial centers and of manufactured products to consumers. Railroads increased the volume and regularity of transport, added to the national income, and created a vast new market for industrial products. Alfred D. Chandler argues that "still another and even more significant contribution to American economic growth" made by railroads is that railroad men pioneered modern business-organization patterns. The railroads set precedents in finance, labor relations, and competition.[12]

THE AMERICAN SYSTEM

The railroad, steamboat, and older textile and weapons industries in the United States established the need for, and helped create, a sophisticated machine-tools industry. American locomotives and tools were being shipped to England and the Continent by the 1840s, even though Europe had a one-generation head start on machine manufacture. The English were the first to realize that there was something new and distinctive about the "American system of manufactures." In 1841, a committee of Parliament investigated the British embargo on the shipment of machinery. One Englishman noted that the "entirely new inventions; . . . come now from abroad, especially America." In answer to the question "Are Americans as skilled as the English?" a witness replied, "It is not possible that they can be, without more experience than they have had at present."

"Are the Americans aware of their inferiority?"

"They will not allow it," was the answer.[13]

At the Crystal Palace Exhibition in London in 1851, British observers were intrigued by the American technique of using interchangeable machine parts to perform the same or different tasks. Samuel Colt further impressed the British when he opened a factory in England in 1853 for the mass production of small arms. A British commission subsequently went to America to purchase machines for the manufacture of army weapons according to the "American system." Americans, if they had not been so before, became acutely aware of their industrial prowess at the Great Exhibition in New York City in 1853. The American system of manufacturing featured interchangeable parts and assembly-line production. It allowed the use of semiskilled labor, maintained a constant flow of products at lower per-unit costs, and made possible the opening of vast consumer markets.

Although Eli Whitney has frequently been cited as the father of the American system of manufacturing, that title is considerably clouded by the facts. Whitney contracted to manufacture for Congress 4,000 stands of arms by September 30, 1799 and 6,000 more by September 30, 1800. His first delivery, consisting of 500 arms, was made in 1801, and the final delivery was not made until 1809. Some historians attribute assembly-line production to Oliver Evans, who developed a "fully automatic" flour mill in 1782. Simeon North used interchangeable parts in pistol manufacturing as early as 1807. In 1811, John Hall patented gun-manufacturing machinery that was subsequently installed in the Harper's Ferry Armory. In a word, the American system of assembly with interchangeable parts and mass manufacture by power-driven machinery designed especially to serve a particular function had developed by the first quarter of the nineteenth century. Although certain pioneers, inventors, and innovators stand out in the development of the American system, this development was a cumulative one. It derived from countless artisans and mechanics, and particularly from the American people's insatiable demand for and ready assimilation of new techniques.

Although the development of industrial technology is ordinarily identified with the Northeast—particularly with the textile industry, as depicted by the

ELI WHITNEY *(1765–1825)*
Inventor of the cotton gin;
firearms manufacturer.
Engraved by D. C. Hinman from a painting by Charles B. King.

Lowell Textile Mills, and gun manufacture—parallel developments occurred in the West and in the southern agricultural region. The machine-tool industry—the mass production of machine components that could be assembled in an infinite variety of combinations to perform distinct tasks—emerged largely from the machine shops of the New England textile industry. The machine-tool industry made possible the diffusion of industrial technology throughout the nation.

A little-observed but very pertinent case of technological development employing mass production occurred in the early years of the South Carolina rice industry. Jonathan Lucas harnessed wind, rivers, and even tidal flows to power rice-milling machinery in the 1780s. By 1787, he had perfected a water-powered mill operated by three men that could mill and package one hundred barrels of rice a day. During his lifetime Lucas became, in effect, a manufacturer of rice mills and rice-milling machinery. His first mills were powered by fresh water stored in reserve tanks or ponds, a number of which were built along the Santee River. In 1792, Lucas built his first mill to be powered by tidal flows. It used a large undershot water wheel, which turned either way with the tidal flow and provided forward thrust for the machinery with a system of alternating gears. In 1822, Lucas built mills in London and Liverpool, England.

An excellent description of Lucas's machinery and milling process is contained in John Drayton's *A View of South Carolina* (1802). One of these mills, Drayton wrote, consisted of "four cog wheels, and one lanthern wheel; a pair of large mill stones, from four to seven feet diameter; fifteen or more pullies working leathern straps; two rolling screens; one or two wind fans; a brush; sets of elevating buckets, and spiral horizontal conveyors," all moved by a huge water wheel 22 feet in diameter and 14 feet wide. Rough rice was elevated in buckets to an upper level, dumped into a rolling screen that removed impurities, and then passed into a hopper that fed the millstones. Fans blew the chaff from the milled rice. The rice was then fed into an elevated bin, whence it was funneled into mortars. There it was beaten by 230-pound pestles that struck the rice at a rate of 32 to 44 times a minute. After this final milling process the rice was again elevated into screens where the broken rice was removed. It was then passed into a funnel where a mechanical brush fed it over a drop for a final winnowing by a fan. The cleaned rice was then passed into a bin, which filled the barrels for shipping.

By the 1830s, many rice mills had converted to steam. Fannie Kemble, a famous actress, spent half a year on a Georgia rice plantation in 1838–39. She was very impressed by the mills, now steam-powered. In the one she investigated, "the whole establishment, comprising the fires, and boilers, and machinery of a powerful steam engine, are all under negro superintendence and direction."[14] Contrary to prevailing myths, black slaves constituted a large portion of the skilled artisans and mechanics in the South. And contrary to other myths in its vast array of gins, mills, iron industries, and railroads the antebellum South experienced an industrial transformation comparable to that of the Northeast.

Southern industrial development was, however, inhibited by cotton, slavery, and
the Civil War.

THE NATIONAL BANKS

Innovation and invention extended beyond mechanical processes and into business and its institutional structures. A particularly important public institution
that facilitated industrial expansion was the national bank. The new American
republic founded a unique national banking system. The closest antecedent of
this system was the short-lived General Bank of France (1716–1720), created by
John Law, son of a wealthy goldsmith and banker of Edinburgh, Scotland. Law
believed that banking should be a public business. A nation should establish a
national bank that would serve as the depository of all national funds. The
deposits would provide the reserve for the issuance of paper currency, which
might, within limitations, be safely issued in greater denominations than the
specie value of the deposits. Although the inflationary and speculative schemes
accompanying Law's banking plans led to a severe financial crash in France, his
organization was sound. Indeed, it prefigured the organization of the First and
Second National Banks of the United States. The Bank of the United States and
the financial policies initiated in 1790 by the First Congress played a significant
role in providing the credit and capital for rapid economic growth in the early
national period.

Hamilton's "Report on Public Credit," presented to Congress in 1790,
indicated an American foreign indebtedness of $11.7 million, on which both
interest and principal payments were delinquent. $40 million in bonds issued by
the Continental Congress were in default to American citizens. These bonds
circulated at about one fifth of their market value. The individual states owed
another $40 million, and it appeared unlikely that this sum would ever be paid.
There was no apparent source of income by which the national government could
pay either principle or interest on these debts. As a revolutionary body, the
national government could reject any obligation to pay the debts of the Continental Congress. Or, as some urged, the government could with a degree of equity
refund the bonds at current market values and thereby erase eighty percent of the
debt. But the new government could not do either and maintain its "good faith
and credit"—that is be able to borrow at reasonable rates. And being able to
borrow was vital. Hamilton presented Congress with a four-point financial program that, when approved, would provide financial stability for the national
government, relieve the states of a burdensome debt, and provide a reservoir for
the borrowing of capital by private banks and business.

The first stage of the program called for refunding the national debt at par
(face) value. Congress approved legislation calling in Continental bonds owed to
foreign and domestic holders and authorizing refunds or the issuance of new

bonds at the face value of the old ones. James Madison led a move in Congress to reimburse the original purchaser of a bond for any loss he incurred if he subsequently sold to a second person. Madison argued that the money of the original investor had financed the Revolution, and that to award a second purchaser windfall profits would be to award the speculator and not the patriot. Hamilton, and finally Congress, rejected Madison's move as involving a breach of contract. Bonds are payable to the bearer on demand. Not to honor such a demand impairs a government's contractual obligations and its "good faith and credit."

One of the most astounding decisions made by the First Congress was to accept Hamilton's proposal that the national government assume the debt incurred by the states during the Revolution. It is virtually unthinkable that the federal government today might voluntarily pay off the enormous bonded indebtedness of the state governments. However, the indebtedness of the states in 1790, compared with their national government's ability to pay, might be comparable to the indebtedness of the states today. Why, then, would a government heavily in debt, with little revenue, agree to enormously expand its indebtedness? Patriotism may have been an inducement. In that the state debts represented a share in the common struggle, the people share the obligations, Hamilton argued. Assumption of the state debts by the national government would also provide a more orderly system of public finance. Selfish interests could, of course, have prompted congressional approval. What state representative would not claim credit for ridding his state of a burdensome debt? But Hamilton's real reason for urging the assumption of state debts by the national government was to commit the vested interests of the creditor to the *national* rather than the state government, and so increase the strength and stability of that government.

Hamilton believed that humans were inherently bad, being motivated primarily by greed and self-interest. "Good"—or order and stability in human society as Hamilton viewed goodness—could come only from bad. Channeling humanity's "bad" nature, or greed, into supporting a strong, stable government underlay Hamilton's financial planning. Thus, the welfare of the bondholder became contingent upon the welfare and sustained existence of the national government.

Congress's approval of the Tariff Act of 1789 provided revenues for the national government and protected American industry from foreign competition. The famous Whiskey Tax provided an excellent source of revenue, and President Washington's decisive action against the ensuing Whiskey Rebellion in western Pennsylvania helped establish the authority of federal law.

A controversial but most successful aspect of Hamilton's program was the establishment of the First National Bank. The bank was chartered by Congress for twenty years with a capital stock of $10 million; $2 million would be subscribed by the federal government, the remainder by private investors. The bank was to be the sole depository of government funds, and was authorized to issue bank notes (paper money) equal in face value to the amount of stock. Such notes were to be receivable in taxes (and hence legal tender) as long as the notes were redeemable at the bank in specie (or gold). During its existence the bank loaned the federal government $13.5 million, maintained a reasonably stable currency, and provided some millions in capital to private interests. It also gave a private group monopoly interests, contributed significantly to the development of political-party alignments, and exercised a substantial degree of central authority over state and local economic interests. Thomas Jefferson's "Opinion Against the Constitutionality of a National Bank" argued that the loose construction of the Constitution advocated by Hamilton in defense of his banking program would impair the authority of the states, lead to the federal government's accumulation of unbridled power, and eliminated a check on the tyranny of a national majority. In large measure because of the bank and Hamilton's other financial programs, Jefferson resigned as Secretary of State in 1793 to lead the Democratic-Republican Party in opposition to the Federalist programs. But by its expiration in 1811, the bank had won many supporters, even among Jeffersonians, and its demise during the critical years of the War of 1812 (1812–1815) led to the creation of the Second National Bank.

Approved by President Madison on April 10, 1816, the Second Bank had a twenty-year charter that provided for a $35-million capital-stock subscription, $7 million to be purchased by the federal government. Twenty directors were to be elected by the stockholders, and five were to be appointed by the government. After some troublesome years in which it overissued paper currency and allowed excessive loans, the bank soon reestablished stable fiscal policies under the direction of Langdon Cheves, a respected South Carolina lawyer. Cheves's policies were too conservative for many stockholders, and he was forced to resign. His replacement was Nicholas Biddle, a brilliant but strong-willed man. Under Biddle the bank expanded its note issue from $3.5 million to $19 million, its domestic bills of exchange from $9 million to $49 million, and its profits to a regular dividend level of 7 percent with comfortable surpluses. The bank, therefore, was at least partly fulfilling the vital role of supplying capital to an expanding economy. But by 1832 the bank had also created enmity among powerful interests. State and local banks chafed under the financial controls imposed by the National Bank. States protested the immunity of branches of the bank from state taxation and the impairment of state sovereignty implied by the *McCullough* v. *Maryland* (1819) decision. Some individuals, including Andrew Jackson, believed that gold should be the only medium of exchange, because bank notes tended to fluctuate in value.

Political inspiration and a host of irritations led to the fatal conflict between the bank and President Jackson in 1832. Led by National Republican supporters of John Quincy Adams (who were soon to become the Whig Party), Congress approved a measure that extended the charter of the bank for twenty years, although the original charter of the Second Bank did not expire until 1836. Jackson was expected to veto the bill, and his political opposition believed that

NICHOLAS BIDDLE *(1786–1844)*
President, Bank of the United States.

this veto would insure his defeat in the election of 1832. The veto came on July 10, 1832. Jackson charged that the bank was a monopoly and granted special favors to the stockholders. He said that it catered to sectional interests, was subject to foreign control, concentrated power in the hands of a few, represented an unconstitutional grant of power by Congress, and abused its power. The veto held. Nicholas Biddle responded by drastically reducing credit and currency. Jackson countered by refusing to deposit federal money in the bank. When Biddle failed to frighten the government into approving a charter, he reversed his policies and flooded the country with paper money and easy credit. The ensuing speculative boom was halted by the Specie Circular, which required payment in gold or silver for public land. The Second National Bank was subsequently given a charter by the state of Pennsylvania, but was forced into bankruptcy in 1841. National banking all but ended from that year until 1863, when the National Bank Act reimposed a degree of regulation of national banking.[15] The passage of the Federal Reserve Act in 1913 established a new central banking facility, but one that has never possessed the power or independence of the National Banks.

It would appear that the National Banks contributed markedly to the economic development of the nation during the critical period between 1790 and 1840. They assisted in the accumulation of private and public capital, helped attract an estimated $300 million to $500 million in foreign investments, and provided reliable standards for domestic trade and commerce. After the demise of the National Banks economic growth occurred even more rapidly, which suggests that the banks imposed excessive restraints on monetary supplies. The "wildcat" banks, on the other hand, being essentially unregulated private or state-licensed institutions that issued unsecured paper currency and made excessive loans, aggravated "boom and bust" cycles in the economy. Partly as a result of this monetary restraint and financial uncertainty, much of America's new investment capital continued to come from England and the Continent.

Although American national and private banking served the needs of the economy imperfectly, that economy continued to grow. Capital formation by public and private agencies and technological innovation greatly expanded the productivity of American labor. But the greatest impetus to economic growth before the Civil War was the rapid expansion in American agricultural production.

Notes

[1]Abbott Payson Usher, *A History of Mechanical Inventions,* rev. ed. (Cambridge, Mass.: Harvard University Press, 1970), p. 9. First published in 1929, this book is the classic work on the history of technology.

[2]George R. Taylor, *The Transportation Revolution, 1815–1860* (New York: Holt, Rinehart & Winston, 1951), p. vii.

[3]See Usher's comments on the impact of transportation on human habitation and development in *A History of Mechanical Inventions,* pp. 1–11.

[4]See Taylor, *The Transportation Revolution,* pp. 22–23.

[5]Usher, *A History of Mechanical Inventions,* pp. 342–43.

[6]These comments appear in John G. Burke, "Bursting Boilers and the Federal Power," *Technology and Culture,* 7 (Winter 1966), 1–23.

[7]See Louis C. Hunter, *Steamboats on the Western Rivers* (Cambridge, Mass.: Harvard University Press, 1949), a classic in the literature on the history of technology. See also Hunter's "The Invention of the Western Steamboat," *Journal of Economic History,* 3 (November 1943), 201–20.

[8]Louis C. Hunter, "The Invention of the Western Steamboat," *The Journal of Economic History,* 3 (November 1943), p. 220.

[9]See John F. Stover, *American Railroads* (Chicago: University of Chicago Press, 1961), for a brief, informative survey.

[10]See Robert W. Fogel, "Railroads in American Economic Growth," *Journal of Economic History,* 22 (June 1962), 163–97.

[11]Stover, *American Railroads,* p. 35.

[12]See Alfred D. Chandler, Jr., ed., *The Railroads, The Nation's First Big Business: Sources and Readings* (New York: Harcourt, Brace & World, 1965), a very good statistical and documentary analysis of railroad development, Robert Fogel, *Railroads and American Economic Growth* (Baltimore: John Hopkins, 1964), is an informative analysis of the interaction of railroads and American industrial growth.

[13]These comments appear in Eugene S. Ferguson, "On the Origin and Development of American Mechanical 'Know-How,' " *Midcontinent American Studies Journal,* 3 (Fall 1962), 3–15.

[14]Frances Anne Kemble, *Journal of a Residence on a Georgia Plantation in 1838–1839,* ed. by John A. Scott (New York: Knopf, 1961), p. 117.

[15]See Robert V. Remini, *Andrew Jackson*, Perennial Library ed. (New York: Harper & Row, 1969), pp. 141–168.

SUGGESTED READING

BOLLES, ALBERT S., *The Financial History of the United States from 1789 to 1860*. New York, 1883.

CALVERT, MONTE A., *The Mechanical Engineer in America, 1830–1910*. Baltimore: John Hopkins, 1967.

GOODRICH, CARTER, *Government Promotion of American Canals and Railroads, 1800–1890*. New York: Columbia University Press, 1960.

GREEN, CONSTANCE, *Eli Whitney and the Birth of American Technology*. Boston: Little, Brown, 1956.

HAMMOND, BRAY, *Banks and Politics in America from the Revolution to the Civil War*. Princeton, N.J.: Princeton University Press, 1957.

HOCHER, LOUIS, *Alexander Hamilton in the American Tradition*. New York: McGraw-Hill, 1957.

HUNTER, LOUIS C., *Steamboats on the Western Rivers*. Cambridge, Mass.: Harvard University Press, 1949.

ROSENBERG, NATHAN, *Technology and American Economic Growth*. New York: Harper & Row, Torchbook ed., 1972.

STOVER, JOHN F., *American Railroads*. Chicago: University of Chicago Press, 1961.

TAYLOR, GEORGE ROGERS, *The Transportation Revolution, 1815–1860*. New York: Harper & Row, Torchbook ed., 1968.

USHER, ABBOTT PAYSON, *A History of Mechanical Inventions*, rev. ed. Cambridge, Mass.: Harvard University Press, 1970.

THE FARMER'S AGE: 1800–1860

 chapter VI

Thomas Jefferson's agrarianism saw America as a nation of small, independent family farmers and derived from both economic and humanistic considerations. Humans had always obtained their livelihood from agriculture, which was the only productive occupation and the true source of wealth. "Cultivators of the earth," Jefferson wrote, "are the most valuable citizens. They are the most vigorous, the most virtuous, and they are tied to their country, and wedded to its liberty and interests by the most lasting bonds." Unlike Alexander Hamilton, Jefferson believed in the innate goodness of humans. This quality derived largely from and was contingent upon the fact that most people were farmers. "I think our governments will remain virtuous for many centuries, as long as they are chiefly agricultural; and this will be as long as there shall be vacant lands in any part of America. When they get piled upon one another in large cities, as in Europe, they will become corrupt as in Europe." Moreover, by its vested rights in property and its apparant guarantee of economic independence, family farming enabled people to enjoy greater liberty, independence, and personal freedom than they could attain in any other way. Jefferson's agrarianism equated personal liberty, capitalism, democracy, and social stability. In that most Americans were, in fact, farmers, and in that vacant lands were, in fact, abundant, agrarianism was a highly practicable social and political ideal.[1] But the agrarianism that envisioned the pastoral ideal of the self-sufficient family farm was inconsistent with the realities of Jefferson's own time.

AGRICULTURE: AN OVERVIEW

Commercial agriculture had long been the dominant industry in America, and it continued to be the major source of national income through the Civil War and well thereafter. Whether the farming was commercial or subsistence, it provided

THOMAS JEFFERSON *(1743–1826)*
President of the United States, 1801–1809.
Painting by Gilbert Stuart, Courtesy Bowdoin College Museum of Art.

a basic element in overall economic growth. Food is the primary raw material of any economy, and although most of the food produced in America before 1860 probably never entered the marketplace directly, it did sustain a burgeoning population. Good public health, a high level of nutrition, and an increase in the labor force are essential to economic growth, and American farms, subsistence or commercial, made these things possible. Thus, in a broad sense agriculture helped provide an unparalleled abundance. Not all Americans, or all farm families, or even most of them, were rich, well off, or even comfortable, but most of them were unusually well nourished.

Agriculture was the central component of the developing national economy before 1860. Rather than acting as hostile economic interests, agriculture, the city, and industry were complementary and interdependent. Farms provided the food and a labor pool for urban growth. The cities provided machined tools, consumer goods, credit, and a marketplace for farm commodities. American cities before the Civil War were primarily centers for the collection, distribution, and processing of agricultural products. The free-market area established in the United States facilitated the maximum utilization of resources and the most efficient application of labor. Improved transportation facilities linked farms to urban markets in America and in Europe by the 1850s. American agriculture prospered not simply because there was an abundance of good arable land, but because of the incentives provided by society and the marketplace and because of the application of human ingenuity and energy. American farms produced the food and fiber needed to sustain a population that increased from 6 million to 31 million between 1815 and 1860.

POPULATION GROWTH

Population increases before the Civil War markedly affected agriculture, less so in providing a labor pool than in creating vast new urban markets for farm produce. Urban market growth, technological change, and an overall population increase were the major determinants of agricultural expansion. In each decade between 1790 and 1860, the population increased by an average of 30 percent. In comparison, during the population "explosion" of the 1950s the American population increased at a rate of 17 percent. Part of the population increase during the period 1790–1860 is accounted for by immigration, but most of it, particularly before 1840, derived from the very high birth rate. Accurate birth-rate data are not available for this period, but the birth rate likely averaged more than 30 per thousand per year before 1860, compared with roughly 20 per thousand per year during the 1960s. Women commonly had eight to ten children, and men, not uncommonly, married several times. The death rate of children was quite high, perhaps three times current levels, and women died far more frequently in childbirth. The median age of the population was 16.5 years in 1820 and 19.2 years in 1850, compared with 30 years in the 1950s and 1960s. Although the rate of immigration into America was high before 1860, immigrants accounted for no more than 15 percent of the American population. The heaviest immigration occurred between 1840 and 1860. In these years about 3 million people entered America from Ireland, 1.5 million from Germany, and .5 million from England. Most of the immigrants settled in the cities along the eastern seaboard. The legal importation of slaves ended in 1808, but the black population in America increased from approximately 1 million to 4 million between 1810 and 1860. The birth rate of the black population was slightly lower than that of the white population, ranging from an estimated high of 29.2 per thousand per year in the decade 1820–1830 to a low of 20.0 per thousand between 1850 and 1860. In summary, it is likely that the United States had the highest sustained rate of population growth in the world between 1800 and 1860.

Although the rural population of America declined from about 95 percent of the total population to 75 percent in the antebellum years, the overall growth in population contributed materially to the increase in the gross national product that occurred during this era. Moreover, this population growth was in part responsible for expanded agricultural production. This increase in farm production, however, derived less from the increase in the farm labor pool than from the increase in the demand for farm produce and the technological innovations in farm equipment. Expanding agricultural production in the period 1800–1860 seems to have been directly related to technological and organizational improvements, which enabled farmers to increase the rate of productivity per unit of labor. It was also related to the availability of new lands: the United States acquired about 1.3 billion acres of land between 1800 and 1860 (see Table 6.1).[2] Moreover, these lands became more accessible as a result of improvements in transportation.

TABLE 6.1

Expansion of Public Domain, 1800–1860 (Area in Acres).

	LAND	WATER	TOTAL	COST
Louisiana Purchase (1803)	523,446,400	6,465,280	529,911,680	$ 23,213,568
Basin of the Red River of the North	29,066,880	535,040	29,601,920	
Cession from Spain (1819)	43,342,720	2,801,920	46,144,640	6,674,057
Oregon Compromise (1846)	180,644,480	2,741,760	183,386,240	
Mexican Cession (1848)	334,479,360	4,201,600	338,680,960	76,295,149
Purchase from Texas (1850)	78,842,880	83,840	78,926,720	15,496,448
Gadsden Purchase (1853)	18,961,920	26,880	18,988,800	10,000,000
TOTAL	1,208,784,640	16,856,320	1,225,640,960	$131,679,222

Source: U.S. Department of the Interior, Bureau of Land Management.

Despite the growth in population and because of the movement of people to the cities and the massive increase in available lands, farmlands remained relatively inexpensive.

LAND DISTRIBUTION

The acquisition and subsequent distribution of land was a matter of high state policy, partisan politics, and sectional and individual interests. The greatest obstacles to expansion were the Indians and foreign powers. Gunpowder, enthusiasm, negligible amounts of money, and that unique phenomenon we label the westward movement—American settlers pressing irresistibly westward of their own volition, irrespective of law or public sanction—resolved the problems of acquisition. Wars and treaties were most often the aftermath of American territorial entry rather than the means to it. Americans walked, rode horses, drove wagons, pushed wheelbarrows, and did whatever else was necessary in their unceasing advance to the unsettled lands to the west. Expansion was popular among most of the population, even though the number of individuals who actually journeyed west was relatively small. The westward movement was a state of mind as much as a physical action. Americans early became addicted to the notion that expansion of any kind is to be equated with opportunity, progress, achievement, and success. But the disposal of the newly acquired territories became a subject of no little public controversy.

Ground rules for the distribution of public lands were instituted by the Land Ordinance of 1785, which provided for the rectangular survey and public sale of land, and by the Northwest Ordinance of 1787, establishing procedures for the transition of unsettled territories into politically equal states. Almost from the first, American land entered the free market and titles were settled in fee simple.

Perhaps nothing was more important to the expansion of agriculture than the open market on the public land. Legislation notwithstanding, the distribution of the public domain was effected largely by the supply and demand factors of the market. This distribution of land was the single most important development in American free-enterprise capitalism, and a phenomenon that did not exist in any European economy in the mid nineteenth century. Only after 1860 did considerations of public welfare markedly affect land-distribution patterns, and then only after most of the public domain had been distributed by the marketplace. Federal land grants to railroads (established by the 1850 precedent of a grant of 2.5 million acres to the Illinois Central Railroad), grants to colleges under the Morrill Land-Grant College Act (established by the precedent of the Land Ordinance of 1785, which specified that one section in each township be reserved for public education), and free land (for which there was no legislative precedent) became major instruments of public land-distribution policy after 1860. Yet even these land policies resulted in the transfer of public lands to private hands.

Land legislation, beginning with the Land Ordinance of 1785, provided for the auction of land in various acreages and specified minimum prices. A limited form of credit was allowed by the earlier land acts, but after 1820 cash payment was required. The Land Act of 1800 maintained the minimum price of $2 per acre specified by the Act of 1796, but allowed sales of half-sections with five years to pay, rather than sales of full sections (640 acres) with one-half down and the balance due in one year. In 1804, the blocks of land available for auction were reduced in size to 160 acres. In 1820, an 80-acre block could be auctioned at $1.25 per acre, minimum, to be paid in cash.

By 1828, the Northeast had become alarmed that cheap land and low tariffs were injuring the development of manufacturing. The famous Webster-Hayne debates of that year began with a discussion of the conflicting economic interests of the Northeast and the Southwest Democratic coalition, and ended in a sophisticated discussion of the nature of the Union. The politics of land and tariffs became increasingly partisan. Henry Clay of Kentucky attempted to fabricate a new political coalition based on these and related economic issues by introducing his American System. Clay favored protective tariffs and low-priced land, and proposed to placate the South and West by using federal income derived from tariffs to underwrite internal improvements, thereby making more land available. The South, however, became increasingly intransigent in its support for free trade. The Northeast became heartily protectionist, and the West began to advocate free land. At the same time, southerners came to identify free land with restraints on the expansion of slavery, the undermining of rights in slave property, and the abolition of slavery. As long as the Southwest political coalition held together, cheap land and low tarriffs prevailed, but by 1850 that alignment was exhibiting unmistakable signs of collapse.

Not only sectional interest but also competitive private interests attempted to shape land-distribution policy. Speculators who wanted first ownership tended to favor governmental sales of large blocks of land at competitive auctions. Farmers usually wanted sales in smaller tracts, with some credit available. Squatters, who held first possession, demanded first rights to buy, preferably at a low price. Many squatters, in fact, equated possession with title, which undoubtedly encouraged the free-land syndrome. Taxpayers and government officials favored land sales as a means of generating government income. Manufacturers favored income from land sales and from tariff revenues as the primary source of public income. Considering the diversity of competing interests, the land auction was perhaps the most democratic and equitable means of land distribution.

The Pre-Emption Act of 1832 injected a new, nonmarket priority into land distribution. Squatters on the public domain were allowed to purchase 160 acres of the land on which they resided at the minimum price of $1.25 per acre, payable in cash. The purchaser had to be the head of a family, a widow, or a single man over twenty-one. Purchasers had to be citizens of the United States—or had to have filed intentions of becoming citizens—could not already own over 320 acres of land, and could not abandon their present landholdings for new lands in the same state. Settlement of the public domain prior to purchase was no longer declared an act of trespass. The advent of preemption precipitated a boom in land sales. The preemption system, which was renewed biennially until it became permanent policy by means of the Pre-Emption Act of 1841, encouraged illegal settlement of the western lands. It reflected a policy of almost complete laissez faire, individualism, and free enterprise. More of the public domain was ultimately distributed under preemption than under any other single policy, including the Homestead Act of 1862. The Homestead Act provided for the distribution of free land after the initial payment of an entry fee and five years residency. The act included an often used preemption clause that allowed the homesteader to purchase 160 acres at the minimum price of $1.25 per acre after six months residency.

Despite the rather liberal policies for the distribution of the public lands, more Americans moved to the cities than to the farms. During the period of the most rapid territorial expansion, between 1840 and 1860, the population of the United States increased about 226 percent, while the population of cities increased 797 percent. In 1780, only 5 cities had a population of more than 8,000; by 1840, 44 cities had exceeded this figure. New York had 312,000. By 1860, there were 141 cities with a population in excess of 8,000 and New York had a population of over one million. Because urban populations increased far more rapidly than rural-farm populations, the domestic demand for farm goods was disproportionately greater than total population increases. But European markets, particularly for cotton, expanded even more rapidly in the antebellum period. Export of American raw materials and crude foods rose from the level of $30 million to $35 million annually in the decade 1820–1830 to exceed $200 million by 1859. By 1860, subsistence farming was rapidly giving way to commercial agriculture under the impetus of urban growth, mechanical invention (including improved farm equipment and transportation facilities) and expanding export markets.

Major farm exports between 1815 and 1860 included cotton, tobacco, wheat and flour, corn and corn meal, rice, beef products, pork products, and timber products. These goods, as a percentage of the value of exported domestic manufacturers, are charted in Figure 6.1.

Improvements in transportation and the natural influence of climate and geography promoted regional specialization in agriculture. Intensive vegetable, fruit, and dairying industries became increasingly prominent in the Northeast. The feed-grain and slaughter industries centered in Ohio. Wheat and food grain were farmed extensively from Ohio to Iowa. In the South, cotton was king but there were important pockets of tobacco, rice, and sugar production. In the Southwest and Southeast the range-cattle industry had become established. Cotton was perhaps the single most important determinant of economic expansion, accounting for the greater part of American exports and maritime freight and the inception of textile-manufacturing industries. Antebellum agriculture, however, is best characterized by small, family farm units that produced grain, meat, and vegetables for domestic consumption. Improved transportation, the growth of urban markets, and mechanization accentuated the trend toward commercial agricultural production in the North and South.

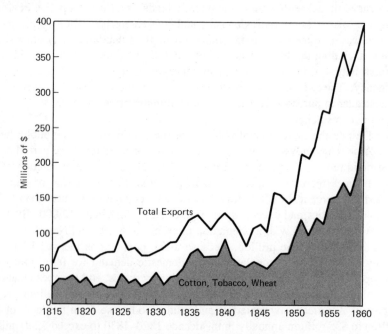

FIGURE 6.1. Value of selected agricultural products (cotton, tobacco, wheat), compared with the value of total exports in millions of dollars, 1815-1860.

Source: *Historical Statistics of the United States Colonial Times to 1970.* Series U 274–294 and U 187–200 pp. 884–886, 897–899.

NORTHERN AGRICULTURE

Wheat was the great cash crop of the northern farm. New York was the major wheat-producing state and milling center until about 1850, by which time heavy production had developed in Pennsylvania and Illinois. The "milling capital" had moved from New York City to Rochester, New York by 1860, and to Minneapolis by 1875. Farms in the Northeast and outside the midwestern plains averaged 40 to 80 acres. Tillage of the often rock-strewn soil was difficult. Farm tools were primitive and labor was scarce. Most small farms, like those in the South, raised corn and food crops on relatively small acreage, and the northern farmer used wheat instead of cotton as his cash crop.[3] As additional acreage was cleared and prepared for cultivation, most of it would be planted in wheat. The wheat growing in the antebellum years was primarily "soft" wheat, which could be milled more readily by the primitive stone-grinding method or even by the mortar-and-pestle method that was necessary in the back-country homestead. "Hard" varieties of wheat, such as Fife wheat, introduced about 1842 by David Fife of Ontario, Canada (via Scotland from the Volga River in Russia), were not easily milled and had a "strong color." However, they required less moisture, were more disease-resistant, and were adaptable to weather changes. Also, hard-wheat flour had a higher protein and vitamin content and absorbed more water in baking processes. Until the adoption of improved milling processes, such as the roller mill, and the opening of the northern plains to wheat in the 1870s and 1880s, hard-wheat flour was 10 to 15 percent cheaper than the soft varieties. By 1900, most American wheat was of the hard variety and the heart of the wheat industry was located in Kansas, the Dakotas, and Minnesota.

Population movements and technological improvements markedly affected northern as well as southern agriculture. A migration of southern farmers between 1800 and 1830 brought settlers into the forested regions of southern Illinois, Ohio, and Indiana. The most formidable task they faced was to clear the land—a slow, costly process. A rather specialized "setup" labor force developed in the Midwest in response.[4] Laborers contracted at five to twenty dollars a day to clear land. The process involved cutting timber, girdling, digging stumps, splitting rails for fencing, and burning the debris. If the farm was accessible to the river, farmers could sell cordwood to the steamboats. Otherwise, much of the timber was burned.

A second migration between 1830 and 1860 brought New England farmers into the yet unsettled great prairies of the Midwest. Farms in the prairies generally were larger, ranging from 80 to 200 acres. Fencing, and breaking the heavy, tough, matted prairie sod were the most critical problems facing the prairie farmer. Another form of specialized labor, the sodbusters, developed in the Midwest. Sodbusters charged two to five dollars per day to open the sod to a depth of about six inches. It often required several days to plow one acre, and such work could be done only in the spring or summer. In the winter, sodbusters often worked as teamsters, hauling produce to market. Hired farm labor was also seasonal employment. Wages were low at fifty to seventy-five cents per day, but board, lodging, and "maintenance" (such as clothes and laundry) were often provided. Seasonal farm hands often ended their employment by driving hogs and cattle to markets such as Cincinnati, and then went to work in the slaughterhouses.

Farm tools improved considerably between 1800 and 1860. Eighteenth-century plows were either flimsy wooden devices or extremely heavy and almost unmanageable iron contraptions that required two to six pairs of horses or oxen to pull them. In 1814 Jethro Wood, a New Yorker, patented a simply constructed, strong, and durable cast-iron plow that had a removable plowshare. It sold at a modest price and was widely copied. By the 1830s, Pittsburgh was probably the leading plow-manufacturing center in the world. But the cast-iron plow had its limitations: it broke often, and prairie sod clung to the share. John Deere was one of those who experimented with polished-steel plowshares. By the 1850s, Deere had become the principal plow manufacturer in the United States. Steel plows, however, were very expensive. The chilled-iron plow, perfected about 1860, performed as well but cost much less. The Prairie Queen plow was adapted especially for plowing virgin prairie soil. Riding on wheels, the Prairie Queen plow used a colter, or cutting disk, ahead of the steel plowshare to cut an opening in the sod for the point of the plow. The first riding plow, a sulky, was developed about 1844, and unsuccessful experiments were conducted with steam-propelled plows in the 1850s. The adaptation of horse-drawn equipment to steam occurred largely in the later 1800s.

Spiked-tooth harrows were commonly used on farms in the North and South before the Civil War, and could easily be fabricated on the farm. The spiked-tooth harrow was at least as old as the Romans. A disc harrow came into use before the Civil War, and a spring-tooth harrow was patented in 1869. A "clod crusher" was widely used. It could be bought, or it could be made on the farm from a log center-bored and fitted on a sleeve so that it would roll when pulled by oxen. Various forms of grain drills, corn planters, and cultivators were devised before the Civil War. The mowing machine with a hinged cutting bar had essentially been perfected by 1860. George Ertel patented a functional hay baler in 1860. The main business of the U.S. Patent Office before the Civil War was, in fact, to approve patents on farm equipment. Improvements in plows and other farm equipment were adopted far more readily in the free-labor North, where the economic imperative to make available labor more productive seemed more urgent than it did in the slave-labor South.

Next to the cotton gin, perhaps the single most important improvement in farm technology before 1860 was the development of the reaper. Until 1850, most wheat in the United States was harvested by hand with a sickle or a cradle (a sickle with wooden teeth that held a sheaf of grain). An expert cradler could harvest four acres of wheat a day at best. Unlike cotton, wheat had to be harvested within days of its ripening. Although there had been earlier experiments at developing harvesting machinery, Cyrus McCormick perfected and patented a workable reaper in 1830. Mass production of his reaper did not occur until McCormick opened a plant in Chicago in 1848. Meanwhile, other reapers had been perfected and put into production, and by the 1850s reliable harvesting machines could be purchased for $100 to $150. The early reaper could harvest fifteen acres of wheat a day, compared with the expert cradler's three to four acres. It is estimated that the reaper saved the farmer at least fifty cents per acre in harvesting costs. It also enabled the farmer to harvest far greater acreages in wheat. The reaper and the twine binder (developed about 1850), which gathered a sheaf of grain and bound it with twine, improved milling processes. Eventually, the steam thresher combined with these innovations to revolutionize the wheat industry in the latter part of the nineteenth century.

Despite improvements in farm equipment, farm labor continued to be scarce and labor costs continued to rise throughout the antebellum period. The large influx of immigrants into the eastern seaboard had little impact on the labor supply in the Midwest before the Civil War, although it was felt after the war. Free Negroes were so few in the North that although they often worked as farm laborers, they had little impact on the labor market. Also, northern farmers preferred white laborers. Blacks, when available, were the last hired and the first fired.

THE AGRICULTURAL SOUTH

Southern farms were comparable to northern farms in their general economic and social characteristics.

Although most white southern farmers may have aspired to slave ownership, by 1860 most did not have slaves. About one fourth of all southern farmers owned slaves. In 1860, representative nonslave family farms ranged in size from 50 to 120 acres. On a 120-acre family farm, an average of 25 acres would be cultivated. Much of this would be devoted to corn, several acres would be allotted to food crops, an orchard, or a garden, several acres would be used for hay crops, and often a small plot was reserved for tobacco and sugar cane. Little more than 3 to 5 acres of cotton were raised, and that provided the small cash income with which the family purchased shoes, coffee, and tools. Chickens, hogs, a small number of cattle, horses, and oxen, which were used most commonly as draft animals, completed the homestead. The southern family farm tended to be a self-sufficient economic unit existing on a near-subsistence level that generated a small cash income from the marketing of cotton, tobacco, grain, or livestock. As in the North, the trend was to expand the volume of commercial production.

Cotton, of course, was not the only commercial crop of the old South. Although not as extensive, rice, sugar, tobacco, and cattle produced profits per unit of production equal to or greater than the profits of cotton plantations. The South of the 1850s actually had substantially larger acreages of corn than of all other crops combined, but relatively little found its way to interstate or foreign markets. In 1855 the corn crop was valued at $209 million, compared with $136 million for cotton. Wheat was also raised extensively, particularly in Virginia and the upper South, though little of it was exported. The value of the wheat crop generally equaled the combined value of the tobacco, sugar, and rice crops.[5]

Tobacco cultivation centered in Maryland, Virginia, and the Carolinas, but by 1860 substantial tobacco crops were being raised in Tennessee and Kentucky. Tobacco farms, which required a small, closely supervised labor force, were rarely as large as cotton plantations, and were operated as efficiently on a small family-labor scale as on a larger scale with slave labor. The tobacco industry was plagued from colonial times by overproduction, depressed prices, high costs, soil exhaustion, and parasitic insect infestations, but with luck, hard work, and efficient management tobacco farming could be profitable.

Rice, unlike tobacco, required large acreages, much unskilled labor, and a substantial capital investment in land and in improvements such as levees, flood-gates, and mills. Most of the rice produced came from 60,000 to 70,000 acres owned by fewer than one thousand planters located along the Savannah, Altamaha, Edisto, Santee and Combahee rivers in South Carolina and Georgia. By 1860, some large rice plantations had developed along the lower Mississippi River in Louisiana. Great fortunes and tremendous investments in land and slaves were accumulated by the successful rice planters on the Golden Coasts of South Carolina. The limited acreage available for rice planting, plus foreign competition, rising slave prices, and the enormous capital requirements of rice production and milling, made the industry an increasingly precarious business by the time of the Civil War. The Civil War and the abolition of slavery effactually ended the eastern rice industry, although some production continued in South Carolina until the twentieth century. Some rice production continued along the lower Mississippi after the Civil War until mechanization and the opening of the coastal plains in Louisiana and Texas in the late nineteenth century revitalized, if not revolutionized, rice production.

Sugar-cane production, which was centered in lower Louisiana, compared with rice production in that it required large acreages, vast amounts of relatively crude labor, and large investments in mills and in land improvements, such as levees to prevent flooding and for drainage canals. Sugar, too, was particularly vulnerable to foreign competition, price fluctuations, and the vagaries of weather. But, as was true of rice, it brought enormous profits to a limited number of planters. Neither rice nor commercial sugar production was suited to small-scale farming operations.

A southern range-cattle industry existed from colonial times, and tended to move westward with the advance of the frontier. Although the "day of the cattleman" came after the Civil War, an open-range cattle industry thrived in the upland ranges of Tennessee, Georgia, and Kentucky, the coastal prairies of southwest Louisiana, and the prairies east of San Antonio, Texas. In 1846 Edward Pipes drove a herd of Texas cattle to Ohio. In the 1850s Texas herds were being driven to Chicago and Illinois markets, to California, and to railheads in Iowa. The Opelousas Trail, which overlay an old Indian track, followed the Gulf Coast to New Orleans markets. One extension of the trail moved northward across the Sabine River to steamboat landings in Alexandria, Louisiana, and herds were occasionally driven on to Natchez, Mississippi for boarding. The Old Government Road, used in the 1840s and 1850s, carried herds from the Texas Red River country to markets in Little Rock, Arkansas. The Shreveport Trail, from Dallas to Shreveport, with extensions to Natchez or Vicksburg, had limited use in the 1850s. Some modern botanists believe it is possible to trace some of the old cattle trails by following lines of plant associations. Cattle droppings caused unusual plant migrations, such as the movement of arid, desert plants into the wetlands. Generally, the cattle industry involved nomadic herding on the open range by family groups, with beef prices and profits varying widely according to local marketing conditions.[6] Considerable quantities of pork, and to a lesser extent beef, were raised on farms throughout the South for domestic consumption and for urban and foreign markert. When Sherman's armies struck into the heart of the Confederacy in 1864 and 1865, the soldiers found enormous stores of pork, bacon, and beef. At the same time, Confederate armies were suffering critical food shortages.

THE COTTON ECONOMY

Although most southern farmers were not directly involved in the "cotton economy," the identification of antebellum southern agriculture with cotton and slavery has great validity. Cotton alone accounted for one third to over one half of the value of all exports each year between 1815 and 1860. Cotton exports were valued at $17.5 million in 1815. By 1860 they had reached a value of $191.8 million. Cotton was the major expansive force in the growth of the antebellum economy, suggests Douglass C. North:

> It was cotton which was the most important influence in the growth in the market size and the consequent expansion of the economy . . . it was cotton that initiated the concomitant expansion in income, in the size of the social overhead investment (in the course of its role in the marketing of cotton) in the Northeast which were to facilitate the subsequent rapid growth of manufactures. Cotton also accounted for the accelerated pace of westward migration as well as for the movement of people out of self-sufficiency into the market economy.[7]

North credits cotton with the strategic role of initiating the interregional flow of commerce. Income received from cotton (as well as sugar, rice, and tobacco) flowed directly into the West and Northeast in the purchase of goods and services. The South, he believes, imported wheat, corn, pork, and beef from the West. Recent studies, however, indicate that much of this trade via the Mississippi was destined for reexport to eastern and European markets. The Northeast provided finance, transportation, and marketing services, and either produced or reshipped the manufactured goods consumed in the South. Northern textile mills bought raw cotton and marketed finished cloth. Strategic inventions stimulating the expansion of the textile industry included Kay's flying shuttle (1733), Arkwright's water frame (1769) for rapidly and evenly spinning coarse yarns, Hargreaves's spinning jenny (1770), Crompton's "mule" (1779), which spun the finest threads, and Cartwright's power loom (1785). Eli Whitney's cotton gin (1793) and the steam engine and steamboat removed the last impediment to mass production and the transportation of raw cotton and cotton textiles. With the close of the Napoleonic wars and the War of 1812, the advent of "King Cotton" precipitated an economic revolution in the United States.

Cotton stimulated expansion in the textile, machine-tool, and derivative industries. It was the major cargo carried by domestic and foreign shippers. The growth in the transportation industries in turn stimulated expansion in the basic iron, steel, and coal industries. Expansion in the cotton industry provided a vital impetus to domestic migration and western expansion. Most significant, cotton stimulated the growth of slavery and the plantation system.

SLAVERY

Slavery became the central issue in the developing sectional conflict. Southern investment in slave property was an estimated $4 billion by 1860. Of the approximately one million white families in the slave states in 1860, one fourth owned slaves. There were even some black slave owners. Black slaves constituted about one third of the South's population. Most slave owners, almost 275,000 of them, owned fewer than ten slaves and farmed on or near subsistence levels. There seems to have been some correlation between family size and slave ownership: the more sons a farmer had, the fewer slaves he owned, given comparative acreages under cultivation. Of the approximately 100,000 farmers who owned more than ten slaves, only 10,000 possessed more than fifty slaves. A planter was generally regarded as one who owned more than thirty slaves. At this level, a slave owner could hire an overseer or manager to supervise the slave force.

The typical labor organization on the plantation included the overseer and field gangs, which were known variously as the plow gang, hoe gang, and trash gang, each supervised by a slave driver. Domestic servants and skilled artisans and craftsmen usually worked under the direct supervision of the planter and his wife. Ulrich B. Phillips, author of the classic study *American Negro Slavery*, believes the severity of the slave system was partially mitigated by the capital

FIGURE 6.2. A place where slaves were sold in Atlanta

Courtesy Library of Congress.

value of the slave. Mistreatment, illness, injury, or runaways depreciated the owner's capital value in the slave. Slavery and the plantation system represented the central form of capital accumulation in the antebellum South, just as the manufacturing plant was the central form of northern capital. Yet in both sections most people were small, independent family farmers, and most of the capital value was in land.

The consensus of historians, although disputed, is that the slave-plantation system was a profitable operation, and that slavery was not, as Phillips suggests, primarily a system for maintaining white supremacy. Among the excellent studies of black history and slavery that have been published in recent decades, perhaps none is more controversial and significant than *Time on the Cross: The Economics of American Negro Slavery*, by Robert W. Fogel and Stanley L. Engerman. A cliometric approach using statistical data analysis, causal models, and paradigm formations (an analysis of models containing a common element), this study has jarred traditional views by arguing that slavery was a rational and profitable economic system that gave no indication of demise before 1860. Southern slave agriculture, say the authors, was more efficient than the northern system of family farming. As an individual laborer, the slave was efficient and hard-working, perhaps more so than his white counterpart. Slaves lived more comfortably than northern free laborers, and were generally as well provided, if not better. Per-capita income, the authors conclude, increased more rapidly in the South in the two decades before the Civil War than in the rest of the nation.[8] Although the specific points raised by *Time on the Cross* and its methodological approach are challenged, the study strengthens the general consensus that slavery was economically profitable.

The new economic history and cliometric methodology provide invaluable tools for the testing of traditional historical hypotheses. Basically, this means that economic historians can amass great quantities of data and by computer analysis can define a model or scale of mathematical probabilities that can be applied to related bodies of data. A simple but representative example is the use of the "survivor technique" in *Time on the Cross* to determine the interregional movement of slaves when no actual raw figures for such movements are otherwise available. The national census reports, particularly for 1850 and 1860, do give a reliable count by age and sex of the slave population. Because of death, some of the slaves in all age groups did not survive from one census to the next. If the survivor rates are calculated, these rates provide a mathematical estimate of survivor rates and birth rates that may be applied to other time frames or to specific geographical areas. Since the importation of new slaves into the United States was illegal between 1810 and 1860, a given slave population in any one state in 1850 should produce a reasonably accurate population projection for 1860 when survivor rates are applied. If the actual census count is greater, or lesser, the difference may be assumed to be the result of the net in- or out-migration of slaves.[9]

Such techniques are obviously not infallible and are susceptible to technical error. They are still contingent upon basic human assumptions in the development of mathematical hypotheses. Indeed, the startling conclusions in *Time on the Cross* have been subjected to serious criticism by historians who argue that the authors' methodology dehumanizes history, and is therefore nonhistorical. Others find the computations faulty. It is argued, for example, that many of the data sources provide too narrow a base for an accurate mathematical projection, or that data such as per-capita income do not provide an accurate index of economic growth for a nonindustrial society. One such criticism is that the use of cotton prices and income as measures of southern wealth in the 1850s gives a false impression of southern agricultural productivity, just as the use of oil-income figures of the OPEC (oil-exporting) nations would provide inaccurate evidence of labor productivity today. Nevertheless, although the new economic history has not as yet solved many of our old historical problems, it has provided a valuable new tool for historical inquiry and has been applied profitably to the problem of slavery.[10]

Slavery was only one of the issues that generated divisive sectional conflicts. The development of the national economy in the antebellum period was paralleled by strong political issues that tended to overshadow the basic interregional and interdependent characteristics of the national economy. The Northeast desired high protective tariffs to discourage ruinous foreign competition with its fledgling industry, and higher prices on land to discourage the migration of labor to the West. The agricultural South and West favored cheap land and low tariffs, which would lower the costs of imported goods. Most sections, but particularly the West and the Northeast, sought internal improvements, especially in roads and railroads, that would facilitate marketing and, for the West, access to more land. However, once the cotton kingdom had reached its apparent geographical limits, which were imposed by the arid lands of the Great Plains, the southern interest in cheap land and domestic territorial expansion cooled. Some southerners, as well as northerners, considered the possibility of overseas expansion into Hawaii, Cuba, and Haiti. Southerners could not envision a cotton kingdom without slaves. Cheap land in the West came to mean free states and the extinction of the slave system. Concurrently, the massive flow of immigrants into the Northeast in the 1850s relieved the manufacturer's concern over the flight of labor to the farms. The organization of the Republican Party and the withdrawal of the southern states from the Union created a new political hegemony of West and Northeast consummated by a free-land policy (the Homestead Act of 1862) and a high protective tariff (the Morrill Tariff of 1863). It would be a gross overstatement to explain the Civil War as a rational economic conflict between the cotton, slave, and plantation interests of the South and the small-farmer, free-labor, and manufacturing interests of the North, as did Charles Beard, but there were, to be sure, substantial economic issues involved.

Notes

[1]See A. Whitney Griswold, *Farming and Democracy* (New York: Harcourt, Brace, 1948), and Merrill D. Peterson, *The Jefferson Image in the American Mind* (New York: Oxford University Press, 1960).

[2]An excellent treatment of land policies is provided in Roy M. Robbins, *Our Landed Heritage: The Public Domain, 1776–1936* (1942; reprint ed., Lincoln, Nebr.: University of Nebraska Press, 1962).

[3]A classic treatment of northern agriculture is Percy Wells Bidwell, *A History of Agriculture In the Northern United States 1620–1860* (1925; reprint ed., Gloucester, Mass.: Peter Smith, 1941). The most useful tools for the study of American agricultural history are the bibliographies published by the Agricultural History Centers at the University of California at Davis.

[4]See David E. Schob, *Hired Hands and Plowboys: Farm Labor in the Midwest, 1815–1860* (Urbana, Ill.: University of Illinois Press, 1975).

[5]For a general résumé of agricultural history and for bibliographic references on specific crop and livestock production, see Paul W. Gates, *Farmer's Age: Agriculture, 1815–1860* (New York: Holt, Rinehart & Winston, 1960). See also the older but excellent study by Lewis Cecil Gray, *History of*

Agriculture in the Southern United States to 1860, 2 vols. (1932; reprint ed., Gloucester, Mass.: Peter Smith, 1958).

[6]See Sam Hilliard, *Hogmeat and Hoecake: Food Supply in the Old South, 1840–1860* (Carbondale, Ill.: Southern Illinois University Press, 1972), and Forrest McDonald and Grady McWhiney, "The Ante-Bellum Southern Herdsman: A Reinterpretation," *Journal of Southern History*, 41 (May 1975), 147–66.

[7]Douglass C. North, *The Economic Growth of the United States, 1790–1860* (New York: Norton 1966; Englewood Cliffs, N.J.: Prentice-Hall, 1961), p. 68. North provides an invaluable analysis of regional economic growth, and of interregional and international trade flows. See also Stuart Bruchey, *The Roots of American Economic Growth, 1607–1861* (New York: Harper & Row, 1965), and Stuart Bruchey, ed., *Cotton and the Growth of the American Economy, 1790–1860* (New York: Harcourt, Brace, 1967).

[8]See Robert W. Fogel and Stanley L. Engerman, *Time on the Cross: The Economics of American Negro Slavery*, 2 vols. (Boston: Little, Brown, 1974), and Ulrich B. Phillips, *American Negro Slavery* (1918; reprint ed., Gloucester, Mass.: Peter Smith, 1959).

[9]See Fogel and Engerman, *Time on the Cross*, Vol. II, pp. 43–54.

[10]For further reference, see Alfred H. Conrad and John R. Meyer, *The Economics of Slavery and Other Studies in Econometric History* (Chicago: Aldine, 1964); Robert W. Fogel and Stanley L. Engerman, eds., *The Reinterpretation of American Economic History* (New York: Harper & Row, 1971); and Herbert G. Gutman, *Slavery and the Numbers Game: A Critique of Time on the Cross* (Urbana, Ill.: University of Illinois Press, 1975).

SUGGESTED READING

BIDWELL, PERCY WELLS, AND JOHN I. FALCONER *A History of Agriculture in the Northern United States 1620–1860*. Washington, D.C.: Carnegie Institution, 1925. Reprint ed., Gloucester, Mass.: Peter Smith, 1941.

GATES, PAUL WALLACE, *The Farmer's Age: Agriculture 1815–1860*. New York: Holt, Rinehart & Winston, 1960.

GRAY, LEWIS CECIL, *History of Agriculture in the Southern United States to 1860*, 2 vols. Washington, D.C.: Carnegie Institution, 1932. Reprint ed., Gloucester, Mass.: Peter Smith, 1958.

GRISWOLD, A. WHITNEY, *Farming and Democracy*, New York: Harcourt, Brace, 1948.

HILLIARD, SAM B., *Hogmeat and Hoecake: Food Supply in the Old South, 1840–1860*, Carbondale, Ill.: Southern Illinois University Press, 1972.

NORTH, DOUGLASS C., *The Economic Growth of the United States, 1790–1860*. New York: Norton 1966.

PETERSON, MERRILL, *The Jefferson Image in the American Mind*. New York: Oxford University Press, 1960.

ROBBINS, ROY M., *Our Landed Heritage: The Public Domain, 1776–1936*. Cambridge, Mass.: Princeton University Press, 1942. Reprint ed. Lincoln, Nebr.: University of Nebraska Press, 1962.

SCHOB, DAVID E., *Hired Hands and Plowboys: Farm Labor in the Midwest, 1815–1860*. Urbana, Ill.: University of Illinois Press, 1975.

WIK, REYNOLD, *Steam Power on the American Farm*. Philadelphia: University of Pennsylvania Press, 1953.

THE CIVIL WAR AND ECONOMIC HISTORY

chapter VII

Did conflict between competing sectional economies cause the Civil War? What was the comparative economic condition of the North and South as each approached the brink of a cataclysmic war? What impact did the war have on economic growth and upon the development of the free-enterprise system? In the 1850s *De Bow's Review*, the preeminent southern commercial magazine, included a note about a day in the life of a typical southern planter. He arose in the morning and shaved with a razor made in the North before a mirror of northern manufacture. He dressed in clothing of northern fabrication, boarded a steamboat made in northern shipyards, and traveled to New Orleans, where he stayed in the finest southern hotel. There, he dined on meat and beans grown in the South and on bread made of northern flour, all served on china made in New England. At night he climbed into an elegant bed imported from the North, pulled a cotton sheet milled in northern mills, and lay down to *dream of southern independence*. A contemporary historian wrote in a similar vein, "Southern planters paid tribute to Northern bankers, Northern merchants, Northern shipowners and Northern manufacturers. A large percentage of the profits of cotton production remained in the North."[1]

Charles Beard, who ascribed a strong economic motivation to historical change, believed that the Civil War resulted from a conflict between economic interests that had a sectional orientation only by geographical accident. The war was fought between the planting interests and the commercial interests, between the agrarians and the industrialists, between the aristocrats and the democrats. It pitted the capitalist, industrialist, small-farmer, free-labor, and democratic interests in the North against the agricultural, slave-labor, aristocratic regime in the South. The Civil War, said Beard, was the "second American Revolution," one in which the urban-industrial interests triumphed over the rural-agrarian interests. It was "a revolution so drastic, so effective," and, because of Radical Reconstruction, "so well protected against the inexorable recoil."[2] The war marked the end of the old order and the arrival of the new. Beard's thesis has been much examined, revised, and rejected. There are in fact many causes and many explanations for the Civil War. Slavery appears to be endemic to them all, to the extent that if there is a historical consensus on the cause of the Civil War, "slavery and slavery alone" is that consensus.

The "peculiar institution" has been the subject of most of the recent historical inquiry about the causes of the war. Slavery alone, however, is not a single causative factor, but has many facets. Was slavery primarily a system of racial control? Was it economically profitable? Did the slave question become such an emotional issue that it generated a "romantic nationalism" in the South and a utopian idealism in the North that produced an unreasoned clash of arms? And is not war basically an irrational act? Would there have been a Civil War had the institution of slavery never existed? All of these questions are pertinent to an understanding of the causes of the Civil War. Although it is impossible to answer each of them here, the questions themselves help formulate an answer to the central issue of this study: Was the Civil War caused by competition between sectional economic interests?

LAND, TARIFFS, AND SLAVERY

There were, to be sure, conflicting economic interests between North and South, prominently involving land policy, internal improvements, tariffs, and slavery. An outstanding example of such conflict is the South Carolina nullification dispute involving the tariff. The Tariff of 1828, called by South Carolinians the Tariff of Abominations, placed an unusually high protective tariff on imported goods. The tariff raised the prices of goods southerners had to buy, whether those goods were bought at home or abroad. To the extent that the tariff reduced American purchases abroad, it reduced the ability of foreign markets to consume American cotton. Moreover in the 1830s South Carolina entered upon hard times, caused in part by competition from cotton planters in the West, in part by soil exhaustion, and in part by erratic prices for cotton, rice, and tobacco. John C. Calhoun and others blamed the tariff. When Congress reaffirmed protectionist principles in the tariff law of 1832, South Carolina adopted a Nullification Ordinance:

> Whereas the Congress of the United States, by various acts, purporting to be acts laying duties and imposts on foreign imports, but in reality intended for the protection of domestic manufactures, and the giving of bounties to classes and individuals engaged in particular employments, at the expense and to the injury and oppression of other classes and individuals . . .
> We . . . do declare and ordain . . . that the several acts . . . are null, void, and no law, nor binding upon this State."

President Jackson announced that the laws of the United States must be executed. South Carolina threatened secession, made preparations for defense, and nullified Congress's "force bill," which authorized Jackson to use troops against South Carolina. A violent confrontation was averted when a new compromise tariff, sponsored by Henry Clay of Kentucky, allowed a gradual lowering of tariff schedules. South Carolina was mollified and the laws were upheld, but Calhoun and others set about building a sense of southern solidarity, which was easily enhanced by the rising conflict over slavery. The slave question had not been a direct part of the nullification controversy, but the tariff issue had brought at least one state to the brink of secession.

Tariffs, slavery, plantations, and cotton fostered a sense of Southern solidarity, but they were not inseparable interests. The South became more firmly entrenched in a one-crop cotton system after the Civil War without slaves than it had ever been before the Civil War with slaves. Hardly fifty thousand southerners in 1860 could be termed planters, and three fourths of the white population did not own slaves. Most southerners, as most northerners, were small, independent family farmers. Yet apart from slavery there were distinctive differences between the North and South in the antebellum era—differences that somehow seemed more acute long after the Civil War, when slavery was dead, than had been true before the war. In 1860 or in 1900 the South appeared backward when compared to the North. The northerner built more factories and more schools, published more books and more newspapers, made more money, lived in closer proximity to more people, built more cities, and seemed more energetic. But the southerner seemed to think his life was richer and more satisfying. He believed himself to be more of an agrarian, conservative outdoorsman and an individualist by temperament and preference, as well as by necessity. The southerner, too, developed different concepts of nationalism and democracy. The quantity and quality of life in the North and the South seemed different before the Civil War, and became more so after the war, despite the resolution by war of some of the more obvious differences between them. These differences had more to do with cultural than with economic distinctions.[3]

Economically, the Northeast, Midwest, and South needed one another. But the more interdependent they became, the more the differences among them chafed. These distinctive sectional attitudes and values had not suddenly developed, but had become more obvious as the economic, political, and cultural values of one section increasingly impinged upon another in the press of a rising national economic and political order. The Civil War was in part the result of the frictions caused by the growth of a national economy and a national as opposed to a sectional or localistic culture. The old, atomistic, Jeffersonian society was giving way to a new, integrated collectivist order. The commercialization of agriculture in the South and in the North, as well as the expansion of industry and commerce, promoted the rising tide of social change and conflict.

ABOLITION

Slavery was an economic issue—and more. It became symbolic of cultural differences, and of change and resistance to change, just as integration has to an extent evolved from a matter of race into an issue involving social change and different conceptions of progress. To oppose integration, or the busing of students to school in order to achieve a racial balance, is often due not as much to racism as to one's hostility to change. White southerners opposed abolition and supported the Confederacy not only because their property values or economic conditions would be affected, but because abolition threatened social change and secession accorded with their view of social order and stability.

Even though only a relatively small part of southern society had a vested financial interest in slavery, the economics of slavery was a legitimate cause for southern opposition to abolition. Southern slave owners invested some $4 billion in slave property. Numerous non–slave owners aspired to acquire property in slaves, which denotes a vested interest. Moreover, many of the non–slave owners who had no aspiration for slave ownership nonetheless feared the economic competition in the labor market that the abolition of slavery would likely, and did, produce. Unrestricted immigration came to mean much the same thing to the northern laborer that the end of slavery meant to the southern free laborer and small farmer—increased competition and lower wages. Slavery was a profitable institution, but free labor, mechanization, and the small family farm were viable and profitable alternatives that had actually been pursued by the great majority of southerners and had been proven by a greater number of northerners. The slave issue was a pertinent economic question, but it was more than profits and property interests alone that set the South on the course of secession and the North on the course of abolition.

Slavery had once been as economically profitable in the North as in the South. The African trade was one of the most lucrative businesses of the seventeenth and eighteenth centuries. As a practical matter, the American Revolution ended the business of slave sales to North America and precipitated American objections to slavery largely because the slave trade was regarded as a part of the British trade monopoly. To oppose the slave trade was to oppose the British. The First Continental Congress declared in 1774 that the colonies would no longer import slaves or purchase imported slaves. After the Declaration of Independence, individual states followed with their own prohibitions on the slave trade, but as a practical matter the Revolution and the British blockade effectually halted the trade. By 1787 every state in the Union but Georgia had enacted legislation prohibiting the African trade, and in 1798 Georgia followed suit. The Constitutional prohibition on the importation of slaves after 1808 endorsed an existing situation. Thereafter, existing circumstances as well as legal and moral considerations proscribed the slave trade. The Napoleonic Wars and the War of 1812 virtually halted American commerce with Europe and Africa. Between

1793 and 1815 there was relatively little opportunity or incentive for Americans to engage in the slave trade. As the economic justification waned, the moral condemnation of the slave trade gained. The abolition of the slave trade could have positive economic benefits even for the slave owners. The importation of more slaves would reduce the value of slaves on hand, and more slaves could mean larger crops, which in turn might produce lower commodity prices. John Adams suggested in 1795 that the abolition of slavery in Massachusetts was "a measure of economy," presumably because of the jealousy and competition from free laborers. Both the defense of slavery and the opposition to it were tangled webs of economic and humanitarian motives.

Generally, where slavery became less and less profitable, support for abolishing the institution increased. Systems of gradual emancipation were adopted in the northern states, beginning in Pennsylvania in 1780. Children of slaves were to remain in servitude until they reached the age of twenty-one, when they would be free. Slaves over twenty-one would remain in bondage. New York adopted similar legislation in 1799, but later emancipated all slaves, effective July 4, 1827. New Jersey converted its remaining slaves to "apprentices" in 1846. Few slaves were freed by northern emancipation, for there were few slaves in the North. Ninety-five percent of all slaves and freedmen lived in the states that would constitute the Confederacy. Yet in the early nineteenth century, support for slavery waned even in the South.

The American Colonization Society, organized in 1817, proposed to free slaves and colonize them in Africa. Virginia and Maryland appropriated state funds for the colonizing efforts, but over a ten-year period the society succeeded in transporting fewer Negroes to Africa than were being born in America each month. Moreover, it appears that by 1830 southern participation in the American Colonization Society derived from different motivations than the southern participation of a decade earlier. Northern members of the society began to suspect that southern members were more interested in strengthening slavery by getting rid of blacks already free than in hastening the end of the institution by encouraging slave owners to free their slaves.

Northern antislave interests soon flocked to the banner of abolition raised by William Lloyd Garrison, Theodore Dwight Weld, and others, who in 1832 founded the New England Anti-Slavery Society. This organization was soon succeeded by the American Anti-Slavery Society. Garrison's newspaper, *The Liberator*, demanded immediate abolition without reimbursement for slave-owners. Meanwhile, the slave states, entering upon a long period of prosperity and expansion, generally adopted the position that slavery was no longer a "necessary evil" but was instead a "positive good." Thereafter, almost every question of public policy became impaled on the horns of slavery.

The "economic conflict between agriculture and business would never have split the Union," suggests Henry Bamford Parkes. "What caused the South to secede was Northern hostility to slavery; and here the propaganda of the abolitionist was of decisive importance." "It is impossible," he wrote, "to attribute any economic motive to these men." Abolitionism was essentially a religious movement retaining a crusading fervor, a narrowness of vision, and a mixture of idealism and intolerance. The South matched abolitionism with racial fanaticism and romantic nationalism.[4] Because of abolition, the mainstream of northerners and southerners became convinced, not as much of the moral good or evil of slavery, but of the righteousness of the one and of the unrighteousness of the other.

By 1850 the slave question and the sectional peculiarities that it symbolized dominated American thought and politics. In that year Congress adopted a compromise providing for the admission of the territories acquired from Mexico at the conclusion of the Mexican War through the Treaty of Guadalupe-Hidalgo. The South had by now formulated the argument that inasmuch as the Constitution recognized rights in slave property, neither Congress nor territorial governments had the authority to abolish slavery within the territories administered under the national government. Abolitionists countered with the proposition that there was a "higher law" than the Constitution. Meeting in Nashville, Tennessee in June, 1850, southern representatives actively considered secession. South Carolina independently approved a resolution calling for secession but retrenched when she discovered that other southern states would not follow. At the same time, every northern state but one adopted resolutions demanding that slavery be banned from the territories. Public meetings throughout the free states called for the abolition of slavery in the territories and the end of the slave trade in Washington, D.C. But most Americans, north and south, sought moderation and compromise. The plan, introduced by Henry Clay and supported by Stephen A. Douglas and Daniel Webster, among others, and approved by Congress, admitted California as a free state and organized the territories of New Mexico and Utah with no mention of slavery. The slave trade was abolished in the District of Columbia, but the enactment of a strong fugitive slave law was taken by the South to mean the permanent recognition of rights in slave property and the final resolution of the slave question. However, the Compromise of 1850 marked only an uneasy truce.

The flow of gold from California, rising prices for wheat and cotton, and increased manufacturing and commerce produced a prosperity that helped quiet the passions of the moment. However, the political base for sectional compromise and negotiation was being undermined. A Free-Soil Party, dedicated to ending the expansion of slavery and to the free distribution of the public lands, had organized. The Democratic Party was losing its national orientation, and the Whig Party was soon to be replaced by the Republican Party, which absorbed the Free-Soilers and committed itself to the restriction of slavery, high tariffs, and free land.

The Kansas-Nebraska Act, the Ostand Manifesto, the publication of Harriet Beecher Stowe's remarkable *Uncle Tom's Cabin*, the Dred Scott decision,

TABLE 7.1

The Slave Controversy to 1860.

1789	Three-fifths Compromise	Provided that for purposes of taxation and representation each slave should be counted as three fifths of a citizen.
1789	Embargo on slave trade	No slaves to be admitted after 1808.
1817	Organization of American Colonization Society	Proposed to gradually end slavery by recolonizing Africans in their homeland.
1820	Missouri Compromise	Efforts to maintain a balance in the number of slave states and free states (eleven) resulted in the admission of Missouri as a slave state and Maine as a free state. Provided that slavery should not exist north of the 36°30' parallel.
1832	Organization of New England Anti-Slavery Society	Dedicated to the immediate abolition of slavery without reimbursement of owners.
1832	South Carolina nullification controversy	Argued states' rights to nullify acts of Congress. Deemed unconstitutional by the Executive.
1850	Compromise of 1850	Admitted California as a free state, organized Mexico and Utah with no mention of slavery. Abolished slave trade in District of Columbia and established a fugitive slave law. Caused political diversions, a threat of secession, and emotional conflicts.
1853	Publication of *Uncle Tom's Cabin*	Contributed to public support for abolition in the North and to southern support for secession.
1854	Defeat in Congress of Homestead Bill	Marked divergence of South and West over free-land issue.
1854	Kansas-Nebraska Act	Admitted Nebraska as a free state. Organized Kansas as a territory. The status of slavery in Kansas was to be settled by popular sovereignty, despite the state's location north of the 36°30' parallel specified in the Missouri Compromise.
1854	Organization of Republican Party	Support free land, high protective tariffs, and the restriction of slavery to its existing locations.
1857	Dred Scott Decision	Prohibited the admission of former slaves to citizenship. Held in an *obiter dictum* that slaves were property and that Congress could not deprive persons of rights in slave property in the territories.
1857	Tariff of 1857	Lowered tariff rates to lowest schedules since 1816.
1857	Presidential veto of Homestead Bill	Regarded by North as additional evidence of southern minority control of national government.

TABLE 7.1 (cont.)

1859	John Brown's raid on Harper's Ferry	Brown proposed to raise up a slave rebellion in the South and force the emancipation of slaves. He was hanged as a traitor, acquired martyrdom in the North, and created widespread sentiment for secession in the South.
1860	Presidential elections	Brought Lincoln, a sectional candidate of a party hostile to the slave, tariff, and land interests of the South, to the presidency.
1861	Organization of Confederate States of America	Firing on Fort Sumter. War.

the Lincoln-Douglas debates, John Brown's raid, the political disintegration marked by the elections of 1860, and the election of Republican Abraham Lincoln to the presidency led to the secession of seven slave states and the organization of the Confederate States of America in February, 1861 at Montgomery, Alabama. After the firing on Fort Sumter, Virginia, Arkansas, Tennessee, and North Carolina joined the Confederacy. Four slave states—Maryland, Delaware, Kentucky, and Missouri—remained with the Union.

Did the Civil War result from competition between essentially hostile sectional economic interests? The best answer at this point is probably not. Secession and the Civil War marked the emergence of a national economic order and a national cultural consensus and the development of a truly federal political structure that had been taking shape over the past hundred years. The old atomistic, individualistic, agrarian order was reluctantly giving way to the new integrated, collectivist society. The roots of war and sectional conflict were deeply imbedded in the society. There was no single cause for that great tragedy. Rather, there were many. Perhaps the British traveler Andrew Burnaby experienced a moment of prescience in 1756 when he reported that

> fire and water are not more heterogeneous than the different colonies in North America. Nothing can exceed the jealousy and emulation which they possess in regard to each other. In short, such is the difference of character, of manner, of religion, of interest of the different colonies that I think if I am not wholly ignorant of the human mind, were they left to themselves, there would even be a civil war from one end of the colony to the other, while the Indians and Negroes would, with better reason, impatiently watch the opportunity to exterminate them all.[5]

ECONOMIC COMPARISON OF THE NORTH AND THE SOUTH

The great disparity in population and industrial prowess between the North and the South preordained the Confederacy to an early extinction, but as Americans have learned in Southeast Asia and other parts of the world, as well as in the United States' own revolutionary experience, the larger and better-equipped armies do not always win. Nevertheless, the Union, once it committed its vast resources to war, held a decided advantage over the Confederacy (Figure 7.2).

The twenty-three states of the Union had a free population of about 22,000,000 and a slave population of 400,000. The eleven states of the Confederacy had a free population of about 9,000,000 plus 4,000,000 slaves. Despite the larger population of the Union, northern armies did not attain a decisive numerical superiority over Confederate armies until 1863. The Confederacy had the manpower to maintain successful warfare in the early years of conflict, but did not have the reserves to sustain those armies. Manpower capacities of both North and South appeared adequate to provide foodstuffs for both civilian and military use. However, the South, unlike the North, lacked the capacity to produce surpluses, nor did it have the capability to market surpluses.

The South's small manufacturing capacity was debilitating but probably not a decisive factor in the outcome of the war. The Union had 110,000 industrial establishments that employed over a million workers and produced goods valued at $1.5 billion in 1860. The Confederacy had some 20,000 industries employing

FIGURE 7.1. President Abraham Lincoln visits General George B. McCellan in the field at Antietam after the indecisive battle of September 1862. The photograph was taken by Mathew B. Brady, October 3, 1862.
Courtesy Library of Congress.

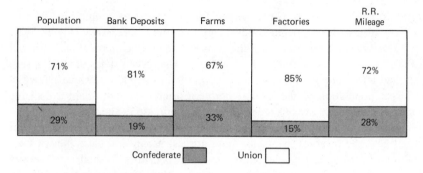

FIGURE 7.2. The Union and the Confederacy: Comparative data.

Source: Bureau of the Census.

somewhat over a hundred thousand workers and producing goods valued at $155 million. Northern manufacturing and production of raw materials—particularly iron, coal, woolens, clothing, salt, guns, and ammunition—expanded rapidly during the war. Southern manufacturing either contracted or was diverted exclusively to the production of war materials. The Tredegar Iron Works of Richmond, for example, had manufactured materials or iron for the fabrication of tools; now it directed its facilities exclusively to war production. By capture, purchase, and through the manufacture of a maximum of 300 rifles per day, compared with the northern manufacture of as many as 5,000 rifles per day, Confederate armies maintained enough firepower to fight and win battles until the close of the war.

The South had little of the financial resources of the North. The Confederate government acquired $1 million in specie from the United States mint in New Orleans, and that specie was allegedly still on hand at the close of the war. The South financed the war through loans, paper money, and taxation. The Confederacy first levied a "quota" on states, rather than a tax. This failed to produce substantial revenues, and in 1863 the Confederate Congress approved a revenue and income-tax measure that allowed for the payment of taxes "in kind." Taxation, it is estimated, produced only about 1 percent of the Confederate government's income. The Confederacy borrowed vast amounts, most of it from its own people. An initial $15-million bond issue was subscribed in gold, and a second issue was subscribed in Europe in 1861. The most famous Confederate loan, the $15 million Erlanger loan, produced only $2.5 million for the government. The Confederacy borrowed to the hilt, and at the end of the war it had accumulated debts of about $2 billion. In addition, it had issued over $1 billion in paper money by 1864. The Confederacy also suffered severe inflation.

The Union followed very much the same financial course as the Confederacy. It financed the war by taxation, loans, and paper money. Taxes provided a negligible part of the total. They were levied on incomes, manufactures, occupations, and sales. Most Union funds were derived from borrowing. The bonded indebtedness of the national government had reached about $2.8 billion by 1865. Current expenses and interest on the debt were often met by the circulation of paper money. The Legal Tender Act of 1862 authorized the issuance of $150 million in paper money. By 1865, this amount had increased to $450 million (about half the amount issued by the Confederacy). The value of these ''greenbacks'' fluctuated widely, causing severe inflation and hardship. But the greenbacks, unlike Confederate currency, floated on a fairly comfortable cushion of specie and private bank notes. Unlike the South, the Union had ready access to specie from the California mines and from sales in foreign markets. There is no doubt that the Union was on a stronger financial footing for war. However, there is some reason to doubt that money was the decisive factor in the defeat of the Confederacy.

Other than the demoralizing effect of inflation, which became notorious in 1864 and which reflected the degenerating military situation, the South's financial programs seemed to accomplish all that any fiscal measures could be expected to achieve. But even if the South had realized $2 billion in gold from its bonds, or even if $1 billion in gold coinage had replaced the same amount of Confederate currency in circulation, it is not clear that this would have markedly affected the South's ability to equip or feed its armies or provide a livelihood for its citizens.

A major factor affecting the Confederacy's economy and its ability to wage war was the Union blockade of Confederate coasts. It is quite likely that had there been no blockade, the South would have been able to buy the ships, guns, and equipment needed for a successful defensive war, and to market sufficient cotton and other agricultural produce to maintain a sound economy. Confederate blockade runners often dealt in the most profitable luxury items rather than in war materials. Manufactured goods of all kinds, such as shoes, paper, flour, cloth, medicines, coffee, and salt, were extremely scarce in the Confederacy. The South lived off of its accumulated goods, and when those were gone it did without. Although military historians emphasize the overwhelming superiority of Union armies after 1863 as the decisive factor in the northern victory, the immediate and vast superiority of Union sea power, the effective use of that sea power in the New Orleans (1862) and lower Mississippi (Vicksburg [1863], Port Hudson [1863]) campaigns, and the loss of European markets resulting from the blockade produced the economic paralysis that assured the ultimate destruction of the Confederacy.

''Cotton diplomacy,'' the southern diplomatic strategy, assumed that if southern cotton were kept from French and British textile industries, the ensuing economic pressure would force the governments of these countries, whose leaders were sympathetic to the Confederacy, to break the blockade, extend recognition to the Confederacy, and intervene in the war. Southern independence would be guaranteed. The Union blockade, southern leaders theorized, supported the

Confederate grand strategy. Throughout the war, Confederate authorities supplemented cotton diplomacy by destroying cotton stockpiles that threatened to fall into Union hands. Union military units, particularly in the Red River campaign in Louisiana, made concerted efforts to capture Confederate cotton, which by 1864 could be marketed for as much as $1.00 per pound. However, cotton diplomacy failed in its objective, for several reasons. The cotton crop of 1859, which generally entered the 1860 export market, was the largest ever produced. England alone imported 2,580,700 bales in 1860, and, thus, manufacturers had a surplus that carried them for some time.

TABLE 7.2

Cotton Production, Exports, and Prices, 1859–1866.

YEAR	PRODUCTION (THOUSANDS OF BALES)	DOMESTIC CONSUMPTION (THOUSANDS OF BALES)	EXPORT (THOUSANDS OF BALES)	PRICE (AVERAGE PER POUND, IN CENTS)
1859	4,310	845	3,535	11.3
1860	3,841	842	615	12.3
1861	4,491	369	10	28.2
1862	1,597	287	23	65.1
1863	449	220	24	91.2
1864	299	344	18	95.2
1865	2,094	615	1,301	44.3
1866	2,097	715	1,402	32.2

Source: Bureau of Agricultural Economics, *Statistics on Cotton and Related Data.* p. 3.

In addition, the blockade and the southern embargo rapidly increased the value of cotton stocks held in Europe. Intervention by European powers would have markedly reduced the value of this cotton. English manufacturers in other industries were also reaping rich profits from the war. Northern wheat was becoming an increasingly important British import. Northern wheat production rose from about 150 million bushels to over 200 million bushels during the war years, much of the surplus going to the British market. England and France also found new sources of raw cotton, notably in Egypt and India. Furthermore, the mass of people in England and France opposed slavery. But not until Lincoln's Emancipation Proclamation of 1863 did public opinion in these two countries shift decisively in favor of the North. Because of the Proclamation, because the tide of battle swung in favor of the North with the vital victories at Gettysburg and Vicksburg, and because Union sea and land power had become increasingly formidable, the possibility of European intervention after 1863 became increasingly remote.[6]

Despite what appeared to be the overwhelming manpower and material superiority of the North, the Confederacy maintained formidable military forces until the close of the war. A northern victory was never a certainty until the surrender of Robert E. Lee's Army of Virginia at Appomattox on April 9, 1865.

THE IMPACT OF THE WAR

The impact of the Civil War on American economic development was profound, but very difficult to measure. Popular opinion tends to believe that the Civil War produced the urban-industrial society and the prosperity associated with modern America. This simplistic view is heightened by the fact that most American history courses end with the Civil War and resume with the study of the rise of big business and the reconstruction politics that undergirded the new industrial regime. The national banking law, high protective tariffs, a contract-labor law, lavish land grants to railroads, the Homestead Act, and the political welding of the defeated southern states to the Republican Party assured the success of the industrial capitalist. Louis Hacker's *Triumph of American Capitalism* stressed the positive effect of the war on mechanization and the growth of heavy industry. The production of iron, machinery, agricultural implements, lumber, shoes, clothing, and food stuffs expanded tremendously. There is some indication, however, that we have read too much of America's present into her past. We like to view the past and the Civil War through the lenses of optimism. We overlook the fact that the Civil War also produced major economic losses and a diversion of energies. Overall, did the Civil War promote or retard industrialization?[7]

The irreplaceable and most immediate loss resulting from the war was that of men. Union and Confederate war dead totaled over 618,000. Almost one fourth (258,000) of the adult white males in the Confederacy died in the war. The decennial rate of increase in population slowed from 35 percent in the 1840s and 1850s to 26 percent in the next three decades, despite a large increase in immigration. Even immigration did not reach prewar levels until the 1870s. It would be fallacious to attribute the continuing decline in the rate of population growth, which reached a low of 7.2 percent in the 1930s, to the Civil War, but it is clear that the war markedly affected the short-term fertility rate and population growth.

Financial losses resulting from the war were great. The abolition of slavery wiped out $4 billion in capital. Confederate bonds valued at $2 billion were repudiated. Few southern banks survived the holocaust; none did in South Carolina. The value of real property in the South declined 50 percent; the value of farm property declined about 70 percent. Two thirds of the South's rail mileage was destroyed. Financial losses incurred by the destruction of such cities as Atlanta, Charleston, and Richmond are inestimable. A substantial portion of the steamboat tonnage that navigated southern waters did not survive the war. In 1870, the production of such staples as cotton, corn, sugar, tobacco, and rice remained well below 1860 levels.

FIGURE 7.3. The ruins of Richmond, Virginia, 1865.
Courtesy Library of Congress.

Despite a remarkable rate of increase in almost every industry outside of the South, Thomas C. Cochran and other contemporary analysts believe the Civil War retarded industrial growth. As Cochran has written, "From most standpoints the Civil War was a natural disaster, but Americans like to see their history in terms of optimism and progress. Perhaps the war was put in a perspective suited to the culture by seeing it as good because in addition to achieving freedom for the Negro it brought about industrial progress." Cochran concluded that war and postwar depression "retarded a curve of production that was tending to rise at a high rate."[8] Total rail construction slowed to a 70-percent rate of expansion during the decade 1860–1870, with only a 15-percent rate of increase between 1860 and 1865. These figures contrast significantly with the 200-percent expansion rate of the 1850s and the average rate of 75 percent for the 1870s and 1880s. Textile production fell by 6 percent in the decade 1860–1870, in contrast with the 47-percent rate of growth in the 1850s. The rate of production of farm equipment changed considerably in each decade between 1840 and 1890, but reached one of its decennial lows during the 1860–1870 period. The constant dollar value of bank loans and bank assets declined below the 1860 level during the war decade. The rate of growth in construction declined from prewar levels. W. W. Rostow supports Cochran's conclusion that by the late 1850s "the United States was a rapidly maturing industrial state" with all of the preconditions for "take-off" into sustained economic growth. It was not the Civil War but the cultural, institutional, and economic conditions established before the war that enabled Americans to achieve a continuing growth in per capita output in the later nineteenth and the twentieth centuries.[9] The war interrupted rather than hastened economic growth.

The Civil War did stimulate growth in specific industries. It did initiate the process by which blacks would participate more fully and share more equitably in economic development. The South's black population undergirded its remarkable economic expansion since World War II. The Civil War did, perhaps, stimulate the cultural assimilation of the ideas of modernization, business, capitalism, growth, and progress. In the long term, the Civil War may well have had a positive impact upon the development of the American free-enterprising system. But in the short term, it retarded an industrial and economic expansion already well under way. The ledgers, however, are still open.

Notes

[1]Henry Bamford Parkes, *The American Experience* (1947; reprint ed., New York: Random House, Vintage Books, 1959), p. 224.

[2]See Charles A. Beard and Mary Beard, *The Rise of American Civilization* Vol. II. (New York: Macmillan, 1933) pp. 52-121.

[3]See Parkes, *The American Experience*, pp. 220–26.

[4]Parkes, *The American Experience*, pp. 225–26. See also Rollin G. Osterweis, *Romanticism and Nationalism in the Old South* (Baton Rouge, Louisiana State Univeristy Press, 1967).

[5]See Rev. Andrew Burnaby, *Tracks Through the Middle Settlements in North America in the Years 1759 and 1760*. (Ithaca, N.Y.: Great Seal Books, 1960).

[6]See Frank Lawrence Ousley, *King Cotton Diplomacy*, 2nd ed. (Chicago: University of Chicago Press, 1959).

[7]See Beard and Beard, *The Rise of American Civilization;* Louis Hacker, *Triumph of American Capitalism* (New York: Columbia University Press, 1940); Thomas C. Cochran, "Did the Civil War Retard Industrialization?" *Mississippi Valley Historical Review,* 48 (September 1961); pp. 197–210; and Harry N. Scheiber, "Economic Change in the Civil War Era: An Analysis of Recent Studies," *Civil War History,* 11 (December 1965).

[8]Cochran, "Did the Civil War Retard Industrialization?" p. 210.

[9]See Walt W. Rostow, *Stages of Economic Growth*, 2nd ed. (Cambridge: Cambridge University Press, 1960).

SUGGESTED READING

CRAVEN, AVERY, *The Coming of the Civil War*, 2nd ed. Chicago: University of Chicago Press, 1959.

DONALD, DAVID, ed., *Why the North Won the Civil War*. Baton Rouge: Louisiana State University Press, 1960.

ELKINS, STANLEY M., *Slavery: A Problem in American Institutional and Intellectual Life*, 2nd ed. Chicago: University of Chicago Press, 1968.

GASTON, PAUL M., *The New South Creed: A Study in Southern Mythmaking*. New York: Knopf, 1970.

GENOVESE, EUGENE, *Roll Jordan Roll: The World The Slaves Made*. New York: Pantheon, 1974.

GUTMAN, HERBERT, *Slavery and the Numbers Game: A Critique of Time on the Cross*. Urbana, Ill.: University of Illinois Press, 1976.

LITWACH, LEON, *North of Slavery: The Negro in the Free States, 1790–1860*. Chicago: University of Chicago Press, 1961.

O'CONNOR, THOMAS H., *The Disunited States: The Era of Civil War and Reconstruction*. New York: Harper & Row, 1972.

OSTERWEIS, ROLLIN G., *Romanticism and Nationalism in the Old South*. Baton Rouge: Louisiana State University Press, 1967.

OUSLEY, FRANK LAWRENCE, *King Cotton Diplomacy*, 2nd ed. Chicago: University of Chicago Press, 1959.

PRESSLY, THOMAS, *Americans Interpret Their Civil War*. Princeton, N.J.: Princeton University Press, 1954.

RANDALL, JAMES G., AND DAVID DONALD, *The Civil War and Reconstruction*, 2nd ed. Boston: Heath, 1961.

ROLAND, CHARLES P., *The Confederacy*. Chicago: University of Chicago Press, 1970.

ROSTOW, WALT W., *Stages of Economic Growth*, 2nd ed. Cambridge: Cambridge University Press, 1960.

STAMPP, KENNETH, ed., *The Causes of the Civil War*. Englewood Cliffs, N.J.: Prentice-Hall, 1959.

A TIME FOR
RECONSTRUCTION:
1866–1876

chapter VIII.

Reconstruction was a time for testing the institutions, political structures, ideas, and values formed before and during the Civil War. The war marked a time of decision on such issues as land sales, the tariff, slavery, and states' rights. The war abolished slavery and eroded state sovereignty, but their ghosts lingered. Land would be free, and tariffs high. Banking would again be a part of the nation's business, in a qualified way. Some railroads would be heavily subsidized by the federal government as well as by state and local public authorities. Most railroads were constructed without public aid of any kind. Financiers, entrepreneurs, and corporations became prominent, but not dominant. The nation's business continued to be primarily agricultural.

Economic indicators for those years, 1866 to 1876, are crude, confusing, and most often unavailable. The population increased about 25 percent in the postwar decade, from 35.7 million to 46.1 million, while the land area remained the same. Thus, population density rose slightly, from about 12 to 15 persons per square mile. The proportion of urban dwellers rose from about 20 percent in 1860 to 26 percent in 1870 and 29 percent in 1880. Most Americans would continue to live in rural areas until 1920. The value of manufactured goods, which remained relatively stable between 1860 and 1865, rose 25 percent between 1866 and 1876. The production of iron ore rose from about 3 to over 4 million tons. Gold production remained relatively stable at about 2.5 million ounces per year for the entire period 1850–1876. Crude-petroleum production, which had been negligible in 1860, came alive in 1861, which witnessed an output of over 2 million barrels. This figure rose to 5 million in 1870, 12 million in 1875, 9 million in 1876, and 26 million in 1880. Crude-petroleum prices declined steadily from an average of $6.59 per barrel in 1865 to $.94 per barrel in 1880. Both bituminous- and anthracite-coal production increased steadily during the war, and rose more rapidly thereafter. In the 1870s, sources of bituminous coal free from sulphur, an impurity that weakened pig iron, were found, and bituminous coal began to replace anthracite in industrial uses. In 1866 the value of exports exceeded the 1860 level for the first time, and the 1876 level was one-third greater. Imports tended to rise more rapidly than exports until 1874. In 1876 the value of exports exceeded that of imports by $120 million.

Perhaps the most interesting indicator of business activity, or of changing attitudes, was the sharp increase in patent applications over prewar levels. In every year from 1866 through 1876 an average of over 20,000 patent applications were filed with the U.S. Patent Office, compared with the 7,600 of 1860 and the 4,000 to 6,000 recorded each year during the war. Among the world's great inventions associated with this decade are the air brake, the carpet sweeper, celluloid, dynamite, the Hotchkiss machine gun, the refrigerated railroad car, and the typewriter. Patent activity indicates rapid expansion in every area of business in the postwar decade, despite the enormous losses incurred by war, the political chaos, and a severe depression. Political, economic, and psychological reconstruction was a national process, not confined to the defeated Southern states.

While Americans outside the South enjoyed the sweet nectar of victory and felt the certitude of self-righteousness, southerners tasted the bitter dregs of defeat. The war, the defeat, and Reconstruction policies bred a legacy of hate that had not dissipated by the twentieth century. As one Virginia planter wrote in his diary in 1865. "I here declare my unmitigated hatred to Yankee rule—to all political, social and business connections with the Yankees and to the Yankee race. Would that I could impress these sentiments, in their full force, on every living Southerner and bequeath them to every one yet to be born!"[1] Then Edmund Ruffin shot himself and died. If they had not done so before the Civil War, many southerners after that war turned away from the "wholesome and practical nineteenth century smell of cotton factories and locomotives" of which Mark Twain wrote, and took refuge in a culture that was "modern and medieval mixed." The South, in part by necessity and in part by choice, failed to participate fully in the economic resurgence of the postwar decade, but "New South" spokesmen were urging industrialization.

POLITICAL RECONSTRUCTION

Republicans differed over the means of reconstructing the South to make it conform more accurately to the northern image of America. President Lincoln and his successor, Andrew Johnson, represented a conservative view supporting a mild peace, the rapid restoration of the defeated states to full political status in the Union, the abolition of slavery, and noninterference in the race relations or internal affairs of the southern states. The conservatives proceeded upon the theory that the defeated southern states had never seceded, and that once the internal revolt was quashed, the states' relationship to the Union was unaltered. The Radicals, led by such men as Thaddeus Stevens and Charles Sumner, believed that the southern states had in fact formed an independent nation, and that as a conquered territory the South held no political rights. In 1864, representatives to Congress from elected Union governments in Louisiana, Arkansas, and Tennessee were denied their seats. Radicals formulated their own plan for Reconstruction in the Wade-Davis Bill, which Lincoln disposed of with a pocket veto. Congress soon passed an embellished Wade-Davis Bill that abolished existing state governments in the former Confederacy, divided the South into five military districts for purposes of military occupation and control, enfranchised the Negro, and disfranchised the former Confederate.[2]

Under the provisions of the Wade-Davis Bill, 703,000 black voters and 627,000 white voters were enrolled and the former Confederacy became a political minion of the Republican Party. As a condition for readmission to the Union the former slave states were required to ratify the Fourteenth Amendment, which they had rejected in 1866 (except for Tennessee), giving the freedman citizenship, and guaranteeing equal protection of the laws. Next, Congress circumscribed the power of the executive with the Tenure of Office Act (1867) and the Command of the Army Act (1867), and failed to impeach President Johnson by only one vote. Johnson was in an untenable political situation, and the Radicals were in power. In 1868, and again in 1872, the electorate ratified the Radical Republican administration with the election of Ulysses S. Grant to the presidency.

THE SPOILSMEN

Thus began what may be referred to as an "age of excess" in politics and in business. Indeed, one characteristic of the era is that business and politics often became indistinguishable. Laissez faire, if it meant the divorce of government from economic activity, was a misnomer if applied to this period. Government was not divorced from business activity, but neither did it exercise control or restraint over that activity. The public largely accepted the idea that government aid to the private sector of the economy produced widespread social benefits. For example, railroad construction, it was believed, benefited the entire nation. There is some evidence that the social rate of return, or the indirect capital gains accrued from massive public investment, were most often less than the public believed them to be. Nonetheless, the "age of excess" is in part explained by the presumption that government had an obligation to extend public aid in order to promote private enterprise. Thus, government's relationship to the private sector of the economy became more consciously and actively promotional. The Senate in particular became a focal point of special interests, such as railroads, sugar, and banking. Senator Zachary Chandler controlled the U.S. Customs Houses in

Michigan by virtue of his patronage, or power to make appointments to federal jobs. He allegedly took a regular levy from the customs' duties for his services. Roscoe Conklin did much the same in New York. Conklin, it is believed, had the power to buy and sell public offices. A federal judgeship could be purchased for $15,000. A term in the New York State Senate cost between $3,000 and $4,000. A seat in the State House sold for $1,500. James F. Casey, Ulysses S. Grant's brother-in-law, exercised similar powers in New Orleans in behalf of the "Customs' House Gang." There the Louisiana Lottery Company, dominated by Radicals and operating on a nationwide basis, returned annual profits of 100 to 200 percent to its shareholders. The Lottery not infrequently used patronage and the power of the purse to determine the outcome of state elections. When the Radicals lost power the Democrats eagerly grabbed the reins of the Louisiana Lottery Company, employing none other than former Confederate General P. G. T. Beauregard as their spokesman and ambassador of good will. California effectually came under the control of the Southern Pacific Railroad, a railroad monopoly that extended its tentacles over the entire southwestern United States. Carpetbaggers—those who utilized political powers to achieve business objectives—were not peculiar to the Reconstruction South. Carpetbaggers believed that a legitimate function of government was to provide opportunities for private profit.

A unique breed of opportunist is exemplified by Jim Fisk, Daniel Drew, and Jay Gould. At their worst, these men were neither politicians nor businessmen, but profiteers on a grand scale. Daniel Drew reportedly made his first $100 as a substitute for someone in the War of 1812. He went into the cattle business and to bolster profits sold stillborn calves for veal. He was perhaps one of the originators of "watered stock," which had a more literal connotation before it was applied to overvalued corporate stock. Drew supposedly kept his cattle from water for a day or two before marketing and fed them salt. Just prior to driving his herd to market he brought them to water and the rangy steers became fat, sleek, heavy, and terribly bloated. They were sold to some untrained and unsuspecting eastern buyer, who soon had nothing but a bunch of rangy, half-starved cattle.

Jim Fisk, who learned about trade from his father, a peddler, and from a short career as a circus barker, became a commission merchant for Jordan & Marsh Company during the Civil War. He made such large profits for the company that he became a vice-president. Jay Gould, often considered the most reputable of the trio, supposedly began his business career with a term paper in grade school entitled "Honesty is the Best Policy." He allegedly decided that it was not. In 1860, Drew, Fisk, and Gould became involved in a "business dispute" with Cornelius Vanderbilt, a rough, tough business tycoon who was busily building a transportation monopoly in ships and railroads around New York City. Drew blocked Vanderbilt's acquisition of the Erie Railroad, a vital transportation artery between New York City and Lake Erie, and obtained control himself. When Vanderbilt attempted to buy Erie securities, Drew, Fisk, and Gould enlarged the capital stock from $17 million to $78 million and sold an estimated $10 million of such watered stock to Vanderbilt. Vanderbilt obtained a court injunction to halt the issuance of the questionable stock, and Drew, Fisk, and Gould obtained a counter-injunction from a higher court. The battle over the authenticity of the stock was carried to the New York legislature, where the competing parties are said to have passed out $2 million in cash to legislators in order to obtain favorable legislation. The Erie Railroad war ended with Vanderbilt, the public, and the railroad poorer but perhaps wiser.

Drew, Fisk, and Gould turned their considerable talents to an attempted corner of the gold market. They wanted to obtain control of a sufficient portion of the national gold supply to drive prices up, and then unload their holdings at an enormous profit. The venture would require the cooperation of the federal government. The trio enlisted the support of James Corbin, another of President Grant's brothers-in-law, who had daily access to the president. They borrowed huge sums, and quietly bought gold at the prevailing price of $133 per ounce. Speculators and the general public were made aware that gold, if hoarded, would soon bring premium prices. The hoarding began. In order that they might reap the benefits of higher gold values in the future, Gould and his friends convinced President Grant that the government's sale of gold should be restricted. The price of gold rose steadily over a period of weeks. On "Black Friday," September 24, 1869, it opened at $145 per ounce and suddenly spurted to $160 per ounce. Inadequate supplies of gold brought panic to the stock exchange, where the little gold available brought premium prices. It appears that the little gold available that day came from the stocks accumulated by Drew, Fisk, and Gould. The trio made substantial profits from this gold during the trading. Before the market opened the following Monday, Secretary of the Treasury George S. Boutwell, under the direction of President Grant, released $4 million in government bullion, and the corner was over. The spoilsmen had used the government to fatten their purses.

RAILROAD CONSTRUCTION

Railroad men actively solicited government financial assistance and subsidies. The juncture of the Union Pacific and Central Pacific Railroads took place at Promontory Point, Utah on May 10, 1869, marking the completion of America's first transcontinental railroad. National pride in this great engineering achievement was marred by revelations of the misuse of government funds. The dream of building a transcontinental railroad antedated the Civil War. The Gadsden Purchase in 1853 was inspired by the need to acquire a suitable southern rail route to California. Stephen A. Douglas was prompted to bring his Kansas-Nebraska Bill before Congress in 1854 in part because of his and his constituents'

FIGURE 8.1. The completion of the first transcontinental railroad, on May 10, 1869, when the last rails of the Union Pacific and Central Pacific (now the Southern Pacific) were joined at Promontory Point, Utah.

Credit: Union Pacific Railroad and Association of American Railroads.

interest in building a railroad from Illinois to California. The organization and settlement of Nebraska would materially aid this objective. Private lobbying and the necessities of war dictated congressional subsidies and charters for construction of the Union Pacific Railroad, which would be built westward from Nebraska, and the Central Pacific Railroad, to be built eastward from California.

Government subsidies in the form of bonds were authorized at $16,000 per mile for construction on level terrain, $48,000 per mile through the mountain ranges, and $30,000 per mile between the ranges. Payments would be due upon the completion of each forty miles of track. The government made an additional grant of a 400-foot right-of-way through public lands, and alternate sections of land along the right-of-way in the amount of five alternate sections per mile on each side of the track. The Union Pacific received a total of 20,000,000 acres of public land, and the Central Pacific 24,000,000 acres. Union Pacific stockholders subscribed to $2,180,000 in capital stock, advancing 10 percent of the total, or $218,000. A contract for construction was awarded to the Crédit Mobilier, a construction company. The Crédit Mobilier in turn purchased the capital stock of the Union Pacific Railroad, advancing $218,000 for the purchase, thereby making the contractors and the railroad shareholders one and the same. The Crédit Mobilier subsequently completed construction of the track and received $93 million in payment from the Union Pacific Railroad, about $60 million of that in government bonds, stocks, and mortgages on land and equipment. A congressional committee concluded in 1873 that the Crédit Mobilier had netted the exorbitant profit of $23 million. In effect, Union Pacific stockholders obtained a railroad and a fortune by risking about $218,000. The committee report concluded,

> It is also said that it is unjust to look at this question in the light of the present; that we should go back to the condition of things before the road was built, when the whole scheme seemed, to the prudent capitalists of the country, visionary and perilous. That is true; and if these gentlemen assumed great risks from which others shrank, and thereby great benefits inured to the public, they should have all due credit. But we think they differ from other capitalists, not in taking a risk, but having discovered that the road could be built at vast profit without risk, the resources furnished by the government being more than ample for the purpose.[3]

The records of the Central Pacific Railroad were not available for careful congressional review, but it was assumed that the construction and financial techniques employed by the Contract and Finance Company were similar. Stockholders of this railroad, including Leland Stanford, Collis Potter Huntington, Charles Crocker, and Mark Hopkins, soon expanded their rail operations and created the massive Southern Pacific system.

Government cash subsidies were awarded only to the Union Pacific and Central Pacific railroads, but federal land subsidies in the nineteenth century totaled 131 million acres, the largest grant being 42 million acres to the Northern Pacific Railroad. States, counties, and cities subsidized construction with enormous, but uncalculated, amounts of land, public-revenue bonds, and depot facilities. Texas alone, which had no federal land within her boundaries, granted 32,153,878 acres of state land to railroads. Public subsidization of private business ultimately forced a new relationship between government and business, and began to erode the laissez faire philosophy.

The conditions surrounding public aid to private business mitigate the popular notion of wrongdoing by railroads. Robert S. Henry has pointed out that less than 8 percent of the total rail mileage in the United States was actually aided by government land grants. Most government loans, such as those to the "Pacific" railroads, were repaid in full. Furthermore, rail construction would not have occurred at the rapid pace it did without public support. And, notes Henry, "whatever may have been its shortcomings, the land-grant policy touched off national and individual energies which in a few short years accomplished the greatest engineering, construction, and colonization project ever undertaken up to that time, a project which transformed the West from a wilderness to a civilized community and welded the nation into one."[4] In our own time, public subsidization of the railroads can best be understood in the context of the massive public aid given to the automotive, trucking, and bus industries, aid in the form of public construction of highways and streets. There could be no modern automotive industry without public roads, and little inland water traffic without the construction and maintenance of rivers and canals by the government.

The public service and general economic benefits afforded by railroads did not excuse the waste, fraud, and extortionate and discriminatory practices sometimes associated with their development. Nor could inequitable and discriminating rate practices be condoned. "These abuses . . . led to a new conception of government regulation of railroads, and this regulation was the first step toward the whole vast system, now prevailing, of government control of the economy."[5]

BANKING AND FISCAL POLICIES

Railroading in the post–Civil War decade was only one manifestation of the changing industrial and political order. New federal banking and fiscal policies contributed to the building of a national economic structure that at times discomfited its various decentralized components. The National Bank Act of 1863 was presumably an effort to expand and stabilize financial services then provided only by a loose and uncertain system of private and state banks. National banks were required to purchase federal bonds in the amount of one third or less of their capital depending upon the size of the community in which the bank was located. Until 1933, the banks were liable to double the par value of their stock for the obligations of the bank. After 1933, liability was limited to par value. Banks had to maintain a required surplus, and were limited in the amount of loans to a single borrower and in the value of loans secured by real estate. There was no central banking authority, and the system served primarily to assure the credibility of the banks. In the opinion of some economists, it contributed to a contraction of the money supply and to fiscal instability. Most of the reserve deposits of the national banks ended up in seven or eight New York City banks. The system generally worked to the advantage of the eastern financial interests, but in bad times, when member banks made unusual demands on their reserves, undue panic would occur in the nation's financial center. The emphasis on short-run profits by the national banks led to overexpansion of credit, which was followed by panic contraction. This, and the general contraction of currency consequent upon federal fiscal legislation, contributed significantly to the Depression of 1873, the second most severe depression in the nation's history.[6]

The national banks were a useful tool in enlarging the scope of business loans to a national scale. Private and state banks, which were chartered under state laws, either by specification or by implication tended to limit their business to state and local services. An amendment to the National Banking Act of 1865 placed a 10-percent tax on state bank notes. This had the overall result of reducing the volume of money in circulation, an unfortunate occurrence in the face of an expanding population and growing money requirements. This currency contraction was alleviated in part by the mid 1870s, when state banks turned to demand deposits in lieu of currency issues. Demand deposits, represented by checks and drafts, opened a vast new medium of exchange. It is estimated that even by 1873, bank deposits approximately doubled the amount of paper currency in circulation. Not until the twentieth century would demand deposits virtually dominate domestic transactions.

United States notes (or greenbacks), national bank notes, and gold coinage in an amount averaging about 10 percent of the face value of notes, were the major forms of money in circulation. Private bank notes, silver, and fractional currency circulated widely during the Civil war, but declined to less than 5 percent of the total money supply by 1870. The money supply contracted in the face of expanding monetary demands. Between 1865 and 1869 the money in circulation contracted about 30 percent. Farmers in particular faced tightening money and credit throughout the nineteenth century. Available capital tended to concentrate in the industrial and financial centers of the Northeast. Wholesale prices and farm prices declined steadily, and the critical shortage of money contributed to the financial panic of 1873, which, among other things, ruined Jay Cooke, the nation's leading financier.

TABLE 8.1

The National Banks, 1863–1880.

YEAR	NUMBER	TOTAL ASSETS OR LIABILITIES (MILLIONS OF DOLLARS)	ASSETS (MILLIONS OF DOLLARS)		
			Loans	*Investments*	*Cash*
1863	66	17	6	6	5
1864	467	252	71	93	86
1865	1,294	1,127	362	394	344
1866	1,684	1,476	550	468	439
1867	1,636	1,494	589	522	361
1868	1,640	1,572	656	507	384
1869	1,619	1,564	686	466	382
1870	1,612	1,566	719	453	361
1871	1,723	1,703	789	456	422
1872	1,853	1,771	872	450	412
1873	1,968	1,851	926	445	439
1874	1,983	1,852	926	451	430
1875	2,076	1,913	973	443	432
1876	2,091	1,826	934	427	400
1877	2,078	1,774	902	431	371
1878	2,056	1,751	835	460	388
1879	2,048	2,020	836	715	398
1880	2,076	2,036	995	452	518

Source: *Historical Statistics of the United States Colonial Times to 1970*, Series X634-655, p. 1027.

TABLE 8.2

Currency in Circulation, by Kind (in thousands of dollars), 1863–1876.

YEAR	STATE BANK NOTES	GOLD COIN	GOLD CERTIFICATES	U.S. NOTES	NATIONAL BANK NOTES
1863	238,677	260,000	—	312,481	—
1864	179,158	184,346	—	415,116	31,235
1865	142,920	148,557	—	378,917	146,138
1866	19,996	109,705	10,505	327,792	296,013
1867	4,484	72,882	18,678	319,438	286,764
1868	3,164	63,758	17,643	328,572	294,369
1869	2,559	62,129	29,956	314,767	291,750
1870	2,223	81,183	32,085	324,963	288,648
1871	1,968	72,391	17,790	343,069	311,406
1872	1,701	76,575	26,412	346,169	329,037
1873	1,399	62,718	34,251	348,464	338,962
1874	1,162	78,948	18,015	371,421	340,266
1875	964	64,446	17,549	349,686	340,547
1876	1,947	74,839	24,175	331,447	316,121

Source: *Historical Statistics of the United States Colonial Times to 1970,* Series X424-437, p. 995.

Federal policy and public preference led to the resumption of specie payments after the Civil War. National bank notes and greenbacks were generally convertible with each other, but not with gold. In 1865, greenbacks carried a gold premium of from 50 to 100; that is, it took from $150 to $200 of greenbacks to buy $100 of gold. There was a public inclination, perhaps inherited from Jacksonian days, to regard gold as "real money" and paper money as fiat, which derived whatever value it had only from governmental sanctions. The resumption of specie payments, authorized by Congress in 1875, made paper money redeemable in gold. By 1879, $4.86 in American paper money or gold could be exchanged for the British pound sterling. Wholesale prices fell almost 50 percent between 1875 and 1879, reflecting the increase in the value of paper money. Total money supplies increased at a rate of slightly over 1 percent per year, but the output of goods and services increased at three or four times that rate, forcing serious price deflation. Silver, although authorized as coinage in 1792, had ceased to circulate because at the legal ratio of 16 to 1 a silver coin of a given designation was worth more than a gold coin of equivalent designation. In 1873 Congress demonetized silver by removing the silver dollar from the coinage list. Thereafter, the United States was on a monometallic or bullion monetary standard, which had in practice already existed, rather than a bimetallic standard. Years later the "Crime of '73"—the demonetization of silver—would be seen as an example of financial and congressional duplicity. It was alleged to have been the product of a conspiracy by financial and creditor interests to exploit the masses, the debtors, and particularly the farmers and laborers. Walter T. K. Nugent suggests that to the contrary, the demonetization of silver was a well-considered scheme to avoid the financial disruption that prospective outpourings of silver from newly developed mines and metallurgy processes, such as the Comstock mines, would bring.[7] Demonetization continued the overall policy of deflation and adherence to the gold standard. "Free silver" would become the great political issue of the 1890s.

Actually, there was little controversy over silver during the Reconstruction era. But there was concern over "Greenbackism." A relatively small but very vocal and disparate group of Americans did not give gold the moral allegiance demanded by others. They believed that legal-tender paper money, inconvertible with bullion, was a just and rational system of exchange, and that the existing monetary, credit, and banking policies were inequitable and discriminatory. For a time, the Greenbackers drew support from labor and labor leaders, such as William Silvis of the Knights of Labor; from manufacturers, represented by spokesmen such as economist Henry C. Carey; and from farmers, who contributed James B. Weaver as the Greenback Party presidential candidate in 1880. The Greenbackers argued that money had *function*, not *form*. Its purpose was to measure the value of production. Money, in itself, need have no value. Labor was the source of all wealth. The role of money was to measure productivity, and if national productivity expanded, so should the money supply. Specifically, Greenbackers opposed the resumption policies favored by Congress and the Republican administrations. They would maintain or expand the greenbacks in circulation and would then make the national debt payable in greenbacks. It was terribly wrong, they believed, to pay a debt contracted in greenbacks with gold, a more valuable currency. Although the Greenback movement attracted a diverse following between 1865 and 1880, after 1873 it became identified more closely with farmer unrest. It is generally identified by historians as a cheap-money panacea similar to the free-silver movement. It was that, and more. In the 1870s, Greenbackers did not identify themselves with silver or gold bullionists, but they did profess some similar principles, such as the belief in a natural law, in progress, and in a just and fair value of exchange.[8]

The historical experience of Americans with paper money, from colonial times through the Civil War, added credibility to the Greenback movement, but the bullionist school won more followers. Greenbackism died as the nation moved positively into a bullion position, and eventually many of the Greenbackers, such as Populist James C. Weaver, advocated the free and unlimited coinage of silver as a means of expanding and inflating the currency supply. Bimetallism offered a more serious challenge to the "gold bugs," since it originated within the framework of the bullionist ideology.

In 1869 and 1870, Congress passed legislation validating and refunding the massive debt contracted during the Civil War. Receipts of the national government exceeded expenditures until the 1890s, and the per capita debt was whittled from about $61 in 1865 to about $12 by the end of World War I. This meant that millions of dollars of government bonds, purchased with "cheap" greenbacks, were eventually repaid in gold. On July 2, 1879, greenbacks and national bank notes were made convertible with gold at par. The result of Reconstruction fiscal legislation was to distinctly aid the nation's financial and banking interests, and to impose heavy burdens on the debtor. These policies stimulated an economic nationalism and a greater degree of financial centralism than previously existed. They also assured the "good faith and credit" of the United States government and increased financial stability. Deflation and currency contraction produced social inequities and contributed to farmer and labor unrest, but in the long run they may also have created a more healthy climate for international trade and economic growth.

New tax policies, as well as monetary policies, adopted during the Civil War and Reconstruction aided entrepreneurs in capital formation and contributed to rapid industrialization and an accelerated growth of output. Congress eliminated the experiment with the income tax and the manufacturers' tax and retained high protective tariffs and excise taxes. The new tax situation, suggests Harry N. Scheiber, raised consumer prices, effected a downward shift in real wages, and reinforced a rise in income disparity.[9]

The Reconstruction years witnessed a proliferation of corporations, which led in 1869 to the founding of the New York Stock Exchange. The primary business of this organization was to provide the capital for industrial expansion. The corporation, long familiar to Americans as a feature of banking and railroading before the Civil War, became identified with manufacturing industries. Several states, particularly New Jersey and Delaware, made it relatively easy to obtain charters of incorporation, and offered special inducements to businesses locating within their confines. The corporate structure facilitated the raising of large amounts of capital and offered the opportunity for wider participation in industry. Its primary inducement was that it limited the risk or liability of the shareholder to the value of his shares, whereas the more traditional proprietary or partnership arrangements included full personal liability. The establishment of the New York Stock Exchange made it increasingly easy to liquidate one's personal business investment, and to raise new capital for expansion.

As corporations such as the transcontinental railroads, United States Steel, and Standard Oil operated on an increasingly national scale, local and state regulation of the corporation became less and less feasible. State regulation, or attempts to do so, became onerous to large-scale enterprise and prompted business to seek and obtain "equal protection of the laws" under the due-process clause of the Fourteenth Amendment. The Supreme Court accepted the argument that a corporation was a "person" under the law in *Santa Clara County* v. *Southern Pacific Railroad* (1886). The corporate structure quickly outgrew the states, and precipitated the trend toward a national economy. National as opposed to state and local sanction and control of business enterprise was not as much the result of conspiracy as the product of corporate growth.

CHANGES IN AGRICULTURE

Whereas manufacturing industries expanded in the size and scope of their activities, farming operations tended to become smaller. This trend was less pronounced in the Midwest and Plains states, and seems to have been reversed around the turn of the century, presumably under the impact of first the steam tractor and then the internal-combustion tractor. The decline in average farm size was particularly notable in the South, where farming did not become mechanized until after World War I. Although many of the plantations were divided or broken up during Reconstruction, many more remained intact and were subsequently broken into many small production units under the sharecropper system.

The abolition of slavery left the southern labor system in a chaotic state. Many if not most of the freedmen wanted to become landowners, and in 1865 and 1866 they anticipated receiving from their liberators or the Freedman's Bureau their "forty acres and a mule." They were to be sorely disappointed. What they obtained instead were work contracts, which represented a joint effort by the Freedman's Bureau and southern state governments to mobilize the black labor force and resume plantation production. Typical labor contracts required one full year's employment on the plantation, specified the wage rate, and reserved half of the wages to be paid at the close of the contract period. Failure by the laborer to complete the contract resulted in the forfeiture of the wages held in escrow. The Freedman's Bureau served as the arbitrating and supervisory agency in the administration of work contracts.

A number of defects in this system doomed the work-contract laws to failure. The first defect, and the one cited most frequently by historians, was that work contracts reinstituted a form of servitude. The work-contract laws were widely assumed to be one more example of the South's refusal to accept Radical control. However, these laws constitute probably the poorest of all examples of southern intransigence. More accurately, they were the result of desperate efforts by both the Freedman's Bureau and southern state governments to bring order out of chaos. In any event, the work contracts were unpopular with blacks, white planters, and the northern public. Money to pay farm-labor wages was essentially unavailable, even under the terms of the work contracts. Wages could not be paid until the crops were marketed, which was taken into account by the long term of the contract. Few, if any, southern planters after the war had the cash to pay wage labor on a daily or weekly basis. In other words, if any wage-labor system would work, the work contract was the most practicable way to implement it.

Another intrinsic failing of the work-contract system is that it was based on the mobilization of labor on the gang basis—the way labor had been organized on the slave plantation. Gang labor permitted specialization and economies of scale. This the freedman objected to most strenuously, for gang labor smacked strongly of the reinstitution of slavery, whether wages were paid or not. Although it became a pernicious system, the sharecrop solution to farm labor was the most expedient solution: it involved absolutely the smallest outlay of money, and it was esthetically more satisfying to the freedman and the white cropper, who at least had the illusion of being independent farmers. By the end of the postwar decade, the work-contract laws had either been invalidated or become inoperative and the South had settled into the quagmire of sharecropping and the crop lien.

The rapid collapse of southern farmland values after the Civil War and their slow recovery meant that land was no longer a mortgageable asset. The crop lien was a mortgage on a future crop, the only asset of value Southern planters had. The cotton factor or broker advanced money to the planter in return for a mortgage on an expected crop and the right to market the crop. The planter, who could not afford wage labor, contracted with farm workers or tenants to farm on shares. Shares were usually based on "thirds": one third of the crop was due for labor, one third for the land, and one third for seed and equipment. The share-cropper received free housing, and provisions were advanced and charged against his share of the crop pending "settlement day." The average sharecropper, white or black, farmed seventeen acres, from which he received one third or two thirds of the crop receipts. Deducted from those receipts were the living expenses charged to his account at the plantation store or commissary. Croppers frequently ended the crop year more deeply in debt, as did the landlord.

As cotton prices continued to decline, the landlord was forced to increase the acreage in cultivation in order to secure a crop lien equal to that of past years. Yet, increasing the acreage in cultivation enlarged operating expenses, and greater production forced increasingly lower prices, which could be compensated for only by expanding production. Between 1870 and 1890, acreage in cotton doubled and prices fell by almost 50 percent. By the 1920s, acreage in cotton had again doubled. However, per-acre yields were relatively unchanged throughout this period, averaging one third to one half of a bale per acre (compared with the 1.5 to 2 bales per acre today). Southern landlords and tenants seemed confined to an inescapable treadmill. As late as 1935, it was estimated that 60 percent of the farmers in the South were tenant farmers, including over 1 million whites and 700,000 blacks.

The share system and small-scale farm operations became increasingly inefficient as farm prices declined and nonfarm prices rose. As late as 1929, 30 percent of the nation's farms, most of them in the South, contributed only 3 percent of the total value of all farm produce. A 1936 Farm Security Administration survey of 287 cotton tenant farmers in Arkansas indicated that total cash income averaged $134 per year and net worth averaged $84.44.[10] Although there were areas of improvement in the South in the Reconstruction era—for instance, the expansion of railroads, the movement into the South of textile mills, tobacco manufacture, and coal and iron industries, the expansion of lumbering—overall the South failed to participate fully in the economic reconstruction of the Union.

One of the more exciting and dramatic agricultural innovations in the South during the Reconstruction era was the expansion of the range-cattle industry centering in Texas. Texas cattlemen began driving herds averaging 2,500 head to northern markets at the close of the Civil War. A dozen cowboys drove the cattle ten to fourteen miles a day over trails such as the Old Shawnee Trail, which ran through Missouri to Quincy, Illinois; the West Shawnee Trail, which ended in Abilene; the Chisholm Trail which led to Dodge City; and the Montana Trail, which cut through Nebraska, Wyoming, and Montana. By 1873 the Missouri-Kansas-Texas Railroad was shipping cattle directly from Texas. Prices fluctuated widely, and the business was very hazardous. Cattlemen operated heavily on borrowed money. Many were wiped out by the panic of 1873, which brought with it a collapse in cattle prices while enormous herds were moving north. By the mid 1880s, drought, a hard winter, Texas fever, the penetration of railheads into the western plains, and fencing had all but wiped out the range-cattle industry. Ranchers began to turn to fenced ranches, blooded stock, animal husbandry, and business management, and began to develop the modern cattle industry. Paralleling the expansion of the cattle industry was the growth of the meat-packing industry, personified by the rise of Armour and Company and Swift and Company and greatly facilitated by the development of the refrigerated railroad car.

TABLE 8.3

Texas Cattle Driven to Northern Markets, 1866–1880.

YEAR	NUMBER	YEAR	NUMBER
1866	260,000	1874	166,000
1867	35,000	1875	151,618
1868	75,000	1876	321,928
1869	350,000	1877	201,000
1870	350,000	1878	265,649
1871	600,000	1879	250,927
1872	349,275	1880	394,784
1873	404,000		

Source: *Texas Almanac*, 1904, p. 119.

Midwestern and northern farmers participated in the expansion of the cattle industry, and were responsible for a tremendous growth in the corn-hog industry. Wheat remained the mainstay of northern agriculture. Between 1873 and 1882 wheat acreage rose from 29 to 41 million acres, and production from 368 to 555 million bushels. England alone annually absorbed from one third to one half of American wheat and flour exports. Improvements in milling processes, such as the roller mill, the purifier, and the adaptation of steam power, paralleled expansion of the industry. Although cash was available for farm operations, interest rates were high. High and often discriminatory freight rates, coupled with declining prices, undermined the profitability of northern agriculture. By the close of the postwar decade, farmers in the North and South were organizing to protest their plight and to seek improvements through legislative and political processes.

Some northern laborers, adversely affected by declining wages and a fall in real earnings in the 1870s, as well as by competition in the labor market, technological innovations, and the massive social changes consequent upon the rise of the urban-industrial world, sought to gain relief by organizing labor unions such as the National Labor Union and the Knights of Labor. Although there was a gradual upward movement of real wages between 1865 and 1900, the output of labor rose faster and labor's grievances and demands grew more insistent.

The United States emerged from the Reconstruction era with a record of tremendous economic development and growth that largely excluded the South. The seeds of industrialization sown before the Civil War had sprouted, but the fruits had not yet been harvested. Some of that fruit would be a bitter harvest. Farmer and labor discontent rose throughout the nineteenth century. Although slavery was abolished, blacks in America were relegated to a secondary economic, social, and political role. On the positive side, America developed a modern transportation system, a sophisticated financial system, and, if it had not had it before, an unquenchable thirst for growth, change, and progress. The Reconstruction era gave birth to the architects of the manufacturing and commercial world that America was becoming, and established the institutional structure upon which that world would build.

Notes

[1]Edmund Ruffin, *An Essay on Calcareous Manures*, ed. J. Carlyle Sitterson (Cambridge, Mass.: Harvard University Press, 1961), p. xxxiii.

[2]See Michael Les Benedict, *A Compromise of Principle: Congressional Republicans and Reconstruction 1863–1869*, New York: Norton, 1974.

[3]*Report of Select Committee on the Union Pacific Railroad and Credit Mobilier*, 42nd Cong., 3rd sess. For a clear, concise statement of government support of railroad construction, see David M. Potter, ed., *The Railroads: Select Problems in Historical Interpretation*, rev. E. David Cronon, and Howard R. Lamar (New York: Holt, Rinehart & Winston, 1960).

[4]Robert S. Henry, "The Railroad Land Grant Legend in American History Texts," *Mississippi Valley Historical Review*, 32 (September 1945), pp. 171–94.

[5]Potter, ed., *The Railroads*, p. xii.

[6]See Rendig Fels, "American Business Cycles, 1865–79," *American Economic Review*, 41 (June 1951), 325–49, and Joseph A. Schumpeter, *Business Cycles* (New York: McGraw-Hill, 1939).

[7]See Walter T. K. Nugent, *The Money Question During Reconstruction* (New York: Norton, 1967), especially pp. 69–92.

[8]See Nugent, *The Money Question During Reconstruction*, pp. 52–64.

[9]See Harry N. Scheiber, "Economic Changes in the Civil War Era: An Analysis of Recent Studies," *Civil War History*, 11 (December 1965), pp. 396–411.

[10]For further discussion of the sharecropping system see especially Rupert P. Vance, *Human Factors in Cotton Culture: A Study of the Social Geography of the American South* (Chapel Hill, N.C.: University of North Carolina Press, 1929).

SUGGESTED READING

BUCK, PAUL H., *The Road to Reunion, 1865–1900*. Boston: Little, Brown, 1937.

DUNNING, WILLIAM A., *Reconstruction, Political and Economic, 1865–1877*. New York: Harper & Row, Torchbook ed., 1962.

FINE, SIDNEY, *Laissez-Faire and the General Welfare State: A Study of Conflict in American Thought, 1865–1901*. Ann Arbor, Mich.: University of Michigan Press, 1956.

FRANKLIN, JOHN HOPE, *Reconstruction After the Civil War*. Chicago: University of Chicago Press, 1961.

NUGENT, WALTER T. K., *The Money Question During Reconstruction*. New York: Norton, 1967.

SHARKEY, ROBERT P., *Money, Class and Party: An Economic Study in Civil War and Reconstruction*. Baltimore: Johns Hopkins, 1959.

SOWELL, THOMAS, *Race and Economics*. New York: McKay, 1975.

STAMPP, KENNETH, *The Era of Reconstruction, 1865–1877*. New York: Knopf, 1965.

UNGER, IRWIN, *The Greenback Era: A Social and Political History of American Finance, 1865–1879*. Princeton, N.J.: Princeton University Press, 1964.

A REVIEW:
AMERICAN
FREE ENTERPRISE

_____ chapter IX __

Relative abundance has been a unique and important condition in American life. Until the Civil War era, American economic endeavor involved primarily an interaction between humans and their primary, natural environment. That natural environment was rich in resources, but its utilization depended upon the application of human energy and ingenuity. A secondary environment, that of human knowledge, technology, and organization, began to make the natural resources "bear fruit and multiply." By the beginning of the Civil War, the American economy had developed a self-generating growth that would allow Americans not only to sustain life but also to constantly improve the style of life. Americans began not only to improve their standard of living but to adopt a cultural mode that readily accommodated if not constantly demanded an improved life-style. Thus, Americans early became a nation of achievers. A level or standard of living having been reached, that achievement became obsolete and demanded the climb to another plateau, a higher standard of living, more education, bigger cars, and a better mousetrap. At least this is one view of the American scene. This view contains an element of truth as well as a degree of prejudice and distortion. American wealth, how it was acquired, how it is allocated, and how it affects the American character is deservedly a vital area for historical inquiry and reflection.

The material wealth of the United States, estimates professor John Hendricks of George Washington University, has increased from a net worth of about $4 billion in 1775 to a net worth of $5,700 billion in 1975. On the basis of those figures, the per-capita wealth of 200 years ago would have been $1,550 and per-capita wealth today would be $26,530, or $106,000 for a typical family of four. Although the American population today is ninety times greater than it was during the Revolution, per-capita income has managed a seventeen fold increase. Americans consume a disproportionate part of the world's energy, and produce a disproportionately larger part of the world's goods and services. The American free-enterprise system as we know it today is the cumulative product of a historical process that reflects the development of a distinctively American culture. Free enterprise is a way of life and an expression of the values, goals, and aspirations of the American people. It is intrinsically capitalistic, but free enterprise invokes liberty, democracy, equality of opportunity, and a degree of humanity precluded in the more narrow concept of capitalism.

An economic system, or a national economy, is a social organization designed to determine for the members of society what to produce, how to produce, and how to distribute the goods and services produced. Economists assume the universal existence of scarcity. Resources are limited in supply relative to wants or needs. Resources, however, are not fixed in absolute terms, and human wants or needs appear to have infinite capacity. Thus, an economic system is a viable and constantly changing social arrangement for the production and allocation of goods and services. Any socioeconomic system affects the realization of nonmaterial wants or objectives, but it is concerned more directly with society's material well-being, or "standard of living." Thus, free enterprise is an expression of American cultural values, and is both a prescription for the business of making a living and a set of values on how to live.

The basic role of an economic order may be illustrated as in Figure 9.1. Resources, actual and potential, vary according to the society's capacity to discover and utilize those resources. The utilization of those resources—that is, the production of goods and services—is contingent upon the actual presence or availability of the resources and the energy and ingenuity applied to them. Wants or needs exceed the availability of goods and services, but they also respond to productive capacities. Wants enlarge as the ability to satisfy them expands. The radiating lines in Figure 9.1 suggest the expansive (and perhaps contractive) nature of resources, goods and services, and wants, and designate the nature of economic systems as being in a constant state of change.[1]

The capitalist economy presumes that the decision of what to produce, how to produce, and to whom and in what quantities the goods and services produced should be allocated is best determined by the marketplace and price mechanisms. Capitalism requires that property, real and personal, be private, autonomous, and transferable. There must be a free market that facilitates the transfer of property

A. Resources   B. Goods and Services   C. Society's Wants

FIGURE 9.1. The basic role of an economic order.

in response to a price set by supply and demand. There must be the technology or knowledge and the institutional framework that supports trade and commerce. There must be free labor and the commercial instruments that service the institutional framework of capitalism. These ingredients of capitalism did not appear all at once, nor did they maintain a static, permanent nature once they developed.

For convenience, the general stages of capitalist development provide a useful historical framework for understanding the growth of the American free-enterprise system. These stages include petty capitalism, mercantile capitalism, industrial capitalism, financial capitalism, and national capitalism, the latter implying a considerable degree of public control over private property. By 1876, Americans had established the foundation of industrial and financial capitalism. In each stage of development there coexisted earlier phases of capitalism, and, indeed, economic structures and values that were noncapitalistic. Though preeminently capitalistic, the free-enterprise system is a *mixed* economic order wherein economic decisions are made by tradition and "authority," or government, as well as by prices and the market.

The American economic system developed in a more intensely capitalistic mold because that system accorded closely with the unique political, religious, and environmental conditions surrounding the development of American society. The Protestant ethic, laissez faire, and a natural abundance complemented the development of the concepts of personal liberty, freedom, democracy, and individual opportunity inherent in a capitalist order.

The American environment offered a distinct opportunity for the satisfaction of human needs. The satisfaction of those needs was at first the product of the application of European and American technology to the special conditions prevailing in the American colonies. Corn, beans, squash, potatoes, tobacco, and cotton were indigenous to America. Americans had to learn to cultivate those crops, as well as to cultivate the "need" for them. They learned by absorbing the knowledge of the native American, by applying the knowledge inherited from Europe, and through innovation. By the time of the Revolution, Americans had a remarkable productive capacity and a substantial market for their produce.

By 1776, the American idea of capitalism, as well as the size and structure of the American economic order, was changing the relationship between the colonies and the mother country. The ponderous structural framework of the British Empire, particularly after the French and Indian War, conflicted with the more individualistic and unregimented American socioeconomic order. Although the Americans had generally become "non-British" by 1776, apart from this they had not developed a homogeneous society of their own. That in itself, perhaps, identified the developing free-enterprise system. That is, this system stressed, at first, individualism, diversity, decentralization, and laissez faire.

The development of the political framework for the preservation and perpetuation of free enterprise began with the Articles of Confederation and carried through the Constitution. Once efforts began to give political form and a national structure to the free-enterprise system, the ship of state began a perilous voyage between the Scylla of individualism and the Charybdis of collectivism. How does government, the force of collectivism, protect individualism? Or as James Madison considered it, how does government protect rights in property that originate from the diversity in the faculties of humans, when that diversity (or individualism) leads to the unequal distribution of property and the division of society into hostile factions? One attempt to resolve that insoluble dilemma—whether by court decision, legislation, or war—has been to transfer authority over property rights and the protection of diversity from local and state control to federal control. This has served more, perhaps, to compound the dilemma than to resolve it.

The growth of the national political structure and the economic order it sustains was the product more of economic and noneconomic "forces" than of rational planning. Although increasingly subject to planning today, technological innovation was a fluid and uncertain element of economic growth, particularly throughout the nineteenth century. Overall, the political and cultural system was highly conducive to technological innovation, and it fostered the ready assimilation of new goods and services by the society. The development and expansion of the railroad, the steamboat, and the American system of manufacture provided a catalyst for an economic revolution in America. That revolution, which even before the Civil War produced an unparalleled standard of living for Americans, was sustained by a dominant and tremendously productive agricultural economy. The cotton industry, suggests Douglass C. North, initiated and stimulated the rapid economic expansion of the first half of the nineteenth century. The expansion of cotton production paralleled and induced the rise of the textile and derivative industries, the expansion of maritime trade, and the westward movement.

Agricultural and urban-industrial growth were interdependent and complementary. Regional specialization characterized agricultural development. Intensive vegetable, fruit, and dairying industries developed in the Northeast as wheat and grain production shifted westward. The corn-hog industry developed prominently in the Midwest. The range-cattle industry had shifted westward to Texas and the Southwest by 1860. Cotton was king in the South, but rice, tobacco, and sugar production were significant commercial crops. Corn was a major crop in the North and the South. But for the corn-hog industry in the Midwest, most American corn was consumed on the farm or by local markets. By 1860, self-sufficient family farming was rapidly being supplanted by commercial agriculture. American farms provided the labor pool and the food and fiber for rapid urban expansion. They made possible an unusually high level of nutrition, enlarging America's human capital resources, and produced a surplus that accounted for the greater part of the value of American exports during the nineteenth century.

Although the agricultural sector of the developing national economy held conflicting policies on such issues as land, labor, and the tariff, the American Civil War derived from many causes, some of them noneconomic. But slavery appeared to be endemic to all of these causes. Secession and Civil War may in a broad sense be attributed to the development of a national economic order, the rise of a national cultural consensus, and the emergence of a more centralized rather than a decentralized political structure. The process of centralization was by no means complete in 1860 or in 1876, but the Civil War and Reconstruction signaled the rise of a new socioeconomic order, born of the old order but cast in a new mold. It was not the Civil War itself but rather the preestablished cultural, economic, and institutional framework that provided the basis for continuing economic growth. Some authorities believe that the war played a negative role in future economic growth, in that it produced enormous human and financial losses and a diversion of energies. On the positive side, it ended slavery and initiated the process by which blacks were assimilated more completely and equitably into the socioeconomic system. It stimulated growth in specific industries and promoted a cultural consensus that embodied an invigorated ideological support for free enterprise.

Reconstruction was a time for redirecting the nation's energies away from war and emotional conflict and toward restoration, rebuilding, and the refining of institutional and financial structures that could accommodate a diverse, expanding, and distinctly national economy. Political institutions were challenged and overhauled. New banking and financial institutions developed. Tax and land-distribution policies were revised. The corporate organization became the dominant form of business enterprise. Transcontinental railroads, built with government financial aid, streamlined the distributive processes and ordained a new relationship between government and business. Meanwhile, the older agricultural America continued to expand its productive capacities. Most Americans continued to live in rural areas and to derive their livelihood from farming, but the industrial manufacture of consumer goods had become the catalyst of economic growth. The South failed to share extensively in this economic transformation. Instead, it became bogged in the quagmire of the crop lien and tenant systems. Reconstruction was a time of experimentation, and of some misdeeds and missteps. But by its close, the nation had generally recovered from the ravages of war and the economy was capable of producing a greater quantity of goods and services than Americans had ever previously known or contemplated.

Although the Civil War and Reconstruction marked a time of transition in the economic life of the United States, American economic development was a historical continuum. The "break" produced by the Civil War and Reconstruction that is intimated by historical study is purely artistic or procedural, and a matter of convenience. America at the close of the nineteenth century was far more like than unlike America at mid-century. But there were differences, and it is these differences that give each age its special character.

The late nineteenth century witnessed a phenomenal surge in industrial expansion. The expansionist impulse of the antebellum years was transferred from a territorial to a business expansion. The city, industry, and commerce became the new frontier in American life. A swell of migration from the farm to the city and a tremendous surge of foreign immigration provided the life blood of urban growth. The telegraph, gaslights, electricity, urban public and private water-power and transportation systems, and soon the radio, the telephone, and refrigeration made possible a new life-style. Within the space of one lifetime, Americans left behind the horse-and-buggy age and entered the jet, television, and atomic age. Americans born around the turn of the century have seen and experienced changes in the quantity and style of life of unbelievable dimensions, changes that Americans born since usually take for granted.

The last quarter of the nineteenth century was dominated by the growth in size and structure of business. United States Steel, Standard Oil, American Tobacco, du Pont, International Harvester, the railroads, and many other industries developed the massive productuve capacity and organizational structure characteristic of big business. That era, too, gave rise to the national farm and labor movements, which inspired twentieth-century reforms. It was a time when things moved very swiftly: critics, writers, and even politicians could hardly offer their objections, analyses, or formulas before the conditions with which they were preoccupied changed. The late nineteenth century sprouted American cities and new urban problems from one side of the continent to the other. Yet it was an age in which most Americans continued to live much as Americans had in ages past.

The first quarter of the twentieth century retained the structures, artifacts, problems, and characteristics of the nineteenth century but exhibited a few new dimensions that made it distinctive. "Giant enterprise" exemplified by the automotive, housing, and food industries, replaced the "big business" of the nineteenth century, some representatives of which—Standard Oil, U.S. Steel, and du Pont, among others—entered the lists as giants. American "consumerism," urged on by radio and mass-circulation newspapers, brought the products of modern life into an ever expanding portion of American households. Reform legislation began to impose a degree of public control over the production and distribution processes in order to assure more Americans of an opportunity to compete in the marketplace for goods and services. There were, nonetheless, those who could not or did not compete and who were ignored and overlooked in the modernization of American life. Overall, however, the life-style of more Americans changed more completely, and usually for the better, than in any other quarter-century, except perhaps the post–World War II era.

The 1920s gave way to the confusion and dislocation of the Great Depression, and then to World War II. In this quarter-century the promise of American life seemed elusive and terribly threatened. The New Deal offered experiments, planning, and new directions in an effort to preserve the free-enterprise system and to temper some of the inequities that its diversities and economic power structures had created. Depression, reform, and war characterize this quarter-century, but beneath the big tent, life, expansion, business, and, despite depression and war, even growth went on much as before. Americans moved from the Model T to the Model A to the V-8.

Once the Great Depression and the war were over, Americans discovered yet new and exciting dimensions in the quality and style of life, and new and terrible dimensions of the complexities of life. The cold war, atomic power, and space flight characterized the new interrelated and sophisticated modern world that had been fired in the forges of World War II. In America the television and the computer replaced the radio and the adding machine. Homes had air conditioning and central heating, autos had automatic transmissions and power steering, hospitals had X-ray machines and antibiotics. Paraphernalia of indescribable kinds and shapes, in plastics, glass, and man-made fibers, became increasingly available and steadily demanded by a rapidly and increasingly affluent population. Americans began having more babies and living longer. And in the face of threatened atomic war, a developing youth culture seemingly disaffected with the established order of things, racial conflicts, chronic energy shortages and environmental pollution, inflation, and spiraling costs of government and welfare, they began to wonder, how long would it last?

The remaining pages of this book deal with this modern world, which is different from but very much a continuation of the past. The government, the laws, and even the people and their perception of free enterprise have been remarkably consistent over two hundred years of change and development.

Notes

[1] John M. Allen's "An Introduction to the American Free Enterprise System: Essentials and Benefits" (unpublished essay, Texas A&M University, 1976) provides useful insights.

AMERICA'S
BUSINESS
IS BUSINESS

_____ chapter X___

The adage that the "nation's business is business" became valid after the Civil War, even though it had been applicable long before. The American colonies, indeed, had been conceived as commercial ventures. Those who signed the Declaration of Independence and framed the Constitution were largely men of commerce and trade. Thomas Jefferson, despite his advocacy of the agrarian society, maintained that agriculture, manufactures, commerce, and navigation were "the four pillars of our prosperity" and were "the most thriving when left most free to individual enterprise." Washington Irving observed that the Americans' "great object of universal devotion" was "the almighty dollar." The "Yankee trader" had become an object of awe and some suspicion before the Civil War. The idea of business inculcated both respect and doubt in the antebellum years. That the businessman was rich and successful was a credit to his initiative, competence, hard work, and state of blessedness. That he acquired his wealth without being a creator or producer of goods, which is to say he lived off of the production of others, was regarded as sinful at worst and indecent at best. Benjamin Franklin, no mean businessman in his own right, noted a basic nineteenth-century objection to business: "There seems to be but three ways for a nation to acquire wealth. The first is by war. . . . This is robbery. The second, by commerce, which is generally cheating. The third by agriculture, the only honest way."

Man had to justify his existence by being a producer. Nineteenth-century Americans thought of production in a tangible form—as goods, not as services. Thus, the businessman was generally considered a nonproducer and a parasite (along with lawyers and teachers) on the social body. But the technological revolution had begun to change this conception of production even before the Civil War, and after the war the general conception of a businessman began to change. He was no longer the shopkeeper or merchant, but the *manufacturer* of *goods*. The character of the nation's business had changed by the late nineteenth century, and "business" became a more fully accepted part of the ideology of free enterprise.

Businessmen continued to be criticized in the late nineteenth century, perhaps more severely than ever before, but then so did farmers and laborers— rural "hayseeds" and urban "cigarette-smoking dudes." In the day of the muck- raker, and in the continuing tradition of democratic journalism, no segment of society was immune from censure. Such criticism did not necessarily denote implacable class hostility or a structural failure of the free-enterprise system. A John D. Rockefeller or an Andrew Carnegie could simultaneously be a "robber baron" and a "sainted benefactor of society." Criticism was most often well deserved, and usually supported free enterprise rather than antagonizing it. Freight-rate rebates, drawbacks, trusts, long- and short-haul discrimination, "money monopolies," blackmail, and cheating were the specific practices of the business sector that were considered injurious to the free-enterprise system. Even in the midst of the most heated journalistic exchanges, farm protests, or labor protests, American businessmen enjoyed an overriding public confidence, which was demonstrated regularly by the election of business representatives to Con- gress, the executive office, state legislatures, and local governing bodies. De- spite the criticism, the nation was becoming increasingly business-oriented.[1] The new business order was also producing some substantial structural changes in American society.

THE "NATIONALIZATION" OF BUSINESS

The railroad, the archetypical big business, created a national market. As rail lines expanded into the rural areas, commodities or raw materials were brought to the city for refining or manufacturing into consumer goods to be sold to farm families. Textiles, flour, and iron products had dominated the earlier marketing processes. By the close of the century, markets had become urban-oriented and manufacturing was dominated by the producer-goods industry—that is, the mak- ing of products for use by intermediate industry rather than by the individual consumer. The iron industry turned from the manufacture of plows and utensils for the farmer to the manufacture of rails and machinery for the railroads. Iron and steel bars and plates were consumed by intermediate machine-tools indus- tries that manufactured machinery for the production of plows, or equipment for refineries. Foundry and machine-shop products, which were second on the list of the ten leading industries in 1900, had not even appeared in the top ten in 1860. Industry tended to become increasingly specialized, bigger if not dominant in its special line of production, and vertically integrated (controlling all proces- ses of production and marketing). Each business tended to develop its own national marketing and financial structure.

Business and commerce became national while the supportive or protective

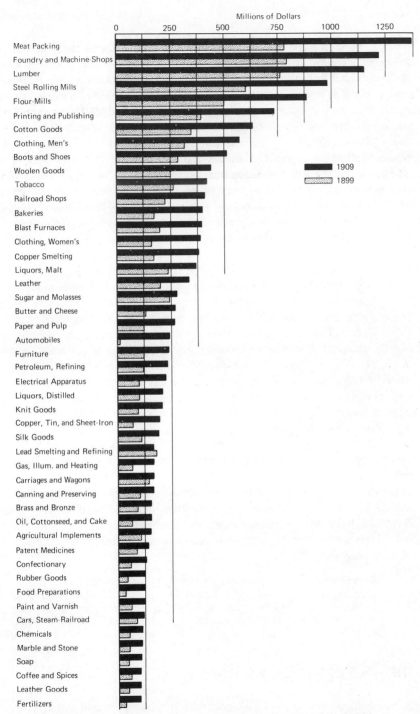

FIGURE 10.1. Value of products for leading industries: 1909 and 1899.

Source: Bureau of the Census, *Statistical Atlas of the United States* (Washington, 1914), Page 415.

political structures and laws remained largely local. Laissez faire, the lack of government control and regulation of business, derived not only from ideological preferences but from the failure of the political framework supporting free enterprise to grow as rapidly as businesses did. The development of national markets and of national corporate structures, such as the trust and the holding company, immunized big business from state control, but also left it more vulnerable to "unbridled competition." The construction of a national legal framework that would regulate or supervise business activity began in the latter part of the nineteenth century with legislation such as the Interstate Commerce Act of 1887, and derived from disparate motives of both businessmen and business critics. The one group sought "standards of competition," the other desired "regulation." Federal legislation usually provided a greater or lesser degree of both. No such legislation was intrinsically destructive of or hostile to business interests.

In addition to the trend toward bigger business structures, national markets, vertical integration, and federal regulation, the later nineteenth century, which marked a watershed for free enterprise, witnessed marked changes in the social order supportive of free enterprise. Whereas one of every four Americans had been an employee in 1800, three of every four Americans were hired hands by 1900. With the rise of the big-business system America was becoming a nation of employees rather than a nation of independent farmers or proprietors. Furthermore, the "big businesses" that existed were corporations that were closely controlled by a handful of stock owners. The day of the giant corporation with wide public stock participation came much later. The rise of big business in the late nineteenth century is in large part the story of the growth and development of the successful small business.

The success of big business may be attributed to a wide range of factors, including prominently the innovative and organizational abilities of the directors and managers, remarkable technological development, the growth of massive urban and foreign markets, and the rise of a "consumer" mentality aided and abetted by the advertising and communications industries. Alfred D. Chandler concludes that in the last quarter of the nineteenth century the basic innovations in business lay more in the creation of new forms of organization and new ways of marketing:

> The great modern corporation, carrying on the major industrial processes, namely, purchasing, and often production of materials and parts, manufacturing, marketing and finance—all within the same organizational structure—had its beginnings in that period. Such organizations hardly existed, outside of the railroads, before the 1880s. By 1900 they had become the basic business unit in American industry.[2]

THE ROLE OF THE ENTREPRENEUR

A macroeconomic analysis of the relationship between income and investments in a country as a whole—a common tool of economic historians—often fails to incorporate the vital, individualistic forces of economic growth and development. A relatively new school of business history seeks to fill this void by examining the historical development of the specific units involved in the production or exchange of goods and services in order to make a profit. A further refinement of business history is to study the role of the entrepreneur in the development of the firm or industry. The entrepreneur has four basic functions: (1) to establish business objectives; (2) to create the organization necessary to achieve those objectives; (3) to establish strategy or policy; and (4) to maintain the structure. He is an innovator whose primary incentive is profit. Business and entrepreneurial history offer microanalyses of a major facet of economic development. Business is shaped and influenced by what is happening in the "external" economy, and the business unit and the entrepreneur have a reciprocal effect on the development of the national economy.[3] Although there is no such thing as a typical business or a typical entrepreneur, a cursory examination of some of the business organizations and business leaders of the late nineteenth century may illuminate some of the finer threads of which the industrial economy was being woven.

Many businesses organized after the Civil War achieved national prominence and success before the close of the century. John D. Rockefeller's Standard Oil Company, James B. Duke's American Tobacco Company, Andrew Carnegie's steel business, and John Pierpont Morgan's financial enterprises are common examples of the successful business. James J. Hill, Edward H. Harriman, Leland Stanford, Mark Hopkins, Collis Potter Huntington, and Charles Crocker are frequently cited as examples of the nineteenth-century railroad magnate. Many businesses organized in the Gilded Age languished as essentially small, independent proprietorships only to "come alive" in later years. Such seemed to be the case with Coca-Cola, Levi Strauss, Kellogg, Eastman Kodak, Sears Roebuck, and R. J. Reynolds, among others. Many more businesses organized in this era thrived only for a time, if at all, and then expired or were absorbed by others. Railroad and oil companies would head this list. Most successful businesses had relatively humble beginnings, offered an innovative product, filled a need that was expanding, and at critical stages were guided by entrepreneurs in a direction that gave them a distinct advantage over competitors.

Levi Strauss

Levi Strauss and Company, the largest pants manufacturer in the world today, began during the California gold rush and was incorporated in 1890. It experienced spectacular growth only when its jeans became popular with the mass market provided by the youth- and leisure-oriented post–World War II society. Prior to that time, "Levi's" were inexpensive work clothes for the farm and factory worker. Levi Strauss, the founder of the company, was born in Germany in 1829, came to the United States when he was fourteen, and lived with relatives in Kentucky. During the California gold rush, Levi was commissioned by his brothers, who operated a dry-goods business in New York, to accompany a cargo

LEVI STRAUSS (c. *1828–1903*)
Clothing manufacturer.
Courtesy Levi Strauss & Co.

of goods sent to California aboard a clipper ship. Levi sold everything at premium prices except for bales of tent canvas. He discovered that miners desperately needed tough pants, and that the conventional woolen, cotton, or even leather breeches failed to stand the stress of rocks, salt, water, and sun. Strauss hit upon the idea of fabricating pants out of his tent canvas, quickly sold the entire stock, and sent back east for an order of denim. He had a desirable product and a market that quickly expanded from the mine to the farm and the factory. As Strauss expanded production he improved the quality and appeal of his clothing, first by introducing the use of a durable indigo dye, and then, in 1873, by using and patenting a copper rivet to reinforce stitched seams. Strauss died in 1902, never having married, and left the management of his companies to four nephews.

Levi Strauss products earned a reputation for durability. After World War II, the management of the greatly expanded Levi Strauss Manufacturing Company capitalized on the proven reputation and on their association of blue jeans with hard work, sun, sod, cowboys, rugged individualism, and adventure to sell hundreds of millions of pants each year to men and women in America and in over fifty foreign countries. Russian athletes, it is said, especially seek out Levi's as the souvenir of their American visits. The jeans mystique and the market for jeans derived from curious external forces, but it was Levi Strauss's innovations that made them possible.

Coca-Cola

Coca-Cola also had humble origins. It began as an experimental concoction made in the 1870s by J. S. Pemberton, an Atlanta druggist, who served it to his friends and customers. At the encouragement of friends, Pemberton adopted the name Coca-Cola for his soft drink (named for the major ingredients, cocoa leaves and cola nuts). He began ''commercial'' production with the manufacture of twenty-five gallons in 1886. In Dallas the same year, Dr. Pepper started. Whereas Dr. Pepper remained essentially a local beverage until 1940, Coca-Cola had developed a national market by 1898, when its sales reached half a million dollars. The growth of Coca-Cola was due to the genius of Asa Griggs Candler, another Atlanta druggist, who bought a two-thirds interest in Coca-Cola from Pemberton in 1887 for the grand sum of $225.00. In 1889 a group headed by Joseph Whitehead acquired bottling rights and began a whole new industry, which stimulated already expanding sales. In 1892 Candler became the sole owner of Coca-Cola. With a nephew, Samuel Candler Dobbs, he launched an extensive advertising and promotion campaign (largely by billboard) that raised sales from the half-million-dollar mark of 1898 to $15.7 million in 1917. Although Pemberton might be identified as an inventor or pioneer, his lack of business expertise fails to qualify him as an entrepreneur. Candler, on the other hand, was a

ASA GRIGGS CANDLER *(1851–1929)*
President, Coca-Cola Company
and Benefactor of Emory University.
Courtesy Emory University.

promoter-entrepreneur who managed an existing idea into a successful business. In 1919 Candler sold his interest to a larger group of investors, who brought fresh ideas and vigorous management. The Coca-Cola Bottling Company introduced local bottling facilities and regional distributorships, and by 1975 Coca-Cola sales to a worldwide market had reached $2.1 billion.

Eastman Kodak

Eastman Kodak probably originated when George Eastman, a 23-year-old bank clerk from Waterville, New York, decided in 1877 to take a trip to the Caribbean. A photograph enthusiast, Eastman wanted to take along his apparatus to record his travels. He discovered that it was a next-to-impossible undertaking. The camera was an enormous, bulky affair, and wet-plate processing required tents, vats, water, and chemicals. Photography, popularized by Matthew Brady and other Civil War and western correspondents, had its limitations. Eastman was aware that a dry-plate process recently developed in England removed some of the bulky impediments to photograph processing. He began experimenting with dry-plate processes and in 1879 developed and patented a machine that would coat the glass plates used in cameras and thereby make the mass production of photographic plates possible.

In 1880 Eastman joined with Henry A. Strong, who provided needed financing, and began the commercial manufacture of dry plates in Rochester, New York. Glass plates, however, were too bulky and fragile for widespread use

GEORGE EASTMAN *(1854–1932)*
Founded Eastman Kodak.

by novice photographers. Eastman kept trying to perfect a durable, easily handled dry plate, and in 1884 perfected a flexible-roll film and holder. The film, however, was virtually useless unless photographers had a camera that was custom-built or hand-made specifically for its use. Eastman worked on this problem and developed a light, portable camera, the Kodak, first produced and priced for a popular market at $25 in 1888. The camera held a reel of film that took 100 pictures, and the photographer simply returned the entire camera to the manufacturer for film processing. Eastman now had an instrument that would have been perfect for his Caribbean cruise.

Eastman Kodak Company was founded in 1889. Eastman did for photography what Henry Ford would do for the automobile—make it available to the masses rather than reserving it as a hobby for the rich or an exclusive business for the professional. By 1900, a Kodak "box" camera was being marketed for $1.00. George Eastman became an extremely wealthy man, and during his lifetime he made philanthropic gifts of over $100 million. Eastman policy stressed mass production at lowest per-unit costs, customer servicing even to the point, some believe, of practically giving away cameras in order to promote film sales, and enticing new customers through extensive advertising. Like Thomas Edison, George Eastman may best be characterized as the inventor-entrepreneur, who converted rudimentary knowledge into a useful consumer product. Eastman Kodak now has international distribution, has diversified into chemical, plastic, and man-made fiber manufacture, and enjoys annual sales in excess of $4 billion.

Montgomery Ward and Sears, Roebuck

Mail order began as an innovative merchandising technique that supplemented, if not replaced, the traditional distribution of goods by traveling salespersons and peddlers to rural and small-town America. Aaron Montgomery Ward, born in Chatham, New Jersey in 1843, became a traveling salesman in the Midwest after the Civil War. He found an eager market for dry goods and utensils among the widely scattered farmsteads, a market limited primarily by time and drudgery involved in visiting customers. Ward decided to improve his status over that of a commissioned salesman by buying goods directly from the manufacturer on his own account for cash, and then selling to his farmer customers for cash. He thus by-passed the usual retail outlet and brought his goods directly to the consumer. Distribution and purchase orders, he decided, could be managed better by the mail than by the salesman. In partnership with George R. Thorn, and with $2,400 in capital and a single-sheet catalog listing a few dry-goods items. Montgomery Ward and Company began their mail-order business in 1872 in the loft of a Chicago livery stable. By the time of Ward's death in 1913, catalog sales by Montgomery Ward exceeded $40 million annually.

Richard W. Sears began work as a railroad telegrapher when he was 16. As a station agent at North Redwood, Minnesota, he sold watches to other railroad employees to supplement his salary. Sales were so brisk that he quit his job in 1886, moved to Minneapolis, and started the Sears Watch Company. Two years later he hired a watchmaker, Alvah C. Roebuck, who soon became a partner, and distributed his first mail-order catalog, which featured only watches. In 1895 Roebuck sold his one-third interest to Julius Rosenwald, a Chicago clothing manufacturer who believed that the mail-order business might be a solution to his marketing problems. The next year, Sears, Roebuck and Company distributed its first general catalog, which offered a greatly expanded line of general merchandise. The company went public in 1906, selling stock to finance expansion. That same year, Sears introduced a new marketing device aimed at developing the expanding urban market—a branch catalog office, in Dallas. After General R. E. Wood joined the company, and with the opening of retail stores in Chicago and Evansville, Indiana in 1925, Sears began to concentrate his sales efforts on urban markets. By the 1970s Sears had become the largest merchandising business in the world, with a net income of over $6.5 billion a year and with stores and affiliates throughout the world. Ward and Sears introduced innovative merchandising techniques.

American Tobacco

James Buchanan Duke was born near Durham, North Carolina in 1856. After the Civil War his father began a small smoking-tobacco business, peddling his hand-rolled cigarettes on the streets of Durham. Sales were good, and the sons joined the father in making cigarettes in a small shed on the family farm. In 1883 James B. Duke introduced the mechanical manufacture of cigarettes, in effect making them a new industrial product. At the same time, he announced a sharp cut in prices. Duke's success resulted from expanding the quantity of production, improving the quality of the product, and lowering the price. In 1884 he opened a factory in New York City and simultaneously began a large-scale advertising campaign. In 1890 Duke organized American Tobacco Company, incorporating in it a number of competitors, who exchanged their stock for American Tobacco stock. Duke added the machinery of the competitors to further expand production, and utilized modern "good-will" advertising and the markets of those firms to enlarge his sales. Duke established a dominant position in the industry by taking advantage of economies of scale. By expanding the scale of operations, he lowered the per-unit costs of manufacturing, sales, and advertising and generally made a better product (so it was assumed until the Surgeon General ruled otherwise), which became available to more people at a lower price.

In 1898 American Tobacco Company produced an offspring, Continental Tobacco Company, which entered the highly competitive chewing-tobacco industry. Duke was a primary innovator in developing "brand" marketing, which identified a brand name with a particular taste, quality, or appeal to more fully exploit consumer preferences. Brand marketing is a dominant modern-marketing technique by which similar products, ranging from soap, beans, and cigarettes to automobiles, may be sold by the same company to a large and diverse consumer market. At the turn of the century Duke used two "fighting brands," "Horse-shoe" and "Battle Axe," to garner control of the chewing-tobacco industry. He gave away huge quantities of free samples in his "plug wars," driving less well funded firms out of business. He then incorporated their holdings into his firm, with full compensation to the owners. In amassing control of tobacco manufacture, Duke also drove tobacco prices on the farm to historically low levels, thereby creating tremendous hardship among tobacco farmers. After organizing a cigar and snuff subsidiary, he established Consolidated Tobacco Company as a holding company for his tobacco empire. Antitrust action forced Duke to divest some of his holdings in 1911. Meanwhile, Duke attempted to control the European tobacco market but was rebuffed after bitter price wars with great European tobacco conglomerates.

Among the companies divested by American Tobacco by court order in 1911 was R. J. Reynolds Tobacco. Richard Joshua Reynolds began manufacturing plug tobacco in Winston-Salem, North Carolina in 1875. By 1899, when Reynolds joined American Tobacco, the company had developed a vertically integrated organization that channeled its products from the farm to the consumer. Reynolds employed tobacco "drummers," who were not as much salesmen as promoters. He was among the first to employ a professional advertising firm to manage his promotions. Reynolds poured as much as half of his earnings into advertising. Reynolds's Camel cigarettes offered a unique tobacco blend that made it the largest-selling cigarette until 1926, when Lucky Strike (American Tobacco) surpassed it. Perhaps one of the "niceties" of Camel advertising was that the camel on the package contains an optically elusive lady and a lion. When Reynolds joined American Tobacco, his company continued to manage its own factories and its own advertising and distribution systems. More recent marketing innovations of R. J. Reynolds Tobacco include the menthol tip, the "hard" pack, moisture-proof cellophane wrappers, and the "little cigar." Recent discoveries of relationships between cigarettes and cancer, and accompanying advertising bans, have failed to diminish tobacco sales but have lowered the advertising costs of the tobacco industry by over one third.

Standard Oil

No nineteenth-century businessman was at once more successful than John D. Rockefeller, founder of Standard Oil Company. Rockefeller was born in New York in 1839. His mother was a strong-willed disciplinarian who raised him; his father was a successful, itinerant medicine man who was rarely home, but who taught John D. to be a "sharp" trader. At the time John D. set up his own commission-merchant business, the older Rockefeller apparently had the habit of lending his son money and then unexpectedly demanding repayment in order to ''test'' his son's financial acumen. John D., a taciturn, resolute, and ''sharp'' trader, never disappointed his father. John D. spent four years as a bookkeeping clerk before joining Maurice D. Clark at the age of twenty in a wholesale business in Cleveland. By 1900, John D. Rockefeller had become one of the wealthiest men in America and his Standard Oil Company controlled ninety percent of the American petroleum-refinery industry. ''Long before his death,'' writes Earl Latham, Rockefeller ''had become a semi-legendary character who appeared to the general public either as a demon of avarice and extortion, crushing without scruple those who stood in his way, or as a high-minded philanthropist, bestowing his bounty with charitable devotion to good works.''[4]

The ''robber baron'' thesis, pursued by Henry Demarest Lloyd in 1894, Ida M. Tarbell in 1904, and Matthew Josephson in 1934, characterizes Rockefeller and his kind as ''plunderers of the public wealth'' whose relentless pursuit of self-interest and employment of Machiavellian guile disrupted the orderly processes of free enterprise and abused individual liberties and personal rights. Defenders, such as Allan Nevins, characterize Rockefeller as a great innovator in industry and philanthropy, an ''industrial statesman'' who brought order and efficiency to the national economy, and specifically to the petroleum industry.[5]

Whale oil was the primary fuel for household illumination from colonial days until the Civil War, but as whales became increasingly scarce and as whalers became forced to make extended voyages, whale-oil prices climbed precipitously. Even by the early 1800s a successful voyage returned enormous profits to the Nantucket captains. By 1850 the price of the superior sperm oil had reached $2.00 to $3.00 per gallon. The average American family turned to the cheaper but often acrid and less effective lard oil. As early as 1825 coal oils were being utilized for illumination, as was camphene, a purified oil of turpentine. In 1854 Dr. Abraham Gesner, a native of Nova Scotia and an errant physician, naturalist, chemist, and inventor, patented a process for distilling petroleum products into three grades of a ''liquid hydrocarbon,'' which he labeled Kerosene ''A,'' ''B,'' and ''C.'' The first two grades were equivalent to gasoline, and the third to the popular lamp fuel kerosene. Kerosene was a fully satisfactory substitute for whale oil, coal oils, and camphene. The North American Kerosene Gas Light Company was organized in 1854 by Horatio Eagle, a merchant, Erastus W. Smith, an engineer, and Philo T. Ruggles, a lawyer. The company retained the services of Gesner and received his patent assignment. Gesner designed buildings and equipment for a plant on a seven-acre tract on the east bank of Newtorn Creek in Queens County, New York, and by 1859 the company was receiving considerable attention from financial writers in New York City.[6] Petroleum, however, was still being secured ''accidentally,'' either in shallow-surface pools or by rigs drilling for salt or fresh water, and was still consumed mainly as a patent medicine.

During the same period, George G. Bissell of New York took a specimen of Pennsylvania "rock oil" to Benjamin Silliman, a Yale University chemist. Silliman reported that the oil was a better illuminant than coal oil. After discussing the possibilities of petroleum but floundering on the problem of how to extract it from the earth, Bissell's business associate, a New Haven banker named James Townsend, sent a railroad conductor, Colonel E. L. Drake, to Titusville, Pennsylvania, with instructions to dig a well. Drake used equipment normally employed in drilling salt wells, and after several years of bumbling and uncertainty he finally hit oil at a depth of seventy feet in August, 1859. During the Civil War fuel prices soared, and a frenzy of drilling activity around Titusville climaxed with the production of 4.8 million barrels of oil in 1869.

In 1860, young John D. Rockefeller visited the Venango County fields as a business agent for a group of Cleveland investors. Rockefeller advised the businessmen to stay out of the producing business and put their money into refining, which he conceived to be the key to the production process. He did so himself, buying part interest in a small refinery operated by Samuel Andrews. When Rockefeller and Andrews Oil Company quickly became a more profitable business than his merchandising business, Rockefeller put all of his money and capital, and that of other business associates, into refining. In 1869 the five small refineries owned by Rockefeller and his associates were organized into Standard Oil Company, with Rockefeller taking two thirds of the outstanding stock. At that time Standard Oil was one of thirty refineries in Cleveland and produced about 600 barrels of oil a day, or 5 percent of the national total.

Rockefeller quickly obtained a marketing advantage over competing companies in Cleveland by contracting with the Lakeshore Railroad to ship all of his oil east with rebates or refunds on freight charges ranging up to 50 percent. Rockefeller later explained this controversial arrangement, which smacked of conspiracy and unfair business tactics, to his critics and competitors:

> [Standard Oil] offered freights in large quantity, car-loads and train-loads. It furnished loading facilities and discharging facilities at great cost. It provided regular traffic, so that a railroad could conduct its transportation to the best advantage and use its equipment to the full extent of its hauling capacity without waiting for the refiner's convenience. It exempted railroads from liability for fire and carried its own insurance. It provided at its own expense terminal facilities which permitted economies in handling. For these services it obtained contracts for special allowances in freights.[7]

The device of rebates, which had originated even before the Civil War, was used with devastating effect by Rockefeller in the petroleum industry. In 1872 the South Improvement Company, a firm controlled by Rockefeller and organized to handle oil shipments by Standard Oil and other leading Pennsylvania oil firms, negotiated contracts with key railroads transporting oil. These contracts authorized rebates and the more vicious "drawback," which in effect gave Standard Oil a rebate on the freight charges of competing oil companies. As a result, the larger the volume of oil shipped by Standard, the lower the per-unit costs of freight, and the more oil shipped by competitors, the greater the per unit cost differential between brand "X" and Standard's oil. Rockefeller ruthlessly drove his competitors out of business or bought them out at the "best possible price." Standard also consistently improved its machinery and refining techniques and sought to lower production costs through economies of scale.

Rockefeller ascribed the success of the Standard Oil Company to "its consistent policy of making the volume of its business large through the merit and cheapness of its product." He improved the quality and quantity of refined petroleum. Prices of petroleum products and kerosene declined throughout the century, but the profits of Standard Oil climbed even more steadily. By 1879 Standard controlled 90 percent of the oil-refining business in America. In 1890, when Rockefeller organized the Standard Oil Trust Company, Standard earned $8 million; in 1904 it earned $57 million. The trust company and later Rockefeller's holding company were declared illegal under the Sherman Antitrust Act, but Standard's earnings and production continued to climb. With the advent of the internal-combustion engine the profits and size of competing firms also grew, and the mechanics of the capitalist system, rather than court action, broke the monopolistic position of Standard Oil. By the mid 1970s Exxon (Standard of New Jersey) was producing 5.7 million barrels of oil per day (about 8 percent of the total U.S. production) and enjoyed annual profits in excess of $25 billion. Texaco, Gulf, Mobil, and Standard of California refined between 2.5 and 4.5 million barrels per day, and earned from $7 to $12 billion annually. And, as in the 1850s, the United States in the 1970s faced a crucial shortage of fuel and rising fuel prices.

Carnegie Steel

Of all the businessmen previously mentioned, Andrew Carnegie was the only one who truly rose from humble origins in the Horatio Alger tradition. Carnegie was an immigrant boy born in Dumfermline, Scotland, in 1835, where his father, a weaver, was displaced by the mechanical looms. In Pennsylvania, Andy got his first job at the age of thirteen as a bobbin boy in a cotton mill. He later became a telegraph messenger boy, picked up enough Morse code to qualify as a telegrapher, and became a Western Union operator. He was then hired by the Pennsylvania Railroad as a private operator at $35 per month. On one occasion Carnegie seized the initiative, in the absence of his boss, to issue train orders in the boss's name, thereby untangling a serious rail traffic jam caused by a wreck. Instead of firing the youth, as he might have, the superior, Tom Scott, took a special interest in Carnegie, advising him in business investments. In 1859 Carnegie replaced Scott as the superintendent of the Pennsylvania Railroad's western division. Carnegie, personally frugal with his money, had tremendous

ANDREW CARNEGIE *(1835–1919)*
Steel magnate, writer, philanthropist.

nerve and daring in financial matters. He borrowed heavily to make investments, and those investments, such as in the Woodruff Sleeping Car Company, the Columbia Oil Company, and the Kloman Axle Company, were returnirg annual dividends of $17,868 by 1863. Carnegie quit the railroad in 1865 and became a bond broker in New York. He continued to plow his capital into new investments, most of them, by accident or design, related to iron manufacturers for railroad and bridge equipment. By 1870 Carnegie was earning $50,000 a year and contemplating retiring from business.

Instead, upon discovering the British preference for Bessemer steel rail rather than the standard iron rail, Carnegie plowed his money into steel. With his associates he built the Edgar Thompson Steel Mill at Braddock, Pennsylvania. Carnegie made steel his one passion and investment. He bought out four of his partners after the 1873 depression and thereafter periodically reorganized his enterprise, adding new partners and buying out old ones, building new mills and acquiring old ones, each time emerging with a larger controlling interest. Carnegie did not manage any of the steel manufacture. Instead, he hired or became a business associate of those who did, such men as Bill Jones and Henry Clay Frick. As John Chamberlain concluded, "All of the allegations that Carnegie grew rich on the labors and ingenuity of men who knew considerably more about steel than he did are perfectly true."[8]

Upon the advice of men such as Frick, Carnegie developed his enterprises into a tight vertical integration, controlling the sources of coke and iron ore, the mills, and an effective portion of the market. Carnegie Steel profits rose from $1 million in 1883 to $40 million in 1900, a year when production reached four million tons, about one half of the American production and one fourth of the world production. Unlike Rockefeller, Cornelius Vanderbilt, Edward H. Harriman, and James J. Hill, Carnegie left the mechanics of production and the day-to-day management of his business in other hands. His great talent was deciding upon the job to be done, selecting the goal to be reached, and picking the right man to do the job. He pursued a "maverick" position within the industry, and waged price wars whenever practicable. He was more the financial capitalist than the industrial capitalist, a man who, like John Pierpont Morgan, anticipated and helped create a new structure in American business development even while the basic industrial structure was emerging. The violent strikes at his Homestead, Pennsylvania plant in 1892 and the ruthless suppression of the strike by his manager, Henry Clay Frick, brought Carnegie public disfavor, which he had previously escaped. His philanthropies for libraries and education tended to offset this disapproval, and Carnegie has generally sustained a better "press" than Rockefeller. His ideas of free enterprise, encapsulated in his *Gospel of Wealth,* provide useful insight into the ideas and motivations of the rising industrial world.

J. P. Morgan, Financial Entrepreneur

J. P. Morgan carried the consolidation of the American steel industry to its final phase. Morgan, a man of grim visage and enormous financial talent, accomplished in finance and banking what Carnegie accomplished in steel. In 1901 Carnegie sold his entire holdings to United States Steel Corporation, a Morgan-created trust, in return for almost $500 million in stock and 5-percent gold bonds. At this point U.S. Steel had 65 percent of the market, but new processes, an expanding demand created by the automotive and construction industries, and, to only a slight extent, antitrust action by federal courts reduced U.S. Steel's dominant market position to its present level of about 25 percent.

Morgan was sixty-four years old when he created United States Steel. "He was a great burly figure with a huge red nose and startling eyes that nobody ever quite dared to stare down. His growl was like thunder," and his word was law, says John Chamberlain.[9] Morgan was raised in a family world of business and finance, was trained for these pursuits, and moved naturally into them. Although Morgan made money in a variety of financial undertakings after the Civil War, his greatest achievement was to bail out "sick" railroads, improve their financial structure through mergers or pruning, and raise profits by preventing unnecessary price competition and the duplication of facilities between railroads. Morgan mobilized the capital to finance the construction of James J. Hill's Great Northern Railroad and his acquisition of the Northern Pacific. After ruinous stock wars and competition between Hill and Edward H. Harriman, Morgan masterminded a combination of their interests through the Northern Securities Holding Company, which linked a substantial part of the rail lines in the West under the joint control of Hill, Harriman, and Morgan. The organization of U.S. Steel brought together the largest accumulation of capital and "money power" the world had ever seen. It linked the Morgan, Rockefeller, and Carnegie fortunes. John D. Rockefeller, who had acquired the Mesabi iron deposits, brought U.S. Steel a vital supply of ore. Morgan pioneered in the new dimension of finance capitalism. The great Morgan combination marked the coalescence of American financial power into the hands of relatively few men. As a contemporary sociologist, Lester Frank Ward, observed, "Competition is growing more and more aggressive, heated, and ephemeral. Combination is growing more and more universal, powerful and permanent. . . . it tends to choke individual freedom and clog the wheels of social progress."[10]

In less than a half-century, America had seemingly been transformed from a pastoral nation of independent farmers and shopkeepers to an urban nation of employees and pawns dominated by corporations, trusts, and rather mysterious financial manipulations. There seemed to be very few men of great wealth at the top and an awesome number of Americans of little wealth at the bottom. Per-capita income, however, doubled between 1870 and 1900, and the gross national product almost quadrupled. The wages paid labor steadily declined, as did the prices paid for farm commodities, but in the nineteenth century prices generally declined more rapidly. Thus, real earnings actually rose, but neither as fast as the wealth of the business elite nor so quickly that the average family could readily acquire the vast new array of products turned out by American industry. Rising expectations, or "needs," rose far more rapidly than the ability to fulfill those needs. With the expanding needs came growing disaffection, social unrest, and progressive reform.

The age of big business witnessed a number of fundamental challenges to the prevailing ideology of free enterprise. Can a "producer" be other than a farmer or laborer? Is wealth the reward of frugality, wisdom, and virtue, the result of exploiting others, or the product of chance? Is bigness in business the result of a conspiracy, or of a great and good natural law? Does a person of wealth owe any obligation to society? Is this wealth a public or a God-given trust? Americans began a continual and agonizing reappraisal of American life as society marched to the tempo of the new age of business.

Notes

[1]William Letwin's "The Past and Future of the American Businessman," *Daedalus*, 98 (Winter 1969), 1–22, provides an excellent historical overview of business development within a social context.

²Alfred D. Chandler, "The Beginnings of 'Big Business' in American Industry," *Business History Review*, 33 (Spring 1959), p. 26. This essay offers basic insights into the dynamic forces and organizational structures of business growth.

³See Herman E. Krooss and Charles Gilbert, *American Business History* (Englewood Cliffs, N.J.: Prentice-Hall, 1972).

⁴*John D. Rockefeller, Robber Baron or Industrial Statesman,* ed. Earl Latham (Boston: Heath, 1949), p. V.

⁵See Henry Demarest Lloyd, *Wealth Against Commonwealth* (Westport, Conn.: Greenwood Press, 1973); Ida M. Tarbell, *The History of Standard Oil Company* (New York: Macmillan, 1904); Matthew Josephson, *The Robber Barons* (New York: Harcourt, Brace & World, 1934); and Allan Nevins, *John D. Rockefeller, The Heroic Age of American Enterprise*, 2 vols. (New York: Scribner's, 1940).

⁶See Kendall Beaton, "Dr. Gesner's Kerosene: The Start of American Oil Refining," *Business History Review*, 29 (March 1955), pp. 28–53.

⁷John D. Rockefeller, *Random Reminiscences of Men and Events* (Garden City, N.Y.: Doubleday, 1909).

⁸John Chamberlain, *The Enterprising Americans: A Business History of the United States* (New York: Harper & Row, 1963), p. 159.

⁹*Ibid.*, p. 165.

¹⁰See the material by Ward in *Government and the Economy: Some Nineteenth Century Views,* ed. E. David Cronon (New York: Henry Holt, 1960), p. 35.

SUGGESTED READING

CAWELLI, JOHN G., *Apostles of the Self-Made Man*. Chicago: University of Chicago Press, 1965.

CHAMBERLAIN, JOHN, *The Enterprising Americans: A Business History of the United States*. New York, 1963.

CLARK, VICTOR S., *History of Manufacturers in the United States, 1860–1914*. New York, 1928.

COCHRAN, THOMAS C., AND WILLIAM MILLER, *The Age of Enterprise*. New York, 1942.

KIRKLAND, EDWARD C., *Dream and Thought in the Business Community, 1860–1900*. Ithaca, N.Y.: Cornell University Press, 1956.

KIRKLAND, EDWARD C., *Industry Comes of Age: Business Labor and Public Policy, 1860–1897*. New York: Holt, Rinehart and Winston, 1961.

KROOSS, HERMAN E., AND CHARLES GILBERT, *American Business History*. Englewood Cliffs, N.J.: Prentice-Hall, 1972.

LIVESAY, HAROLD, *Andrew Carnegie and the Rise of Big Business*. Boston: Little, Brown, 1975.

MARTIN, ALBRO, *James J. Hill and the Opening of the Northwest*. New York: Oxford University Press, 1976.

MCCLOSKEY, ROBERT, *American Conservatism in the Age of Enterprise, 1865–1910*. Cambridge, Mass.: Harvard University Press, 1951.

MILLER, WILLIÁM, ed. *Men in Business: Essays on the Historical Role of the Entrepreneurs.* Cambridge, Mass.: Harvard University Press, 1952.

PORTER, GLENN, *The Rise of Big Business, 1860–1910.* New York: Thomas Y. Crowell, 1973.

WALL, JOSEPH, *Andrew Carnegie.* New York: Oxford University Press, 1970.

WYLLIE, IRVIN G., *The Self-Made Man in America.* New York: Free Press. 1966.

SOCIAL DARWINISM
AND REFORM

———————————————— chapter XI ——

The idea of a self-adjusting, untouchable economy suited the vast majority of Americans conditioned by experience, environment, and creed to individualism, personal liberty, and free enterprise. For most of these Americans, economics had never been a question of ideology or philosophy, but rather a pragmatic acceptance of "the American way of life." As that way of life began to change markedly in the later nineteenth century, they became more concerned about economic philosophy and about the nature and purposes of the changing economic order. Despite the great diversity of ideas among the rising schools of economists, political scientists, and sociologists, those who tended to defend the business system, such as Andrew Carnegie and William Graham Sumner, as well as those who criticized it, including Lester Frank Ward and Henry George, argued in behalf of personal freedom and free enterprise. The crux of the debate over the nature of the economy was whether individual freedom could best be assured through unrestricted competition or by social regulation.

Lester Frank Ward argued that "competition suppresses; it tends to choke individual freedom and clog the wheels of social progress."[1] Under the prevailing system of laissez faire, he said, competition was becoming ephemeral or meaningless and self-destructive. Combination was "growing more and more universal, powerful and permanent." The paradox, he said, is that *individual freedom* can come only through social regulation. Ward's proposition underscores the great debate of the following century. And reform, when it came, proposed to restore equality of opportunity and individual freedom through social regulation. Although there were exceptions, the reformer and the critic both sought to preserve free enterprise in America, which drew its sustenance from over two centuries of cultural experience and from the philosophic underpinnings of the Protestant ethic, laissez faire, and social Darwinism.

SOCIAL DARWINISM

Social Darwinism, which applied Charles Darwin's biological theories of evolution to society, may be attributed to Herbert Spencer, a British philosopher (1820–1903), whose *Synthetic Philosophy* (1860), argued that social progress derived from the natural law of evolution. A natural process of selection operated in both nature and society, resulting in the survival of the fittest. Thus, the giants of business, such as Standard Oil, the Southern Pacific Railroad, and American Tobacco, and the successful businessmen, such as Carnegie, Rockefeller, and Vanderbilt, Americans could believe, were the most fit, those who had thrived the best in the competitive world. Government should do nothing to interfere in the natural order of things, for that natural order assured social progress. Social Darwinism complemented the Protestant ethic, which argued that God's blessings, including wealth, properly went to the elect, who testified to their election by hard work, thrift, and religious decorum.

William Graham Sumner, an ordained Episcopal minister and professor of political science and social science at Yale University in the 1870s and 1880s, offered the strongest defense of natural selection and laissez faire and embraced the pessimism of Thomas Robert Malthus. Humankind's standard of living bore a direct relationship to the density of population. The scarcer the population, the higher the standard of living, and the higher the standard of living, the more

WILLIAM GRAHAM SUMNER *(1840–1910)*
Economist, sociologist.
Courtesy Yale University News Bureau.

imminent the population increases that lead to relative scarcity. The greater the population, the greater the struggle for self-preservation. Poverty, misery, and class antagonism were natural concomitants of social progress. The inequality in the distribution of capital was "at once the proof and reward of unequal effort and virtue." Private property, said Sumner, is aimed against nature: "it is from her niggardly hand that we have to wrest the satisfactions for our needs, but our fellow men are our competitors for the meager supply." Competition is the law of nature. Nature is entirely neutral and grants her rewards to the fittest—to "those who most energetically and resolutely assail her." Individuals earn, or have and enjoy, in proportion to their works: "we cannot go outside of this alternative: liberty, inequality, survival of the fittest."[2]

The doctrine of social Darwinism, which at first found favor in the minds of many Americans, increasingly came to be the private philosophy of the few rather than the many. To be sure, relatively few Americans, including business-men, became economic philosophers or adopted any consistent or cogent ideol-ogy. Most preferred to leave the business of synthesis and abstract thought to the professors and writers. The average American, whose thoughts touched upon such concrete matters as money, monopoly, freight rates, tariffs, prices, and profits, was nonetheless persuaded by, or found reinforcement in, the growing dialogue about the nature of the economic order.

One of the few defenses of social Darwinism from the ranks of the businessman, and perhaps the most incisive, was Andrew Carnegie's *Gospel of Wealth,* which, while embracing social Darwinism, escaped the pessimism of Sumner and Malthus. Carnegie acknowledged that under the competitive system friction developed between the employer and employee, between capital and labor, between the rich and the poor. Society tended to coalesce into hostile "castes." There developed an "inequality of environment" and the concentra-tion of business in the hands of the few. Carnegie escaped the Marxian notion of inevitable class conflict and revolution by arguing that although the price society pays for the law of competition is great, the advantages are greater. Social progress through natural selection is not for the few but for the many. Competi-tion and the rise of big business brings "wonderful material developments" in its train. Carnegie rejected Malthusian pessimism and equated the rise of the new urban-industrial order with the promise of American life—the material well-being of more and more Americans.

"Today," Carnegie wrote, "the world obtains commodities of excellent quality at prices which even the generation preceding this would have deemed incredible." Luxuries have become the necessities of life. The laborer has more comforts than the farmer had a few generations ago. The farmer enjoys a better life and is better housed and clothed than a few generations ago. The landlord now enjoys the material comforts that even a king could not previously obtain, he wrote.[3] Not just the few but rather the whole of society benefits from the process of natural selection. Thus, Carnegie posed but did not pursue, perhaps because he failed to really understand it, a solution to the intellectual dilemma that social Darwinism in America contained: progress could be equated only with the deprivation and despoilation of the masses. Social Darwinism contained a proposition that was inherently undemocratic, un-Christian, and "un-American." But the inference that the changing economic order could unshackle the masses from their eternal struggle for animal sustenance and survival and make them truly free and fully human accorded with the basic goal of individual freedom. Americans supported the idea of "wonderful material development." They questioned the growing inequality, the developing concentration of wealth and power, the declining wages and farm prices (failing to understand that there were not necessarily indicative of falling real income), and the alienation of those who were less and less free, independent, and participatory agents in society.

Trusts and monopolies patently threatened individual opportunities and personal liberties. Low prices for farm goods and low wages paid to labor were intrinsically discriminatory and begat dependence and servitude. Slums and poverty in the face of wealth and opulence suggested exploitation. Urban growth and the concentration of population threatened the agrarian sense of social order. Critics and reformers sought not to destroy the free-enterprise system but to purify it and restore its promise of individual opportunity.

REFORM DARWINISM

Was it indeed the *fit* who survived and grew rich and powerful? Although Americans believed that individuals should earn according to their ability and that an individual's wealth and property reflect hard work and efforts, the American democratic experience also implied that people sprang from a common mold and that their ability to work, produce, and earn was a thing of degree and not of absolutes. Great and unusual wealth as well as great and unusual poverty were easily suspect in the fundamentally equalitarian society of the nineteenth century.

Henry George

Henry George probably had more to do with undermining the moral position of wealth than any other individual in the nineteenth century. George was born of rather poor parents in Philadelphia before the Civil War. He became self-supporting at fourteen, which was probably characteristic of nineteenth-century American society. At sixteen he shipped out to sea and discovered that he vigorously preferred land. He, and presumably most Americans, believed in the Protestant ethic: hard work and thrift were divinely ordained, and each person should receive according to his or her effort, energy, or productiveness. As a young man George went to California seeking "opportunity," which was very elusive. He found misery and poverty, and eventually a wife and a profession—journalism. Later, as an established journalist whose optimism was tempered by those early, bitter years, he happened to visit New York City. There he was struck, as he had never been in California, by the glaring contrast between the rich and the poor. Was it hard work, energy, and ability that explained the enormous chasm between the few who had so much and the many who had so little?

Returning to California, George began to observe things he had previously overlooked but that now appeared obvious. Wealthy Californians, he decided, almost invariably derived their fortune from an increase in the value of land. Land values, he believed, seemed to increase according to their proximity to the railroad. Those who owned land of little value often became wealthy if a railroad was constructed across it, although they had nothing to do with the course or the construction of the railroad. This increase in the value of land was not the result of hard work or thrift. Rather, this "unearned increment" could be explained only by chance or monopoly. Wealth not earned by honest toil was undeserved. The free-enterprise system promised to each according to ability. If, then, there was an "unearned increment," equity, justice, and social Darwinism demanded the removal of that increment in order to restore equality of opportunity and survival of the fittest. George thus opened a serious crack in the intellectual armor of social Darwinism, using that philosophy's own rhetoric to do so. Perhaps more than just "the fit" were surviving.

George developed his thesis, employing vivid examples of social problems and crises, in *Progress and Poverty* (1886). This book failed to attract readers until British excitement over George's analysis of the Irish land problem in a British journal generated American interest in the idea of the unearned increment. George advocated a *single tax* to remove the unearned increment. If an individual sold land for more than he paid for it, he was entitled to the increase in value or rent derived from his labor, risk, or planning. He was not entitled to any increase deriving from factors beyond the control or management of the individual, such as social or population pressures or unanticipated intrusion, as by a highway or a railroad. George's book soon became widely read, even among farmers, who believed that spiraling land prices were caused by speculators who prevented farmers from acquiring cheap land for agricultural purposes. In 1886 George ran for mayor of New York. He finished second, ahead of Theodore Roosevelt. In the 1890s Henry George "Single Tax Clubs" sprang up in all parts of the United States, offering the "Single Tax" as a panacea for almost all social ills. The tax was actually implemented in some local governments as a tax base. George still had a sufficient following in 1897 to make another unsuccessful try for the New York mayor's office. The administration of a single tax proved unworkable, but the idea did provide a strong impetus for the adoption of the income tax. George argued that wealth was a form of social benefit as well as deriving from individual endeavor. If society participated in the individual's acquisition of wealth, then society had the right to consume a portion of that wealth in taxes.

George's significance lies less in establishing a new economic principle or in precipitating a new tax policy than in challenging the moral primacy of wealth. Great wealth did not necessarily demonstrate the moral or productive measure of a person. Chance and social benefits should be eliminated from the competitive system in order that individual initiative and ability be accurately measured. Free enterprise meant that an individual should earn only according to ability—no more. George and the social Darwinists were intrinsically concerned with individual freedom. He suggested that social problems did exist, and did not derive from a "natural order of things." Society created those problems, both the wealth and the poverty, and society had the obligation to remove the inequities in order to restore individual freedom and opportunity.

Edward Bellamy

Edward Bellamy, a contemporary of Henry George and also a professional journalist, wrote one of the most popular critiques of the nineteenth-century American economic order—*Looking Backward*. This widely read book is essentially a science-fiction novel, which perhaps made his criticisms more oblique and thus more palatable to the public. The book offered neither technical explanations nor realistic solutions for economic situations or problems. Rather, its

EDWARD BELLAMY *(1850–1898)*
Author of *Looking Backward.*

message was that an economic problem existed and that society could and should do something about it.

Published in 1888, Bellamy's book characterized the competitive, laissez-faire system as savage, un-Christian, and an obstacle to social progress. His leading character is an ordinary nineteenth-century American, Julian West, who returns home after a regular working day to relax in his subterranean study. Dr. Pillsbury, a "remarkable mesmerist," casts him into a deep sleep, from which he is awakened in the year 2000. In conversation with leading individuals of that time, such as Dr. Leete, West is astounded at the immense social and economic progress that has occurred. By the year 2000 all competition has ceased. All production is owned and managed by the state, which uses a computerlike device to match each worker to his or her most efficiently completed and most satisfying task. The result is a "nationalist" utopia in which all persons have material comforts and enjoy the best of all possible worlds.

West is amazed that nineteenth-century America failed to see the crudeness, inefficiency, and waste of its "stagecoach" economy. The competitive system of that century, he relates, is like a stagecoach traveling over a bumpy road in which only a few ride while the masses pull or push it along. Those on the ground are eager to climb aboard but are at a distinct disadvantage. On rare occasions a rider will be thrown off and someone may get on, but for virtually all of the masses there is no opportunity, only unending drudgery and hopelessness. But now, by the year 2000, humankind has substituted the law of "tooth and fang" with the law of helping one another, and has finally achieved a state of economic well-being. Whereas Henry George questioned that laissez faire and social Darwinism achieved an equitable distribution of wealth as promised, Bellamy questioned the efficiency of unrestrained, undirected competition. He believed that humanity could and should try to control its environment and regulate and administer the natural wealth in the interest of better promoting individual welfare.

Andrew Carnegie

Andrew Carnegie and many other Americans believed that individuals of great wealth served as trustees or custodians of that wealth, and should, and most often did, administer that wealth to the general advantage of society. Carnegie noted, for example, that there were only three ways to dispose of surplus wealth: first, it can be left to heirs; second it can be bequeathed to the state; third, it can be administered for the public good during the life of its possessor. Carnegie rejected the first as essentially aristocratic and degenerate. In the second case, the world must wait before any good is derived and the objectives of the bequest are usually thwarted. Interestingly, Carnegie believed that increasing use of the inheritance tax was a "cheering indication" of changing public opinion about

posthumous bequests. Carnegie believed that a person of wealth had an obligation to administer that wealth during his lifetime so that it could best be directed
to the common good. "In bestowing charity," he said, "the main consideration
should be to help those who will help themselves; to provide part of the means by
which those who desire to improve may do so, . . . to assist, but rarely or never
to do all."[4]

In his condemnation of an aristocracy of wealth, in his support of the
inheritance tax, and in his belief that surplus wealth should be used to encourage
others to help themselves, Carnegie is remarkably close to the Populist-
Progressive view of free enterprise. Their difference lay more in the mode of
accomplishing an objective than in the objective itself. "Reformers," whether
Populist or Progressive, believed that government should help others help themselves, and that a few individuals of great wealth could not, or would not, do
this. By the twentieth century many Americans believed that the accumulation of
great wealth could not, of itself, serve the common good.

Thorstein Veblen

This opinion was fortified by the writings of the ubiquitous, sometimes
"crackpot realist" Thorstein Veblen. Veblen was born in Wisconsin in 1857, the
son of Norwegian immigrants. At the age of eight Veblen moved to Minnesota,
where his teachers considered him bright but possibly "unsound." He pursued
graduate studies at Johns Hopkins and Yale, where he received a doctorate in
1884. There was no job for him after graduation, so he returned to his father's
farm, where he reportedly lived for the next seven years in "idle curiosity."
After marriage he returned to Cornell for more studies, and then obtained his first
job teaching at the University of Chicago. There he got into difficulty because of
extramarital activities and was asked to leave. Girls liked Veblen, and Veblen did
not object.[5] He went to Stanford, and then to the University of Missouri, where
he did much of his writing. He obtained local notoriety in Columbia, Missouri
by, among other things, labeling the town a "woodpecker hole" in the "rotten
stump of Missouri."

In his *Theory of the Leisure Class*, Veblen questioned whether the accumulation of great wealth by an individual served any useful social purpose whatever,
thus questioning the central proposition of Carnegie's *Gospel of Wealth*. Writing
at the turn of the century, Veblen said that every society, from the barbarian to
the modern, developed a "leisure class," whose main sign is that they regard
manual labor as the exclusive occupation of the inferior class. Even the American
Indian had a leisure class—the warrior—whose primary occupation was to hunt,
fight, and engage in politics, sports, religion, or learning. The women did the
manual labor. The hunt, though it served a useful purpose in providing food, was
viewed by the warriors as a skill or sport, as was war. Its object was not to be

THORSTEIN BUNDE VEBLEN *(1857–1929)*
Economist, educator.

productive, but to show "good form." A leisure class, Veblen said, is concerned primarily with consuming time nonproductively and with showing "good form" or status. One demonstrates his status before others by "conspicuous consumption"—that is, by doing those things that are nonproductive, expensive, and unnecessary. Thus, war and sports are highly prized modes of conspicuous consumption, being very expensive and wasteful. The point is to demonstrate to others that one no longer has to struggle in order to survive. Veblen labeled a number of favored modes of conspicuous consumption:[6]

> *The dog:* "He is the filthiest of the domestic animals in his person and the nastiest in his habits." Because he is an item of expense, serves no useful purpose, and symbolizes the chase, people value him highly in the race for conspicuous consumption.
> *The Horse:* "The case of the fast horse is much like that of the dog. He is on the whole expensive, wasteful and useless."
> *Handmade products:* They have high standing because they are expensive and more often less useful than machine-made products.

Clothing fashions, hat designing, interior decorating, the dead languages, and alcoholic beverages are all common modes of conspicuous consumption because they are generally expensive and serve no useful purpose.

Veblen's "crackpot realism" would lead him to argue that a place setting of fine china, crystal, linens, and silver served no purpose other than to demonstrate one's status before others; a tin plate and spoon were far more efficient. He would suggest, were he living today, that a modern football or baseball game, which brings in hundreds of thousands of dollars in gate receipts and costs millions more in clothing, travel, liquor bills, coaches' salaries, and the like, is totally nonproductive and wasteful, and thus preeminent in the race for conspicuous consumption. He would probably compare the fast, fancy automobile to the "fast horse"—on the whole, expensive, wasteful, and inefficient. And he would probably say that neckties, like jewelry, are expensive and useless status symbol. Although Veblen never endeared himself to the American public, through the years he has inspired a continuing reexamination of American social and economic life and has influenced such contemporary economists and writers as John Galbraith and Vance Packard.

Veblen's critique of wealth was not from the point of view of equality of opportunity or democracy. Rather, he believed that wealth and competition were inherently inefficient. For the most part, competition meant conspicuous consumption—just spinning the wheels. Veblen believed that the creative force of the scientist and engineer would bring progress and achievement. The idea of conspicuous consumption was particularly nettlesome in the ideological hide of accumulated wealth: it argued against inefficiency, and businessmen prized efficiency as much as they did laissez faire and social Darwinism.

A corollary to the idea that success or wealth is accorded those who are most fit, productive, or virtuous is, of course, that those who become impoverished are *ipso facto* unfit, nonproductive, and likely immoral or irreligious. The critiques of the developing free-enterprise system approached not only the "problem" of wealth but the problem of poverty. The free-enterprise ethic presumes that poverty, within the context of social Darwinism and the Protestant ethic, is justified only if the impoverished are, in fact, unproductive and unworthy. But what if the poverty is inflicted by purely external factors having nothing to do with individual ability or godliness? That chance could lead to impoverishment was a commonly recognized social condition. A laborer could be maimed or the family wage earner might die an accidental or premature death. Fire could destroy a home or a business. Crops could fail, and disease could wipe out livestock. By the mid nineteenth century private and mutual insurance companies and societies had become well-established institutions for safeguarding the individual against natural hazards and accidents. The existence of insurance reflected a consensus that misfortune and impoverishment were often the products of external forces beyond the control of the individual. It was implicitly recognized that poverty was not invariably self-inflicted and was thereby justified even within the context of survival of the fittest. Chance had a role in determining poverty.

Thus, the reform Darwinism inherent in the social justice and social gospel movements derived in part from established views about poverty and professed a general commitment to individualism, self-sufficiency, and personal liberty. On a less philosophical plane, people simply wondered why the harder the farmers worked, the larger the crops they grew, and the more virtuous they appeared to be, the poorer they often seemed to become, and why the urban laborer appeared to work longer and longer hours for less and less pay.

The Social Gospel

It was difficult, if not inconceivable, for the rural preachers or the urban ministers to tell their faithful that their poverty was a sign of God's wrath or of their personal sin. The minister began to frame a new perspective of poverty, one that reversed the traditional view that poverty was evidence of an individual's damnation. The blame for poverty lay not upon the individual but upon the external forces of society. Sin did not lead to life in a slum, but life in an urban slum could lead to sin. Since society had created the slum, society had an obligation to clean up the slum in order to preserve the Christian life.

Prominent in the new social gospel movement was Washington Gladden, a Congregational minister from Columbus, Ohio. Gladden argued that unbridled competition was contradictory to the concept of Christian love. But he did not attack private property or free enterprise. Society, he said, needed to be Christianized, not socialized. Walter Rauschenbusch, a New York reform minister, argued eloquently in his books in behalf of "Christian socialism." The social gospel is exemplified in *In His Steps*, a novel written in 1882 by another minister, Charles M. Sheldon. In this book Sheldon depicted flagrant social problems, such as the condition of the urban poor, and attempted to answer the question "What would Jesus do?" By 1933, over 23 million copies of the book had been sold. The point of the social gospel was that poverty, disease, and unemployment were beyond the control of the individual, but were within the scope and responsibility of society as a whole. The churches had a new mission.

Under the impetus of the social gospel, churches began to sponsor educational and recreational activities. Sunday schools, youth organizations, and a new social consciousness carried the message of Christian love and financial aid to the needy. Poverty was regarded as a temporary social or environmental condition, not evidence of eternal damnation. None portrayed the new gospel as fully as the Salvation Army, a movement imported by America from England in the 1880s. Indigence, poverty, slums, and drunkenness led to sin but were not intrinsic evidence of sin. Sober the drunk, feed and house the poor and unemployed, and you help them overcome their temporary, socially induced handicap and restore them to the paths of righteousness. The Young Men's Christian Association and Young Women's Christian Association, founded in America, held that a better environment made a better Christian. In a similar vein, modern churches of every denomination attracted youth to a more wholesome environment by providing gyms, swimming pools, and recreational facilities. The social gospel, along with the social justice movement, was instrumental in removing both the stigma of charity and the hopelessness of poverty.

Social Justice

The social justice movement was the secular arm of reform Darwinism. It is distinguished from the social gospel only in that its objectives are secular and not religious. It advocated a better, more productive, prosperous society, not a more religious one. It included prominent ministers, lawyers, teachers, and women who generally sought public or government assistance in lessening the evils and hardships afflicting the individual in an industrial society. Social justice followers believed, for example, that long hours of labor by women and children prevented social progress and undermined the health and regenerative capacities of society. They advocated laws that would regulate the employment of women and children. Industrial injury, they believed, was partially the fault of the society that condoned the development of the industry, partially the fault of the employer who failed to institute adequate safeguards to protect an employee from injury, and perhaps in part the responsibility of the employee who accepted the work and who may have been careless in its performance. The supporters of social justice advocated workmen's-compensation laws that would protect the individual from the environmental hazards of the industrial world. Thus, such laws require contributions from each of the contributors to industrial injury—the laborer, the employer, and the society (or government). Social security presumes a similar tripartite responsibility: the incapacity to work because of aging is in part individual, in part environmental, and in part social.

Social justice concepts also undergirded the conservation movement. The depletion of natural resources—clean air, water, forests, and minerals—would ultimately contribute to a "bad environment" in which even the fit could not survive. Impure foods and drugs are an environmental hazard against which the individual is defenseless and must be protected by society. Although social justice advocates could still ostensibly believe in survival of the fittest, they could, and did, advocate controls over competitive enterprises in order to preserve the opportunity to compete. Thus, both the social justice and social gospel movements grew within the ideological framework of free enterprise. Their paramount concern was for the individual, not the group, and for the preservation of the individual's opportunity to compete on an equitable basis.

The nineteenth-century women's suffrage movement and the modern women's equal-rights movement hold that legal and social sanctions prevented a woman as an individual from achieving her full capabilities. Inequities such as suffrage restrictions, property-holding proscriptions, male-only qualifications, and discrimination in employment prevent a woman from achieving according to her ability. The modern civil-rights movement, whether pertaining to women, blacks, or ethnic minority groups, would guarantee to each individual the right to compete on an equitable basis.

The presumption of the social justice and social gospel movements is that individual freedom can best be achieved through social regulation. Progressive legislation in the early twentieth century and much of the modern legislation affecting slum clearance, job retraining, medical care, the environment, and civil rights draw their philosophical sustenance from the social gospel and social justice movements. Although these movements were critical of the developing free-enterprise system, their criticism was in a spirit of reform rather than one of radicalism and revolution. Most nineteenth-century Americans believed in individualism, personal liberty, and a free-enterprise system that awarded each according to his or her ability. Few challenged the "rightness" of material abundance or rejected the idea of social progress. The question was how to administer that abundance more equitably, or how best to promote human progress and retain individual freedom.

There were, to be sure, radicals who believed that individual welfare and personal property must give way to the "common good," and that free enterprise and individual freedom tended to destroy social progress. Socialists and communists were cheered by the trend toward social regulation, but their basic tenets were incompatible with the philosophy of the mainstream of American reform. Pressure from the left, as from farm and labor organizations and social critics, stimulated reform. But opposition from truly radical groups, such as the Molly Maguires, the Wobblies (the International Workers of the World), socialists, and anarchists, who stood outside the philosophical framework of free enterprise and who advocated or resorted to violent practice that threatened the capitalist system, was usually met by strong suppression and widespread public condemnation. Reform, when it came, was achieved within the conceptual framework of free enterprise. The real testing of the form and fiber of the developing urban-industrial society was done not by the philosophical supporters or the literary critics but by the farmers, laborers, shopkeepers, and manufacturers who were involved in the everyday business of making a living.

Notes

[1] See the material by Ward in *Government and the Economy: Some Nineteenth-Century Views,* ed. E. David Cronon (New York: Holt, Rinehart & Winston), p. 35.

[2] See the material by Sumner in *Government and the Economy,* p. 20.

[3] See the material by Carnegie in *Government and the Economy,* p. 23.

[4] Ibid., p. 27.

[5]See introduction by C. Wright Mills in Thorstein Veblen, *The Theory of the Leisure Class* (New York: New American Library, 1953), pp. viii-ix.
[6]Thorstein Veblen, *The Theory of the Leisure Class* (Boston: Houghton Mifflin, 1973), pp. 141-143, 159.

SUGGESTED READING

BELLAMY, EDWARD, *Looking Backward, 2000–1887*. New York: New American Library, 1960.

BREMMER, ROBERT H., *From the Depths: The Discovery of Poverty in the United States*. New York: New York University Press, 1956.

CRONON, E. DAVID, ed., *Government and the Economy: Some Nineteenth-Century Views*, rev. ed. New York: Holt, Rinehart & Winston, 1963.

DORFMAN, JOSEPH, *The Economic Mind in American Civilization*, Vol. III. New York: Viking, 1949.

FINE, SIDNEY, *Laissez-faire to General Welfare State: A Study of Conflict in American Thought, 1865–1901*. Ann Arbor, Mich.: University of Michigan Press, 1956.

GEORGE, HENRY, *Progress and Poverty*. New York: Modern Library, 1929.

HOFSTADTER, RICHARD, *Social Darwinism in American Thought*. Rev. ed., Boston: Beacon Press, 1955.

KIRKLAND, E. C., *Dream and Thought in the Business Community, 1860–1900*. Ithaca, N.Y.: Cornell University Press, 1956.

KOLKO, GABRIEL, *The Triumph of Conservatism: A Re-interpretation of American History, 1900–1916*. New York: Free Press, 1963.

McCLOSKY, ROBERT, *American Conservatism in the Age of Enterprise, 1865–1910*. Cambridge, Mass.: Harvard University Press, 1951.

RISCHIN, MOSES, ed., *The American Gospel of Success, Individualism and Beyond*. Chicago: Quadrangle, 1965.

VEBLEN, THORSTEIN, *The Theory of the Leisure Class*. Boston: Houghton Mifflin, 1973.

FARM AND
LABOR DISCONTENT
TO 1914

_____ chapter XII __

The farm and labor movements of the turbulent half-century between the Civil War and the American entry into World War I are commonly regarded as evidence of a mass reaction to and discontent with the rising urban-industrial system. They are more accurately evidence of rising expectations—often frustrated. The nineteenth-century farm and labor movements gave new form to the free enterprise system. Between 1870 and 1910 the gross national product grew from $7.4 billion to $35.3 billion. Per-capita income doubled even while the total population expanded from 40 million to over 92 million. In these years the agricultural labor force rose from 5.5 million to 10.5 million. The ranks of nonagricultural labor swelled from 5.1 million to 19.5 million. The output per man-hour for manufacturing almost doubled, and farm output increased by one third. But per-capita farm income tended to decline before 1900. Real industrial wages occasionally declined, but in the long term they rose. The farm and labor movements were essentially class actions that derived from the fact that although the economic situation of farmers and laborers might not be worsening, it seemed to be improving little, if at all. In contradiction to the "promise of American life," there seemed to be no way that individual farmers and laborers could raise their level of material well-being to their level of expectancy, try as they would. Inasmuch as their problems appeared to be collective in scope, the solutions to those problems, farmers and laborers increasingly came to believe, required the formation of national associations for the protection and advancement of their individual interests.

Shortly after the Civil War, farmers and laborers began to develop national organizations that would seek solutions to their economic problems. Although both farmers and laborers held common grievances and sought similar goals or legislation, the farm and labor movements maintained their independence from each other. Indeed, there was a basic conflict of interest between them. The farmer, most often a property owner, was interested in higher food and commodity prices, more profits, and a higher standard of living. The laborer, a wage earner and most often propertyless, sought higher wages, lower living costs, and a higher standard of living. The farmer's interest in higher commodity prices was in direct conflict with the laborer's desire for lower living costs. The laborer's interest in obtaining higher wages was in conflict with the farmer's interest in lower production costs. In addition, the laborer retained a closer ideological affinity with industry and the city than did the farmer. Although there were exceptions, both farmers and laborers intrinsically supported the free-enterprise system and held nonradical goals and objectives.

THE UNION MOVEMENT

The American labor movement has been predominantly conservative, and it has been a minority movement.

TABLE 12.1
Number of Laborers in Unions, 1897–1915.

YEAR	NUMBER (THOUSANDS)	% OF CIVILIAN LABOR FORCE
1897	440	1.6
1900	791	2.8
1905	1,918	5.9
1910	2,116	5.8
1915	2,560	6.5
(1974)	(21,643)	(23.8)

Source: Bureau of the Census, *Bicentennial Statistics*. Reprinted from Pocket Data Book, USA 1976, table 607.
See Table XVI.5.

Throughout the nineteenth century the vast majority of Americans were not dependent upon industrial wages. Furthermore, many of those who worked in the factories failed to identify themselves with industrial labor, but were in fact simply farmers who had met economic adversity by "hiring out." They fully expected to return one day soon to the farm. In an intriguing way, industry became the "safety valve" for farmer discontent more than the farm functioned as a safety valve for labor discontent. Throughout the nineteenth century farm-reared Americans were rapidly leaving the fields and going to work in the factory. American labor, despite its many grievances, generally enjoyed higher wages and better living conditions than labor in other parts of the world. Labor,

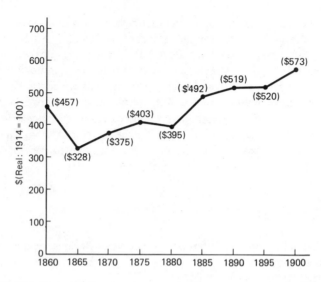

FIGURE 12.1 Real average annual earnings for non-farm employees 1860–1900.

Source: Bureau of the Census, *Historical Statistics of the United States*, Series D 735–738, p. 165.

particularly skilled labor, remained relatively scarce in the rapidly expanding late-nineteenth- and early-twentieth-century American industrial economy.

After the Civil War the conditions of labor worsened, due to the rapid expansion of assembly-line production, the "American system" of manufacturing, a great influx of immigrants, and the impersonal forces of industrialization and urbanization.[1] Labor's problems were not exclusively economic, but were in part social. Industrial labor was a relatively new phenomenon in America, and had yet to establish its values or social "position." Individual laborers tended to lose their individuality in the faceless crowd. Aside from its basic economic objectives, the labor union served as a social outlet: it gave the individual a sense of belonging and identification and opportunities for friends, fellowship, and leadership, if desired.

The historical antecedents of labor unions were the very ancient craft guilds of Europe. Unions were organized in America before the Civil War. One of the first unions was a society of shoemakers organized in Philadelphia in 1792. Early unions were organized on the craft principle—that is, those having common skills united—but their objectives were usually quite modest and their tactics extremely conservative. They sought largely to retain rather than advance wage levels and provided an apprenticeship system for prospective artisans.

Output per man-hour doubled between 1870 and 1910. Money wages paid nonfarm labor increased about 10 percent, but real wages in manufacturing actually increased about 50 percent between 1870 and 1910. Hours of employment varied from ten to eighteen per day for a six- or seven-day work week, depending upon the industry. Insecurity, however, resulted from the constant efforts by employers to lower wages. Salary cuts were common throughout the era. Cuts resulted, in part, from falling price levels and the rise in monetary values. It was undoubtedly difficult for a laborer to understand how he might be financially "better off" when his salary was being lowered. In the short term, his buying power was less following a wage cut. Examples of labor's problems include Jay Gould's across-the-board pay cut of his railroad employees in 1885, the Carnegie (Homestead) Steel lockout and strike of 1892, and Buck Stove and Range Company's increase in the labor day for metal polishers from nine to ten hours without additional pay in 1906. Despite the tremendous increase in the number of industrial employees between 1870 and 1910, workers believed with some justification that they generally failed to share in the "wonderful material benefits" that were being derived from the expanding economy.

Perhaps the best indicator of labor's plight in the nineteenth century is a simple comparison of what laborers can expect today and what they could expect then. In the nineteenth century, labor did not have the forty-hour work week, minimum wages, or overtime. Children were commonly employed in industry, particularly in textile manufacturing. Women and children invariably received lower pay than men for the same work. There was no retirement program or social security, no unemployment compensation, no workmen's (accident) insurance, no employer liability, no safety or health codes, and for all practical purposes no union contracts or collective bargaining. Whatever problems skilled labor confronted, they were compounded for the unskilled laborer.

The National Labor Union

The first attempt to consolidate some of the local independent unions into a larger organization was the creation of the National Labor Union in 1866 under the leadership of William Sylvis. Organized on the craft principle as a confederation of skilled craft groups, the National Labor Union sought higher wages, the eight-hour day, the abolition of the use of convict labor, and restricted immigration. The union also supported the establishment of producer and consumer cooperatives, advocated equal rights for women and Negroes, and favored cheap money. Sylvis believed that labor should take political action to win its objectives. Most of the announced objectives of the National Labor Union became persistent labor demands throughout the century.[2]

Although the purposes of higher pay and the eight-hour day are obvious, labor policies concerning convict labor, immigration, and cooperatives need some explanation. Labor's opposition to the use of convict labor derived far less from humanitarian considerations than from purely economic motivations. Convict labor was bonded or cheap labor, which drove free-labor wages down. The abolition of the convict-labor system would, in effect, increase the demand for and the wages of labor. Similarly, organized labor desired to halt or restrain immigration in order to reduce the supply of labor, particularly cheap labor, and thus raise the wages paid domestic labor. The cooperative movement, which became particularly popular with farmers, was intended to raise the laborers' standard of living by lowering the cost of food and provisions (or in the case of marketing cooperatives, to increase profit margins), thus increasing the purchasing power of earnings. The consumer cooperative was a cost-sharing, profit-sharing enterprise that eliminated the "middleman," or retailer, and passed profits back to the consumer. In its advocacy of equal rights for women and blacks and in its support for cheap money and political action, the National Labor Union committed itself to goals that were essentially nonlabor. By drawing support from diverse nonlabor interests the National Labor Union weakened its position as a bargaining agent and spokesman for labor.

After Sylvis's death in 1869, the National Labor Union began to disintegrate. Crusaders having no real labor affiliation had been attracted to it as a vehicle to promote cheap money and women's or Negro rights. The Union's demise came with its nomination of David Davis of Illinois as a presidential candidate in 1872. As a political party, the union compromised its remaining claims to being a labor organization. Davis's disastrous defeat in the election was the death knell of the union. Its decline, however, was hastened by the growth of a rival union, the Knights of Labor, organized by Uriah Stephens in 1869.

The Knights of Labor

The Knights rejected the craft system of alliance and organized on a purely industrial base. Skilled and unskilled workers alike were admitted to the national body. Interestingly, lawyers, saloonkeepers, prostitutes, and bankers were prohibited. The Knights adopted an elaborate and secret ritual. Secrecy was much in vogue then, and was also useful in safeguarding workers from being fired by their employers (both employers and the press regarded labor unions as subversive). Instead of promoting union recruitment, secrecy served only to thwart the growth of the union by discouraging Catholic laborers from joining. The Catholic Church actively opposed the Knights because of its secret rituals, and this particularly discouraged recruitment among Irish Catholic laborers. Finally, in 1879, after Terrence Powderly became Grand Master, the Knights eliminated secrecy and their membership greatly expanded. Powderly was a particularly vigorous organizer and recruiter who believed that labor could not achieve its objectives through political action.[3] He preferred the boycott and arbitration to the ultimate weapon of the strike in the union's pursuit of labor's goals.

The Knights supported the eight-hour day, equal pay for women, the graduated income tax, free land, producer and consumer cooperatives, restricted immigration, and the abolition of convict labor. Free land was seen as a device to attract would-be farmers away from the labor pool, thus diminishing the supply of labor and forcing wages higher. Under Powderly's aggressive leadership the Knights enrolled over 100,000 members in 1885.

The same year, a dramatic confrontation between the Knights and railroad magnate Jay Gould rocketed the prestige and membership of the Knights to unbelievable levels. Gould, who then held controlling interest in the Missouri Pacific, Missouri-Kansas-Texas, and Wabash Railroads announced an across-the-board wage cut. Powderly reciprocated with an across-the-board strike that completely paralyzed the lines and forced Gould, who was in temporary financial straits, to rescind his wage cut. It was the largest and most successful strike in history. It attracted over 600,000 new members to the Knights, but it also fostered the ill-conceived belief that the cherished objectives of organized labor, particularly the eight-hour day, were within reach. That *success* could be achieved simply by retaining an existing wage level is indicative of the severe economic pressures on labor and the inherent weakness of labor's position. Strikes, paradoxically, were more effective in times of full employment, when a labor scarcity existed (and when a strike was least required), than in periods of rising unemployment and falling wages, when labor's hardships were most severe.

An immediate by-product of the Gould strike was a growing resolution that labor should participate in a great, universal strike in support of the eight-hour day. While labor took heart, the public and the press took an extremely dim view of the idea, pronouncing it a great radical and revolutionary movement to overthrow established law, order, and rights in private property. As the newspapers hammered away at the great danger of the class revolution inherent in a universal strike and in the very concept of labor unions, Powderly and more reflective labor leaders refused to sanction the universal strike, now being set for a specific date—May 1, 1886. But radical, socialist, and Marxist leaders in Chicago continued to promote the idea.

A great fear swept the nation as tensions in Chicago mounted. Eighty thousand Chicago workers actually participated in the strike, but the day passed without serious incident. Two days later there was a local strike at the McCormick plant in Chicago. Police were called in to break the strike and in the melee four workers were killed. Labor called a mass protest meeting in Haymarket Square for May 4. Speakers stood on a wagon in the square; police stood by; the mayor and the city officials were on hand, and affairs proceeded peaceably enough. After several hours officials and police left the scene, but soon afterwards a cordon of police from the nearby precinct station marched toward the wagon with the intent, seemingly, of ending the meeting. As they moved forward, someone suddenly tossed a bomb into the police ranks and a deadly riot ensued. Seven police and four workers were killed; hundreds were injured. Public revulsion was widespread, and the blame was laid on a number of anarchists in particular and labor unions in general.

The bomb thrower was never identified, but eight known anarchists were seized and brought to a speedy trial. Seven of them were sentenced to death, despite inconclusive evidence. One committed suicide in jail, four were hanged, and Governor John P. Altgeld of Illinois freed the remaining three in 1894 on the grounds that the evidence presented in the trial was insufficient to obtain a conviction. The prestige and effectiveness of the Knights of Labor were eroded by the Haymarket Riot, despite Powderly's efforts to disassociate the Knights from it, by severe setbacks in strikes sanctioned on Gould's railroads and in the Chicago meat-packing industry, and by a recession in 1886. By 1893 membership had dwindled to about 75,000.

The American Federation of Labor

Contributing to the decline of the Knights was the organization in 1886 of the American Federation of Labor. Headed by the redoubtable Samuel Gompers, the new union organized on the older craft principle with each affiliate retaining a considerable degree of autonomy.[4] The AF of L was a "bread and butter" union: it sought primarily higher pay and shorter hours. The union intended to abstain from political action, and would bar reform groups and political parties from affiliation. Gompers particularly believed that the primary tool for labor advancement must be collective bargaining—the negotiation of a union contract by union representatives. In some ways Gompers may have been as laissez-faire-oriented as Andrew Carnegie. He opposed government regulation of hours and wages or government interference in labor disputes. Although the AF of L continued to press for the eight-hour day, Gompers proposed to achieve it by having one large union, or trade, strike each year. The first such strike, by the Carpenters Union, was called for May 1, 1890. It achieved some success, but the day, the anniversary of the Haymarket Riot, reverberated to become a labor anniversary, celebrated by international socialists and communists.

In 1892 the AF of L was almost destroyed by a series of strikes. In the most serious incident the labor contract for the Carnegie Steel Mills in Homestead, Pennsylvania expired. The union demanded higher wages. Henry Clay Frick, Carnegie's manager, offered lower wages or no jobs and gave laborers twenty-nine days to decide. Carnegie, meanwhile, left for Europe. When the union refused the terms, Frick locked the workers out, and they in turn refused to let new employees in. Frick brought in Pinkerton detectives to break the strike, and in the ensuing violence a dozen workers were killed. Frick himself was almost assassinated. Finally, federal troops were sent in to halt the violence and, not incidentally, to break the strike.

The next year, at the height of the 1893 depression, George Pullman began lowering the wages of his workers at the Pullman Palace Car Company. Eugene V. Debs, who headed the American Railway Union, called a strike in 1894. Debs asked the AF of L to join the strike, but Gompers refused to commit the entire union to what he believed to be an untimely confrontation. The strike by the American Railway Union succeeded in paralyzing railroad transportation. Finally, President Grover Cleveland, backed by a court-ordered injunction issued under the authority of the Sherman Antitrust Act, sent federal troops to end the strike. The Sherman Antitrust Act, designed to curb the monopolistic practices of big business, had become a tool of big business to thwart collective bargaining by labor. By 1900 the union movement appeared to be on the brink of collapse, and some laborers, including Debs, were advocating more radical, if not revolutionary, action.

Among the most militant of the radical groups was the International Workers of the World, or "Wobblies." Organized in 1905, this group sought the overthrow of the capitalist system and condoned the use of violence. Violence became the trademark of the Western Confederation of Miners, headed by "Big Bill" Hayward. Daniel De Leon, a leader in the Socialist Labor Party, sought government ownership and operation of industry by revolutionary and violent means, if necessary, while Eugene V. Debs pursued socialism through political action in the Socialist Party of America. Perhaps the only point of agreement among the more radical labor groups was that the AF of L should be done away with as a tool of the capitalist. Meanwhile, the National Association of Manufacturers, organized in 1895, agreed that all unions should be eliminated, the AF of L in particular.

Business fought unions with considerable success through court action. In 1908, the Supreme Court ruled in the Danbury Hatters' Case that a secondary boycott was a conspiracy in restraint of trade. Also that year Samuel Gompers was sentenced to prison for defying a court-ordered injunction against the AF of L to desist from an advertising campaign against Buck Stove and Range Company, and to stop blacklisting its products. However, Gompers was never forced to serve his term. Perhaps the most effective method of resisting unionism was to undermine the appeal of unions by offering to labor special company benefits. Company-sponsored health- and accident-insurance plans, retirement programs, and workmen's-compensation programs began to appear. The corporations became aware of public and employee relations and personnel management. The change in employer-employee relations was slow and inauspicious, but in the long run it alleviated the economic discontent of industrial labor. More important, it began to make the impersonal world of machines and manufacturing more humane.

In the short run organized labor fared badly. Between 1900 and 1914 union membership declined. In the interim, the pay for skilled workers increased slightly but the pay for nonskilled labor decreased. State and national woman- and child-labor legislation brought some social improvement. Nonetheless, the AF of L became an enduring and ultimately successful labor organization, and by 1914 organized labor had experience, leadership, and, more important, a vast new labor force from which to recruit.

THE FARM MOVEMENT

It was little consolation to the laborer that the farm movement fared less well. There were 2.6 million farms in 1870 and 6.3 million in 1910. There were good and bad years for farm profits during these forty years, but the bad far outnumbered the good. Over the long term farm prices fell and farm operating costs rose. The number of farmers more than doubled, and total farm production almost quadrupled, but total farm income remained relatively unchanged. The farm problem derived in part from simple overproduction. The dimensions of the farm problem may be appreciated by noting that the 10-million-bale crop of 1894 marketed for fewer dollars than the 4-million-bale crop of 1870; the 1894 wheat crop of 541 million bushels sold for little more than the 1876 crop of 210 million bushels; and the 1895 corn crop, three times the 1876 crop size, brought the same price. To be sure, real farm income did increase as the value of the dollar increased, but farmers never enjoyed prosperity and generally became mired in indebtedness and tenancy. By 1910 farm income accounted for less than one fourth of the total national income, even though half of the American people derived their livelihood from agriculture.[5]

TABLE 12.2

Gross Farm Output, 1870–1900
(in current and real values).

YEAR	CURRENT $ (MILLIONS)	1910–1914 $ (MILLIONS)
1900	4,298	6,409
1890	3,397	4,990
1880	3,263	4,129
1870	2,774	2,694

Note: The real value of total farm product increased far more rapidly than did the dollar value of the product after approximately 1873. Note that in 1870 the inflated dollar receipts have less real value. Farm dollar income could have theorectically remained stable after 1870 while real farm income would increase.

Source: Bureau of the Census, *Historical Statistics of the United States*, Series K 240–250, p. 482.

The farm movement, as did the labor movement, had social as well as economic implications. Farming in the nineteenth century was as much a way of life as it was a business, and the mystique of the ''agrarian ideal'' was equally as influential as the profit motive. Ultimately, the profit motive overrode other considerations, for the story of American agricultural history is predominantly the story of the commercialization of agriculture, and of how relatively fewer and fewer farmers could provide the food and clothing for an ever expanding population. Commercial agriculture was nothing new in America; it was simply that subsistence and marginal farm operations became less feasible. Mechanization was something new in the nineteenth century, although it was not until after World War II that all sectors of the agricultural economy became mechanized. The farm movement, which is usually identified with the Grange, Alliance, and Populist organizations, in fact had dual motivations: one, purely commercial, was concerned with profits and prices; the other, essentially esthetic, was concerned with farming as a way of life and with social order and stability.

The farm protest was in one sense, as John D. Hicks argued, an effort to save "agricultural America from the devouring jaws of industrial America."[6] Its values were those of the older, individualistic, atomistic, and agrarian America that were becoming increasingly out of harmony with the values of modern, urban-industrial society. Yet these agrarian ideals were based intrinsically on free-enterprise capitalism. Late-nineteenth-century farmers generally accepted the same philosophy of free enterprise that a Carnegie, Rockefeller, or Duke did. They believed that a person earned according to his ability and production. They believed that hard work, thrift, and a God-fearing life would be rewarded. Farmers worked harder, planted more acreage, produced larger crops, earned increasingly smaller profits, and often accumulated greater debts. This did not mean that in the farmers' mind free enterprise was a false doctrine, but rather that through some unfair practices—trusts, conspiracies, or monopolies—each person was not receiving his proportionate earnings. The farm movement was essen-

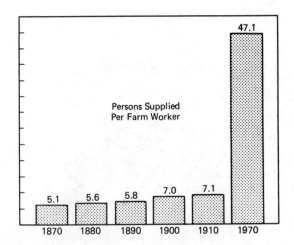

FIGURE 12.2 Output per farm worker 1870–1910.

Source: Bureau of the Census, *Historical Statistics of the United States*, Series K 407–413, p. 498.

tially a conservative movement in that it sought to make free enterprise work as it was supposed to work. It was reactionary to the extent that farmers believed that the only true producers were farmers, and that the rural life was in fact more virtuous, wholesome, and democratic.

The Grange

The National Grange of the Patrons of Husbandry, organized in 1867 by Oliver Hudson Kelley and some associates in the Bureau of Agriculture, began as a social and educational organization but soon spilled over into economic and political issues. Farmers in the Midwest were the first to take up the Grange banner, and by 1873 the organization had spread into almost every state of the Union. Midwestern Grangers were convinced that their "farm problem" derived heavily from the high freight charges of railroads. They believed that railroads, by charging arbitrary and monopolistic rates, obtained larger profits from agriculture than farmers did. Southern Grangers were less concerned about railroad freight charges, for throughout the nineteenth century most of them enjoyed the competitive rates charged by steamboats. But southern farmers, as did farmers everywhere, desired lower tariffs, easier farm credit, more money in circulation, and controls on land speculators. They believed that discriminatory legislation and trade practices deprived farmers of fair returns on their labor.

    Beginning in the Midwest, Grange organizations began to advocate legisla-

OLIVER HUDSON KELLEY *(1826–1913)*
Founded National Grange
Courtesy National Grange.

tion to regulate the weighing and grading of staple commodities and to impose fair and uniform railroad freight rates and grain-elevator charges. Their rationale was that rates imposed by railroads were monopolistic and arbitrary, and that government regulation did not mean intervention in the economy but merely restored competition and sustained free enterprise. Railroads contested the legality of such laws, arguing that they impaired rights in private property and were unconstitutional. In 1876 the Supreme Court upheld the constitutionality of state legislation in a series of cases, the most important of which was *Munn* v. *Illinois* (1877). Beginning in 1886, however, in *Wabash, St. Louis and Pacific* v. *Illinois* the Supreme Court began overturning Grange legislation on the grounds that such state legislation affected the regulation of interstate commerce, and so interfered with the constitutional grant to Congress of exclusive power over interstate commerce.[7] The new court position belatedly recognized that commerce and transportation were integral parts of the national economic order, and gave notice that the federal government could no longer abstain from exercising authority. The railroads, as well as farmers and small businessmen, began to seek national, as opposed to state, regulation, but from widely different motives. Railroads, as did corporate structures generally, regarded state legislation as inherently restrictive of national commerce and trade, but they also regarded federal legislation as a means of eliminating unprofitable and burdensome competition among themselves. Farm interests believed that federal legislation might more fully achieve "fair returns" and higher farm profits.

The result was congressional passage of the Interstate Commerce Act of 1887. This act prohibited rebates, pools, drawbacks, and long- and short-haul discrimination. Rebates and drawbacks had become burdensome to the railroads themselves. Farmers had particularly protested the railroad's practice of charging higher freight rates on short hauls than on long hauls, although railroads justified the apparent inequity on the basis that per-unit costs were in fact often higher for short runs than for long runs. The requirement that railroads publish their rates did discourage flagrant discrimination and inequities. The law established a five-person Interstate Commerce Commission authorized to review rates to see if they were fair and reasonable, but the commission could seek remedy only through the courts. As a result of procedural delays, rules of evidence, and the judiciary's favorable treatment of railroads, the law had little effect before 1900.

The Farmers' Alliance

By 1887, the Grangers had been all but supplanted by the Farmers' Alliances, which had more of a business orientation and less of a social educational orientation. The Southern Farmers' Alliance originated in Lampasas County, Texas in 1872 and by 1880 had replaced the Grange as the largest Texas farm organization. It was originally named the Texas Farmers' Alliance.[8] The Texas Alliance created the largest consumer and producer cooperative program then in existence, and even entered into the manufacture of farm equipment. Under-capitalized and overextended, the great Texas cooperative crashed in 1891, but the Southern Farmers' Alliance, which had grown beyond the boundaries of Texas, continued to expand under the dynamic leadership of Charles W. Macune. In 1887 Macune met with leaders of the Louisiana Farmers' Union and in January the two organizations merged to become the National Farmers' Alliance and Cooperative Union of America, better known as the Southern Farmers' Alliance. The Alliance soon absorbed the Arkansas Agricultural Wheel and the South Carolina Brothers of Freedom and developed affiliations throughout the South and in the Midwest. Under the leadership of Milton George, a Chicago newspaper publisher, an independent National Farmers' Alliance (the Northern Alliance) was organized in 1880. It did not acquire the membership or aggressive leadership of the Southern Alliance, although in most respects its objectives were identical, as were those of the Negro Alliance, organized in Houston, Texas in 1886.

The Alliances advocated cooperatives, the use of paper money as legal tender, the unlimited coinage of silver, government control or ownership of the railroads and telegraph systems, lower tariffs, a graduated income tax, the Australian or secret ballot, the direct primary (which eliminated the convention system of nominating party candidates), the direct election of United States senators, and expanded public education. Macune particularly promoted the idea of a federal subtreasury system, which he believed would eliminate the most burdensome farm problems, including inadequate and expensive credit, speculation and irregular marketing, currency contraction, and crop storage. The plan proposed to establish federal commodity banks in every region of the country. These banks would lend farmers up to 80 percent of the value of their crop at 1 percent interest. The loans would be in the form of bills that would circulate as legal tender, a practice that would in effect underwrite paper money with commodities instead of specie. The farmer could store or market his crop at his discretion, thereby providing orderly marketing and avoiding seasonal gluts that depressed prices. Although the plan failed to receive serious legislation attention, it helped define farm problems and was at least in part a theoretical precedent for the Federal Reserve System and the Commodity Credit Corporation of later days.

The Populists

Although the Northern and Southern Alliances failed to merge, they did develop a common list of objectives. These objectives, usually styled the Ocala Demands, were formulated in 1891 and became the platform of a more militant farm movement—the People's Party of America, or the Populists. The Populists sprang from the Farmers' Alliances almost spontaneously in 1891. They advocated immediate political action to achieve farmers' goals. The deepening depression (cotton at five cents per pound and wheat at fifty cents per bushel) promoted a radical fervor among Populists and a reform press and rhetoric that appeared threatening to the established political order. Populists advocated government ownership and operation of the railroad, telegraph, and telephone systems and public ownership or control of utilities. They sought electoral reforms, which they believed would restore "rule to the people," and a solution by the people of "the great questions of finance and commerce." Currency contraction, the crop lien, and the furnishing merchant, coupled with the conservatism of the major political parties, led farmers to Populism. The Populist revolt was grounded in the cooperative crusade of the Alliance, which imported a sense of self-worth and organic democracy. Populism was deep-rooted only in areas where the cooperative movement was strong. Elsewhere, as in Nebraska, Populism was but a shadow movement whose members failed to accept the essential commitment to the cooperative movement and to the greenback monetary ideas that characterized true Populists.

The Populist Party nominated James B. Weaver for president in 1892, and was sufficiently encouraged by the election returns to develop substantive organizations on the state level. Between 1892 and 1896 Populists ran for state and federal offices in most states of the South and West and succeeded in electing one governor, one U.S. senator, and a number of U.S. congressmen. The Populists narrowly failed to sweep several states with "fusion" tickets in hotly contested, disputed, and often violent elections.

In 1896 the Populist nominating convention, narrowly dominated by free-silver "shadow" Populists, with great reluctance backed William Jennings Bryan, the presidential nominee of the Democratic Party. Bryan Democrats supported free silver, the direct election of senators, the graduated income tax, and further regulation of railroads. The elections marked the collapse of the Populist Party.[9] The demise of Populism remains a hotly debated phenomenon. There is reason to believe that although Bryan undermined Populism, he nonetheless was responsible for directing rural discontent into more politically effective channels.

The farm movements, including the Populists, failed to achieve any significant or permanent relief for the plight of farmers. Farm prices did recover after 1898 and surged upwards with the outbreak of World War I. Farmers and youths continued to flock to the cities for better opportunities. The farm movements had, however, created a new social consciousness and, indeed, a better political climate for effective reform. There had been some positive accomplishments, which may in part be attributed to agrarian reform. Most states had developed railroad and utility commissions and ballot reforms. Federal legislation beneficial to agriculture included not only the Interstate Commerce Act but also the Hatch Act of 1886, which created Agricultural Experiment Stations and rejuvenated the faltering system of land-grant colleges established by the Morrill Act. Between 1900 and 1914, the Interstate Commerce Act was strengthened and the Federal Highways Act, the Federal Reserve System, the Smith-Lever and

Smith-Hughes acts, (which created agricultural-extension and vocational agricultural-training programs, respectively), and the lower Underwood-Simmons Tariff all alleviated farm distress.

Subsequently, farmers and laborers flourished for a brief time (especially between 1917 and 1919) as a result of the soaring farm prices and escalating wages that accompanied the advent of war in Europe. Indeed, Henry Ford captured the headlines from the announcement of war in Europe by voluntarily implementing a remarkable wage increase from $2 to $5 per day at his Ford Motor Plant. This was not a case of benevolence, but one of business. Nothing denoted the end of the old age and the beginning of a new one as much as the advent of the automobile. By 1920 America had emerged as an urban-industrial society, a world power, a creditor nation, and a country with still unsolved farm and labor problems and complex new problems involving urban growth, suburban sprawl, slums, housing, immigration, expanded public services, and land use.

Notes

[1] For a study in cultural perspectives of the labor movement, see Herbert Gutman, *Work, Culture and Society in Industrializing America* (New York: Knopf, 1975).

[2] A good survey of the labor union movement is Henry Pelling, *American Labor* (Chicago: University of Chicago Press, 1960).

[3] See Terrence V. Powderly, *The Path I Trod* (New York: Columbia University Press, 1940).

[4] See Philip Taft, *The AF of L in the Time of Gompers* (New York: Harper & Row, 1957).

[5] Vernon Carstensen, ed., *Farmer Discontent, 1865–1900* (New York: John Wiley, 1974), p. 13.

[6] John D. Hicks, *The Populist Revolt* (Lincoln, Nebr.: University of Nebraska Press, 1959), p. 237.

[7] For an excellent discussion of the origin of the Granger Laws, which had some non-Grange beginnings, see George H. Miller, "Origins of the Iowa Granger Law," *Mississippi Valley Historical Review*, 40 (March 1954), 657–80.

[8] See Ralph A. Smith, "The Farmers' Alliance in Texas, 1870–1900," *Southwestern Historical Quarterly*, 48 (January 1945), 346–69; and Robert C. McMath, Jr., *Populist Vanguard: A History of the Southern Farmers' Alliance* (Chapel Hill, N.C.: University of North Carolina Press, 1975).

[9] The literature on the Alliance and Populist movements is extensive. For references, see Henry C. Dethloff, ed., *A List of References for the History of the Farmers' Alliance and the Populist Party* (Davis, Calif.: Agricultural History Center, University of California–Davis, 1973). The best study of the Alliance-Populist movement is Lawrence Goodwyn, *Democratic Promise: The Populist Movement in America* (New York: Oxford University Press, 1976).

SUGGESTED READINGS

Bogue, Allan G., *Money At Interest: The Farm Mortgage on the Middle Border*. Ithaca, N.Y.: Cornell University Press, 1955.

BRUCE, ROBERT, *1877: Year of Violence*. (Indianapolis: Bobbs-Merrill, 1959).

FITE, GILBERT, *The Farmer's Frontier, 1865–1900*. (New York: Holt, Rinehart & Winston, 1966.

GOODWYN, LAWRENCE, *Democratic Promise: The Populist Movement in America*. New York, Oxford University Press, 1976.

GROB, GERALD, *Workers and Utopia*. Evanston, Ill.: Northwestern University, 196:.

GUTMAN, HERBERT, *Work Culture and Society in Industrializing America*. New York: Knopf, 1975.

MALIN, JAMES C., *Winter Wheat in the Golden Belt of Kansas*. Lawrence, Kans.: University of Kansas Press, 1944.

MANDEL, BERNARD, *Samuel Gompers: A Biography*. Yellow Springs, Ohio: Antioch Press, 1963.

POLLACK, NORMAN, *The Populist Response to Industrial America*. Cambridge, Mass.: Harvard University Press, 1962.

POWDERLY, TERRENCE V., *The Path I Trod*. New York: Columbia University Press, 1940.

SHANNON, FRED, *The Farmer's Last Frontier: Agriculture, 1860–1897* New York: Farrar & Rinehart, 1945.

TAFT, PHILIP, *The AF of L in the Time of Gompers*. New York: Harper & Row, 1957.

THERNSTROM, STEPHEN, *Poverty and Progress: Social Mobility in a Nineteenth-Century City*. Cambridge, Mass.: Harvard University Press, 1964.

THE CITY
IN AMERICA

chapter XIII

The America that was once a wilderness became a city. The growth of the city was both physical and ideological. In the beginning America's cities were in Europe, and many Americans, such as Thomas Jefferson, preferred that they remain there. "The mobs of great cities," wrote Jefferson in 1781, "add just so much to the support of pure government, as sores do to the strength of the human body. . . . let our workshops remain in Europe." Neither the workshops nor the cities remained in Europe. By 1920 most Americans lived in cities and the national economy had effectively become a metropolitan economy wherein virtually all enterprise was tied to urban markets, urban manufactures, or urban finances. The rapid spread of urban life is the dominant development in American history over the past century. An understanding of the phenomenon of urban growth in America requires some review of broad historical precepts about the city.

URBAN DEVELOPMENT

Americans understandably compare cities to industrialization, but urbanization and industrialization are distinctly different historical processes. In America, however, unlike in Europe and Asia, industrialization and urbanization were superimposed. The agricultural revolution and the domestication of animals made possible the rise of the city in ancient times, perhaps as early as 7,000 B.C. The city, according to Lewis Mumford, was largely woman's creation, for it provided the collective nest for the care and nurture of the young. As a container, it provided security and tenure for human life. It was a granary, bank, arsenal, library, store, moat, aqueduct, drain, and sewer. By 3,000 B.C. the city had become the dynamic structure in human organization. It made possible the mobilization of manpower, expanded communication and transportation facilities, promoted an outburst of invention and a rise in agricultural productivity, and produced ''an enormous expansion of human capabilities in every direction.''[1] Early cities organized existing life forms into a new state of dynamic tension and interaction.

The city imposed a novel economic order on humans. The institution of private property was an innovation of urban life, in contrast with the communal, tribal concept of possession or use common to primitive, nomadic, hunter-gatherers. The Code of Hammurabi of 1700 B.C., for example, details laws concerning transfer and rights of property. The city established divisions of labor and introduced the idea of the specialization of labor. Specialization, division, compulsion, and depersonalization produced inner and previously unknown tensions in human society. In modern times, industrialization has aggravated the negative influences of the city, and the generally better life made possible by the city has begun to be offset by the rapid deterioration of the human environment.

The context and structure of the traditional city has changed under the impact of technological revolutions. The situation may not be as dire as Mumford projects it, but his observations are startling:

> We live, in fact, in an exploding universe of mechanical and electronic invention, whose parts are moving at a rapid pace ever further and further away from their human center, and from any rational, autonomous human purposes. This technological explosion has produced a similar explosion of the city itself: the city has burst open and scattered its complex organs and organization over the entire landscape. . . . we are witnessing a sort of devolution of urban power into a state of randomness and unpredictability. In short, our civilization is running out of control, overwhelmed by its own resources and opportunities, as well as by its superabundant fecundity.[2]

The dilemma is perhaps best illustrated by Ray Ginger's observation that the automobile that made the modern city possible has become self-defeating: ''With so many cars you can't move. And you can't stop moving because you can't park your car.''[3]

The city can no longer be distinguished from society. Ours is an urban society bound together by rapid transportation and communication and stressing in every economic endeavor the specialization of labor, mass production and consumption, mechanization, and standardization. In sum, the traditional concept of city itself has changed. America has become one big city.

The process has been twofold. In the nineteenth century and the first half of the twentieth century the growth of cities derived from natural population increase, net migration, and enlargement of boundaries. Natural population increase was the least significant of these factors. High mortality rates and low birth rates were characteristic of American cities until recent years. Migration, mostly from the farm, accounted for swelling urban populations, but foreign immigration brought an estimated 28 million newcomers to American cities between 1860 and 1920. Domestic population increases maintained the proportion of foreign-born residents at about 14 percent of the total population, a ratio that has declined since World War II with the advent of stringent immigration quotas. Until 1896, most immigrants to the United States came from England, Ireland, and Germany. The "New Immigration" after 1896 brought in more immigrants from southern and eastern Europe—Italy, Austria-Hungary, Poland, and Russia. The immigrant provided a source of cheap, largely unskilled labor, tended to settle in the city in ghettos or enclaves, and, contrary to myth, failed to assimilate rapidly into the new society.

Between 1870 and 1970 the population of the United States increased from 40 million to 203 million. Population density increased from 13.4 to 57.5 people per square mile. In 1840 only one twelfth of the American people lived in cities of 8,000 or more. By 1860 city dwellers constituted one sixth of the total population, by 1900 one third, and by 1920 one half. The decennial rate of increase of urban population averaged 40 percent between 1870 and 1910, with a high of 56.6 percent in the decade 1880–1890. After 1910 the rate of increase slowed to an average of about 20 percent, with a low of 7.9 percent in the depression decade 1930–1940.

Table 13.1 illustrates the growth of the nation's 100 largest cities. Raw data depicting city growth is deceptive, particularly for the years since 1920.

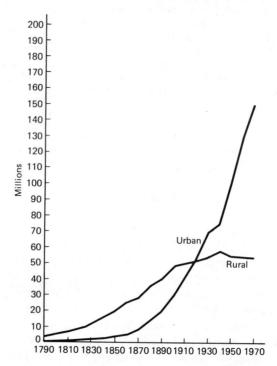

FIGURE 13.1 U.S. population in urban and rural areas, 1790–1970.

Source: U.S. Bureau of the Census, *Bicentennial Statistics* Reprinted from Pocket Data Book, USA 1976.

Throughout the twentieth century, urban growth has been more rapid outside the central city than within it. The city has literally spilled over the entire landscape. Improved modes of transportation, especially the automobile, have speeded the growth of the population adjacent to cities at a far greater pace than the population within cities. The suburbs now house the greater part of the urban population and increasingly account for larger shares of commercial and manufacturing enterprise.[4]

The flight to the suburbs has created enormous new transportation and inner-city problems. The abandonment of the central city by more affluent segments of society has left behind a high incidence of poverty, crime, and physical decay. Correspondingly, while the costs of urban welfare, education, police, and public services have risen, the revenue base of the city has declined. In turn, some sociologists argue that although suburbanites enjoy relatively high levels of food, clothing and shelter, they have lost the vibrant, cultural contact with the traditional city. The suburbs, it is alleged, have become the Peyton Places and Happy Valleys of America—places where people live in sheer, hopeless boredom characterized by a continual round of golf, bridge, sex, and commuting. Others argue that on the contrary, the suburbs reflect a higher level of living and have in fact reinforced the traditional institutions of family and community. In any event, the city is no longer what it once was. This urban transformation is partially acknowledged by the broader census delineation of the metropolis and the megalopolis.

The metropolis includes the older central city and the densely populated areas adjacent to it. The Bureau of the Census has identified 265 Standard Metropolitan Statistical Areas in the United States. The top 20 SMSAs appear in Table 13.2

Approximately one third of the American population lives in the 20 largest metropolitan areas. Another third lives within the remaining 245 metropolitan areas, and the remaining one third lives in nonmetropolitan areas. The suburbs have grown at a rate of 25 percent in each decade since World War II, whereas the central city and nonmetropolitan areas have grown at little more than 7 percent, or less than half the rate of total population increase. Furthermore, actual central-city growth may be even less than 7 percent, in that much of this figure can be accounted for by the expansion of city boundaries.

Contiguous metropolitan areas constitute a megalopolis, or "super-city." Under this definition the northeastern United States, the Ohio Valley, the Great Lakes area, the Florida coasts, the central Gulf Coast, California, and the Seattle area are megalopolises. Reversing the nineteenth-century trend, populations are now increasing more rapidly along the coastal regions than in the interior. In addition, migration currently appears to be shifting away from the traditional south-north, east-west axis to a north-south, north-southwest axis.

Perhaps a more realistic definition of "city" should disregard population density and concentrate instead on a simple time continuum. An urban environ-

TABLE 13.1

How the Cities Grew.

RANK	CITIES	1970	1960	1950	1900	1850	1790
1	New York, N.Y.	7,895,563	7,781,984	7,891,957	3,437,202	696,115	49,401
	Bronx	1,471,701	1,424,815	1,451,277	200,507	8,032	1,781
	Brooklyn	2,602,012	2,627,319	2,738,175	1,168,582	138,882	4,495
	Manhattan	1,539,233	1,698,281	1,960,101	1,850,093	515,547	33,131
	Queens	1,986,473	1,809,578	1,550,849	152,999	18,593	6,159
	Richmond	295,443	221,991	191,555	67,021	15,061	3,835
2	Chicago, Ill.	3,368,357	3,550,404	3,620,962	1,698,575	29,963	—
3	Los Angeles, Calif.	2,809,813	2,479,015	1,970,358	102,479	1,610	—
4	Phila., Pa.	1,949,996	2,002,512	2,071,605	1,293,697	121,376	28,522
5	Detroit, Mich.	1,513,601	1,670,144	1,849,568	285,704	21,019	—
6	Houston, Tex.	1,232,802	938,219	596,163	44,633	2,396	—
7	Baltimore, Md.	905,787	939,024	949,708	508,957	169,054	13,503
8	Dallas, Tex.	844,401	679,684	434,462	42,638	—	—
9	Washington, D.C.	756,510	763,956	802,178	278,718	40,001	—
10	Cleveland, Ohio	750,879	876,050	914,808	381,768	17,034	—
11	Indianapolis, Ind.	746,302	476,258	427,173	169,164	8,091	—
12	Milwaukee, Wis.	717,372	741,324	637,392	285,315	20,061	—
13	San Francisco, Calif.	715,674	740,316	775,357	342,782	34,776	—
14	San Diego, Calif.	697,027	573,224	334,387	17,700	—	—
15	San Antonio, Tex.	654,153	587,718	408,442	53,321	3,488	—
16	Boston, Mass.	641,071	697,197	801,444	560,692	136,881	18,320
17	Memphis, Tenn.	623,530	497,524	396,000	102,320	8,841	—
18	St. Louis, Mo.	622,236	750,026	856,796	575,238	77,860	—
19	New Orleans, La.	593,471	627,525	570,445	287,104	116,375	—
20	Phoenix, Ariz.	581,562	439,170	106,818	5,544	—	—
21	Columbus, Ohio	540,025	471,316	375,901	125,560	17,882	—
22	Seattle, Wash.	530,831	557,087	467,591	80,671	—	—
23	Jacksonville, Fla.	528,865	201,030	204,517	28,429	1,045	—
24	Pittsburgh, Pa.	520,117	604,332	676,806	321,616	46,601	—
25	Denver, Colo.	514,678	493,887	415,786	133,859	—	—

TABLE 13.1 (cont.)

RANK	CITIES	1970	1960	1950	1900	1850	1790
26	Kansas City, Mo.	507,330	475,539	456,622	163,752	—	—
27	Atlanta, Ga.	497,421	487,455	331,314	89,872	2,572	—
28	Buffalo, N.Y.	462,768	532,759	580,132	352,387	42,261	—
29	Cincinnati, Ohio	451,455	502,550	503,998	325,902	115,435	—
30	Nashville, Tenn.	447,877	170,874	174,307	80,865	10,165	—
31	San Jose, Calif.	446,537	204,196	95,280	21,500	—	—
32	Minneapolis, Minn.	434,400	482,872	521,718	202,718	—	—
33	Fort Worth, Tex.	393,476	356,263	278,778	26,688	—	—
34	Toledo, Ohio	383,105	318,003	303,616	131,822	3,829	—
35	Newark, N.J.	381,930	405,220	438,776	246,070	38,894	—
36	Portland, Oreg.	379,967	372,676	373,628	90,426	—	—
37	Oklahoma City, Okla.	368,377	324,253	243,504	10,037	—	—
38	Louisville, Ky.	361,706	390,639	369,129	204,731	43,194	200
39	Oakland, Calif.	361,561	367,548	384,575	66,960	—	—
40	Long Beach, Calif.	358,879	344,168	250,767	2,252	—	—
41	Omaha, Nebr.	346,929	301,598	251,117	102,555	—	—
42	Miami, Fla.	334,859	291,688	249,276	1,681	—	—
43	Tulsa, Okla.	330,350	261,685	182,740	1,390	—	—
44	Honolulu, Hawaii	324,871	294,194	248,034	39,306	—	—
45	El Paso, Tex.	322,261	276,687	130,485	15,906	—	—
46	St. Paul, Minn.	309,714	313,411	311,349	163,065	1,112	—
47	Norfolk, Va.	307,951	304,869	213,513	46,624	14,326	2,959
48	Birmingham, Ala.	300,910	340,887	326,037	38,415	—	—
49	Rochester, N.Y.	296,233	318,611	332,488	162,608	36,403	—
50	Tampa, Fla.	277,753	274,970	124,681	15,839	—	—
51	Wichita, Kans.	276,554	254,698	168,279	24,671	—	—
52	Akron, Ohio	275,425	290,351	274,605	42,728	3,266	—
53	Tucson, Ariz.	262,933	212,892	45,454	7,531	—	—
54	Jersey City, N.J.	260,350	276,101	299,017	206,433	6,858	—
55	Sacramento, Calif.	257,105	191,667	137,572	29,282	6,820	—
56	Austin, Tex.	251,808	186,545	132,459	22,258	629	—

TABLE 13.1 (cont.)

RANK	CITIES	1970	1960	1950	1900	1850	1790
57	Richmond, Va.	249,431	219,958	230,310	85,050	27,570	3,761
58	Albuquerque, N. Mex.	243,751	201,189	96,815	6,238	—	—
59	Dayton, Ohio	242,917	262,332	243,872	85,333	10,977	—
60	Charlotte, N.C.	241,178	201,564	134,042	18,091	1,065	—
61	St. Petersburg, Fla.	216,159	181,298	96,738	1,575	—	—
62	Corpus Christi, Tex.	204,525	167,690	108,287	4,703	—	—
63	Yonkers, N.Y.	204,297	190,634	152,798	47,931	—	—
64	Des Moines, Iowa	201,404	208,982	177,965	62,139	—	—
65	Grand Rapids, Mich.	197,649	177,313	176,515	87,565	2,686	—
66	Syracuse, N.Y.	197,297	216,038	220,583	103,374	22,271	—
67	Flint, Mich.	193,317	196,940	163,143	13,103	—	—
68	Mobile, Ala.	190,026	194,856	129,009	38,469	20,515	—
69	Shreveport, La.	182,064	164,372	127,206	16,013	1,728	—
70	Warren, Mich.	179,260	89,246	727	350	—	—
71	Providence, R.I.	179,116	207,498	248,674	175,597	41,513	6,380
72	Fort Wayne, Ind.	178,021	161,776	133,607	45,115	4,282	—
73	Worcester, Mass.	176,572	186,587	203,486	118,421	17,049	2,095
74	Salt Lake City, Utah	175,885	189,454	182,121	53,531	—	—
75	Gary, Ind.	175,415	178,320	133,911	—	—	—
76	Knoxville, Tenn.	174,587	111,827	124,769	32,637	2,076	—
77	Virginia Beach, Va.	172,106	8,091	5,390	—	—	—
78	Madison, Wis.	171,769	126,706	96,056	19,164	1,525	—
79	Spokane, Wash.	170,516	181,608	161,721	36,848	—	—
80	Kansas City, Kan.	168,213	121,901	129,553	51,418	—	—
81	Anaheim, Calif.	166,408	104,184	14,558	1,456	—	—
82	Fresno, Calif.	165,972	133,929	91,669	12,470	—	—
83	Baton Rouge, La.	165,921	152,419	125,629	11,269	3,905	—
84	Springfield, Mass.	163,905	174,463	162,399	62,059	11,766	1,574
85	Hartford, Conn.	158,017	162,178	177,397	72,850	13,555	2,683
86	Bridgeport, Conn.	156,542	156,748	158,709	70,996	6,080	—
87	Santa Ana, Calif.	155,762	100,350	45,533	4,933	—	—
88	Columbus, Ga.	155,028	116,779	79,611	17,614	5,942	—
89	Tacoma, Wash.	154,407	147,979	143,673	37,714	—	—
90	Jackson, Miss.	153,968	144,422	98,271	7,816	1,881	—

RANK	CITIES	1970	1960	1950	1900	1850	1790
91	Lincoln, Nebr.	149,518	128,521	93,884	40,159	—	—
92	Lubbock, Tex.	149,101	128,691	71,747	—	—	—
93	Rockford, Ill.	147,370	126,706	92,927	31,051	—	—
94	Paterson, N.J.	144,824	143,663	139,336	105,171	11,334	—
95	Greensboro, N.C.	144,076	119,574	74,389	10,035	—	—
96	Youngstown, Ohio	140,909	166,689	168,330	44,885	—	—
97	Riverside, Calif.	140,089	84,332	46,764	7,973	—	—
98	Fort Lauderdale, Fla.	139,590	83,648	36,328	—	—	—
99	Huntsville, Ala.	139,282	72,365	16,437	8,068	2,863	—
100	Evansville, Ind.	138,764	141,543	128,636	59,007	3,235	—

Source: Bureau of the Census.

202 The City in America

TABLE 13.2

The Top Twenty Standard Metropolitan Statistical
Areas in the United States (1974).

1	New York, N.Y.–N.J.
2	Los Angeles–Long Beach, Calif.
3	Chicago, Ill.
4	Philadelphia, Pa.–N.J.
5	Detroit, Mich.
6	San Francisco–Oakland, Calif.
7	Washington, D.C.–Md.–Va.
8	Boston, Mass.
9	Nassau–Suffolk, N.Y.
10	St. Louis, Mo.–Ill
11	Pittsburgh, Pa.
12	Dallas–Fort Worth, Texas
13	Baltimore, Md.
14	Cleveland, Ohio
15	Newark, N.J.
16	Houston, Texas
17	Minneapolis–St. Paul, Minn.–Wis
18	Atlanta, Ga
19	Seattle–Everett, Wash.
20	Anaheim–Santa Ana–Garden Grove, Calif.

Source: Bureau of the Census.

ment certainly exists when communications between any two points or individuals has little or no physical or geographical impediment. In this sense whoever has a telephone, television, or radio has instant communication. The airplane and automobile have also served, albeit imperfectly, to overcome traditional barriers of space and time. The modern press and satellite communication make newsworthy items equally accessible to the hinterlands and the suburbs. The city as a geographical entity no longer retains an advantage in rapid communication. Urban transportation between terminals is increasingly efficient in terms of time, but delays between the terminal and central-city destinations become greater as terminals move to outlying areas. The costs of interurban transportation resulting from fuel consumption, expropriation of land, and construction are rising relatively faster than the increasing utility of the transportation medium. Urban problems involving transportation, housing, land use, taxation, and public services are becoming more acute. Cities, nonetheless, remain the most efficient means of economic and social organization.

The International City Managers' Association has broadly classified cities by function, as follows:

Manufacturing: 50 percent or more of the aggregate employment is in manufacturing, and less than 30 percent is in retail trade.

Industrial: 50 percent or more of the aggregate work force is in manufacturing, and over 30 percent is in retail trade.

Diversified-retailing: employment is greater in retailing than in manufacturing, but manufacturing accounts for at least 20 percent of the total.

Retailing: retail employment is greater than manufacturing or any other component of the aggregate work force, and manufacturing is less than 20 percent.

Dormitory: aggregate employment is less than 67 percent of the resident labor force.

The ICMA has also identified a small number of cities whose primary endeavor is wholesaling, mining, transportation, the resort trade, government administration, the armed forces, professional service, hospitals, education, or social service. Urban populations are by necessity consumer-oriented. The greater the degree of specialization of labor is, the more dependent the individual is upon others to satisfy his wants and needs. The taxi driver, policeman, banker, insurance broker, retailer, garbage collector, and librarian are specialists who perform services that others cannot or will not perform but that are vital to survival. The "marketplace" determines, through wages and prices, the value of each service performed.[5]

In its size and complexity the urban marketplace may be less efficient than the town or country marketplace. The ratio of work accomplished in the city to the energy or product ultimately supplied by the city appears enormous. But economic development and growth are not related solely to efficiency. According to one authority, "The conditions that promote development and the conditions that promote efficient production and distribution of already existing goods and services are not only different, in most ways they are diametrically opposed."[6] Greater efficiency often derives from a rigid stratification of effort—one building type, one automobile, one retail outlet, one large loan instead of thousands of small ones, and the elimination of duplication and competition—but such effort also generates stagnation and the curtailment of growth and development. Perhaps one of the inherent characteristics of cities is that in their environment of flux and change new problems constantly emerge, and where the problems are solved growth occurs. When there is no solution there is stagnation. The problem of the cities, then, may not be one of progress, but the failure to respond to progress. It is at that point that the city becomes stagnant.[7] The paradox is that economic inefficiency is necessary for growth and development. The pundit might observe that if problems are what makes the city grow, America can expect an awesome urban growth in years ahead, for we have ample problems to solve.

CASE STUDIES OF PROMINENT AMERICAN CITIES

In attempting to classify cities in America, it is good to remember that each city is in fact unique: it has a history, character, economic structure, architecture, and layout that may be similar to but is never identical with another. Each city is a unique case in historical and cultural development. A brief "case study" of prominent American cities reflects the overriding homogeneity of urban life, but distinguishes as well the unique development of any single city. For example, New York City, Chicago, New Orleans, Houston, San Francisco, and Los Angeles are diverse in their origins, culture patterns, and development, but retain many similarities in their economic base and physical development.

New York City

For the past 200 years, New York City has been the nation's largest city and greatest seaport. The Port of New York handles 200 million tons of cargo per year, but its port trade is eclipsed by its banking and finance. It is the largest banking and financial center in the world. The assets of New York's commercial banks generally exceed the combined assets of all other commercial banks in the United States. Organized in 1869, the New York Stock Exchange is the world's largest marketplace for corporate stocks and bonds. Trading on the exchange has risen from thousands of shares in its early years to 140 million shares in 1900, to more than 4 billion shares annually today. Eighty companies traded on the exchange have each recorded annual sales or revenues in excess of $2 billion. The population of New York first exceeded 1 million people in 1860, and the metropolitan population now exceeds 16 million. Metropolitan New York covers nine counties in New York and eight in New Jersey. Its "central city" is the island of Manhattan, first settled by the Dutch in 1626. British forces occupied New Amsterdam in 1664, and the already thriving settlement was renamed New York for the Duke of York, who became King James II of England in 1685. By 1700 the city had a population of 7,000 and was already the busiest port in America.

Foreign trade continued to dominate New York business over the next century, but New York found itself in intensive competition with Boston and later with Philadelphia. New York's primary exports in the seventeenth and eighteenth centuries included flour, baked bread (biscuits), and furs. A thriving intercolonial trade brought furs and grain from the interior and tobacco from Delaware. New York established a monopoly on flour milling and crafting by refusing to buy milled or packed flour. The monopoly was effectively broken about 1700 when the New York Assembly, representing interior farmers and towns, authorized any person to engage in milling, baking, and packing. Boston, too, undercut the New York City flour trade by refusing to buy New York flour, opening its own mills, and buying New York grain with clipped or depreciated coinage. The decline of the flour trade in the eighteenth century, the rapid growth of Philadelphia, and the growing carrier trade of Boston, among other factors, reduced New York's earlier advantages.[8]

From the advent of the American Revolution through the close of the Napoleonic Wars the foreign trade of Boston and New York suffered most severely. The westward shift of population and farming and the decline of the fur trade in the East further undermined New York City's commercial advantages, although the city continued as a major exporter of flour and grain. A growing volume of midwestern trade was flowing south on the Mississippi River to New Orleans or eastward over the Cumberland Road to Philadelphia and Baltimore, New York's trade rivals.

Perhaps the two factors that contributed most significantly to New York's commercial survival and growth in the first half of the nineteenth century were the flood of immigration into the city, which brought vast supplies of cheap labor, and the opening of the Erie Canal. Of these, the completion of the Erie Canal in 1825 was the more dramatic. Constructed at a cost of almost $7.5 million, the canal earned over $1 million in tolls in its first season of operation. By the 1850s, tolls had reached almost $3 million annually and 2 million tons of cargo flowed through the canal each year. The canal provided a direct artery for the flow of goods from Europe via New York to the Mississippi Valley, and for the export of products of the interior to Europe via New York City. New York City's successes, however, began to fade before the onslaught of the railroads, as Boston, Philadelphia, and other rival cities began to make direct rail connections to the Midwest. New York persisted in a "canal mentality" until the 1850s, even to the point of prohibiting the shipment of freight by rail on lines paralleling the Erie Canal. Finally, in 1853, the New York legislature authorized the merger of independent lines into the New York Central System, which improved rail transportation and reduced total dependence on the canal.

As long as water power was the primary source of energy, New York City did not have the energy capacity for industrial manufacturing. Converting to steam and coal allowed the city to develop industrially in the antebellum years, but heavy industry, including the textile, iron, and steel industries, never became dominant. Rather, New York City's industrial base derived from, and continues to be based on, labor-intensive manufacturing. The clothing industry, for example, developed rapidly between 1850 and 1900. It sprang almost naturally from the large immigrant labor supply. The immigrant men and women possessed at least one universal skill—the ability to cut, sew, and make clothing. Mass production of clothing depended primarily on organizing the labor force and involved a relatively low capital investment in machinery, tools, and housing. Today New York City manufactures over 25 percent of America's wearing apparel. Other highly labor-intensive manufacturing processes in which New York City excels are furniture and toy manufacture, millinery, furs, and food products and packaging. On a more sophisticated level, printing, book publishing, communications, and banking are in effect highly labor-intensive processes requiring relatively larger man-hours per unit of product than is true in most other manufacturing processes.

New York City's historic attraction to immigrants derives in part from its strategic geographic location as a port city, but also from its unique ethnicity. The Dutch, who founded the city, were international traders who admitted all comers. The British, by accident or design, continued this policy after taking the city from the Dutch in 1664. Thus, by 1700 eighteen different languages were spoken among the city's 7,000 inhabitants. The international flavor of New York City is among its most distinguished cultural characteristics. The city has a greater variety of ethnic groups than any other city in the world. The old story that New York City has more Jews, Italians, Germans, Irish, Africans, and Puerto Ricans than any city in the homeland of those peoples contains an element of truth. The early concentration of aliens in the city acted as a magnet to later immigrants, who sought the cultural identity in America that they had in their homeland. New York early became a host of identifiable ethnic communities— Little Italy, Chinatown, Harlem, the Bowery, and others—which changed according to the patterns of immigration and the gradual assimilation of new peoples. Overall, immigration may have been the most significant factor in New York City's economic growth and unique cultural development. Immigration was the wellspring of the creativity and innovation important to both capitalism and culture. The location of the United Nations in New York is a fitting capstone for this world city.

Chicago

Chicago, the third largest metropolitan area in the United States, following New York City and Los Angeles, and the fourteenth largest metropolitan area in the world, was until recent decades the fastest growing city in America. Founded two centuries after New York City, Chicago was incorporated in 1837 with a population exceeding 4,000. Its condition at that time was reported to be "one chaos of mud, rubbish, and confusion." Chicago was created out of the speculative land booms of the 1830s. It became the crossroad for settlers moving from the East to the midwest and for the goods and produce that began to flow between these two regions. The opening of the Erie Canal shortened the journey from east to west by weeks, and made Chicago the westernmost trade terminal. Federal and state appropriations in the 1830s and 1840s enabled the city to develop a ship channel and improve its harbor facilities. Although depressed conditions followed the initial decade of feverish growth, by the mid 1840s Chicago had become the center of a rapidly growing grain trade. The first grain-storage facilities in the city were built in 1841. Grain was purchased by eastern buyers for shipment to New York and eastern mills, although limited quantities of wheat were being milled by Chicago mills established in 1841 and powered by wind. More significant than its export functions, Chicago served as a supply center for the rapidly growing midwestern farm population. As early as 1833, local blacksmiths such as Asahel Pierce began manufacturing plows and other farm tools, a movement that culminated in the construction of the McCormick Reaper plant in 1850. Over the next decades the reaper and improvements in plows and often farm equipment transformed the prairies into the breadbasket of America.[9] Chicago served as the central gathering and distribution point for midwestern grain.

Chicago became the center of a thriving pork-slaughter and packing industry in the 1830s and 1840s, but by the mid 1840s beef rivaled pork in volume. Complementing the packing industry was a rising lumber business, which provided staves and barrels. Offspring of the livestock industry included lard-oil, tallow, candle, and shoe and leather industries. By 1850 Chicago had grown to a city of 30,000. The first railroad to serve Chicago began operation in 1848, and in 1856 the Illinois Central made possible direct rail connections between Chicago and the eastern seaboard. The completion of the Union Pacific in 1869 gave Chicago a direct rail link with San Francisco. In the 1850s Chicago's population surged to over 112,000. The Civil War brought a business boom, and prices for beef, pork, and wheat skyrocketed. The completion of the Chicago Union Stockyards in 1865 made the city the meat market of the world. By 1870 Chicago's population had reached 300,000.

In 1871 the Great Fire, reportedly begun when Mrs. O'Leary's cow kicked over a lantern, destroyed much of the central city.[10] But Chicago rebuilt and began two decades of unprecedented growth. Its population reached half a million in 1880 and topped one million in 1890. Meat packing, milling, and lumbering exhibited phenomenal growth, which was nonetheless surpassed by the development of heavy manufacturing, the products of which included railroad equipment, iron, and steel. The Columbian Exposition held in Chicago in 1893 found the city on the threshold of yet another phase of economic growth, a phase that included the development of the automotive, chemical, petroleum, retail, insurance, publishing, and finance industries. Strategically located on one of the great natural trade arteries of North America, endowed with a rich agricultural hinterland and abundant supplies of water and minerals, and aided by improvements in its port, rail, and highway connections, Chicago became the second largest city in the United States in 1900.

New Orleans

Geography dictated the emergence of New Orleans as one of the great port and trade cities of North America in the nineteenth century. New Orleans's growth, as Chicago's, was reciprocal with the growth of mid-America. The city was founded by the French in 1718 as a guardian of the Mississippi Valley from foreign intrusion. It was also viewed as a means of developing the rich agricultural and trade possibilities in the lower Mississippi Valley. New Orleans was beset with enormous difficulties for most of its first 100 years. The alluvial plain on which the city stood was subject to flooding and mosquito infestation. Drainage was an unending problem; even cemeteries had to be built above ground. The colonizing ventures were never adequately financed, and speculative enterprises sponsored by John Law and Antoine Crozat in the early decades resulted in financial ruin for thousands of investors. Most grievous was the crumbling state of the French and Spanish monarchy in the eighteenth century. Spanish governors after 1763 were more successful in stabilizing the Louisiana colony. Sugar cane, rice, furs, lumber, and hides became important articles of trade. Spain reluctantly allowed New Orleans greater trade license than was common with colonial possessions, but this stimulated growth. Building codes and more responsible government began to improve living conditions in the city. Most important, trade with Americans on the upper Mississippi was approved by the Pinckney Treaty in 1795. River trade grew steadily, but was closed again in 1802, leading President Jefferson to attempt to buy the Isle of Orleans. The French had acquired the colony by the secret treaty of San Ildefonso in 1800, although Spanish governors continued to rule in Louisiana. In 1800, the city of New Orleans had a diverse population of some 8,000 persons and prospered largely as a gathering and distributing center for a very localized agricultural economy.[11]

Duties, tariffs, trade restrictions, and political confusion declined with the American purchase of the Louisiana Territory in 1803. New Orleans was quickly assimilated into the world's largest free-trade area, and by 1850 this strategically located port city had become the fifth largest city in the United States, with a heterogeneous population of 116,000. In the 1850s exports from the Port of New Orleans exceeded those from New York. Cotton, sugar, rice, and tobacco came to New Orleans from the lower Mississippi and its tributaries. Wheat, flour, pork, beef and hides reached the city from the Ohio, Missouri, and upper Mississippi river systems. The steamboat accomplished for New Orleans what the Erie Canal did for New York City: it unlocked the Mississippi River system to midwestern trade. The value of produce New Orleans received from the interior rose from about $22 million in 1830 to almost $200 million in 1860. Over the same three decades its exports increased in value from $15 million to $108 million. While the real volume of New Orleans's trade rose throughout the antebellum period, the relative volume of trade between the city and points in the Midwest declined as rail traffic, particularly after 1850, began to divert grain and meat traffic directly to eastern points.

Unlike New York and Chicago, New Orleans never developed a substantial industrial base in the nineteenth century. There are a number of explanations for this, perhaps none of them wholly satisfactory. The city did not have fuel (coal) in reasonable proximity. Coal would have to have been transported down the Ohio or Tennessee rivers, and the cost of this would have been prohibitive; river transportation for alternative commercial cargoes would produce far better returns than a cargo of coal. Investment capital, in other words, was better spent on commerce than on manufacturing. Labor, too, especially skilled labor, was relatively scarce in New Orleans throughout the century, despite substantial population increases in the antebellum period. New Orleans lay outside the regular immigrant route from England, Ireland, and northern Europe to the United States before the Civil War. Although immigrants did arrive in New Orleans from those points, they were relatively few. The institution of slavery undoubtedly discouraged the movement of free laborers to southern cities. After the Civil War, investment capital in the South was increasingly scarce, although New Orleans likely did better than other southern cities. Available capital continued to be plowed into the production and marketing of staple commodities. The growth of the city was and is, moreover, physically limited by a lack of land. Of the 363.5 square miles constituting the modern city, 163 are under water. The early name "Isle of Orleans" has a literal connotation for the city, although the phrase originally applied to a much broader territory.

New Orleans is perhaps unique in that its basic economic functions and cultural identity have changed relatively little since the early nineteenth century. The city continues to trade heavily in staples and raw materials, and Mississippi River traffic continues to dominate port activity. The Port of New Orleans handles more than 125 million tons of cargo each year. Cotton, sugar, and grain remain major export items. The advent of the petroleum and petrochemicals industry on the Gulf Coast has provided a new dimension to trade and created a modern industrial base. New Orleans, Baton Rouge, and much of the Louisiana coast are an amalgam of chemical industries and petroleum production and refining. These industries, like the lumber, salt, and sulphur industries, are primarily extractive rather than finished manufacturing processes, and they require relatively small input of labor per unit of product. More intensive manufacturing processes have developed rapidly since World War II, particularly in the areas of food processing and paper products. Trade between New Orleans and Latin America has intensified from the late nineteenth century to the present. But since 1900 New Orleans has experienced growing competition in this area and in the export of staples with the Port of Lake Charles and particularly with the Port of Houston.

Houston

Settled in 1836, Houston is among the newest and fastest-growing cities in the United States. In the nineteenth century Houston was an inland village and later a commercial appendage linked by rail to Galveston, after New Orleans the second busiest Gulf port in that century. By 1900 Houston had a population of only 44,000 and was primarily an agricultural center for the highly productive cattle and cotton area to the north and west. But in 1915 the city completed the fifty-mile Houston Ship Channel and opened the Port of Houston. Over the next sixty years, but particularly after World War II, Houston "happened."[12] By the mid 1970s the city had become the fifth largest in the nation. It had replaced New

Orleans as the petroleum and banking center of the central Southwest. Indeed, its petroleum production was the highest in the world. Port-of-Houston trade now ranks third in the nation. Unlike New Orleans, Houston has spilled out over former boundaries with relative ease. It now encompasses a metropolitan area and a population almost twice as large as those of New Orleans. It has also developed a diversified economic base, one that includes metals, plastics, foods, insurance, entertainment, medicine, and the Lyndon B. Johnson Space Center. Houston is a preeminent example of the fact that cities do not just happen; people make them happen. Geography is clearly a determinant, but technological development—be it a canal, port facility, ship channel, railroad, steamboat, or fuel-resource development—can be crucial.

San Francisco and Los Angeles

Los Angeles, like Houston, is new in age and in character, it lacks a well-defined central city, and its functions and services are sprawled in a seemingly incongruous manner. When San Francisco gained prominence with the gold rush in 1850, Los Angeles was a small farming and fishing community of little more than 2,000 persons, and it remained that way for many years. By 1900 Los Angeles had grown to slightly over 100,000 and had developed an economy based largely on fishing, farming, and vacation resorts. San Francisco, meanwhile, was growing with tremendous vigor, which was stimulated first by gold and then by silver, the railways, and the expanding Pacific markets. The city was destroyed by fire, triggered by the earthquake of 1906, but was rebuilt on its old foundations and in its old pattern. By 1919 San Francisco was known around the world; Los Angeles was little known outside of its immediate neighborhood. Over the next fifty years San Francisco increased its manufacturing output fourfold, but was surpassed by Los Angeles in production and population by a ratio of three to one. The population of Los Angeles exceeded 3.5 million in 1970, and the metropolitan population trailed only those of New York and Chicago. San Francisco occupies 44 square miles of a peninsula, Los Angeles 463 square miles, confined only by county lines. The resort, recreation, and agricultural base of Los Angeles was transcended by the movie industry during the first three or four decades of the twentieth century, and that industry in turn was eclipsed by the aerospace, petroleum, and metalworking industries. Essentially man-made port facilities, created for the most part since World War II, extend 46 miles along the beach from Los Angeles to Long Beach. Clothing, electronics, printing, furniture, and diversified manufacturing contribute to a complex industrial sprawl interlaced with military complexes, residential areas, and highly productive farms and ranches.[13]

Los Angeles and Houston are particularly appropriate examples of urban explosion in that their complex organs have been scattered over their entire landscape. Unlike Chicago, New York, New Orleans, and San Francisco, these two cities have been less restrained by geography and by older institutional and cultural patterns. Like all cities, they integrate components of regional growth and the national economy and are vastly affected by technological innovations and world trade patterns. Perhaps the outstanding feature of the modern city, unlike the older one, is its structural impermanence and constantly changing economic character. Survival increasingly requires flexibility, growth, and change, all of which increase the tensions and volatility of the society. The modern city continues in the function of the old as a major economic and cultural stimulant and catalyst. Unlike the old city, it may overstimulate to the point of frustration and alienation. Once the hallmark of quality, culture, and pastimes, the city is endangered by the sheer quantity and intemperance of urban life. But the failure may be less that of the city than that of humans to conquer the cities they have created.

Notes

[1] See Lewis Mumford, *The City in History: Its Origins, Its Transformations, and Its Prospects* (New York: Harcourt, Brace & World, 1961), pp. 12–31.

[2] *Ibid.*, p. 34.

[3] Ray Ginger, ed., *Modern American Cities* (Chicago: Quandrangle Books, 1969), p. 21.

[4] See Gurney Breckenfeld, " 'Downtown' Has Fled to the Suburbs," *Fortune,* October, 1972, pp. 80–162.

[5] See Advisory Commission on Intergovernmental Relations, "The Pattern of Urbanization," in *Urban Studies: An Introductory Reader,* ed. Louis K. Lowenstein (New York: Macmillan, 1971) pp. 3–40.

[6] Jane Jacobs "The Valuable Inefficiencies and Impracticalities of Cities," in *Urban Studies,* ed. Lowenstein; (New York: Macmillan, 1971), pp. 45.

[7] See Jane Jacobs in Lowenstein, *Urban Studies,* pp. 41–57.

[8] See Curtis Nettels, "The Economic Relations of Boston, Philadelphia, and New York, 1680–1715," *Journal of Economic and Business History,* 3 (February 1931), pp. 185–215.

[9] See Bessie Louise Pierce, *A History of Chicago,* Vol. I (Chicago: University of Chicago Press, 1975).

[10] See Pierce, *A History of Chicago,* Vol. II.

[11] See John G. Clark, *New Orleans, 1718–1812: An Economic History* (Baton Rouge: Louisiana State University Press, 1970), and Joy J. Jackson, *New Orleans in the Gilded Age: Politics and Urban Progress, 1880–1896* (Baton Rouge: Louisiana State University Press, 1969).

[12] See Marilyn M. Sibley, *The Port of Houston; A History* (Austin: University of Texas Press, 1968).

[13] See R. L. Duffus, "The Two States of California," in *Modern American Cities,* ed. Ginger, pp. 52–60.

SUGGESTED READING

BLUMSTEIN, JAMES F., AND EDDIE J. MARTIN, *The Urban Scene in the Seventies*. Nashville: Vanderbilt University Press, 1974.

CHUDACOFF, HOWARD P., *The Evolution of American Urban Society*. Englewood Cliffs, N.J.: Prentice-Hall, 1975.

DAVIES, RICHARD O., *The Age of Asphalt: The Automobile, the Freeway, and the Condition of Metropolitan America*. Philadelphia: Lippincott, 1975.

GLAAB, CARLES N., and A. THEODORE BROWN, *A History of Urban America*, 2nd ed. New York: Macmillan, 1976.

JACOBS, JANE, *The Economy of Cities*. New York: Random House, 1969.

LOWENSTEIN, LOUIS K., ed., *Urban Studies: An Introductory Reader*. New York: Macmillan 1971.

McKILNEY, BLAKE, *The Urbanization of America, 1860–1915*. New Brunswick, N.J.: Rutgers University Press, 1963.

MUMFORD, LEWIS, *The City in History: Its Origins, Its Transformations, and Its Prospects*. New York: Harcourt, Brace & World, 1969.

REPS, JOHN W., *The Making of Urban America: A History of City Planning in the United States*. Princeton, N.J.: Princeton University Press, 1965.

STEFFINS, LINCOLN, *The Shame of the Cities*. McClure's Magazine, 1904. Reprint ed., New York: Peter Smith, 1948.

THERNSTROM, STEPHEN, *Poverty and Progress: Social Mobility in a Nineteenth Century City*. Cambridge, Mass.: Harvard University Press, 1964.

THERNSTROM, STEPHEN, AND RICHARD SENNETT, *19th Century Cities: Essays in the New Urban History*. New Haven: Yale University Press, 1969.

AN AGE
OF AUTOMOBILES
AND PROGRESSIVES

_____ chapter XIV__

The automobile altered the course of America in the twentieth century as the steamboat and the railroad had done in the century before. It made possible the rise of the modern city and its suburbs, and provided the incentive for a revolution in American industry. The steel, petroleum, lead, paint, glass, rubber, concrete, and housing industries exploded under the stimulus of automobile manufacturing. A major part of the modern advertising, banking, and insurance business is accounted for by the automobile. Since 1900 a substantial portion of public expenditures by local, state, and federal authorities has been for highway construction and maintenance. An estimated 10 percent of the national wealth is accounted for by the automobile. Americans own half of the automotive vehicles in the world.

The automobile industry paced the economic growth of the nation through the first quarter and much of the first half of the twentieth century. The value of production of the industry, compared with that of other industries, rose in rank from 150th in 1900 to 1st in 1925. Six percent of the total value of American manufacturing in 1925 was contributed by the automobile industry. The automobile, electric-power, and chemical industries were primary leaders in industrial growth after the turn of the century. These industries affected changing structural and productivity patterns in related industrial sectors, and altered American life-styles and social patterns.

The first decades of the automotive age were also a time when the relationship between government and the economy was altered by Progressive reforms and the social unrest of the recent past. Automobiles, urbanization, the consolidation of business units, and Progressivism were the major social forces affecting the development of the economy in the early 1900s.

THE PROGRESSIVES

The Progressives were urban, upper-middle-class, twentieth-century reformers who had a deep ideological commitment to America and free enterprise. They believed intensely in the right to profits, private property, and the proposition that each should earn according to ability. Individual freedom and personal liberty were supremely important. The Progressives believed that the growth of big business through monopolistic and conspiratorial practices threatened free enterprise and individual freedom. They believed with equal or greater fervor that the socialism of radical labor and farm groups also threatened the free-enterprise system. They tended to accept the social gospel–social justice idea that the social environment affected the individual's opportunity to earn a living and to accumulate wealth. Wealth or poverty did not always result from the individual's energy, ability, productiveness, or "state of grace." Either could be the product of chance, monopoly, misconduct, or crime. If so, it was clearly unearned and undeserved. The Progressives wanted to preserve individual freedom and to save free enterprise both from the collectivist within the system and from the socialist without.[1] To do so, they increasingly called upon government to impose a competitive, "equal-opportunity" environment, and they slowly began to weave a web that contained some of the patterns of state capitalism but retained many of the threads of individualism. As Lester Frank Ward had observed decades earlier, the paradox was that individual freedom seemingly could come only through social regulation.

Theodore Roosevelt

Theodore Roosevelt, an outspoken advocate of Progressivism, believed in hard work, individualism, and "Americanism." He believed that positive government and strong executive leadership were needed to promote national strength and to assure each individual the opportunity for honest and rewarding labor. Born of a patrician family, Roosevelt felt a deep sense of responsibility for the downtrodden and an equally deep fear of the "mob." "T. R." overcame youthful frailties as an asthmatic, sickly child to become a cowboy, soldier, writer, statesman, and preeminent politician. He served three terms in the New York legislature, lost the New York mayor's race in 1886, and retired to a ranch in the West, where he lived the life of a cowboy and wrote seven books. In 1889 he returned to the East to serve as a member of the newly organized Civil Service Commission. In 1895 he became head of New York City's police commission. In this capacity he conducted a personal campaign against crime and corruption, and achieved considerable publicity and a bit of notoriety. He was appointed Assistant Secretary of the Navy in 1897 and became a proponent of war against Spain. When war came, Roosevelt rushed off to organize the Rough Riders and

THEODORE ROOSEVELT *(1858–1919)*
President of the United States, 1901–1909.

won distinction and fame in the Cuban campaign. New Yorkers elected him governor after the Spanish-American War, but shortly thereafter state political bosses wishing to get him out of their way supported him for the Republican vice-presidential nomination in 1900. His election to that office reportedly occasioned the remark by Mark Hanna, "Don't you realize there is only one life between this madman and the White House?" Soon that life was gone. Theodore Roosevelt became president on September 6, 1901.[2]

Roosevelt's election frightened big-business interests, but by the end of his first term he had won most of them to his side while projecting the image of a Progressive reformer. Roosevelt was not against big business, but he did not want big business to run the country. He feared that unbridled competition might lead to drastic reactions against the free-enterprise system. As he informed Congress in 1902, "Our aim is not to do away with corporations; on the contrary, these big aggregations are an inevitable development of modern industrialism. . . . We draw the line against misconduct, not against wealth."[3] Roosevelt hoped to restore to health the Sherman Antitrust Act of 1890, which stated: "Every contract, combination in the form of trust or otherwise, or conspiracy in restraint of trade or commerce among the several states, or with foreign nations, is hereby declared to be illegal." The act had become virtually inoperative by virtue of Supreme Court rulings such as in the *United States* v. *E. C. Knight* (1895), which held manufacturing to be distinct from commerce and thus excluded from Congress the authority to regulate most business enterprises.

215

One product of the fight between James J. Hill and Edward H. Harriman over the northern railroads was the organization of a holding company, the Northern Securities Company, that exercised control over $400 million of railroad stock and a substantial portion of the nation's rail business in the West. Attorney General Philander C. Knox directed the government's case against the Northern Securities Company and in 1904 won an order from the Supreme Court dissolving the company as a conspiracy in restraint of trade. In another case Knox successfully attacked the Beef Trust. Comprising the Swift-Armour packing monopoly, this trust engaged in price fixing, the blacklisting of rebellious independents, and the use of railroad rebates. In 1903 Roosevelt established the Department of Commerce and Labor and obtained congressional authority to create the Bureau of Corporations, which would investigate the "organization, conduct, and management of the business of any corporation, joint-stock company, or corporate combination." The successful antitrust actions and the creation of regulatory agencies theoretically established the opportunity for federal control of business activity. In practice, there was little curb on the size, rate of growth, or activity of corporations.

Roosevelt also interposed the authority of the national government in settling a strike involving the United Mine Workers headed by John Mitchell. In the past the premise underlying executive intervention, as in the Homestead and Pullman strikes, had been that strikes were in fact an illegal conspiracy in restraint of trade. In this case the United Mine Workers sought a 20-percent wage increase, the eight-hour day, and union recognition. Anthracite-coal operators flatly refused to meet the demands. The resulting strike created severe shortages of coal—which was used then for heating and cooking—particularly in New York City. As public suffering increased, more radical political elements in New York began demanding government ownership and operation of the mines. The conflicting interests portrayed the classic Progressive dilemma. On the one hand, labor attempted to obtain a greater share in the fruits of free enterprise and concurrently impose restraints on the use of private property. On the other side stood the employer and his inherent rights in property. In the center was a large public sector facing hunger and cold—a hostile environment beyond its apparent ability to control. In the shadows were those who would undermine rights of property in order to achieve relief. There was no perfect solution, but a resolution was imperative in order to protect both the public and rights in property. Roosevelt called for arbitration between labor and management, threatened government operation of the mines unless a settlement was made, used the personal and financial influence of J. P. Morgan with the companies, and effected a negotiated settlement that gave labor a nine-hour day and a 10-percent wage increase and reopened the mines and the flow of coal to the consumer, albeit presumably at a slightly higher price. The settlement enhanced Roosevelt's stature as a great Progressive leader without seriously alienating business.

In 1904 Roosevelt won election to the presidency in his own right and announced a "Square Deal" for all Americans. Typical of Square Deal Progressive philosophy was the passage of the Hepburn Act of 1906, which extended the jurisdiction of the Interstate Commerce Commission to include sleeping and express cars and pipelines, prohibited public passes and rebates, prescribed a uniform system of bookkeeping for railroads, and placed the burden of proving rates to be fair on the railroads rather than on the commission. Previously, the Elkins Act of 1903 had required railroads to publish standard rates and fares, which theoretically eliminated unfair or unequal charges. The Hepburn Act supposedly benefited the railroads by eliminating some of the burdensome competitive practices and the consumers benefited by having more "equality of opportunity." The "benefits" to either railroads or consumers were debatable, but the idea of such acts was not to impose government direction and control but rather to create a more equitable and free economy.

The conservation movement became full-blown in the Progressive era. By the turn of the century lumber and mining companies were rapidly stripping the nation's forest and mineral resources. The "public domain," that land area under federal jurisdiction and subject to sale and disposal by auction and grant, had dwindled almost to nonexistence. The frontier was gone. Its disappearance provoked the realization that future generations would not have the opportunities of earlier Americans and that the depletion of the nation's resources might lead to an environment in which no one, irrespective of abilities, could successfully compete or survive. Conservation, Progressives believed, was necessary to preserve the free-enterprise system. Roosevelt acted to forestall the depletion of resources by transferring vast tracts of public domain to a national preserve. The transfer of such lands undermined profit opportunities, particularly in the undeveloped, raw-material-supplying states of the West, where exploitation seemed far more important than conservation. In 1907 Congress passed a bill prohibiting the further transfer of lands by the president to a preserve. But before the bill became law Roosevelt added an additional 125 million acres to the national forests and restricted the sale of minerals from 4.7 million acres of phosphate lands and 68 million acres of coal deposits. Acting under the philosophy that government could do some things for the people better than the people could do for themselves, an idea that had strong Populist connotations, Roosevelt reserved 2,565 water-power (dam) sites for the national government, thus keeping them out of the hands of private power interests. This action was perhaps least consistent with Square Deal programs in that it represented a significant philosophical departure from the essential view that what government did was on behalf of preserving opportunities for private enterprise. It also foreshadowed the more radical Rooseveltian ideas of the New Nationalism.

The Meat Inspection Act and the Pure Food and Drug Act of 1906 reflected more accurately the Progressive idea that government regulation was sometimes necessary to assure equality of opportunity. The acts required government inspection and certification of meat, food, and drug products. On the one hand, contaminated foods and mislabeled or dangerous drugs constituted a "bad social environment" over which the ordinary individual had no control. Society must provide everyone with the environment in which they can compete most equitably and effectively. On the other hand, to be sure, these acts were not inspired wholly by Progressive or humanitarian considerations. Great Britain, for example, was seriously considering banning American meat products from British markets because of contamination. To avoid this catastrophic blow, meat packers urged Congress to act. Besides, government inspection of meat, food, and drugs provided a more marketable stamp of approval and transferred at least part of the financial burden of inspection from private businesses to the public. The meat, food, and drug laws were passed with the general approval of, rather than over the objections of, the industries affected. Nonetheless, like much of the Progressive legislation they placed government in a new relationship to business.

Despite the political schisms that developed during the administration of President William Howard Taft, some important Progressive legislation further altered the complexion of the free-enterprise system. The Weeks Act of 1911 allowed the national government to purchase or exchange lands for the creation of new national forests. More important, it authorized the National Forest Service to enter into cooperative agreements with the states in order to protect "forested watersheds of navigable streams," a phrase given the broadest construction. This act provided federal support and incentive for the creation of state-forest-service programs. The Physical Valuation Act of 1913 imposed stronger Interstate Commerce Commission regulation over railroads, and presumably a fairer and more competitive rate structure, by authorizing the ICC to make independent assessments of railroad properties (rather than accepting railroad evaluations) in order to determine fair returns, rates, and ultimately railroad profits. Thus, some private industries became increasingly affected, if not regulated, by government policy.

Theodore Roosevelt's bold new reform program of 1912, the New Nationalism, raised the old question of whether or not rights in property have primacy over all other rights. Roosevelt, the presidential candidate of the Progressive Party, supported the paramount position of government over private property, saying that government is the steward of national wealth. Private property or wealth derives its rights and authority only from society or government. Individuals use property during their lifetime, the apportionment of wealth or the amount of property used depending upon one's ability and productivity. Roosevelt, by his advocacy of the graduated income tax and inheritance tax, seemed to hold that wealth, or at least a portion of it, was a part of the "public domain." To be sure, this doctrine had ancient precedents in western capitalism, such as the writ of eminent domain, which gives the state a certain priority over private property. But Roosevelt's New Nationalism, having split the Republican Party, led only to his own defeat and that of the regular Republican candidate, William Howard Taft, and to the election of Woodrow Wilson, a Democratic "dark horse," as president.

Woodrow Wilson

Some historians suggest that the key difference between the Democratic Party and the Progressive Party in 1912 was one of personality rather than one of principle. Roosevelt was flamboyant, aggressive, and very personable. Wilson was aloof, tense, and Messianic. For him, in politics or in religion there were the righteous and the unrighteous. He was a natural crusader and an idealist. Although his programs were similar to those advocated by Roosevelt, his was a different brand of Progressivism, tinctured by a healthy Jeffersonian fear of government. Individual rights, including rights in property, might be threatened by big government as much as they might by business combination or monopoly. The duty of government was to restore equality of opportunity, competition, and free enterprise but not to maintain surveillance or regimentation.[4]

Wilson, formerly president of Princeton University, destroyed the New Jersey political machine that helped him win the governor's seat in 1910. He then implemented a rigorous reform program that included a revision of election laws, workmen's compensation, utility regulation, and educational reform. As a presidential candidate, he stressed individual freedom and opportunity in his New Freedom program. Wilson declared in 1911, "The great monopoly in this country is the money monopoly. So long as it exists, our old variety and freedom and individual energy of development are out of the question."[5] In 1913 a House investigating committee headed by Congressman Pujo of Louisiana reported that the twenty largest banks and trust companies in New York City controlled 43 percent of the nation's financial resources. The Morgan-Rockefeller interest

WOODROW WILSON *(1856–1924)*
President of the United States, 1913–1921.
Courtesy New York Historical Society.

alone controlled an estimated $22 billion, or 10 percent of the national wealth. The Federal Reserve Act of 1913 reflected Wilson's fear of strong central government and also his distrust of the private money monopoly. The act created twelve virtually independent Federal Reserve Banks. A central board held advisory powers only. Each bank was required to maintain certain reserves, could issue Federal Reserve notes, and, by setting the rediscount rate (the rate of interest on loans to member banks), could alter the volume of money and credit. The Federal Reserve System, despite its weaknesses and limitations, provided more credit and equitable banking opportunities to more people.

In the corporate realm the Clayton Antitrust Act echoed New Freedom sentiments. It prohibited interlocking directorates, price discrimination, exclusive contracts, and combinations by competing firms. One section of the act specifically exempted labor unions from antitrust prosecution. The Underwood-Simmons Tariff, by lowering tariff levels an average of 30 percent, encouraged free trade and expanded competition. The Graduated Income Tax law of 1913 was designed to restore equality of opportunity and individual competition by attacking the private monopoly of wealth. But its intent was not to impose government regulation over wealth, for the New Freedom held that private competition rather than government direction could best maintain individual opportunity.

Predicated on the classic Progressive idea that an unfavorable or unhealthy social environment affected the individual's ability to earn and thereby not only limited his opportunities but diminished his contributions to society, New Freedom legislation sought to remove inequities in the financial and social institutions affecting the individual's ability to earn. New Freedom programs incorporated a shift in government policy from a concern solely with existing business structures to a concern with social structures. The economically disadvantaged came to be regarded as effectually outside the business system. They needed to be incorporated within the system in order to receive its blessings. Education came to be of vital concern to Progressives on both the state and national levels. On the national level, the Smith-Lever Act established the Agricultural Extension Program. The Smith-Hughes Act funded vocational agricultural training, which was designed to help the farmers help themselves and improve their ability to earn. Recent emphasis on federal aid to education, research grants, school integration, and bussing assume that equal educational opportunities best help individuals to help themselves. Admittedly, equality of environment also hoists the double-edged sword of a regimented equalitarianism that could limit individual opportunities. But that is more a concern of our time than of the Progressive era.

The Wilson administration's Federal Farm Loan Act of 1916 offered self-help by insuring bank loans to high-risk farmers. The Keating-Owen Child Labor Act prohibited child labor in industries involved in interstate commerce, but because of court and legislative exceptions this act set little more than a moral tone. The La Follette Seaman's Act would improve the physical accommodations and rights of merchant seamen, and the Adamson Act granted the eight-hour day to railroad employees. Perhaps least characteristic of New Freedom legislation was the Federal Trade Commission Act, which reflected a more New Nationalist or Hamiltonian view of government-business relationships. The FTC was to be a bipartisan commission appointed by the president to maintain surveillance of "unfair methods of competition in commerce." Although it suggested constant government policing, the act presumed that free competition and not government direction could best maintain individual opportunity. The Federal Trade Commission Act, like most Progressive legislation, resurrected attempts to safeguard individual and free enterprise through collective action. The national government not only must protect the American's right to diversity but must guard against the dangers of factionalism engendered by the different quantities and kinds of property derived from that diversity. Under Progressivism, government began to supervise and regulate the use of private property in order to protect rights in property.

THE AUTOMOTIVE INDUSTRY

The Federal Highways Act recognized the advent of the automobile age in America and helped implement it. The act provided matching federal funds to states for the construction of paved highways. Relatively few miles of paved roads existed in America before 1916, but by 1930 most cities and larger towns in the United States could be reached on such roads. Most of this enormous highway construction occurred after the close of World War I, and it contributed heavily to the economic boom of the Roaring Twenties. By 1930 automobile manufacture had become America's biggest business. In the next three decades the industry reached maturity. It became the leading sector of economic growth, stimulating production and innovation in the petroleum, glass, paint, steel, rubber, concrete, electronics, and other supporting industries. It was the cutting edge in a social revolution that made Americans more mobile and independent than ever before. Family structures and modes of courtship bent under the influence of the automobile. The city became outward-bound as automobiles made possible suburban living, shopping centers, and drive-ins. The expansion of the automotive industry may be briefly evaluated in three distinct phases: (1) the pioneering stage, between 1893 and 1900; (2) the mass-production phase, between 1900 and 1925, which emphasized the central problems of production and capital accumulation; and (3) the era of maturity, from about 1925 to the present, when emphasis shifted to marketing, labor relations, and more recently to safety standards and environmental impact.[6]

The first "horseless carriage" makers were mechanics, often bicycle mechanics who—like the Duryea brothers, who made the first American automobile—mounted an internal-combustion engine on a chassis. For them the automobile was a hobby or toy rather than a business. Their experiments corresponded to the refinement stage of the invention process—that is, the production of an efficient, useful machine. In the early decades steam, electric, and gasoline propulsion appeared to be viable alternatives and vehicles using each system were developed. Steam engines proved more dangerous and electric engines proved less efficient because of inadequate batteries, their heavy weight, and the need for constant recharging. By World War I the gasoline engine had proved its superiority and dependability. It was lighter, it produced higher speeds, and it was relatively simple to operate. During the pioneer "tinkering" phase of automobile production, vehicles were custom-built for a very limited market.

Ransom Olds

Ransom E. Olds was the first to attempt to mass-produce motor vehicles. He began building gasoline engines in his machine shop, and in 1897, with credit from local banks, he began producing a limited number of automobiles in Lansing, Michigan. His business failed, in good part because of his lack of capital and a limited local market for his product. He attempted without success to attract investors in the East, but finally obtained a $200,000 capital-stock subscription from S. L. Smith, which left Olds a 5-percent interest in the business. Olds began to manufacture a rather complicated and high-priced automobile in Detroit in 1899. He left Detroit after a year and moved back to Lansing, where, still financed by Smith, he began to manufacture the Oldsmobile in 1901. Instead of attempting to machine-tool each part, he bought parts in quantity from suppliers and engaged primarily in the assembly of vehicles. He divided his labor into special tasks and instituted a rudimentary moving assembly line. It was Olds rather than Henry Ford who actually pioneered the mass production of automobiles. His Oldsmobile sold at a then highly competitive $650. During the first three years of Oldsmobile manufacture Olds paid investors 105 percent on their securities. In 1904, a year in which 5,000 Oldsmobiles were sold, he and Smith parted over the then classic question of whether the automobile should be built in limited quantities for the luxury market or mass produced, as Olds desired, for the "common" market.[7]

In general, the auto makers who chose to mass-produce lower-priced vehicles had a higher survival rate. Those who compromised between mass production and luxury, such as Duesenberg, Wills–St. Clair, Stutz, Pierce Arrow, and most recently Packard, survived somewhat longer. But mass production and low prices by no means guaranteed success. Finance, management, purchasing, and technical proficiency in design could also spell the difference between profit and loss. Since 1900 there have been over 1,500 manufacturers of cars and trucks. Of these the survivors can be counted on the fingers of two hands. Three of these survivors, General Motors, Ford, and Chrysler, produce an estimated 90 percent of the cars and trucks manufactured in America today.

Automobile sales climbed from 4,000 in 1900 to almost 2 million in 1920 and continued to grow dramatically until the 1950s (see Table 14.1).

TABLE 14.1

Factory Passenger-Car Sales, 1900–1975.

Year	Number	Value in Dollars
1900	4,192	$ 4,899,443
1905	24,250	38,670,000
1910	181,000	215,340,000
1915	895,930	575,978,000
1920	1,905,560	1,809,170,963
1925	3,735,171	2,458,370,026
1930	2,787,456	1,644,083,152
1935	3,273,874	1,707,836,325
1940	3,717,385	2,370,654,083
1945	69,532	57,254,655
1950	6,665,863	8,468,137,000
1955	7,920,186	12,452,871,000
1960	6,674,796	12,164,871,000
1965	9,305,561	18,380,036,000
1970	6,546,817	14,630,217,000
1975	6,713,000	* * *

Source: Motor Vehicle Manufacturers Association

Henry Ford

Despite the precedent set by Olds, Henry Ford is substantially responsible for the mass production of the automobile. Ford's ambition was to produce an automobile for the multitude at a price that would compare to the price of a "good horse and buggy." Born on a farm that was soon to be swallowed up in the city of Detroit, Ford had little serious affection for school and studies but a great interest in tinkering and mechanical things. Between the ages of fourteen and twenty-eight Ford held a variety of jobs, including sawmilling, farming, and tinkering. His mechanical ability was such that in 1891 he was hired as the night engineer by Edison Illuminating Company in Detroit at $45 a month. Subsequently, he rose to the position of chief engineer at $100 per month. During these years Ford built his first automobile, in his home workshop. To get the vehicle out of the shop, he had to knock down part of a brick wall. The car ran, and after making some modifications Ford sold it for $200. In 1899, with $15,000 contributed by backers, Ford organized the Detroit Automobile Company, which was defunct within a year. Ford then became interested in building racing cars, and apparently his successful entries attracted new capital, which resulted in the organization of the Henry Ford Company. Ford was given the title of chief engineer and $10,000 in stock. However, he continued to build racing cars, and the stockholders fired him a year later. Under the management of Henry M. Leland, the company was renamed the Cadillac Automobile Company.[8]

In 1903 Ford, backed by a local coal dealer and with a dozen partners, organized the Ford Motor Company. He rented a building for $75 per month and developed his first assembly line. Basically, the assembly line brought parts to a central location for assembly. Ford paid his workers the relatively good wages of $1.50 per day. By 1908 the company was producing 100 low-priced cars per day and was financially solvent. But Ford's partners were dissatisfied, believing that the best market was for higher-priced, luxury, and custom cars—which for the moment appeared to be the case. It was obvious to most people that the automobile was a toy for the rich and would have little use or significance for the ordinary citizen other than to visually accentuate the great gulf between the rich and the poor. Ford, of course, as well as Olds and some others thought the contrary. The automobile was a horseless carriage, nothing more and nothing less, but it was far more tractable, manageable, and cleaner than a horse. Ford bought the interests of five of his dissatisfied partners, thereby putting himself for the first time in financial control of the company. He also redesigned his automobile and began constructing a new plant that would contain the first complete assembly-line production system. As Ford remarked, this system would take "the work to men instead of the men to the work—as Olds has done."

The new automobile was the Model T. Ford built it from 1908 through 1927, never changing the basic design, mechanics, models, or even the color of the paint—black. The one thing he did change was the price. In 1909 the Model T touring car entered the market at $1,000. By 1914 a Model T could be bought for $490, somewhat near the price of a good horse and buggy. By 1914 Ford and his efficiency experts had so improved the assembly processes that the basic assembly time for a completed automobile had been reduced from 12.5 to 1.5 hours. In 1914 Ford voluntarily raised the wages of his employees from an average of $2.00 per day to $5.00 per day. In giving this raise Ford acted not as a philanthropist or humanitarian but as a shrewd businessman and employer. There were certain strings attached to the raise. All Ford employees were required to buy a Model T, which undoubtedly they were delighted to do. This measure not only returned a part of the workers' wages to the company treasury but also put more Fords on the road and brought more favorable advertising and goodwill to Ford products than any professional promotion could have brought. More important, the workers Ford hired at $5.00 per day—a figure that doubled many other prevailing wage levels—had to be skillful, hard-working, and much in earnest about their labor or they were summarily fired. Ford established one of the first corporate employee-relations departments, stressed clean, safe, and sanitary working conditions, established wage and employee classifications, and voluntarily instituted the eight-hour day. For many decades he got the pick of skilled laborers and diligent workers. For these and other reasons labor unions were hesitant to organize Ford's workers. Only after 1935 did the newly organized Congress of Industrial Organizations promote the development of the United Auto Workers Union, which negotiated contracts with General Motors and Chrysler in 1937 and finally with Ford in 1941.[9]

Ford sales and production climbed steadily from about 12,000 cars in 1909 to over 800,000 in 1917. By the close of World War I, Ford had garnered 50 percent of the American car market. Ford tactics throughout this period focused almost exclusively on increased production and more efficient production at a lower per-unit cost. Expanded sales were geared to continually declining prices. By 1920 the touring car sold for $440, and in 1923 the price reached a low of $290.

The Model T was an efficient, well-engineered piece of machinery. According to the U.S. Board of Tax Repeals in 1928, the car's

> principal distinguishing features were a planetary transmission, a rear axle of unusual design, a magneto built into the flywheel as an integral part of the motor, the use of vanadium steel, and relative lightness and power. Incorporation of the magneto as a part of the flywheel reduced the weight of the car. Vanadium steel was used in the car to make it stronger and lighter, increasing the ratio of horsepower to the weight and making the car cheaper to operate. The car was simple of design, making it easy to operate and easy to maintain and repair. The parts were so precisely manufactured that a number of cars could be dissembled, the parts mixed, and the same number of cars rebuilt from the parts. It is said that this could not be done with any other car in the low-priced field as late as 1913.[10]

FIGURE 14.1 Ford automobile assembly line about 1914.

Courtesy of the Ford Archies, Henry Ford Museum, Pearbom, Michigan.

By the mid 1920s the automobile industry had ended its growth stage and entered the competitive stage, in which it came to emphasize marketing rather than production. By that time automobile manufacturers could produce 6 million cars a year, but sales between 1921 and 1941 leveled off to an average of 3 million cars a year. Ford's single-minded devotion to efficient manufacturing processes—which included the decentralized manufacture of parts, the fabrication of special machinery to perform specific operations, and efficient assembly-line production—coupled with lower prices, failed to meet the challenge of a saturated market. While Ford stuck to time-honored policies of production and direct management, General Motors, Chrysler, and other industries adopted innovative marketing and management policies that were better geared to the more sophisticated modern market. Ford's share of the automobile market plummeted from 55 to 19 percent between 1921 and 1940 while General Motors' share rose from 13 to almost 50 percent.

Ford and General Motors

By 1924 the market for automobiles was a replacement market. More sophisticated and affluent car buyers wanted a stylish, prestigious, and comfortable vehicle, not just a cheap, efficient car. William D. Durant, an experienced carriage manufacturer, moved into the automotive industry in 1904 with the purchase of Buick Motor Company. In 1908 he united Buick, Oldsmobile, and Cadillac and organized General Motors Corporation. Through rapid financial combinations, mergers, and acquisitions, he established a network of suppliers, assembly plants, and distributors. Overextended in 1910, Durant was forced out of General Motors. He then acquired Chevrolet, and with the backing of Pierre du Pont and John J. Raskob regained control of General Motors in 1915. In 1920 the postwar recession caught General Motors and Durant in an overextended financial position. Durant lost most of his fortune and the control of General Motors, but the company survived. Alfred P. Sloan, the new president of General Motors, instituted a sweeping reorganization that streamlined the administrative and planning structure while providing substantial autonomy to division managers.

Although Ford dealers clamored for autos with "sales appeal," Ford stuck resolutely to the manufacture of the Model T; the 1927 model was visually unchanged from the 1909 model. Meanwhile, General Motors offered a variety of models, styles, colors, and innovations, including electric starters, sealed-beam lights, automatic transmissions, hydraulic brakes, cigarette lighters, radios, and attractive interiors. The organization of General Motors Acceptance Corporation in 1919 facilitated the sale of the more attractive cars on easy credit terms. In 1927 Ford closed his production line for six months in order to redesign and retool for the production of the Model A. A vigorous advertising campaign and a more stylish product resulted in the sale of 500,000 Model A's before the first car left the assembly line, and Ford sales resurged in 1928 and 1929. But it was not enough. In 1929 Chevrolet introduced the six-cylinder engine. Thereafter, the race was on in engineering improvements, suspension, engines, and overall design and ornamentation. Despite the introduction of the Ford V-8 in 1934, Ford sales continued to decline: the company lost an average of $1.4 million each year between 1931 and 1941. A saturated market, the Great Crash of 1929, and the depression that followed reduced the number of auto manufacturers from about forty in 1926 to hardly a dozen in 1941.

The economic impact of the automobile went far beyond the profits and losses of the manufacturers. The petroleum, rubber, steel, glass, and machine-tool industries virtually became subsidiaries of the automobile industry. Joseph Schumpeter and others attributed a substantial portion of the phenomenal economic growth of the United States between 1897 and 1929 to the automobile. By the 1960s, over 800,000 businesses were directly engaged in the manufacture, distribution, and service of automobiles and employing one out of every six

FIGURE 14.2. "Reliable Motoring at a Cost Millions Can Afford."(This advertisement appeared in the *Saturday Evening Post,* May 30, 1925.)

Courtesy of the Ford Archives, Henry Ford Museum, Dearborn, Michigan.

members of the American labor force. By the 1950s there was some substance to the alleged remark by Charles E. Wilson, former president of General Motors, that what was good for General Motors was good for the country. Upon the election of Dwight D. Eisenhower and a Republican administration in 1952, Democratic nominee Adlai Stevenson admonished the public that "while the New Dealers have all left Washington to make way for the car dealers, I hasten to say that I for one, do not believe the story that the general welfare has become a subsidiary of General Motors."

While the automobile was adding a new dimension to economic growth, business structures, marketing, and social life, the relationship between government and business was being altered, first by the Progressive movement, which sought to preserve established standards of democratic opportunity and free enterprise, and second by economic dislocation and depression. Progressives reacted essentially to the problems of a rapidly changing economic and social order. In the face of expanding productivity, worker income and consumer purchasing power tended to lag behind. Economic dislocation and cyclical unemployment increased concurrently with the growth of manufacturing. Labor shifted from agriculture to industry, and families moved from the farm to the city. Economic power became increasingly concentrated. The great problems of the Progressive era concerned trusts, banking, labor, and agriculture. These problems became even more acute in the depression decade.

Notes

[1]The literature on the Progressive movement is extensive. Interpretations vary. Especially recommended for initial study are Richard Hofstadter's *The Age of Reform; From Bryan to FDR* (New York: Knopf, 1955) and *The American Political Tradition* (New York: Knopf, 1948). See also Eric F. Goldman, *Rendezvous with Destiny* (New York: Knopf, 1952); Harold U. Faulkner, *The Decline of Laissez-Faire, 1897–1917* (New York: Harper & Row, 1951); George E. Mowry, *The Era of Theodore Roosevelt and the Birth of Modern America, 1900–1912* (New York: Harper & Row, 1958); and Robert H. Wiebe, *The Search for Order, 1877–1920* (New York; Hill & Wang, 1967).

[2]The most useful studies of Roosevelt are Mowry, *The Era of Theodore Roosevelt*; Henry F. Pringle, *Theodore Roosevelt: A Biography* (New York: Harcourt, Brace & World, 1931); and John M. Blum, *The Republican Roosevelt* (Cambridge, Mass.: Harvard University Press, 1954).

[3]Quoted in Hofstadter, *The American Political Tradition*, p. 226.

[4]Recommended studies of Wilson include Arthur S. Link, *Woodrow Wilson and the Progressive Era* (New York: Harper & Row, 1954), and John M. Blum, *Woodrow Wilson and the Politics of Morality* (Boston: Little, Brown, 1956).

[5]See Hofstadter, *The American Political Tradition*, pp. 238–260.

[6]See Herman E. Krooss and Charles Gilbert, *American Business History* (Englewood Cliffs, N.J.: Prentice-Hall, 1972), p. 295.

[7]See Krooss and Gilbert, *American Business History,* pp. 300–301.

[8]See Krooss and Gilbert, *American Business History*, pp. 302–3.

[9]See Alfred D. Chandler, Jr., ed., *Giant Enterprise: Ford, General Motors, and the Automobile Industry* (New York: Harcourt, Brace & World, 1964), pp. 17–19, and cited for remaining commentary on Ford and General Motors.

[10]Quoted in Chandler, ed., *Giant Enterprise*, pp. 28–29.

SUGGESTED READING

CHANDLER, ALFRED D., JR., ed., *Giant Enterprise: Ford, General Motors, and the Automobile Industry*. New York: Harcourt, Brace & World, 1964.

DAVIES, RICHARD O., *The Age of Asphalt: The Automobile, The Freeway, and the Condition of Metropolitan America*. Philadelphia: Lippincott; 1975.

FAULKNER, HAROLD U., *The Decline of Laissez-Faire, 1897–1917*. New York: Harper & Row, 1951.

HAYS, SAMUEL P., *The Response to Industrialism, 1885–1914*. Chicago: University of Chicago Press, 1957.

KOLKO, GABRIEL, *The Triumph of Conservatism: A Re-interpretation of American History, 1900–1916*. New York: Free Press, 1963.

LINK, ARTHUR S., *Woodrow Wilson and the Progressive Era, 1910–1917*. New York: Harper & Row, 1954.

MOWRY, GEORGE E., *The Era of Theodore Roosevelt and the Birth of Modern America, 1900–1912*. New York: Harper & Row, 1958.

O'NEILL, WILLIAM L., *The Progressive Years: America Comes of Age*. New York: Harper & Row, 1975.

WIEBE, ROBERT H., *Businessmen and Reform*. Cambridge, Mass.: Harvard University Press, 1962.

WIEBE, ROBERT H., *The Search for Order, 1877–1920*. New York: Hill & Wang, 1967.

WIK, REYNOLD M., *Henry Ford and Grass-roots America*. Ann Arbor, Mich.: University of Michigan Press, 1973.

ORIGINS OF
THE GREAT DEPRESSION

_____ chapter XV___

In the six weeks following Thursday, October 24, 1929, corporate stocks traded on the national exchanges lost 40 percent of their value, banks became insolvent, and factories and businesses closed. Unemployment spiraled upward: between 1931 and 1940 from 14 to 25 percent of the working people were without jobs. By 1932 farm income had slipped to almost one third of its already depressed 1930 level. The value of goods and services declined by one half between 1929 and 1932. Capital investment almost stopped. The golden fabric of the Roaring Twenties lay in tatters. Coming as it did upon the heels of the most expansive and prosperous decades since the Civil War, the Great Depression produced a severe cultural and economic shock. Faith in the free-enterprise system was severely shaken. On March 3, 1933 (the day before he assumed office) President Franklin D. Roosevelt said, "The mechanics of civilization came to a dead stop." But former President Herbert Hoover rejoined that "if civilization came to a dead stop the press missed a great piece of news that day."

Table 15.1 illustrates the decline in the output of goods and services from 1929 to 1933, and then a gradual improvement such that production in 1939 matched that in 1929. For a decade Americans experienced a non-growth economy and real economic hardship.

Economists loosely fall into two schools of thought about the causes of the Great Depression. One may be called the "spending hypothesis," the other the "money hypothesis." The spending school holds that the depression was caused by a fall in autonomous spending—that is, investment generated by innovation in either the structure or mix of the factors of production or in the technology of production. Among the variety of factors contributing to the decline, falling farm income, the severe reduction in new housing after 1925 because the supply of housing exceeded the demand, the saturation of the automobile market, and the stock market collapse in 1929 all sharply reduced spendable income. The spend-

TABLE 15.1

Gross National Product, Total and Per Capita, 1920–1940 (1958 prices).

YEAR	TOTAL (BILLIONS OF DOLLARS)	PER CAPITA (DOLLARS)
1920	140.0	1,315
1921	127.8	1,177
1922	148.0	1,345
1923	165.9	1,482
1924	165.5	1,450
1925	179.4	1,549
1926	190.0	1,619
1927	189.8	1,594
1928	190.9	1,584
1929	203.6	1,671
1930	183.5	1,490
1931	169.3	1,364
1932	144.2	1,154
1933	141.5	1,126
1934	154.3	1,220
1935	169.5	1,331
1936	193.0	1,506
1937	203.2	1,567
1938	192.9	1,484
1939	209.4	1,598
1940	227.2	1,720

Source: *Historical Statistics of the United States, Colonial Times to 1970*, Series F 1–5. p. 224.

ing view holds that the "mal-distribution of wealth" resulted in "underconsump-tion" by the broad spectrum of society and overinvestment in the production of goods and services by those wealthier segments of society whose personal con-sumption of goods and services had long reached maximum limits. The fall in income and prices resulting from reduced spending in turn decreased the demand for and the supply of money. The "money supply" school holds that a "normal" cyclical recession or depression was converted into a long-term disaster by the collapse of the banking system and the severe retraction of the money supply.

One school holds the banking collapse as a cause of the depression, the other as a symptom. One holds that declining consumption was a product of the depression, the other that it caused the depression. One holds that the stock of money declined because the demand for it declined, the other that the actual supply of money fell first. One school stresses falling international monetary stocks, the other declining export markets and consumptions patterns. Both schools investigate essentially the same body of available information, and all economists admit intangible and entangled factors underlay the causes of the depression.[1]

FARM PROBLEMS

Economic dislocations induced by World War I, particularly in the areas of agricultural prices and export markets, contributed to the depression. During World War I, farm production and farm prices soared. More than 77 million acres of cropland were added to farms between 1910 and 1920. Yields also increased significantly, largely because of increased mechanization and improved farming practices. The Smith-Hughes Act (vocational agricultural training) and the Smith-Lever Act of 1913 (agricultural extension) contributed to higher farm production. Exports of American agricultural products more than doubled during the war years. Prices of farm commodities and agricultural land increased even more rapidly than production. On a 1914 base, the index of agricultural prices stood at 170 in April, 1920. By the end of the year the index had skidded to 80. Cotton prices, which stood at 41.4 cents per pound on the New Orleans market in April, slipped to 14.6 cents in December. The average price per bushel of wheat in 1921 was about half that of 1919 and 1920. Overall, the level of farm prices was less than half that of a year earlier, while farmers had committed themselves to the purchase of new equipment and to capital outlays. For rural-agricultural America a very real depression began in 1921 and lasted almost two decades.

There were ameliorating circumstances behind the slump in farm prices in the 1920s. Perhaps most significant, industrial expansion continued to draw surplus labor from the farm to the city. Despite the higher rural birthrate, farm population declined by 1.5 million persons between 1920 and 1930. Mechanization, higher yields, and continually expanding acreage produced larger volumes, which in part offset declining farm prices. Land prices generally increased throughout the early 1920s, giving the farmer a more favorable equity position despite declining prices. Unfortunately, these circumstances evaporated with the collapse of the money markets in 1929, which doubly aggravated the farm crises. Farm mortgage loans averaged almost $10 billion each year between 1921 and 1931, three times pre–World War I levels. Farmers who had borrowed heavily on their land in order to maintain income levels or to expand production were often unable to make mortgage payments after 1929. Almost one million farmers lost their land from mortgage foreclosures between 1930 and 1934. To compound the farm problem, for the first time since 1900 there was a reverse migration of unemployed industrial workers back to the farm. This movement occurred after 1930. Thus, the Great Depression compounded an already critical situation in agriculture.

At a ten-day meeting beginning April 11, 1921, farm leaders, legislators, and government officials discussed ways to relieve the crisis in agriculture resulting from the disastrous postwar commodity-price slump. Subsequently, a group of senators organized a bipartisan "farm bloc" designed to initiate farmer-desired legislation and shepherd it through Congress. Included in the legislative

TABLE 15.2

Farm Population, Farm Acreage, and Value of Farm Product, 1929–1940.

YEAR	POPULATION (IN MILLIONS)	ACREAGE (IN MILLIONS)	VALUE OF GROSS FARM PRODUCT (IN BILLIONS OF 1958 DOLLARS)
1929	30,580	6,512	23.8
1930	30,529	6,295	22.5
1931	30,845	6,608	24.4
1932	31,388	6,687	23.5
1933	32,393	6,741	23.4
1934	32,305	6,776	20.2
1935	32,161	6,812	22.5
1936	31,737	6,739	21.5
1937	31,266	6,636	24.7
1938	30,980	6,527	24.9
1939	30,840	6,441	26.0
1940	30,547	6,102	26.2

Source: *Historical Statistics of the United States, Colonial Times to 1970,* Series K 1–16, K 220–39. pp. 457, 481.

package were proposals relating to credit, commodity financing, incentives to farm cooperatives, tariffs, farm roads, and the regulation of meat-packing companies, commodity-futures dealers, and fertilizer manufacturers. A looser, less-structured, bipartisan coalition soon developed in the House of Representatives. Over the next few years federal legislation affecting most of these areas was approved by Congress, and much of that legislation was framed on the Progressive proposition that the role of government was to help farmers help themselves, to preserve the basic tenets of laissez faire and individualism, and to avoid paternalism and regimentation.

Believing that what was good for business should be good for agriculture, congressmen began to include produce in tariff bills. The Fordney-McCumber Tariff of 1921, for example, tacked a 42-cent tariff on wheat to bolster sagging prices. There appear to have been short-term commodity-price increases, perhaps attributable to the tariff. But in the long run, because the United States exported much of its annual wheat crop, protective tariffs encouraged increased farm production and eroded both domestic and export market prices. The Agricultural Credits Act (1921) and the Federal Intermediate Credits Act (1923) provided government insurance for private farm loans. By 1930, over $3 billion had been loaned to farmers under these programs. In 1923 the Capper-Volstead Act exempted farm cooperatives from antitrust prosecution while the Department of Agriculture, through its extension services and credit policies, encouraged the organization of cooperatives. As a result, producer and consumer cooperatives proliferated throughout the remainder of the decade, which helped reduce the farmers' cost of living and doing business. Farmers shifted from party politics to pressure-group politics in the 1920s.

The McNary-Haugen bill, first introduced in Congress in 1924, combined the ideas of cooperatives, protection, and low-cost government finance in a comprehensive farm program. Devised primarily by George N. Peek of the Moline Plow Company, the bill would have established a giant marketing cooperative financed by $200 million of low-interest government loans. The cooperative would be authorized to buy farm produce at a parity price, and parity would elevate domestic farm prices to a par, or equality, with nonfarm prices. Five distinct bills embodying this program were introduced to Congress in 1927 and 1928, two of them passing Congress to be vetoed by President Calvin Coolidge.

Farm problems were still the paramount economic consideration when Herbert Hoover became president in 1929. Hoover, like Coolidge, opposed the privileged position of agriculture in the McNary-Haugen plan and the massiveness and rigidity of the cooperative marketing structure it would establish. Hoover favored a more decentralized, unstructured arrangement that would employ existing producer cooperatives and federal credit. In 1929, prior to the stock-market crash, Congress approved the Agricultural Marketing Act. This act established the Federal Farm Board, which would administer a $500-million revolving fund. This money would be loaned to cooperatives so that they could buy, store, and market commodities in a more effective manner. The act rejected price fixing and accepted the principle that government's role was to help farmers help themselves. But the act included a proviso that marked a significant departure from this self-help philosophy: the Federal Farm Board was authorized to establish its own marketing facilities (the Wheat Stabilization Corporation and the Cotton Stabilization Corporation) and, in emergencies, to buy on its own account. This meant that government assumed a direct responsibility for economic welfare. By 1932 government warehouses were full of grain and cotton and the Farm Board had exhausted its financial resources. Although cotton and wheat prices were temporarily stabilized by government purchases in 1930 and 1931, by 1932 the price of cotton had dropped from the 1929 high of 18 cents per pound to a historic low of 4.6 cents per pound. In the same period wheat slipped from about 70 cents to 36 cents per bushel. The belief that Farm Board operations to strengthen the position of agriculture would stabilize the general economy had been disproved.[2]

American foreign sales of both agricultural and manufactured goods declined from the wartime high following the Armistice. But throughout the 1920s exports generally exceeded imports by about $900 million annually, creating a severe trade imbalance that drained the financial resources of importing nations and softened the long-term market for American goods. Moreover, European countries who were primary markets for American goods were already heavily debt-ridden from World War I. The protective-tariff policy of the decade, which

HERBERT CLARK HOOVER *(1874–1964)*
President of the United States, 1929–1933.
Courtesy Library of Congress.

culminated in the all-time high Hawley-Smoot Tariff, appears to have markedly reduced American exports and imports at a particularly inappropriate time and stimulated restrictive trade barriers around the world.

REAL-ESTATE SPECULATION

A collapse in real-estate values centering in Florida but having nationwide ramifications occurred after 1926. Having experienced a dizzying real-estate boom between 1921 and 1925, Florida suffered the most severe decline in land prices. Hotels, cities, and suburbs were laid out and often partly constructed from Jacksonville south to Miami on the east coast and from Tampa to Sarasota on the west coast. Cities sprang into existence on palmetto flats and dredged dunes. Prices and profits, most of the latter on paper, skyrocketed. At one time Miami had 2,000 real-estate offices and 25,000 salesmen marketing lots or acreage. But oversale and an untimely hurricane burst the paper pyramids of real-estate speculation.[3]

What happened in Florida occurred in many other parts of the United States. The automobile produced a frenzy of suburban developments near almost every city in the United States. High profits attracted large investments in construction. By 1925 more new homes were being built than the market could absorb. But new construction continued, and eventually forced a decline in real-estate values, raised credit liabilities, and froze capital assets. Independently

235

or jointly, agricultural crises, trade imbalances, and the decline in construction and real-estate values could not, it is believed, have caused the Great Depression. Income from agriculture constituted only about one fourth of the national income, and the reduction of that income by even as much as one half would not have affected the total economy so disastrously as to cause a financial collapse. Population increases would soon have absorbed unsold housing units after 1926. Nonetheless, these situations contributed to the depression.

THE GREAT BULL MARKET

The most spectacular collapse, and the event that many believe to be the trigger if not the cause of the Great Depression, was the stock market crash of 1929. The crash brought an end to "the greatest fantasy in an age filled with illusion."[4] It also brought an end to the great bull market of the 1920s. This decade was an age of unbridled optimism. Americans had fought the war to end all wars, and won. The United States had become a world power, militarily and financially. The new age of science and technology was affirmed by such symbols as the Scopes Trial, which established the inescapable truth of human evolution and progress, and by tangible entities such as electricity, automobiles, refrigerators, radios, indoor plumbing, and supermarkets. All of these advances, and more, became reflected in the great index of American optimism and progress, the stock exchange. By 1924 the confusion and uncertainties of the postwar resettlement had ended. Over the next five years the volume and value of stocks traded on the New York Stock Exchanges soared (see Tables 15.3 and 15.4).

TABLE 15.3

Volume on the New York Stock Exchange, 1923–1929.

YEAR	VOLUME (SHARES)
1923	237,276,927
1924	282,032,923
1925	452,211,399
1926	449,103,253
1927	576,990,875
1928	920,550,032
1929	1,124,990,980

Source: *Dow Jones Investors' Handbook, 1966*, pp. 50–51

TABLE 15.4

Dow-Jones Industrial Averages, 1923–1931.

YEAR	HIGH	LOW
1923	105.38	85.76
1924	120.51	88.33
1925	159.30	115.00
1926	166.64	135.20
1927	202.40	152.73
1928	300.00	191.23
1929	381.17	198.69
1930	294.07	157.71
1931	194.36	73.79

Source: *Dow Jones Investors' Handbook, 1966*, pp. 50–51.

The most conservative $1,000 investment in stocks made at the high in 1924 would have returned over $3,000 if sold at the 1929 high, or a 40-percent annual return, not including stock dividends. The national economy was a dynamic economy in the 1920s, and the market more than reflected this condition.

Comparative annual high prices of a half-dozen leading corporate stocks between 1924 and 1929 (Table 15.5) indicate the apparent infallibility of market investments. At least this is what the general public could and did readily conclude at almost any time before October, 1929.

TABLE 15.5

Prices of Selected Corporate Stocks, 1924 and 1929.

STOCK	1924 HIGH	1929 HIGH
American Can	163 1/2	184 1/2
Eastman Kodak	114 7/8	264 3/4
General Electric	322	403
International Harvester	110 1/2	142
Standard Oil (N.J.)	42 1/4	83
U.S. Steel	123	198 3/4

Source: Robert Sobel, *The Great Bull Market, Wall Street in the 1920s*. (New York: Norton, 1968), pp. 105, 120.

But there was more to the market than the general upward trend of stock prices and corporate earnings. Bull markets and enthusiastic optimism have occurred since the 1920s, but the stock market in that decade was subject to several important conditions that have not prevailed since. Intrinsic to an understanding of the excesses of the bull market of the 1920s is an understanding of margin buying, the investment trust, and the climate of national banking. Buying on margin simply means that the purchaser borrows a part of the purchase price of the stock from the seller, usually a broker. A 50-percent margin means that a purchaser pays half the market price—in the case of a $10,000 transaction, $5,000. A 10-percent margin enables a buyer to obtain $10,000 in stock for a $1,000 investment. The "call rate," or interest on the "call loan"—the difference between the purchase price and the collateral—has in recent years amounted to one or two percent more than the regular bank-loan rate, but in the 1920s it fluctuated widely, often between 10 and 30 percent. If the value of a stock declines below the margin requirements, the broker issues a call on the buyer requiring him to renew his margin or sell his holdings. Thus, if $1,000 stock on a 10-percent margin declines to $900, the buyer must pay an additional $90 margin and he loses his original $100 investment. The higher the percentage of the loan, the greater the likelihood of a call. Between 1920 and 1929 the volume of brokers' loans rose from approximately $1 billion to $9 billion. This meant that stocks of at least that value were not paid for, and that a market decline might force at least twice that volume of stocks to be sold. The market thus has a built-in reverse leverage: falling prices generate an increasingly greater volume of sales. Since World War II margin requirements have rarely dropped below 75 percent. On just a few occasions, in the mid 1970s, they dropped to 50 percent. Often, they have equaled 100 percent; in effect, no margin existed. In the 1920s, margin requirements were rarely more than 50 percent, on occasion they were as low as 5 percent, and often they were 10 percent. Purchasing on margin gave the buyer unusual leverage, which in a rising market meant handsome profits with minimal investments. For example, the investor could have purchased 100 shares of General Electric at 81 in January, 1927 for a collateral of $810, and sold it in September at 146, realizing a profit of $6,500, or 800 percent, in an eight-month period

The investment trust institutionalized and popularized margin buying. Developed in England in the nineteenth century, the investment trust became recognized, popular, and truly public in the United States only in the 1920s. Much like contemporary mutual funds, but without their stringent regulations and financial-accounting requirements, the investment trust sold shares in its own name and invested the receipts in shares of other companies. The small investor was encouraged to buy perhaps $500 in stock in an investment trust such as United States and Foreign Securities or Goldman, Sachs Trading Corporation by investing $200 (often borrowed) on a 40-percent margin. The trust would then buy $2,000 in corporate stock with the original $500 on a 25-percent margin. In this way the investor piled one margin on top of another. Stocks in the trust were traded on the exchanges and bore little or no relationship to the market values of the stocks retained as its capital investment. Speculation in trust certificates could be as rampant as speculation in industrial issues. Between 1927 and 1930 more than 700 investment trusts were formed in the United States. The height of investment-trust speculation was the investment by one trust company in the shares of another, the result, as Robert Sobel writes, was the piling of "margin on margin on margin on margin."[5]

The call-money market, where interest rates often exceeded corporate dividends, soon became one of the most attractive investments for banks, investment trusts, and corporate funds. Banks, trusts, and conservative businesses began to invest in brokers' loans, which they used to buy stock in their own companies, thereby driving prices higher and higher and creating the demand for yet more margin buying and larger loans. All such investments occurred within the legitimate market. Purely fraudulent operations also existed—corners, market manipulations, and schemes such as Charles Ponzi's Old Colony Foreign Exchange Company, which used new investors' money to pay "profits" to old investors. Somewhere, sometime, the sands of the hourglass had to run out.

In the 1920s there was no Securities Act or Securities and Exchange Commission to regulate trade or impose a degree of uniformity in corporate accounting or reporting procedures. Speculation was blatantly encouraged by a call-money market fed by the Federal Reserve Banks, private banks, and the corporations themselves, and by minimal brokerage margins, often as low as 10 percent. Furthermore, the wild growth of investment trusts in the late 1920s inflated both the volume and the value of corporate securities traded. Finally, private bankers and even the Federal Reserve Board either abdicated responsibility for controlling speculation or, by their inaction and sometimes their positive encouragement and incitement, fed the speculation. This financial environment interrelated with the pervasive mood of national optimism.

The Federal Reserve Board and even political and financial authorities could have done several things to check the boom and alleviate the bust. Most certainly, they could have prevented the panic. This does not mean that such action could have halted a depression, but it could have made it less severe and shorter in duration. As early as 1924, governmental actions stimulated an already optimistic and rising market. In that year Congress approved the Soldiers Bonus Bill, which injected an estimated half-billion dollars into the economy, and approved the Revenue Act urged by Secretary of the Treasury Andrew Mellon, which reduced maximum tax brackets from 50 to 25 percent. Mellon himself is said to have saved $800,000 in taxes from this reduction in 1925 alone. In 1927, as the housing and real-estate market turned down, industrial production, consumer purchases, and corporate profits declined. The national economy showed strong symptoms of recession. Yet in the face of these conditions corporations actually increased their dividends. However, they retained little of their earnings for expansion, reasoning that further expansion of plants and equipment was unwise in a saturated market. The Federal Reserve Board lowered the rediscount rate to 3½ percent, and borrowing by member banks and businesses rose markedly. Much of the new money produced by higher dividends and easier credit found its way into the call-money market and produced sharply higher stock prices in spite of the downtrend in earnings.[6]

By 1928 there was considerable sentiment among investors that "stock prices had risen too high, too fast."[7] Moody's Investment Service, the Harvard Economic Society, Bernard Baruch, Joseph Kennedy, and apparently President Coolidge, despite his repeated protests that the nation's business had never been better, were among those who believed that a readjustment of market prices, perhaps a violent one, was imminent. Grace Coolidge is said to have replied to the question of why her husband wanted to leave the White House in 1928 with the comment, "Poppa says there's a depression coming."[8] There *was* a short-lived decline in 1928, but it was followed by yet another galloping bull market. Federal Reserve Board Chairman Benjamin Strong responded by raising the rediscount rate from 3½ to 5 percent over the next eight months, but the flow of money into the call-money market continued to rise, fed now by corporate and investment-trust funds bidding for the 10-to-15 percent interest rates. The market appeared to be out of the control of the Federal Reserve Board. Yet throughout 1928 and most of 1929 there were strong and repeated public statements from bankers such as Charles Mitchell of the National City Bank and the New York Federal Reserve Bank, John J. Raskob of General Motors, and Treasury Secretary Mellon urging continued optimism and investment.[9]

Voices of caution and conservatism were drowned in the market stampede. John Galbraith argues that although there were reasonable excuses for the Federal Reserve Board's failure to seriously attempt to slow the boom in 1928 and 1929, the board "was helpless only because it wanted to be." Its most obvious weapon, he believes, would have been to obtain congressional approval of a grant of power to the board to set margin requirements. "An increase in margins to, say, 75 percent in January 1929, or even a serious proposal to do so, would have caused many small speculators and quite a few big ones to sell. The boom would have come to a sudden and perhaps spectacular end."[10] Galbraith suggests that even a strong attempt at moral persuasion by the board could have checked the boom. He points to a sharp break in market prices in March, 1929 that derived solely from the fact that the board was conducting daily meetings but issuing no statements. This break was easily overridden by a pronouncement from Charles Mitchell that the National City Bank was committed to supporting the call-money market.[11] It is doubtful that Congress would have acted on a board request for authority over margins, or that "jawboning" by banking or political figures could have stayed the final great bull market. There was too much financial commitment to a rising market, and too little political profit in a market break or a recession. In this respect, the present is not unlike the past.

THE CRASH

The Great Crash occurred on Thursday, October 24, 1929. The market was swamped by the sale of 12,894,560 shares of stock, twice the volume of the previous daily record of 6,000,000 shares. Prices plummeted so fast that there was often a spread of from ten to thirty points between the price of stock being quoted on the exchange floor and the price printed on the ticker tape. Not until evening would hundreds of thousands of investors and speculators discover they were ruined. Six to seven billion dollars in values were erased. But before the close of the trading day the widespread panic eased and the market was stabilized by the bankers. Then on Tuesday, October 29, "the most devastating day in the history of New York stock market," 16.4 million shares traded hands as prices plunged. The market lost another $8 billion to $9 billion in values. Over a period of six weeks market prices declined an average of 40 percent. Paper values, credit, and money disappeared.

Over the next twelve months the rate of bankruptcies, foreclosures, and simple business cessation rose. Business failures involved liabilities of $483

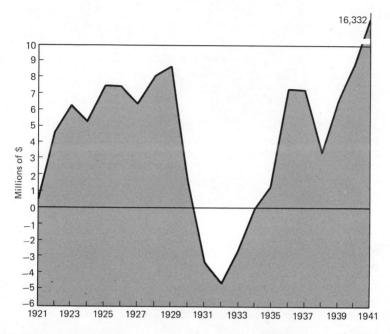

FIGURE 15.1 Corporate net income, (Millions of dollars), 1921–1941.

Source: Bureau of the Census, *Historical Statistics of the United States Colonial Times to 1970.* Series Y 381–392, p. 1109.

million in 1929 and $668 million in 1930. In 1929 corporate profits were $8.7 billion; in 1932 corporate losses were $5.6 billion (see Figure 15.1). Unemployment climbed steadily for four years (see Table 15.6).

In the summer of 1931 depression rocked Europe. European banking structures collapsed. Despite loans of $650 million from the United States, the Bank of England defaulted on its payments to foreign creditors. By the close of the year most European nations left the gold standard, and as Europeans began buying gold a heavy drain was imposed on American gold supplies. The domestic depression was capped by a worldwide depression. President Hoover believed that recovery could best be achieved through natural processes: "Our first duty as a nation is to put our governmental house in order, national, state and local. With the return of prosperity the government can undertake constructive projects of both social character and in public improvement. We cannot squander ourselves into prosperity."[12] As the depression deepened, Hoover began to initiate certain emergency programs. In meetings with business, farm, and labor leaders he sought voluntary action to stem unemployment. New commodity purchases were made by the Federal Farm Board. The Reconstruction Finance Corporation, created by the Hoover administration in 1932 to promote economic stability, loaned $1.5 billion to banks, railroads, and businesses. Another $1.5 billion was

TABLE 15.6

Unemployment 1929–1943.

YEAR	NUMBER	PERCENTAGE OF LABOR FORCE
1929	1,550,000	3.2
1930	4,340,000	8.7
1931	8,020,000	15.9
1932	12,060,000	23.6
1933	12,830,000	24.9
1934	11,340,000	21.7
1935	10,610,000	20.1
1936	9,030,000	16.9
1937	7,700,000	14.3
1938	10,390,000	19.0
1939	9,480,000	17.2
1940	8,120,000	14.6
1941	5,500,000	9.9
1942	2,660,000	4.7
1943	1,070,000	1.9

Source: *Bureau of the Census, Statistical Abstract, 1954*, p. 195.

allocated for 1933, and $300 million was loaned to the states for direct relief. Additional loans were released through the Federal Home Loan Agency and the Federal Credit Agency. In 1931 Hoover obtained a moratorium on war-debt and reparations payments to help stabilize the German and European economies, and in 1932 war debts were scaled down. Economic disaster caused Hoover to break with the tradition of laissez faire and to make government responsible for maintaining the nation's economic welfare.

By July, 1932 Hoover believed that a recovery had begun. Hoover based his position on several factors. Between July and October of 1932 more banks reopened than failed. Gold began to reenter the country. Exports increased each month. Farm prices, industrial production, factory payrolls, employment, and stock prices rose steadily during the same period. However, the rejection of Hoover at the polls in November, 1932 brought new uncertainties, and a slump. In February and March of 1933, prior to Franklin D. Roosevelt's inauguration, bank and money panics swept the nation. Hoover attributed this crisis to Roosevelt, labeling it the "Great Fear." Factory employment and commodity prices sank to an all-time low. The nation was in the depths of the most severe and prolonged depression in its history. Why? The following list reviews some of the factors:

A. Collapse of the banking system and a retraction of the money supply.
  1. American tariff policy and American investments abroad restricted the ability of foreign countries to buy from the United States.

2. Overspeculation and the buying of stocks on margin.
3. Weaknesses of European economies resulting from World War I.
4. Decline in agricultural prices.
5. Collapse in land values.
6. A series of domestic and international banking crises.
7. Decline in income.

B. Fall in autonomous spending.
    1. Unequal distribution of income produces "underconsumption" (see Table 15.7).
    2. Too much capital investment and production capacity for the existing purchasing power results in declining investments after 1927.
    3. Growth of credit buying helps hide declining purchasing power.
    4. Declining farm income.
    5. Speculation in land.
    6. Speculation in stocks.
    7. Decline in the value of American exports.
    8. Growth of monopolies and other forms of combination causes price fixing and production to be controlled by the producer rather than by demand.

TABLE 15.7

Income Distribution in 1929.

INCOME GROUP	PERCENTAGE OF TOTAL FAMILIES AND UNATTACHED INDIVIDUALS IN GROUP	PERCENTAGE OF TOTAL INCOME BY INCOME LEVEL
−1,999	65.0	31.0
2,000–2,999	17.0	17.0
3,000–3,999	8.0	11.0
4,000–4,999	4.0	7.0
5,000–9,999	5.0	15.0
10,000 and over	1.0	19.0

Note: According to this tabulation, 10 percent of the families earned 41 percent of the national income in 1929.
Source: Bureau of the Census, *Historical Statistics of the U.S. Colonial Times to 1970*, Series G 269–82, G 283–96.

Economic historians of many points of view have examined the same statistical and narrative data of the predepression and depression eras. Two dominant explanations have emerged: the decline in spending and the decline in the money supply. The two explanations are closely interrelated: spending and the money supply interact. Which has primacy?

THE TEMIN TEST

Recent attempts to unravel the degree of interdependence of the money supply and spending have produced some surprising but still incomplete conclusions. An econometric, macroeconomic analysis of depression data tests the relationship of banking panics to the fall in income, and the impact of a decline in the money supply to a decline in consumption. Explanations of the Great Depression rely on counterfactual models or hypothetical alternatives: if the money supply had been greater, there would have been no depression or a less severe one; if consumption had been greater, there would have been no depression or a less severe one. The "new" economic historians attempt to test historical explanations by developing explicit mathematical counterfactual models that can be applied to different bodies of data in order to derive quantitative results.

Peter Temin's one- and two-year econometric perspective of three distinct economic cycles reveals inconsistencies in consumption and in the apparent money supply as represented by investments and exports (Table 15.8). In 1930, unlike in 1921 and 1938, consumption declined in conjunction with GNP, investment, and exports.

TABLE 15.8

Percentage of Change in Real Macroeconomic Variables in Three Periods.

	1920–21	1929–30	1937–38
GNP	− 2.4	− 8.9	− 5.4
Consumption	+ 6.4	− 5.4	− 1.6
Investment	−41.7	−35.6	−53.1
Exports	−14.2	−19.1	+ 1.7
	1919–21	1928–30	1936–38
GNP	− 3.5	− 3.4	+ 2.3
Consumption	+11.6	− 0.2	+ 2.1
Investment	−30.7	−27.8	−26.4
Exports	−19.7	−15.7	+29.8

Note: All variables are in 1929 prices. "Investment" refers to gross private domestic investment. "Exports" refers to merchandise exports.

Source: Peter Temin, *Did Monetary Forces Cause the Great Depression?* (New York: Norton, 1976), p. 64.

An examination of the interrelationship among housing and construction investment, autonomous investment, exports, and the stock-market crash and the decline in spending tentatively reveals no consistent variable or equation. This suggests that the fall in consumption was truly autonomous, or that it requires other explanations than those we have reviewed. Similar tests indicate that the demand for money actually fell more rapidly than the supply during 1930 and the first three quarters of 1931. This finding suggests that the demand for money or spending had more of a deflationary impact than the supply of money. These tests conclude then, that changes in spending or consumption patterns are better explanations for the Great Depression than a contraction in the supply of money.[13]

Depression, however, may not be subject wholly to economic analysis. Data and econometric analysis still basically explain *what* happened, not necessarily *why* it happened. Depression and economic expansion are clearly functions of people's expectations. The psychology of depression is not subject to quantification, but pessimism, insecurity, dejection, the absence of motivation, and human inactivity are clearly elements of the Great Depression. Depressions have to do with both the quantity and the quality of life. The New Deal sought to improve the human situation on both levels through programs that would expand the quantity of money and spending, and through reforms that would generate broad-based optimism and participation in the free-enterprise system. The debate about the causes of the Great Depression has been eclipsed by the controversy over what impact the New Deal had on both the depression and the free-enterprise system.

Notes

[1]For a general statement of these two schools, see Peter Temin, *Did Monetary Forces Cause the Great Depression?* (New York: Norton, 1976), pp. 14–103. Also, see especially Milton Friedman and Anna J. Schwartz, *The Great Contraction 1929–1933* (Princeton, N.J.: Princeton University Press, 1965), for an emphasis on money; and Arthur M. Schlesinger, Jr., *The Crisis of the Old Order, 1919–1933* (Boston: Houghton Mifflin, 1964), and John Maynard Keynes, *Treatise on Money* (New York: Harcourt, Brace, 1930), Vol. 2, for an emphasis on spending.

[2]See Gilbert C. Fite, *George N. Peek and the Fight for Farm Parity* (Norman, Okla.: University of Oklahoma Press, 1954), pp. 221–42, and Murray R. Benedict, *Farm Policies of the United States, 1790–1950* (New York: Twentieth Century Fund, 1953), pp. 239–40, 257–67.

[3]See Frederick Lewis Allen, *Only Yesterday* (New York: Harper & Brothers, 1931), pp. 191–205.

[4]Robert Sobel, *The Great Bull Market: Wall Street in the 1920s* (New York: Norton, 1968), p. 21.

[5]*Ibid.*, pp. 92–93.

[6]See Sobel, *The Great Bull Market*, pp. 104–12.

[7]*Ibid.*, p. 113.

[8]*Ibid.*, p. 118.

[9]John Galbraith, *The Great Crash 1929* (Boston: Houghton Mifflin, 1954), p. 37.

[10]*Ibid.*

[11]*Ibid.*, p. 116.

[12]Herbert Hoover, *The Memoirs of Herbert Hoover*, Vol. III (New York: Macmillan, 1952).

[13] See Temin, *Did Monetary Forces Cause the Great Depression?* pp. 62–64, 169–78.

SUGGESTED READING

ALLEN, FREDERICK LEWIS, *Only Yesterday* New York: Harper & Row, 1931.

FITE, GILBERT C., *George N. Peek and the Fight for Farm Parity.* Norman, Okla.: University of Oklahoma Press, 1954.

FREIDEL, FRANK, *Franklin D. Roosevelt: The Triumph.* Boston: Little, Brown, 1956.

FRIEDMAN, MILTON, AND ANNA J. SCHWARTZ, *The Great Contraction, 1929–1933.* Princeton, N.J.: Princeton University Press, 1965.

FUSFELD, DANIEL, *The Economic Thought of Franklin D. Roosevelt and the Origins of the New Deal.* New York: Columbia University Press, 1956.

GALBRAITH, JOHN, *The Great Crash, 1929.* Boston: Houghton Mifflin, 1954.

GRAHAM, OTIS, *Encore for Reform: The Old Progressive and the New Deal.* New York: Oxford University Press, 1967.

HICKS, JOHN D., *Republican Ascendency, 1921–1933.* New York: Harper & Row, 1960.

LEUCHTENBURG, WILLIAM E., *The Perils of Prosperity: 1914–1932.* Chicago: University of Chicago Press, 1958.

PROTHRO, JAMES WARREN, *The Dollar Decade.* Baton Rouge: Louisiana State University Press, 1954.

SCHLESINGER, ARTHUR M., JR., *The Crisis of the Old Order, 1919–1933.* Boston: Houghton Mifflin, 1964.

SOBEL, ROBERT, *The Great Bull Market: Wall Street in the 1920s.* New York: Norton, 1968.

THE NEW DEAL

_____ chapter XVI__

Did the New Deal reflect a radical excursion in Keynesian compensatory fiscal spending? Was it an attempt to squander ourselves into prosperity? Did the New Deal inaugurate a "welfare state"? Did it significantly redistribute the wealth of the country? Did it change the role of government in the economy? Did it alter the structure of the free-enterprise system? Did New Deal policies effect economic recovery? As Americans have become increasingly remote and detached from the trauma of depression and the partisanship of a now distant politics, the New Deal has assumed a more definitive form. Yet additional econometric analysis of New Deal taxation, spending, and monetary programs are needed to sharpen our perception and understanding.

ROOSEVELT'S NEW DEAL

In his inaugural address of March 4, 1933 Franklin D. Roosevelt observed with candor that "Values have shrunken to fantastic levels; taxes have risen; our ability to pay has fallen . . .; the means of exchange are frozen in the currents of trade; the withered leaves of industrial enterprise lie on every side; farmers find no markets for their product; the savings of many years in thousands of families are gone. . . . Only a foolish optimist can deny the dark realities of the moment." The unscrupulous moneychangers, said Roosevelt, have "fled from their high seats in the temple of our civilization." His plan for economic recovery included (1) putting people to work; (2) correcting the "overbalance of population in our industrial centers"; (3) raising the value of agricultural production; (4) strictly supervising banking, credits, and investments, ending speculation, and providing for an "adequate but sound currency"; and (5) balancing the national budget. International trade relations, he said, are secondary to the establishment

FRANKLIN DELANO ROOSEVELT *(1882–1945)*
President of the United States, 1933–1945.
Courtesy Library of Congress.

of a sound domestic economy. New Deal programs ultimately had far broader ramifications and diversity than Roosevelt's inaugural address denotes, and not a few contradictions, but the five points cited above indicate the central thrust of New Deal legislation.

Historians have delineated two distinct phases of the New Deal. A "first" New Deal (1933–1935) emphasized relief and recovery through cooperative planning by government and business. This New Deal had a strong Hamiltonian orientation. A "second" New Deal (1935–1937) emphasized reform based upon precepts of Jeffersonian democratic opportunity, and was characterized by a determined fight against business domination. Although the distinction between a first and a second New Deal has lost its epochal qualities, it provides a useful frame of reference for examining New Deal legislation.[1]

THE FIRST NEW DEAL

On March 6, 1933, two days after assuming office, President Roosevelt declared a four-day bank holiday that temporarily halted a run on the nation's banks precipitated by inflationary fears and the uncertainties surrounding Roosevelt's fiscal policies. On March 9 Congress confirmed this action in the Emergency Banking Act, which gave the president power to regulate financial transactions and to license Federal Reserve Bank members for reopening. Prior to reopening, banks were hastily checked by examiners, loaned money by the Reconstruction

Finance Corporation when justified, and provided a license that amounted to a federal certification of soundness. By mid-March 90 percent of the banks closed by executive order had reopened for business, but these banks constituted less than half the number of banks in business in 1929. On March 10 Roosevelt forbade the export of gold unless approved by the Treasury Department, and in April he prohibited the hoarding of gold and gold certificates. These measures finally halted the export of gold. In June Congress voided obligations to pay debts in gold, an action that effectively removed the United States from the gold standard. In October the Reconstruction Finance Corporation began to purchase gold in the domestic markets on an erratic but rising price schedule designed to depreciate the dollar such that by January 1, 1934 cotton would be selling at 10 cents per pound, corn at 50 cents a bushel, and wheat at 90 cents a bushel. In November the New York Federal Reserve Bank began to purchase gold in international markets. After the price of gold stabilized at $35 an ounce, Congress officially fixed the value of the dollar at 59.06 percent of its 1900 value. Although stock values generally rose in accord with the 40-percent annual rate of inflation, commodity prices rose only 20 percent. Inflation failed to restore a balance between agricultural and industrial prices, as had been anticipated. Nonetheless, through these initial market actions the administration relieved the burden of the debtor, eased credit, placed more money in circulation, and ultimately stabilized the value of the dollar, which had appreciated during the past few years. Despite protests that the end of the gold standard would spell the doom of civilization, the inflationary measures were generally in accord with the views of conservative economists and many business leaders, such as J. Pierpont Morgan.[2]

The Glass-Steagall Banking Act, approved by Congress in June, 1933, separated investment and savings institutions from parent banks and established the Federal Deposit Insurance Corporation to insure bank accounts. This act, following upon the Emergency Bank Act of March, 1933, contributed substantially to financial stability. The Banking Act of 1935 expanded Federal Reserve Board control over the reserve requirements and credit policies of member banks while lessening political influence over board policies.

Finally, the Securities Act of 1933 required that every security listed on a national exchange be listed as well with the Federal Trade Commission, and that full financial information be furnished. The Securities Exchange Act of 1934 created the Securities Exchange Commission and empowered it to regulate trade, brokerage practices, and margin requirements. By 1935 Roosevelt had essentially completed his specific banking and monetary reforms, all of which sought to strengthen existing banking and investment institutions and to provide a broader and more equitable financial structure. But even though New Deal policies eased the constriction of the money supply, there was little increase in investment.

In his structural analysis of the Great Depression John B. Kirkwood concluded that the effectiveness of monetary policy appears to be proportionate to the demand for money: "As interest rates fall, larger and larger increases in the money stock are needed to produce the same absolute reduction in short-term rate."[3] The sharp decline in business investment that had occurred by 1931 forced interest rates to such low levels that small increases in the supply of money failed to stimulate even lower interest rates, new investment, or a rise in income. In other words, Roosevelt's fiscal policies did provide some relief but failed to stimulate recovery, because the problem of the 1930s was less the shortage of money for capital investment and the production of goods and services than the shortage of money in the pockets of the consumer. Furthermore, federal expenditures expanded only in 1931 and 1936, and those exceptions reflected the distribution of veterans' bonuses and not administration policy. Until at least 1937 Roosevelt believed in a balanced budget. Between 1933 and 1937 the Keynesian idea of compensatory public spending had not been accepted as a part of New Deal policy.[4]

Although the federal government incurred a deficit each year between 1933 and 1940, only in 1934, 1936, and 1938 was the deficit greater than the 1932 deficit of $2.73 billion incurred by Hoover. Only after 1940 did the necessities of

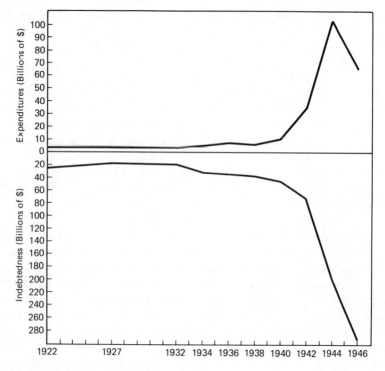

FIGURE 16.1. Total federal expenditures and indebtedness (billions of dollars), 1922–1946.

Source: Bureau of the Census, *Historical Statistics of the United States Colonial Times to 1970,* Series Y 335–338, Y 339–342, pp. 1104–1105.

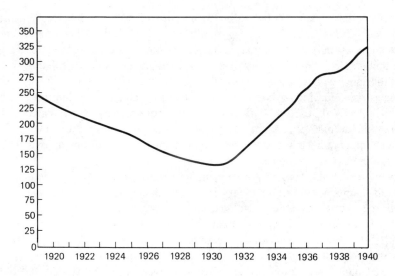

16.2. Per-capita debt of the federal government (dollars), 1920–1940.

Source: Bureau of the Census, *Historical Statistics of the United States Colonial Times to 1970*, Series Y 493–504, p. 1117.

war generate massive public expenditures and prodigious public indebtedness. By 1940 the per-capita debt of the United States was approximately $100 greater than it had been in 1920. (See Figures 16.1 and 16.2.)

It is generally agreed that Franklin Roosevelt and his economic advisors were not strongly influenced by John Maynard Keynes's ideas of compensatory public spending.[5] Keynes (1883–1946) was a Cambridge economist who, in company with a small number of economists in the 1920s and 1930s, questioned the orthodox economic view that national economic growth, or growth in real income, was proportionate to expansion in land (capital accumulation), labor (population growth), and capital (technology). Because of the closed circular flow of an economic system, in accord with Say's Law and conventional wisdom, supply invariably equals demand. But Keynes rejected this theory, arguing that an equilibrium in the circular flow of goods and income could be attained below the level necessary to achieve growth, and indeed could occur at stagnation levels. Real investment—the actual expenditure of savings for capital goods the productuion of which generates employment—need not reflect the propensity to consume. Keynes believed that the problem of the 1930s was overinvestment in the production of durable goods and underconsumption. The solution to the depression was to increase consumer spending power by new injections of money—welfare spending.

Real investment is responsive to interest rates, which in turn are determined by the *liquidity preference* and the *marginal utility of money*. The liquidity preference suggests that despite attractive interest rates or investment opportunities, business may choose to retain money for operations rather than spending it for capital expansion, fail to invest because of an overriding pessimism, or hoard for future speculative opportunities even while ignoring present sound investment conditions. The marginal utility of money calculates the rate of return on the increase in the quantity of money invested. Given an established market equilibrium, each new increment to the supply factor (capital investment) creates greater risks and higher costs, or alternative investment opportunities and new risks appear with each new increment of investment. Keynes recognized a tendency of the market economy to maintain a given level of economic flow, or stagnation. Furthermore, stagnation could occur in times of unemployment, despite the obvious existence of a propensity to consume. In such cases, he believed, it was the task of government to generate the aggregate demand that would maintain full employment. The government should "prime the pump" until the normal investment cycle sustains growth in national income.

Keynesian economics was revolutionary primarily in that it viewed the capitalistic economy from an aggregate or collective perspective rather than from the individualistic, per-unit view of the classical economists, and in that Keynes advised public regulation of the investment cycle through taxation and public spending. In down-cycles, when private investment declines, public spending should expand in order to stimulate employment and renew consumption. In upward swings, in order to prevent overinvestment and inflation public spending should be reduced and taxes increased. Government should assume the responsibility for containing economic growth, sustaining profits, and maintaining high employment levels. Keynes did not advocate nationalization of industry, the conscription of wealth, or a wholesale revision of the free-enterprise system. He did advocate planning and collective controls over the economy, but he believed that the fundamental components of the economy continued to be individual initiative and freedom, and private property.

Keynesian economics has had a pervasive if not revolutionary impact on modern economic thought. Although there is considerable disagreement as to the mechanics and degree of governmental planning, it is both fashionable and proper to use Keynesian precepts to test the New Deal, particularly New Deal taxation and spending policies.

New Deal programs were, to be sure, largely a matter of accident and experimentation, and they often seemed to embody a mass of contradictions.[6] Their net result was a substantial increase in government spending, compared with predepression levels. Large expenditures were made in an effort to stimulate agricultural relief and recovery. The Agricultural Adjustment Act, approved by Congress on May 12, 1933, created the Agricultural Adjustment Administration (AAA), which assumed, with substantial modifications, the program of the Federal Farm Board. The AAA entered into voluntary agreements with farmers for the reduction of acreages of basic crops, and made cash advances for crops stored on the farm. As part of the contract, the AAA agreed to purchase or support basic commodities at a "parity" price, the cost of the program to be met by a "processing tax" on commodities.[7] Because some crops were already in the ground and

because hogs had already farrowed, the AAA programs began with the seemingly opprobrious action of plowing up every third row of cotton and "killing
little pigs." The idea of creating scarcity when so many were in want was
incongruous. But price supports, production controls, and marketing quotas
(which were established by the Bankhead-Jones Act of 1934) have become
permanent features of federal farm programs, even though the first AAA was
declared unconstitutional in 1935.

The list of New Deal agricultural programs is quite extensive, and each of
these programs fully merits its own intensive analysis and evaluation. All that
can be done in the present study, however, is to identify the programs and the
amounts of federal monies spent on them (Table 16.1).

TABLE 16.1
New Deal Agricultural Agencies, 1933–1939.

PROGRAM	PURPOSE	YEAR OF INCEPTION	EXPENDITURES, 1933–1939 MILLIONS OF DOLLARS
Agricultural Adjustment Administration	Farm price supports in commodity marketing and production	1933 (Soil Conservation and Domestic Allotments Act 1935–1938) (also, Agricultural Adjustment Act of 1938)	2,862.8
Farm Security Administration	Aid to migrant labor, homestead communities	1937 (Absorbed Resettlement Administration organized 1935)	272.7
Soil Conservation Service	Soil erosion, conservation, interim payments to farmers after Supreme Court rejection of AAA in 1935	1935	109.2
Federal Surplus Commodities Corporation	Relief-foods distribution	1933 under Federal Emergency Relief Administration; transferred to Dept. of Agriculture, 1935.	196.5

TABLE 16.1 (cont.)

PROGRAM	PURPOSE	YEAR OF INCEPTION	EXPENDITURES, 1933–1939 MILLIONS OF DOLLARS
Farm Credit Administration	Farm mortgage, production, marketing, and cooperative loans	1933	3,958.6
Commodity Credit Corporation	Loans for AAA controls, surplus storage	1933	1,159.7
Farm Security Agency	Tenant Loans	1937	450.0
Rural Electrification Administration	Electric-cooperative loans	1935 by Executive order; 1936 by act of Congress	122.5

Source: Office of Government Reports, Statistical Section, Report 10, Vol. II. mimeographed (Washington, D.C., 1940).

Several other organizations aimed at relief and recovery in the first New Deal. The Civilian Conservation Corps (CCC) recruited unemployed and unmarried young men eighteen to twenty-five years of age to work in the national forests and on conservation and road-building projects. The Federal Emergency Relief Administration (FERA), headed by Harry Hopkins, provided funds to states for relief projects. The Public Works Administration (PWA), under Harold Ickes, funneled some $6 billion into public construction projects such as roads and public buildings between 1933 and 1939. The Tennessee Valley Authority (TVA) not only assumed permanent government ownership and operation of nitrate and power projects on the Tennessee River, but also initiated a multifaceted program of regional rehabilitation that included flood control, conservation, and resettlement. The TVA represented a totally new, and highly controversial, dimension in government economic activity, economic planning, and regional political authority.[8]

The National Industrial Recovery Act of 1933 established the National Recovery Administration (NRA) under Hugh S. Johnson. This act typified the philosophy of the first New Deal that big government, big business, and labor ought to cooperate to promote recovery. Industrial representatives sat down with government and labor representatives to draw up codes of fair competition that would provide for price minimums, production quotas, and market allocation. Business was to accept maximum working hours, minimum wages, and prohibition of child labor, and under Section 7A of the act was to recognize the right of labor to bargin collectively. The government pledged to support the codes in the courts and to encourage consumer patronage of industries that adopted the codes and displayed the NRA's symbol, the "Blue Eagle." Industry was in effect exempted from antitrust prosecution, and government exerted strong moral suasion on consumers to patronize only those businesses entering into cooperative agreements.

The Blue Eagle produced chaos in almost every direction. Labor and independent businesses participated at a great disadvantage if they participated at all, and if they failed to participate immediately, they suffered from the organized competition. Some industries received conflicting directives from different government agencies. Many businesses capitalized upon the situation by obtaining more-than-adequate price structures and marketing monopolies. What is generally regarded as one of the "bad" New Deal experiments finally collapsed under a court order in the Schecter Poultry Case of 1935. The NRA bolstered rising criticism that the New Deal had "sold out" to giant enterprise on the one hand and imposed too much regulation and regimentation on the other.

HUEY P. LONG

By 1935 the colorful but dangerous Huey P. Long of Louisiana had become one of the most formidable critics of Franklin Roosevelt. Although Long likely accepted the Populist-Progressive persuasion of progress, individual initiative, and equal opportunity, and although he suspected that great wealth was probably unearned and hence undeserved, as a "mass leader" he tended to ignore ideology and developed a homespun kind of political and economic radicalism. As governor of Louisiana, he pushed through new spending and tax bills; expanded public schools; provided for free textbooks, roads and bridges, and educational institutions; expanded utility services; and, unprecedented for the era, instituted old-age pensions. As a senator Long was at first a strong supporter of FDR. But he soon became the president's most rigorous critic, promoting a "Share-Our-Wealth" movement that spearheaded his own drive toward the presidency and the derailment of the New Deal. "So long as America has, or can produce, an abundance of the things which make life comfortable and happy," said Long, "none should own so much of the things which he does not need and cannot use, as to deprive the balance of the people of a reasonable proportion of the necessities and conveniences of life."[9]

Long's Share-Our-Wealth plan would conscript personal wealth in excess of $1 million, limit individual annual income to $1,800,000 "to be subject to present income taxes," and redistribute the wealth through a variety of public-service programs:

1. Every family would be given $5,000 with which to buy a house, a car, and a radio.
2. Each family would be guaranteed a $2,500 annual income.
3. Hours of industrial labor would be regulated to prevent overproduction.
4. Old-age pensions would be paid to persons over 60.
5. The government would store farm surpluses.
6. Veterans' benefits would be provided.
7. A college education would be provided for youths of proven ability.

There is no question that Long attracted a host of followers and that Franklin Roosevelt considered him a serious political threat in the election of 1936, a threat aborted by Long's assassination in Louisiana in September, 1935.[10]

    Long, of course, was not the only radical critic, nor did he have the only formula for recovery. Father Charles Coughlin advocated inflation and the nationalization of banks, utilities, and natural resources. Dr. Francis E. Townsend would have given every person over 60 a $200-per-month pension that had to be spent each month. Others simply advocated flying over the country in an airplane and scattering money to the winds. None of these individuals had the strong political base from which Long operated, but the sum of all the criticism from the "left" was simply that the New Deal had not provided relief, recovery, or reform. It was in part the pressure from this sector that pushed Roosevelt into the stronger reform stance leading to the second New Deal.

THE SECOND NEW DEAL

A "wealth tax" introduced in Congress in 1935 was to be Roosevelt's answer to Long's Share-Our-Wealth plan. It would raise taxes on inheritances and gifts, provide a steeply graduated income tax, and establish a corporate income tax. The bill that finally passed did substantially alter the tax structure, but was a much modified version of the original proposal. The "soak-the-rich" bill elicited stinging criticism from the press and business interests, but it seems to have mollified the more liberal and radical supporters of the New Deal. However, the new tax structure did not redistribute the wealth at all. In fact, it created a more regressive tax system, one that imposed relatively greater burdens on mass consumers and low-income groups than on the wealthy.

    Although taxes were higher on larger incomes, a quick comparison of 1928 tax rates with 1940 tax rates indicates that taxes on the lowest bracket in 1940 were 15 times those of 1928; taxes on the $10,000 bracket were 11 times those of 1928; taxes on the $20,000 bracket were 4.5 times those of 1928; and taxes on the $50,000 bracket were 3.3 times those of 1928; and taxes on the $1,000,000 bracket were 3 times those of 1928. From 1930 to 1939 corporate income taxes,

TABLE 16.2

Individual Income Tax: Comparable Rates for Selected Years, 1920–1940.

NET INCOME GROUP (FOUR EXEMPTIONS)	$5,000	$10,000	$20,000	$50,000	$1,000,000
	Effective percentage rate of taxation by income bracket.				
1920	2.1	5.6	9.8	18.3	66.3
1924	1.0	1.4	4.7	12.1	43.0
1928	0.1	0.4	2.4	8.3	23.1
1932	1.4	4.2	8.1	17.1	57.1
1934	1.0	3.4	7.3	17.2	57.1
1936	1.0	3.4	7.3	17.2	67.8
1940	1.5	4.4	10.7	27.5	71.7

Source: Bureau of the Census, *Historical Census of the United States Colonial Times to 1970* Series Y 412–39.

including the excess-profits tax, ranged from 11 to 14 percent of total American income tax receipts, which indicates little change in real assessments by the New Deal tax measures.

Moreover, some large corporations used the depression to reduce debts and raise liquid capital while incurring paper operating losses, suspending dividends, and avoiding taxes. In addition, tax loopholes for both corporations and the wealthy were greater then than later. Thus, New Deal tax policies did not depart from "the realm of rhetoric and psychological warfare."[11]

Although it is difficult to quantify or accurately assess the results of New Deal policy in terms of simple wages and increases in union membership, the National Labor Relations Act of 1935 (NLRA; also known as the Wagner Act) did contribute ultimately to an income redistribution, perhaps more so than any other single piece of legislation. This act conclusively established the right of collective bargaining, legalized the closed shop (which required that as a condition of employment the laborer be a member of the union), imposed fair employment practices, and established the National Labor Relations Board (NLRB) to supervise employment practices and arbitrate labor disputes. The act presumed that by strengthening the bargaining power of labor, unions could effectively raise the wages of labor and thereby increase the purchasing power of workers. The Fair Labor Standards Act of 1938 imposed minimum wages, maximum hours, and child-labor constraints on industries engaged in interstate commerce. To be sure, many industries, including agriculture and retail sales, were excluded by law or by subsequent court interpretation from the provisions of the Wagner Act and the Fair Labor Standards Act.

Although there is no conclusive evidence that New Deal legislation was primarily responsible, the real earnings of employees rose approximately 15 percent between 1935 and 1940. Union membership rose 150 percent during this period and a further 100 percent between 1940 and 1945. The changed institutional framework established by the Wagner Act and supplemented by the Fair Labor Standards Act—but more especially World War II—induced labor shortages and contributed to the markedly improved income levels of the industrial labor force between 1935 and 1945. To be sure, the Clayton Antitrust Act (1913), the Norris–La Guardia Act (1932), and the National Industrial Recovery Act established important precedents for the Wagner Act.

Affirmed by the Supreme Court in *NLRB* v. *Jones & Laughlin Steel Corporation,* 1937) after the famous "court-packing" battle by Roosevelt, the "new unionism" promoted by the NLRA precipitated a jump in union membership and jurisdictional rivalries between unions. The most notable development within the new unionism was the "deaffiliation" of the Committee for Industrial Organization, which had been established by John L. Lewis, Sidney Hillman, Homer Martin, and others within the American Federation of Labor for the purpose of organizing nonskilled and nonaffiliated workers. Suspended from the AF of L in 1937, the new Congress of Industrial Organizations (CIO) aggressively expanded union membership and won important labor contracts by using the new and controversial tactic of the sit-down strike. For example, the United Automobile Workers (UAW), a CIO affiliate, won recognition from General Motors in 1937 and from Ford in 1941. The Ford settlement effectually meant that Ford and the UAW were in business together, with the union having jurisdiction over the 130,000 Ford employees below the rank of foreman. Under the settlement the Ford Company granted (1) wage increases of from 5 to 30 cents per hour; (2) abolition of a Ford "service department" that carried on antiunion activities; (3) a shop-steward system with a steward in charge of every 550 workers; (4) time and a half for all work over eight hours a day plus double time for Sunday and holidays; (5) two hours pay for call-in workers who received no work assignment; (6) a strict seniority system governing layoffs and rehiring; and (7) reinstatement of employees previously fired for antiunion activities. Finally, every Ford product was entitled to bear a "union-made" label.[12] By 1941, the AFL and CIO, each enrolling some 4 million members, had unionized the major American manufacturing industries.

Although New Deal administrators tended to regard both the NLRA and the Public Works Administration (PWA) as joint efforts to stimulate employment, the Works Progress Administration (WPA) created by Executive Order in May, 1935, operated in a context totally different from that of the NLRB. Operating on the theory that people wanted work, not welfare, the WPA administered direct federal work-relief programs. By 1939 the WPA had spent some $10 billion on materials and wages and had employed over 7.5 million persons for varying periods. Employment rolls generally exceeded 2 million at any one time. Projects ranged from writing history books to building roads, bridges, and schools to producing plays, writing music, and painting pictures. The WPA obtained strong support from many sectors of the public but received an equal

TABLE 16.3

Civilian Labor Force, Union Potential, Actual and Real Union Membership, for Census Years, 1900 to 1950.

YEAR	CIVILIAN LABOR FORCE*	UNION POTENTIAL†	UNION POTENTIAL AS PERCENT OF CIVILIAN LABOR FORCE	ACTUAL UNION MEMBER-SHIP‡	REAL UNION MEMBER-SHIP (PERCENTAGE COLUMN 5 IS OF COLUMN 3)
1900	29,030,000	14,236,000	49.0	868,500	6.1
1910	37,194,000	20,397,000	54.8	2,021,100	9.9
1920	41,010,000	25,392,000	61.9	4,780,600	18.8
1930	48,462,000	31,237,000	64.5	3,189,300	10.2
1940	51,798,000	33,701,000	65.1	7,873,900	23.4
1950	58,999,000	42,783,000	72.5	13,304,100	31.1

*1900–1940, from Alba M. Edwards, *Sixteenth Census of the United States: 1940, Population, Comparative Occupation Statistics for the United States, 1870 to 1940*, U. S. Bureau of the Census (Washington: G. P. O., 1943). For 1900, Table 8; 1910, 1920, and 1930, Table 4; and 1940, Table 23. Armed forces were deducted from the totals. For 1950, from U.S. Bureau of the Census, *U. S. Census of Population: 1950*, Vol. II, *Characteristics of the Population*, Part 1, Chapter C (Washington: G. P. O., 1953), Table 124.

†For 1950, the following categories were subtracted from the experienced civilian labor force: farmers and farm managers; farm laborers and foremen; managers, officials, and proprietors, except farm (except railroad conductors and postmasters); private household workers; among professional, technical and kindred workers—physicians and surgeons, lawyers and judges, clergymen, dentists, funeral directors, therapists and healers (n.e.c.), optometrists, chiropractors, veterinarians, and osteopaths; among service workers, except private household—boarding and lodging house keepers, housekeepers and stewards, policemen and detectives, sheriffs and bailiffs, marshalls and constables, midwives; among sales workers—real estate agents and brokers, hucksters and peddlers, auctioneers. There were also deducted from the included occupations, the self-employed and unpaid family classes of workers (except for the self-employed male craftsmen and kindred workers and male barbers, beauticians, and manicurists). See *ibid.*, Tables 124, 128.

For 1940 and earlier years, the list of occupations deducted was as close as possible to that given above. For the occupational distribution of the work force for these years, the major source was Edwards, *op. cit.* For 1940, the deductions for self-employed and unpaid family workers were obtained from the U. S. Bureau of the Census, *Sixteenth Census of the United States: 1940, Population. The Labor Force (Sample Statistics), Occupational Characteristics* (Washington: G. P. O., 1943), Table 6.

For 1930, 1920, and 1910, Table 4 (gainful workers 14 years old and over) and, for 1900, Table 8 (gainful workers 10 years old and over), of Edwards' work were used. (It was impossible to deduct self-employed and unpaid family workers from the included occupations, since these classifications first came into use by the Bureau of the Census in 1940.) For 1920 and 1910, the size of a few occupations had to be determined from Edwards' list by estimates based on 1930 relationships. Considerably more estimation was required for 1900, most of it based on 1910 relationships.

‡For 1900–1930, from Leo Wolman, *Ebb and Flow in Trade Unionism* (New York: National Bureau of Economic Research, 1936), p. 16. For 1940 and 1950, from Irving Bernstein, "The Growth of American Trade Unions," *American Economic Review*, Vol. 44, June 1954, Table I, pp. 303–304. Totals for 1910 and succeeding years were reduced by Canadian membership of American international unions, obtained from Canadian Department of Labour, *Labour Organization in Canada*, annual issues. The 1910 total was reduced by the 1911 Canadian membership, since this was the first year this information became available.

Reprinted with permission from Benjamin Solomon, "Dimensions of Urban Growth, 1900–1950," *Industrial and Labor Relations Review*, Vol. 9, No. 4 (July 1956), p. 546. Copyright © 1956 by Cornell University. All rights reserved.

amount of hostility from business and labor leaders who protested WPA competition. Work relief was a novel form of public welfare, but its impact was overshadowed by that of Social Security.

The Social Security Act, approved by Congress on August 14, 1935, professed to secure "the men, women, and children of the nation against certain hazards and vicissitudes of life," prominently old age and unemployment. This multifaceted act included provisions for the blind and for dependent and crippled children, maternal benefits, vocational rehabilitation, and public-health services. The original bill excluded agricultural and domestic laborers and the self-employed. Since 1935 the coverage, benefits, and costs of the programs have been markedly expanded. Through fiscal year 1973–1974 over $423 billion in old-age and survivor benefits were disbursed. Since 1973, annual Social Security payments have run well over $50 billion and are rising. Hospital and medical insurance began in 1966. The Social Security Act had relatively little impact in the 1930s, but by the 1970s, if interest on the national debt be excluded, government disbursements under Social Security and health-care services accounted for approximately one half of all public expenditures.

Applying the New Deal to the American economy was somewhat like putting an automatic transmission in a "stick-shift" automobile. In its early stages, during the 1930s, the transmission was often rough, erratic, slow, and undependable. It was also more expensive. Many preferred the old manual shift. But by the 1950s and 1960s the automatic transmission, still expensive, had become universally acceptable and was providing a generally smoother ride. In its basic structure, design, and purpose, though, the vehicle was unchanged. The New Deal clearly initiated a major change in the style of the national economy and added a new component to its structure. Government, which had always assumed the responsibility of promoting and protecting individual economic opportunity, now assumed the responsibility of securing individual economic welfare. Expanding government spending and government taxation established certain constraints on free enterprise and altered the environment within which the capitalist system functioned, without changing the basic structure of the system. Like a by-pass valve used in a heart operation, governmental welfare machinery supplements and slightly reroutes the flow of money in the economy while sustaining the system. Public welfare in effect became a form of government insurance for the capitalist economy.

Old-age insurance, unemployment compensation, health insurance, and other public services represent money moving through a by-pass valve. If the flow through that valve becomes too large, the body dies, but as long as the flow is adequate, the system works better and consumes more than it otherwise could. Public welfare generates a sustained consumption of goods and services by those elements of society who would otherwise be unable to consume. Social Security, for example, provides not only individual freedom for vast numbers of the aged but also a sustained market for housing, automobiles, television sets, food, travel, and medical services. It, like other welfare services, stimulates consumption and higher profits, but too much flow through the by-pass valve can generate a severe economic crisis.

The New Deal, then, did generate something new, but not something radical. It created a new institutional structure to protect capitalism from cyclical economic "booms" and "busts" such as had occurred in 1929 and during the subsequent Great Depression. Government assumed a new obligation to underwrite continuing economic growth, but the New Deal did not redistribute the wealth. It did not alter the structure of the economy, but it created a more rigid institutional structure by establishing political-economic bureaus and agencies that gave business, farmers, and labor a vested interest in government. The New Deal did not bring about economic recovery during the 1930s. In 1940 14.6 percent of the labor force was unemployed. Manufacturing output was about 60 percent of capacity. The total value of farm products was less in 1940 than in 1930. The New Deal did provide relief for many from the economic hardships of the depression, but even this was minimal.

New Deal programs, including the Social Security legislation, were largely experimental. Some failed to provide anything more than confusion. Many were contradictory in their techniques and in their goals. There was precious little planning, but then there were few guidelines with which to plan. Keynesian economics, then as now, contained many variables and unknowns. Economic conditions at any one time are unique because the economy is an amorphous, constantly changing set of relationships, knowledge, and technology. The New Deal did not embrace Keynesian economics or a new body of knowledge, but it did institute tax and spending policies that added a Keynesian dimension to the economic system. The impact of these policies was little felt until after World War II.

The post– World War II American economy was so altered from the economy of the 1930s that it is difficult to determine how much that change derived from New Deal legislation. There was very clearly a convergence in the way of life of the rich and the poor. There were to be many more rich and somewhat fewer poor, but the style of life and the goods and services available to Americans were more comparable in quality than ever before. But that had little to do with New Deal policies. By the "logic of mass production" clothing styles, hair styles, foodstuffs, education, and entertainment became standardized in the new mass-consumer economy. In part, the convergence was a by-product of the Progressive era, wherein expanded public education had enhanced the nation's social capital. In part, the depression itself had a leveling influence. While those in the lowest economic strata moved up a bit, many of those at the top moved considerably lower. Welfare services may have given a slight upward lift to those at the bottom, but only slight. Union activity and organization contributed to a rising standard of living among millions of laborers. Mass communications and modern advertising both stimulated and democratized consumer appetites. Americans were taught to want more things and to want basically the same kinds of things. Wartime prosperity affected almost every economic stratum of American life. Americans produced more and spent less during World War II than in any comparable period of time.[13] Perhaps in the short run, war helped resolve the old crises of depression, but it also plunged Americans deeply into a new maelstrom.

Notes

[1]Arthur M. Schlesinger, Jr., *The Politics of Upheaval* (Boston: Houghton Mifflin, 1960), pp. 385–408.

[2]John Morton Blum, *From the Morgenthau Diaries, Years of Crisis 1928–1938* (Boston: Houghton Mifflin, 1959), pp. 63–77, 120–125.

[3]John B. Kirkwood, "The Great Depression: A Structural Analysis," *Journal of Money, Credit and Banking*, 4 (November 1972), p. 829.

[4]See Lewis H. Kimmel, *Federal Budget and Fiscal Policy, 1789–1958* (Washington, D.C.: Brookings Institution, 1959), pp. 213–28.

[5]Keynes's classic study is *The General Theory of Employment, Interest and Money* (New York: Harcourt, Brace, 1936). For a good analysis of Keynesian economics see A. H. Hansen, *A Guide to Keynes* (New York: Norton, 1953).

[6]See Arthur Smithier, "The American Economy in the Thirties," in *Issues in American Economic History*, ed. Gerald D. Nash (Boston:, Heath, 1964), pp. 445–60. See also the critical evaluation of New Deal policies by Gardiner C. Means on pp. 461–64 of this book.

[7]For a good, brief review of Farm Board operations, see Murray R. Benedict, *Farm Policies of the United States, 1790–1950* (New York: Twentieth Century Fund, 1953), pp. 239–75. For an excellent background study of New Deal farm policy, see Gilbert C. Fite, *George N. Peek and the Fight for Farm Parity* (Norman, Okla.: University of Oklahoma Press, 1954). For an intensive study of the implementation of AAA programs, see Van L. Perkins, *Crisis in Agriculture: The Agricultural Adjustment Administration and the New Deal, 1933* (Berkeley and Los Angeles: University of California Press, 1969).

[8]See Philip Selznick, *TVA and the Grass Roots: A Study in the Sociology of Formal Organization*, 2nd ed. (New York, 1966).

[9]*Congressional Record*, 74th Cong., 1st sess., 1935, Vol. 79, pp. 8040–43.

[10]See T. Harry Williams, *Huey Long* (New York: Knopf, 1970), and Henry C. Dethloff, *Huey P. Long: Southern Demagogue or American Democrat* (1967; reprinted. Lafayette, La.: University of Southwestern Louisiana, 1975).

[11]Paul K. Conkin, *The New Deal* (New York: Thomas Y. Crowell, 1967) p. 65.

[12]See Alfred D. Chandler, Jr., ed., *Giant Enterprise: Ford, General Motors, and the Automobile Industry* (New York: Harcourt, Brace & World, 1964), pp. 218–66.

[13]See Frederick Lewis Allen, *The Big Change: America Transforms Itself, 1900–1950* (New York: Harper & Row, 1952), pp. 209–23.

SUGGESTED READING

BELLUSH, BERNARD, *The Failure of the NRA*. New York: Norton, 1945.

BERNSTEIN, IRVING, *The Turbulent Years: A History of the American Worker, 1933–1941*. Boston: Houghton Mifflin, 1970.

BLUM, JOHN MORTON, *From the Morgenthau Diaries: Years of Crisis, 1928–1938*. Boston: Houghton Mifflin, 1959.

BRAEMAN, JOHN, ROBERT H. BREMNER, AND DANIEL BRADY, eds., *The New Deal, Vols. I and II* Columbus, Ohio: Ohio State University Press, 1975.

BURNS, JAMES M., *Roosevelt: The Lion and The Fox*. New York: Harcourt, Brace, 1956.

CONKIN, PAUL K., *The New Deal*. New York: Thomas Y. Crowell, 1967.

FINE, SIDNEY, *The Automobile Under the Blue Eagle*. Ann Arbor, Mich.: University of Michigan Press, 1963.

FREIDEL, FRANK, *Franklin D. Roosevelt: Launching the New Deal*. Boston: Little, Brown, 1973.

FUSFELD, DANIEL, *The Economic Thought of Franklin D. Roosevelt and the Origins of the New Deal*. New York: Columbia University Press, 1956.

HAWLEY, ELLIS W., *The New Deal and the Problem of Monopoly: A Study in Economic Ambivalence*. Princeton, N.J.: Princeton University Press, 1966.

KIRKENDALL, RICHARD S., *The United States, 1929–1945*. New York: McGraw-Hill, 1974.

LEUCHTENBURG, WILLIAM E., *Franklin D. Roosevelt and the New Deal*. Chicago: University of Chicago Press, 1963.

SCHLESINGER, ARTHUR M., JR., *The Age of Roosevelt*, 3 vols. Boston: Houghton Mifflin, 1957–1960.

SHANNON, DAVID A., *Between the Wars: America, 1919–1941*. Boston: Houghton Mifflin, 1965.

WAR, RECONSTRUCTION, AND A NEW POLITICAL ECONOMY

_____chapter XVII__

Our world today was brewed in the maelstrom of World War II. It is a world in which the United States emerged with military prowess and wealth second to none. The war contributed to a technological explosion. New industries formed in such areas as plastics, electronics, pharmaceuticals, metal alloys, synthetic fibers, and appliances. In electronics alone the new technology created giant enterprises in computer, television, sound equipment, and communications, and utilized transistors, radar, sonar, laser, and microwave components. The advertising, insurance, education, and food industries attained proportions undreamed of before World War II. Aeronautics, space-related industries, and nuclear engineering, previously nonexistent, achieved an impressive size and sophistication in two decades. A population explosion, a "baby boom," new products, and a host of eager consumers created a new dimension in American economic life.

In startling contrast with the depression decade, relative abundance, widely distributed, became a basic and seemingly permanent condition of American life. Depression, the New Deal, and war contributed to the development of the federal government as an adjunct of the economy and to its firm commitment to a sustained defense posture and to economic growth and public welfare.

MOBILIZATION FOR WAR

American mobilization began, in limited fashion, well before the Japanese attack on Pearl Harbor on December 7, 1941. When war began in Europe in 1939, National Guard and Regular Army forces were expanded to about half a million men each. Congress lifted the prohibition by the Neutrality Act (1937) of sales of munitions to belligerents. The Selective Service Act and a $6-billion military appropriation raised army personnel to 1.5 million by the close of 1940. In June, 1940 President Roosevelt made large transfers of World War I equipment to

Britain, and in September he exchanged fifty destroyers for bases in British possessions in the Atlantic. In March, 1941 Congress approved the Lend-Lease Act, which purported to make America the "arsenal of democracy." The act authorized the release of some $25 billion in war materials to Britain (who received 58 percent of the total), Russia (23 percent), France (8 percent), China (7 percent), and other nations. But when war came to the United States, the country was still ill prepared. Industrial production was less than 60 percent of capacity; six million Americans were unemployed; munition, ship, and aircraft production was marginal. The structure of mobilization closely followed World War I patterns.

The War Production Board, established in January, 1942, controlled the use of raw materials, machine tools, and industrial facilities, as had the War Industries Board in World War I. The War Shipping Administration, cooperating with the British Ministry of War Transport, allocated shipping among the combined British and American merchant fleets. The Office of Price Administration administered wage and price controls. Under the general supervision of the Office of Defense Transportation, railroads maintained private control, unlike in World War I, and performed an outstanding job of internal rail transport. In 1943 the Office of War Mobilization, headed by James F. Byrnes, assumed supervisory and coordinating control over the myriad war boards and agencies. Rationing, particularly of sugar, gasoline, and rubber, and government allocation of steel, copper, and aluminum helped establish a more efficient distribution of critical war materials.

War-materials production in 1943 was valued at approximately $60 billion, three times the 1941 level, and constituted 31 percent of the GNP, compared with 9 percent in 1941. Military-aircraft production in 1943 was twice that of 1941. In 1941 shipyards turned out 4 battleships, 1 carrier, 8 cruisers, 81 destroyers, 34 submarines, 600 Liberty ships (a figure that doubled in 1943), and some 7,500 lesser craft. By 1943 approximately 7 million Americans had entered the service. Military personnel peaked at about 12 million in 1945. A total of 14 million men and women wore the uniform. Unemployment dropped to 1 million in 1943, or 1.9 percent of the civilian labor force. By the close of the war one third of the civilian labor force consisted of women. Wages rose 50 percent, and prices, restrained by government-imposed ceilings, rose 30 percent. The index of industrial production rose to 239 (1935–1939 = 100), and the index of durable manufactured goods rose to 360. Farm production was 50 percent greater than that of World War I, and per-capita production rose 25 percent. The GNP expanded from about $100 billion in 1940 to $121 billion in 1945. Government expenditures for goods and services rose from 10 percent of the GNP in 1940 to over 50 percent in 1943 and 1944, and averaged 42 percent for the duration of the war. Defense expenditures during the war totaled approximately $315 billion, of which 44 percent was raised by tax levies and the remainder by borrowing. The public debt rose from $50 billion to $260 billion. Statistics, to be sure, cannot reflect the commitment, the sacrifice, the dislocation, the hard work, and the

FIGURE 17.1. The cloud of the Atomic Bomb at Hiroshima.
Courtesy of the National Archives and the U.S. Office of War Information.

personal losses of all Americans. Victory did not come easily, and it brought new problems.

Table 17.1 demonstrates the downturn in employment levels, production, and disposable personal income that occurred during the postwar conversion period. Congress and the public were very fearful that this postwar recession might turn into a full-fledged depression. The deteriorating domestic and international situations also created the fear of radicalism and communism that underlay the McCarthy era. But the economy was on a much stronger base than most believed, and the dramatic economic recovery that became evident in 1950, coupled with European recovery and greater stability abroad, began to calm the disquiet.

POSTWAR CONVERSION

The postwar conversion from military to civilian production idled factories and employees. By 1946 5 million men and women had been released from the military and civilian employment had declined 2.5 million. Many businessmen

TABLE 17.1

Trends in Employment, Per-Capita GNP, and Disposable Personal Income, 1945–1955.

YEAR	PERCENTAGE OF UNEMPLOYED	PER-CAPITA GNP (1958 PRICES)	DISPOSABLE PERSONAL INCOME (1958 PRICES)
1945	1.9	$2,538	$1,642
1946	3.9	2,211	1,606
1947	3.9	2,150	1,513
1948	3.8	2,208	1,567
1949	5.9	2,172	1,547
1950	5.3	2,342	1,646
1951	3.3	2,485	1,657
1952	3.0	2,517	1,678
1953	2.9	2,587	1,714
1954	5.5	2,506	1,795
1955	4.4	2,650	1,839

Source: Bureau of the Census, *Historical Statistics of the U.S. Colonial Times to 1970,* Series F1–5, F6–9, F17–30, D 85–86.

anticipated a severe depression, and despite the obvious shortage of consumer goods they refrained from new capital investment or hiring. Although the Office of Price Administration (OPA) held the lid on sharp price increases during the war, average prices rose 33 percent between 1945 and 1947. The cessation of hostilities created an intense demand for both price and wage hikes. While wages were rising 50 percent during the war, rationing and the virtual shutdown of the consumer durable-goods industries were pushing personal savings to all-time highs. With the war's end there were real shortages, a resurgent demand for goods and services, and plenty of liquidity to bid prices to new highs. Price controls became increasingly ineffective and unpopular through 1946. Nevertheless, President Truman insisted on an extension of price controls beyond their June, 1946 expiration date. When Congress passed a drastically weakened control law, Truman angrily vetoed the measure. Congress passed an acceptable law in July, but in the thirty-day interim in which no controls existed prices rose 10 percent.

Organized labor, now on the lagging end of the wage-price spiral, experiencing layoffs and the loss of overtime, and chafing from the voluntary and involuntary wage controls of the war, erupted with a series of wage demands and strikes in 1946. On May 23 the Brotherhood of Locomotive Engineers and Railway Trainmen called a general strike, their first in more than half a century. Truman and the public considered the strike a national emergency. The president demanded an end to it and asked Congress for authority to draft the workers and court-martial them if they refused to work. The strike ended without this drastic action, but in November John L. Lewis announced a United Mine Workers strike in the bituminous-coal industry, an industry that technically remained under government wartime controls. Despite a court-ordered injunction and the president's threat to draft the mine workers, the union struck. Lewis and the union workers were cited for contempt of court and ordered back to work. During the period of government operation of the mines most of the strikers' demands were met by the government.

The Taft-Hartley Labor Management Relations bill, approved by the Eightieth Congress in the spring of 1947, proposed to curb the "excesses" of the labor movement and impede the postwar wage-price spiral. The bill outlawed the "closed shop," the union practice of requiring membership in the union as a condition of employment. It required formal notification of a contract termination, or strike, sixty days prior to the termination—a "cooling-off" period—and authorized the president to apply an injunction to any strike that endangered national safety or health. The bill prohibited unfair union practices, such as secondary boycotts and the refusal to bargain in good faith, and required unions to register with the secretary of labor and submit annual financial reports. Truman declared the bill a "shocking piece of legislation" and issued a ringing veto in June, 1947: "It is unfair to the working people of this country. It clearly abuses the right, which millions of our citizens now enjoy, to join together and bargain with their employers for fair wages and fair working conditions."[1] Congress decisively overrode the president's veto, and the bill became law.

TRUMAN'S ECONOMIC PLAN

Truman's domestic economic programs had three major objectives: (1) inflation must be halted; (2) labor, business, and agriculture must receive a fair share of the national income; (3) every American should be assured the opportunity to achieve a decent standard of living. Truman consistently emphasized the interdependence of labor, business, agriculture, and government and their responsibility for promoting economic growth.

The uncertainties and social disruptions brought by the conversion from war to peace produced a host of divergent and often extreme attitudes, particularly as to the future role of government in the economy. Conservatives such as Senator Robert A. Taft of Ohio pointed to the loss of the old individualism and personal freedom that government involvement threatened. At the other extreme Henry A. Wallace, Secretary of Agriculture, accused the administration of selling out to a "monopoly capitalism" that threatened the right of each individual to "peace and abundance." Wallace wanted to organize for peace, not war. Southerners, fearful of "big government" and the disruption of segregation patterns in the South, organized to defend "states rights." The disquietude, uncertainties, and confusion of those years were enormous. Yet certain patterns and resolutions were clearly emerging. One certainty was that government would play a much greater role in promoting both international and domestic welfare.

The Employment Act of 1946 in many ways presaged the development of the new peacetime political economy. It escaped serious attack and scrutiny largely because of its basically passive machinery, but its provisions clearly addressed the policy of ''economic stabilization through government supplementation of private activity.'' The act contained four major provisions:

1. A declaration that it will be the continuing policy and responsibility of the federal government to coordinate and utilize all its plans, functions and resources with a view to creating and maintaining, in a manner calculated to foster and promote free competitive enterprise and the general welfare, conditions under which there will be afforded useful employment opportunities, including self-employment, for those able, willing and seeking to work, and to promote maximum employment, production and purchasing power.

2. A provision for the submission each year, by the President, of an Economic Report setting forth the current and projected levels of employment, production and purchasing power, the levels required to achieve the objectives outlined in the declaration of policy and recommendations as to which action should be taken to strengthen the economy.

3. Authorization of a three-man Council of Economic Advisors to serve as an analytical and advisory unit to aid the President in performing the functions outlined above.

4. The establishment of a joint Committee on the Economic Report consisting of seven members from the Senate and seven from the House.[2]

Truman attempted to pierce the clouds of doubt and uncertainty by assuring the public that ''our peace-time economy cannot equal our war-time economy, but can surpass it.'' Truman reminded Americans that the economy of 1947 was far more healthy than that of 1929, the peak year of prewar economic activity. The volume of production was 71 percent greater. Agricultural production was 32 percent higher, employment was 10 million greater, and the national income had more than doubled. Personal income had risen from $654 per individual to $1,090. But prosperity, Truman said, could be assured only by curbing the violent rise in wholesale and retail prices since 1945. Truman advocated high taxes, rent controls, export controls, and credit controls by government in the fight against inflation.[3] Domestic difficulties, however great, seemed slight against the backdrop of the international disorder and destruction left in the wake of World War II.

THE MARSHALL PLAN

The close of hostilities left European economies in a state of collapse. The breakdown of business structures was complete. England was wholly dependent upon outside food supplies, and had virtually no peacetime consumer products to offer in world trade in order to generate vital income for imports. Italy, France, and Greece were beset with communist movements that fed upon the economic prostration and sought total political collapse. Germany lay literally in ruins. The wealth of the Western world was largely in American hands. As one author noted, the end of World War II left the United States in the role of the world's banker, with most of the world's money in the bank.[4]

Secretary of State George C. Marshall addressed the problem in June, 1947:

> In considering the requirements fot the rehabilitation of Europe the physical loss of life, the visible destruction of cities, factories, mines, and railroads was correctly estimated, but it has become obvious during recent months that this visible destruction was probably less serious than the dislocation of the entire fabric of European economy.
>
> . . . The truth of the matter is that Europe's requirements for the next 3 or 4 years of foreign food and other essential products—principally from America—are so much greater than her present ability to pay that she must have substantial additional help, or face economic, social and political deterioration of a very grave character.[5]

Moreover, it appeared imperative to stabilize the economies of Europe in order to thwart communist takeovers of existing governments. The Marshall Plan, presented to Congress by President Truman in December, 1947, proposed to provide $17 billion for European recovery between April 1, 1948 and June 30, 1952, with periodic supplements to be appropriated by Congress in 1948. The plan

FIGURE 17.2. President Truman signs putting the Marshall Plan into effect.

Courtesy of the Harry S. Truman Library by permission of the United Press-International News Photograph.

resulted in the expenditure of $15.7 billion by the end of 1953. Another $7.7 billion in military aid under the Truman Doctrine and other programs was provided by the close of 1953. By 1960 United States foreign-aid programs totaled almost $73 billion, with increasingly larger expenditures devoted to military assistance after the Korean War. By the end of the decade following World War II, European economies had staged a surprising recovery, as had the Japanese economy. American economic assistance to Europe magnified the cold war, but without this assistance American and European foreign trade, security, and economic expansion would have been irreparably weakened, if not destroyed. The United States experienced a sizable credit balance in foreign trade throughout the 1950s, but large foreign expenditures and investments produced a deficit in the American balance of payments each year except 1956. As the Western-bloc economies recovered, and as Soviet and American power each coalesced along distinctive ideological lines in Europe, the underdeveloped nations in the Middle East, Latin America, Africa, and Asia became the focus of cold-war economic and political struggles.[6]

Marshall Plan aid subsequently allowed European countries to purchase American capital equipment, consumer goods, and arms. Such purchases absorbed surplus American production and stimulated higher production and employment in the United States. There were, to be sure, highly advantageous "economic strings" attached to Marshall Plan aid. By 1948 American consumer prices were stabilizing, more because of the "excess liquidity" created by personal savings during the war being depleted than because of the imposition of federal controls or because of exports to European markets.

TABLE 17.2

Consumer price indexes,
1945–1957 (1967 = 100).

YEAR	ALL ITEMS
1945	53.9
1946	58.5
1947	66.9
1948	72.1
1949	71.4
1950	72.1
1951	77.8
1952	79.5
1953	80.1
1954	80.5
1955	80.2
1956	81.4
1957	84.3

Source: *Historical Statistics of the United States Colonial Times to 1970,* Series E 135–66, p. 210.

INTERNATIONAL INSTABILITY

The fear of depression and the disillusionment with Truman's domestic and foreign policies began to evaporate in late 1948, a time when Truman's reelection to the presidency appeared doubtful. Truman won new respectability and popular support by his handling of the Berlin crisis in June of that year. Russia had clamped a tight military blockade around West Berlin, which was under American and allied occupation. Truman's choices seemed to be either to relinquish control over the city to Russia or to attack and launch the Third World War. Neither alternative was palatable. The United States extricated itself from the dilemma by launching a "Berlin Airlift," which over the next two years flew sufficient supplies into the beleaguered city to save it from starvation and from "capture" by Russia. This move also forced the decision for war or peace onto Russian shoulders. The rapidly deteriorating international situation seemed to require the hand of an experienced war leader at the helm. Voters rejected the notion that "to err is Truman," and reelected him president in November, 1948.

The years 1948–1952 witnessed a resurgence of prosperity clouded by international instability. International crises during this era largely overshadowed domestic programs. Chiang Kai-shek and his Chinese Nationalist army fled China for Formosa. More ominous, Russia exploded an atomic device in September, 1949. The same year, Western Europe and the United States formed the North Atlantic Treaty Organization (NATO), a defensive alliance. Also in 1949, the United States provided financial assistance through Point Four programs, which were designed to give technical, scientific, and managerial expertise, as well as machinery and equipment, to the underdeveloped nations of the world. In 1950 Truman announced the hydrogen-bomb program, directed the seizure of railroads by the army to prevent a general strike, and suspended trade agreements with communist China. Senator Joseph McCarthy led an errant crusade against communism and radicalism. In 1950 American soldiers were committed to military action in Korea. A European coal and steel agreement in 1951 began a series of developments that led to the formation of the European Common Market.

THE FAIR DEAL

The Fair Deal denoted the preservation, if not the extension, of the New Deal principles of direct government participation in the promotion of the general welfare. The Truman administration implemented The Agricultural Act of 1949, which established high mandatory price supports for farm commodities. Congress approved programs for federally subsidized low-income housing, grants for slum clearance and rural housing, and increased appropriations for the TVA. But Truman's programs for a strong civil-rights program, federal health insurance, and federal aid to education were defeated. In 1952, at the laying of the keel of the nuclear-powered submarine *Nautilus*, Truman perceived Americans to be on the threshold of an age "in which poverty, hunger, and war are banished once and for all."[7]

DWIGHT D. EISENHOWER

Truman left the presidency and the resolution of the Korean War to the Republican administration of Dwight D. Eisenhower. Great was the jubilation of the Republicans on returning to power in 1952 after 20 years of exile; greater still the consternation and sense of disaster of the fallen Democrats. There would be, however, no return to "normalcy." A truce in Korea produced the threat of a recession at home. Eisenhower's administration reacted with tax cuts, an easing of credit, and an extension of Social Security coverage. To be sure, there would be little expansion of government's domestic economic role, but neither would there be retrenchment.

The Progressive principles of decentralization, limited liability on the part of the federal government, and indirect stimulation of private enterprise came back into vogue. Thus, instead of federal power development, private enterprise received incentives for the construction of power projects, as in the Hell's Canyon and on the Snake River. Criticizing public health insurance as "socialized medicine," Eisenhower introduced a plan to underwrite private insurance com-

DWIGHT DAVID EISENHOWER *(1890–1969)*
President of the United States, 1953–1961
Courtesy Library of Congress.

panies issuing health policies. A school-construction bill would have established the federal government as the guarantor of local and state school bonds. Neither measure passed Congress.

The Interstate Highways Act, approved in 1954, provided for a new matching-funds road-building program to modernize the nation's highways. The federal government was to pay 90 percent of the cost of construction. A new sliding scale was substituted for the rigid price supports of the farm program, and the Soil Bank extended government income guarantees for farmers in the mode of the New Deal's Soil Conservation and Domestic Allotments Act of 1935. When decentralized controls over the new Salk polio vaccine proved impracticable, rigid national controls were instituted. Under Public Law 480 (1954) federal farm surpluses were released for school lunches, relief agencies, and sale to foreign countries in their own currencies which could be spent only in those countries.

In the field of civil rights, Eisenhower completed the desegregation of the armed services and promoted integration in government and in the District of Columbia. In 1954 the Supreme Court rejected the "separate but equal" doctrine of *Plessy* v. *Ferguson* (1896). "In these days," said the Court, "it is doubtful that any child may reasonably be expected to succeed in life if he is denied the opportunity of an education. . . . Separate educational facilities are inherently unequal."[8] Thus began the judicial realization of that basic civil right recognized by President Truman in 1948: "We believe that all men are entitled to equal opportunities for jobs, for homes, for good health, and for education."[9]

The hotly contested Civil Rights Act of 1957, the first such measure since Reconstruction, established a Federal Civil Rights Commission and a division in the office of the Attorney General that was empowered to obtain injunctions to protect those rights guaranteed under the act. In that year a confrontation at Little Rock, Arkansas demonstrated federal authority and executive determination to enforce civil rights. The civil-rights movement ultimately began to unleash some of the nation's greatest underdeveloped resources—women, blacks, minority groups, and the poor generally—and a potential resource became an actual resource for long-term economic growth. Civil-rights legislation and court orders concurrently extended federal control and authority over the use of private property to an extent that tax and welfare programs never did.[10]

THE NEW POLITICAL ECONOMY

Depression, war, and reconstruction created a new political economy. Government supplemented the allocation of goods and services by the free marketplace with a public allocation of goods and services. Defense and welfare spending significantly broadened the role of government in the economy. The renewed commitment of government to the maintenance of a "war economy" and expanded public services was much less an ideological choice—that is, it was due less to the triumph of either "New Dealism" or "Keynesianism" than to military and demographic necessity. It was no coincidence that through the Fair Deal and the Eisenhower, Kennedy, Johnson, and Nixon administrations the role and scope of the public sector of the economy continued to expand. But so too did the dimensions of the private sector. Table 17.3 compares GNP with public expenditures in order to illustrate the relationship of the public sector of the economy to the private sector. Table 17.4 lists the proportion of total government expenditures devoted to defense.

Partially as a result of New Deal legislation and more directly as a result of war costs, government postwar expenditures had a built-in growth factor. Needless to say, political decisions negating farm subsidies, defense spending, GI benefits, Social Security, foreign aid, and deficit spending could have been forthcoming, but were not. Thus federal expenditures remained on an upward curve.

TABLE 17.3

Federal Expenditures as a Proportion of GNP, 1940–1960
(Billions of Dollars, Current Prices).

YEAR	TOTAL FEDERAL EXPENDITURES	GNP	FEDERAL EXPENSES AS A PERCENTAGE OF GNP
1940	$ 9.0	$ 99.7	9.0
1941	13.3	124.5	10.7
1942	34.0	157.9	21.5
1943	79.4	191.6	41.4
1944	95.0	210.1	45.2
1945	98.3	211.9	46.4
1946	60.3	208.5	28.9
1947	38.9	231.3	16.8
1948	33.0	257.6	12.8
1949	39.5	256.5	15.3
1950	39.5	284.8	13.8
1951	44.0	328.4	13.3
1952	65.3	345.5	18.9
1953	74.1	364.6	20.3
1954	70.9	364.8	19.4
1955	68.5	398.0	17.2
1956	70.5	419.2	16.8
1957	76.5	441.1	17.3
1958	82.6	447.3	18.5
1959	92.1	483.7	19.0
1960	92.2	503.7	18.3

Source: *Historical Statistics of the United States Colonial Times to 1970*, Series F 1–5, and Y 457–65, pp. 224, 1114.

TABLE 17.4

Defense Expenditures as a Proportion of Total Federal Expenditures, 1940–1960 (Billions of Dollars, Current Prices).

YEAR	DEFENSE EXPENDITURES	TOTAL FEDERAL EXPENDITURES	DEFENSE EXPENDITURES AS A PERCENTAGE OF TOTAL EXPENDITURES
1940	$ 1.8	$ 9.0	20.0
1941	6.2	13.3	46.6
1942	22.9	34.0	67.4
1943	63.3	79.4	79.7
1944	75.9	95.0	79.9
1945	80.5	98.3	81.9
1946	43.2	60.3	71.6
1947	14.8	38.9	38.0
1948	12.0	33.0	36.4
1949	14.0	39.5	35.4
1950	13.4	39.5	33.9
1951	20.9	44.0	47.5
1952	40.6	65.3	62.2
1953	44.1	74.1	59.5
1954	40.6	70.9	57.2
1955	35.6	68.5	52.0
1956	35.7	70.5	50.6
1957	38.7	76.5	50.6
1958	39.9	82.6	48.3
1959	44.6	92.1	48.4
1960	44.0	92.2	47.7

Source: *Historical Statistics of the United States Colonial Times to 1970*, Series Y 457–65, p. 1114.

      Tax revenues also rose, but not as fast as expenditures. The proportion of net national income paid in taxes rose from one fifth in 1940 to one third in the 1960s. This meant that a larger proportion of national income was being spent on the basis of nonmarket decisions. Traditional market controls, such as Federal Reserve interest rates, became increasingly imperfect mechanisms for expanding or contracting total spending, inasmuch as market controls affected a smaller segment of the economy. Conversely, tax policy would become an increasingly effective mechanism for regulating private spending because of the greater elasticity of disposable income after taxes. After a certain portion of income goes to taxes, the remaining income is increasingly responsive to tax policy. Tax rebates or cuts tend to generate new spending, and tax increases curb private investment or spending.

      Controls over public expenditures by the legislative and executive branches were actually circumscribed by the fact that a major portion of the federal budget comprises relatively fixed costs, such as interest, Social Security, operating expenses, and veterans' benefits. Even defense appropriations have rather well defined built-in cost parameters. Moreover, the persistent lag of tax revenues behind expenditures, which as persistently enlarged the national debt, generated constantly rising nondiscretionary public spending in the form of interest costs.

State and local governments, too, had curtailed spending during the war, and were forced into rapid expansion of schools and public services after the war. Greater social mobility and a widening urban sprawl required expanded public services. A population explosion—the 39 million American babies born between 1947 and 1957—fueled the expansion in both the public and private sectors of the economy. Improved living standards and technological breakthroughs in medicine alone meant that more Americans would be living longer and needing both public and private goods and services, ranging from food, housing, clothing, and automobiles to highways, education, medical care, and old-age security.

Government regulation of the marketplace by wage and hour laws, labor and civil-rights legislation, tax policies, and eventually energy and environmental programs increasingly directed the use and distribution of both property and income. Yet the overriding justification remained, as always, that private property, a free market, and personal liberty were the basic elements of the American free-enterprise system. As long as government intervention broadened the base and increased the growth and security of the private sector, the ancient conflict between expanding central authority and personal liberty remained unobtrusive. Unprecedented economic growth in the 1950s mitigated the expanding role of government and enlarged the base and structure of the underlying free-enterprise system in absolute terms. War, welfare, and big government began to fade from the public consciousness as the economy began to experience a remarkable rate of growth.

During the "miracle decade" 1947–1957, Americans earned 2.6 trillion dollars, paid $290 billion in personal taxes to federal, state, and local governments, poured $50 billion into foreign aid, and $270 billion into defense expenditures, and devoted $190 billion to personal savings. Population increased from 144 million to 172 million, and although the median age declined to almost twenty-five, older Americans were living longer. There was a net increase of 25 million automobiles, and superhighways were built to accommodate them. Drive-in banks, restaurants, movies, and hotels appeared. The automobile spawned self-service and the proliferation of suburbs. Shopping centers, with their more adequate parking, replaced "downtown." The two-car garage and two-car family became commonplace. Automobiles came in varying sizes and shapes, mostly larger, and sported automatic transmissions, power steering, power brakes, tubeless tires, and even air conditioning, features largely nonexistent in 1946.[11]

Americans spent $113 billion on recreation from 1947 to 1957. "Recreation became big business. People bought 4 million power boats, 500,000 sailboats. More than 15 million hunters bought guns and licenses, while 4 million took to golf and 18 million bought tackle and went fishing."[12] Eighty million civilian Americans traveled abroad. Although the sale of radios continued to rise, the radio was eclipsed by FM, the TV, and the stereo. The 78-rpm Bakelite record gave way to plastic "LP's" and "45's." Old-fashioned cigarettes yielded to filtered and menthol cigarettes, and soap became detergent.

Eleven million new homes were built in this decade, mostly on the rambler or split-level design and almost all with picture windows and a garage. Increasing numbers of them were air-conditioned and had central heating. The kitchen featured a panoply of modern appliances, including dishwashers, ranges, and ovens. Many had freezers and garbage disposals, and all could quickly serve a frozen dinner or instant tea. The prefab and the mobile home appeared, as did high-rise apartments and condominiums. One in two families became home owners.

The pattern of consumer expenditures changed noticeably in the postwar era. Whereas the average household spent almost 50 percent of its outlays on food and clothing in 1946, it expended not quite 38 percent in 1957. Expenditures on housing, transportation, medical care, and recreation rose.

Americans put more money into education than into defense. From 1947 to 1957 12.3 million young people acquired high-school diplomas and 3.2 million received college degrees. Enrollment in graduate studies rose steadily. Education became one of the affordable "necessities" of life. Adolescence was extended ten years and the youth culture was born. Moreover, the market for technically trained youths seemed unsatiable. Over 8 million new jobs existed at the close of the decade, more than had existed at its start. Many jobs were in the electronics, plastics, and computer-technology fields, which had never previously existed. Airplanes broke the sound barrier, and the piston-powered civilian aircraft engine gave way to the jet. The United States was on the threshold of the space and atomic age.[13] Most Americans were buffeted by the changes in life-style. Many, but not all, participated in the unprecedented prosperity.

"New metals and other new materials, new products, inventions, and new methods," predicted the *U.S. News and World Report* in 1957, "point the way to revolutionary changes in the near future."[14] Research and development became an integral component of business enterprise and generated far-reaching changes in the structure and finance of business. Public and private research became a long-term commitment to economic growth. Chapter XVIII briefly reviews the impact of the new technology and the growth of modern business enterprises within the framework of the new political economy.

Notes

[1]*Vital Speeches of the Day*, 13 (July 1, 1947), 547.

[2]60 Stat. 23, approved February 20, 1946. See also Murray R. Benedict, *Farm Policies of the United States, 1790–1950* (New York: Twentieth Century Fund, 1953) pp. 467–69.

[3]See *Vital Speeches of the Day,* 13 (May 1, 1947), 423–25.

[4]Eliot Janeway, *The Economics of Crisis: War, Politics, and the Dollar* (New York: Weybright & Talley, 1968), p. 236.

[5]Remarks of Secretary of State George C. Marshall at Harvard University, June 5, 1947; reprinted in *Congressional Record*, June 30, 1947, p. A3248.

[6]See Harold G. Vatter, *The U.S. Economy in the 1950s: An Economic History* (New York: Norton, 1963), pp. 17–21, 258–81.

[7]*U.S. Department of State Bulletin,* 26 (June 30, 1952), 1007–8.

[8]*Brown* v. *Board of Education of Topeka,* 347, U.S. 483 (1954).

[9]80th Cong., 2nd sess., House Document No. 516, p. 1.

[10]The economics of integration is a much neglected area of inquiry. A useful introductory study is Roy Lubov, ed., *Poverty and Social Welfare in the United States,* (New York: Holt, Rinehart, & Winston, 1972).

[11]See "10 Amazing Years: 1947–1957," *U.S. News and World Report,* December 27, 1957, pp. 42–53.

[12]*Ibid.,* p. 44.

[13]*Idid.,* pp. 43, 46, 50.

[14]*Ibid.,* p. 42.

SUGGESTED READING

GALBRAITH, JOHN KENNETH, *American Capitalism: The Concept of Countervailing Power,* rev. ed. Boston: Houghton Mifflin, 1956.

GALBRAITH, JOHN KENNETH, *The Affluent Society.* Boston: Houghton Mifflin, 1969.

HAMBY, ALONZO, *Beyond the New Deal: Harry S. Truman and American Liberalism.* New York: Columbia University Press, 1973.

LUBELL, SAMUEL, *Revolt of the Moderates.* New York: Harper & Row, 1956.

LUBELL, SAMUEL, *The Future of American Politics.* New York: Harper & Row, 1952.

POTTER, DAVID M., *People of Plenty.* Chicago: University of Chicago Press, 1954.

VATTER, HAROLD G., *The U.S. Economy in the 1950's: An Economic History.* New York: Norton, 1963.

WHYTE, WILLIAM H., JR., *The Organization Man.* New York: Simon & Schuster, 1956.

WILSON, SLOAN, *The Man in the Gray Flannel Suit.* New York: Simon & Schuster, 1955.

GIANT ENTERPRISE: ASPECTS OF ECONOMIC POWER

_____ chapter XVIII __

The growth in the economic power wielded by government in the decades since World War II is in part matched by the increasing concentration of economic power in the private sector during the same period. Economists and politicians differ on how extensive or irreversible these trends are, as well as on how they may be altering the free-enterprise system. The trend toward greater governmental control over private property seems to divorce ownership from control and create what some economists refer to as "people's capitalism" or "national capitalism." The concentration of industrial production within relatively fewer and larger firms, as well as the growing separation of management from ownership, has also altered the traditional relationship between private property and control over that property. The growth of big government and the growth of big business have been largely autonomous. That is, independent forces have affected the development of each. There have also been common stimulants to the growth of big government and big business. War, for example, certainly stimulated the growth of both big government and giant industry. Automation and the emergence of a mass-production, mass-consumption society motivated enlargement in private plants and production. Population growth and democratic values encouraged expansion in government services. Overlaying the problem of identifying and defining the changes within the structure of both government and business is the problem of deciphering the changing relationship between government and business, between the public and private sectors of the national economy.

GOVERNMENT AND THE ECONOMY

On the one hand, some economists and perhaps most laymen see a sharp dichotomy between the economy and government. They are two separate and, perhaps in the Jeffersonian view, innately hostile social structures. Others believe that big government and giant enterprise have fused to form a "military-industrial complex" that endangers personal liberty, democratic processes, and the free-enterprise system. Somewhere in the center of the spectrum is the "collectivist" view, which regards the modern free-enterprise system as a collection of competitive but inherently democratic politicized economic interest groups. It is not too difficult to support any one of these social theories with the diverse evidence and models available. Nor is it difficult to detect a basic continuity in the growth and development of the American free-enterprise system over the past 200 years. Rights in property have been expanded more than they have been constrained; the base of individual material welfare has been broadened; individual opportunity, competition, innovation, and growth are perhaps greater and more evident today than at any time in the past. While the modern business world is one of change, it is clearly built upon the precepts and structures of the past.

This chapter briefly evaluates the dimensions of the growth of business enterprises in the postwar era, offers case histories of some of the participants in the new technological revolution, and attempts to provide some insight into the changes that are occurring in business, in government, and in the relationships between the two. The growth, prosperity, and problems of the "miracle decade" 1947–1957 blend into an era of continuing stability and growth, but an era in which growth is slower and more painfully achieved. During the 1960s unemployment, interest rates, and inflation rose. Cyclical recoveries were more short-lived, and the economy was less resilient. The GNP almost doubled in the ten years between 1960 and 1970—from $503.7 billion to $977.1 billion, or in 1958 constant dollars, $487 billion in 1960 to $722 billion in 1970. This increase represents a real growth rate of 5 percent per year. During the same period the labor force rose by 13 million persons, a gain of 18 percent, and the total population increased by almost 30 million. But although the economy was healthy and growing, the bloom was fading on the bush.

Numerous factors may be attributed to the slowdown in the dynamics of the postwar economy. Certainly a temporary saturation of the marketplace was a factor. The variety of products in the supermarkets and department stores approximately doubled between 1945 and the close of the 1960s. Most products in supermarkets came in different form or wrappings than they had ten years earlier, and could be expected to have changed again ten years later. Americans not only had more, but could be more selective. Market saturation generated yet more innovation, and less appreciation for the new product. There was something of a "psychic inundation" of goods, war, and change that may have generated a degree of "future shock." Americans became somewhat less preoccupied with acquisition and more concerned about order, stability, and the quality of life. Business became increasingly disposed to enter into the overseas market where saturation was distant, but where marketing problems and competition were more severe.

The costs of developing new products—that is, research costs—continued to rise with the sophistication of the product and the consumer, sometimes resulting in a lower rate of return and often increasing the imperative to constantly develop new products. The automation of research—or as some refer to it, ''bureaucratized research''—involves a large capital outlay that is not quickly recouped in the market and that often, but not invariably, raises the price of the product to the consumer while softening the market for the product.

American businesses not only directed their energies to foreign markets, but in the American market concentrated more resources on the supply of services and less on the production of nondurable goods. This was accompanied by sustained expenditures on capital equipment, which tended to improve the quality of labor while diverting labor to the service industries. Between 1960 and 1970 personal-consumption expenditures for durable goods increased 100 percent, expenditures for nondurable goods rose about 75 percent, and expenditures for services climbed 127 percent. The postwar economy in the 1960s was accelerating the transition to a service economy.

Increased foreign competition after 1950 unquestionably decelerated the American economic growth rate. Whereas output per man-hour in the United States doubled between 1950 and 1975, in other countries it increased far more rapidly:

Japan					+834 percent
Germany				+290 percent	
France			+246 percent		
Britain		+106 percent			
United States	+98 percent				

While the productive capacity of the United States was enormous and growing, that of competitive economies was growing relatively faster, having a smaller base to build upon. The expansion of newer, underdeveloped economies, it may be anticipated, will be a constant factor in world trade, but one that stimulates rather than retards economic growth in the long run. The enormous expansion of the Japanese, West German, French, and British economies in the postwar era bolstered the rate of American economic growth throughout most of the third quarter of the twentieth century.

As the wealth of developing countries increases, so does their purchasing power. Members of the Organization of Petroleum Exporting Countries have experienced substantial increases in per-capita wealth since 1972 as a result of forming an international cartel to raise the price of crude oil. These price hikes have added enormously to energy costs in oil-importing countries, which include most industrialized nations, but have also stimulated consumer purchases and investment sectors never before represented. Although the long-term effects of the new wealth of OPEC nations on world trade are still obscure, there is some speculation that increased energy costs will be offset by higher OPEC imports and investments in the industrial nations.

Despite its affluence, the United States ranked sixth among nations in per-capita income in 1975, according to preliminary figures from the Union Bank of Switzerland. In 1974 approximately 20 nations, comprising 412 million persons, had per-capita incomes exceeding $5,000. In contrast, 75 nations, populated by 2.3 billion persons, had per-capita incomes of less than $500, and another 33 nations, with a population in excess of 1.2 billion, earned less than $200 per capita. The underdeveloped nations represent a reservoir of markets and world economic growth that industrial nations must nourish in their own self-interest as well as in the broader context of humanitarianism.

One possible explanation for the declining rate of growth in the American economy is government. Taxation, labor legislation, civil-rights constraints, antimonopoly laws and rulings, and a sometimes tangled bureaucracy unquestionably affect investment decisions by business firms as well as work and consumption patterns by individuals. Yet for every instance in which these accouterments of big government have deterred investment or consumption, numerous instances of the active stimulation of business by government can be cited, ranging from GI educational benefits to Lockheed Aircraft subsidies, and from tax rebates to Federal Housing Administration loans. Much of the investment in research and development has been allocated by government, ostensibly for defense requirements. But these requirements have perhaps been more than offset by payoffs from this investment in the consumer marketplace. U.S. weather-satellite systems and privately owned communications satellites are excellent examples of how defense-related expenditures have generated business profits. It was government that institutionalized research and development as a central component of the modern economy. To be sure, whatever government gives, it has first taken.

GIANT ENTERPRISE

The concentration of industrial production in the hands of a relatively small number of very large firms is also suspected of contributing to lower efficiency and a declining rate of growth. In 1962 there were about 180,000 corporations and 240,000 partnerships and proprietorships engaged in manufacturing in the United States. The combined assets of these business units was about $300 billion, of which $295 billion, or 98.4 percent, were corporate assets. In testimony before Congress, Willard F. Mueller, director of the Bureau of Economics of the Federal Trade Commission, pointed to the "high degree of concentration in American manufacturing'': ''The 20 largest manufacturing corporations had $73.8 billion in assets, or an estimated 25 per cent of the total assets of all U.S. manufacturing companies. The 50 largest corporations accounted for 35.7 percent, the 100 largest 46.1 percent, the 200 largest for 55.9 percent, and the 1,000 largest for almost three-fourths (74.8 percent) of the total assets of all manufacturing companies.''[1] Mueller pointed out that the 20 largest manufacturing companies held assets equal to those of the 419,000 smallest firms. ''These data,'' said Mueller, ''indicate unmistakably that, regardless of the measure used, a relatively few immense corporations hold the great bulk of the financial resources of American manufacturing.''[2]

The classical presumption has been that the concentration of economic power in governmental or private hands prevents competition, precludes the maximum efficient utilization and allocation of resources, and produces economic stagnation. This presumption is being challenged and tested by economists who argue that oligarchy and monopoly can in fact be more efficient in terms of production and unit price than pure competition (utilities and telephones often being a case in point). Other economists, such as John Kenneth Galbraith, believe that the institutional structure of monopoly and oligopoly are deceptive, and that ''countervailing power'' constantly acts as a check on exploitation and inefficiency by giant enterprise. Thus, a monopolistic position by manufacturers begets a countervailing power structure by suppliers, labor, and consumers. Experiences with price rises in the 1970s suggest, however, that if a countervailing power develops, it does so belatedly and provides no short-run response to monopolistic practices. In the long run, however, monopoly is necessarily a transient situation in a free-market economy.

Yet another form of unobtrusive but effective competition lies in technological innovation and the marginal utility of a product. In energy, for example, petroleum competes with coal, water power, wind power, solar energy, and atomic energy. A ''monopoly'' in one sector may disintegrate when the efficiency of one energy form becomes less than that of another—when it pays to use lignite instead of petroleum, for example. Innovations constantly affect the distribution of economic power among firms. Indeed, some economists argue that technological competition among a few large firms is most conducive to human progress, and that research and innovation eventually destroy monopolistic market controls. The contradictory facts are that business history does suggest a constant trend toward concentration and combination by established firms rather than dispossession or destruction of the old by the new; there is a distinct tendency by the larger firm to enter in and destroy the smaller firm in its own technological ball park. Thus, Continental Can entered the paper-container industry, International Business Machines the quick-copy industry; and Kodak the one-step photographic-process business. But the issue here is not resolved as clearly as adherents on either side often presume. Innovative processes have

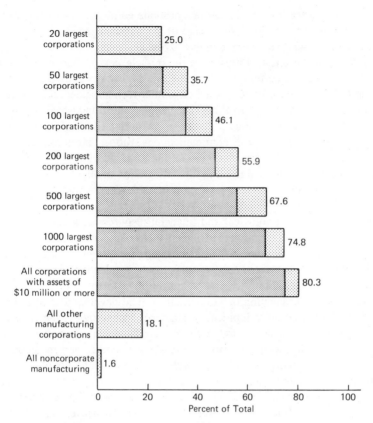

FIGURE 18.1. Percentage of total manufacturing assets accounted for by various groups of firms, 1962.

Source: Testimony of Willard F. Mueller, Economic Concentration, Part I, *Overall and Conglomerate Aspects,* Hearings before the Subcommittee on Antitrust and Monopoly of the Committee of the Judiciary, U.S. Senate, 88th Cong., 2nd sess. (Washington, D.C.: Government Printing Office, 1964, p. 114).

given rise to new giant enterprises and have forced older firms into more competitive and dynamic production and marketing practices.

By 1957 Americans had come to believe that economic growth could be taken for granted. The total annual sales of the 500 largest industrial corporations rose from $136.8 billion in 1954 to $834 billion in 1974 which, discounting inflation, meant a real net increase of 6.5 percent annually. Unadjusted for inflation, profits grew at an average rate of 8.7 percent and assets at a rate of 9.2 percent. The number of employees of "the 500" almost doubled, and accounted for 74 percent of all industrial workers, despite automated production techniques and the rising productivity rate. The share of total industrial sales by the largest corporations rose from one half to two thirds, and earnings increased from two thirds to three quarters of total industrial corporate earnings. Giant corporations accounted for an increasingly larger share of the national product.[3]

The corporation that emerged in the 1970s, however, often bore a different complexion from the one that existed in the miracle decade starting in the late 1940s. The new giant corporation tended to be highly diversified. That is, it manufactured dissimilar products based on similar technological and production processes, and decentralized into almost autonomous multi-industrial complexes. The most intensive diversification occurred in the more technologically advanced industries, such as the chemical, communications, rubber, electrical, and transportation industries. A notable exception to this trend was the petroleum industry, where the stress continued to be on total integration of all processes from raw material to consumer. But even here, considerable diversification of product occurred.[4]

The larger the technological and financial resources of a corporation, the greater the pressure, and the ability, to diversify. As old markets waned, corporations sought new product lines. The depression, for example, stimulated the search for markets; war created opportunities for the production of new products; and war-generated technology created again the investment imperative and the opportunity for the production of new products. The development of synthetic rubber helped stimulate development in chemical technologies, particularly in plastics. Radar and sonar research opened new fields in electronics. Breakthroughs occurred in metal fabrication, aircraft production, and medicine. Increased attention to an investment in research and development, coupled with the postwar market demands, triggered an avalanche of new products.[5] Although new industries emerged and an array of new corporations appeared within those industries, most products came from established industries that had the technological and financial sophistication to manufacture and market them. Thus, in a sense the big corporation necessarily became bigger. Expansion, however, necessitated diversification and decentralization.

du Pont

E. I. du Pont de Nemours (du Pont) offers a classic example of the transition in the structure of the modern industrial corporation. Organized in 1802, du Pont was a family business that manufactured black gunpowder and explosives for the first 100 years of its existence. In 1912 antitrust action forced the dismemberment of the parent company into three parts, with Hercules and Atlas Powder separating from du Pont. During and after World War I du Pont began to acquire chemical companies that supplemented its main product—explosives. The technology that was acquired in the production of picric acid, nitric acid, and cellulose for munitions began to pay unusual dividends in the development of rayon, nylon, cellophane, paints, and adhesives. By planned research and development, and occasionally by accident, du Pont enlarged its product line to the point that explosives represent a small part of its production today.

Du Pont began to investigate the possibilities of synthesizing long-chain molecules, or polymers (cellulose was a natural carbon polymer associated with oxygen or nitrogen atoms), when it hired a group of organic chemists, including Wallace Hume Carothers, about 1927. These men engaged in pure research on the production of synthetic polymers containing atoms of oxygen (polyesters) or nitrogen (polyamides). Six years of laboratory work produced some interesting but nonfunctional results, nonfunctional primarily because the products had extremely low melting points, and for a time the work was abandoned. In 1935 Carothers was encouraged to return to his polymers, and he soon developed a superpolymer "66" that could withstand temperatures of over 500° F. A variety of new synthetics were soon being developed. Du Pont directors now decided to manufacture Carothers's "66" even though yet better polymers might be synthesized. The new product, *nylon*, entered the market less than five years after its discovery.[6] Research and development were coming of age.

The "accident" of invention also added to du Pont's repertoire. In 1941 a du Pont chemist, Roy J. Plunket, was assigned to investigate the properties of C_2F_4, a gas related to Freon that had been developed by Kinetic Chemicals, then jointly owned by General Motors and du Pont. Plunket synthesized a quantity of C_2F_4 and stored it in a cylinder. When he opened the cylinder several weeks later it contained particles of polymerized gas. This substance was discovered to be

ELENTHÈRE IRÉNÉE du PONT *(1771–1834)*
Founder of E. I. du Pont de Nemours & Co.

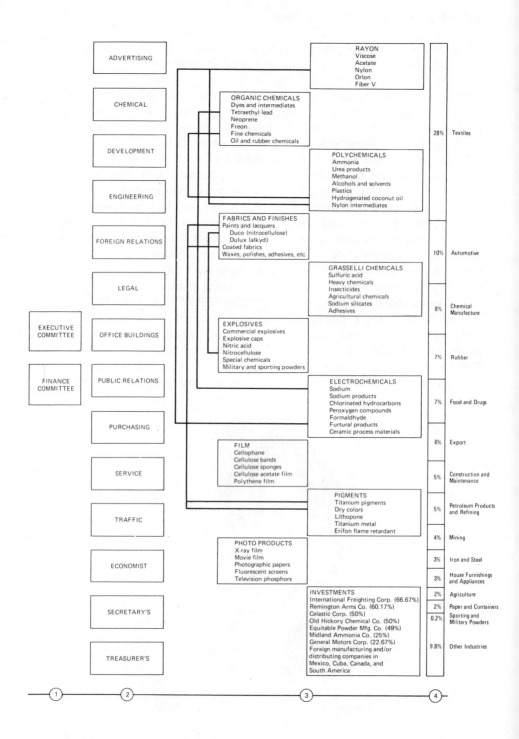

ADVERTISING

CHEMICAL

DEVELOPMENT

ENGINEERING

FOREIGN RELATIONS

LEGAL

EXECUTIVE COMMITTEE

OFFICE BUILDINGS

FINANCE COMMITTEE

PUBLIC RELATIONS

PURCHASING

SERVICE

TRAFFIC

ECONOMIST

SECRETARY'S

TREASURER'S

RAYON
Viscose
Acetate
Nylon
Orlon
Fiber V

ORGANIC CHEMICALS
Dyes and intermediates
Tetraethyl lead
Neoprene
Freon
Fine chemicals
Oil and rubber chemicals

POLYCHEMICALS
Ammonia
Urea products
Methanol
Alcohols and solvents
Plastics
Hydrogenated coconut oil
Nylon intermediates

FABRICS AND FINISHES
Paints and lacquers
    Duco (nitrocellulose)
    Dulux (alkyd)
Coated fabrics
Waxes, polishes, adhesives, etc.

GRASSELLI CHEMICALS
Sulfuric acid
Heavy chemicals
Insecticides
Agricultural chemicals
Sodium silicates
Adhesives

EXPLOSIVES
Commercial explosives
Explosive caps
Nitric acid
Nitrocellulose
Special chemicals
Military and sporting powders

ELECTROCHEMICALS
Sodium
Sodium products
Chlorinated hydrocarbons
Peroxygen compounds
Formaldhyde
Furtural products
Ceramic process materials

FILM
Cellophane
Cellulose bands
Cellulose sponges
Cellulose acetate film
Polythene film

PIGMENTS
Titanium pigments
Dry colors
Lithopone
Titanium metal
Erifon flame retardant

PHOTO PRODUCTS
X-ray film
Movie film
Photographic papers
Fluorescent screens
Television phosphors

INVESTMENTS
International Freighting Corp. (66.67%)
Remington Arms Co. (60.17%)
Celastic Corp. (50%)
Old Hickory Chemical Co. (50%)
Equitable Powder Mfg. Co. (49%)
Midland Ammonia Co. (25%)
General Motors Corp. (22.67%)
Foreign manufacturing and/or
distributing companies in
Mexico, Cuba, Canada, and
South America

28%   Textiles

10%   Automotive

8%   Chemical Manufacture

7%   Rubber

7%   Food and Drugs

6%   Export

5%   Construction and Maintenance

5%   Petroleum Products and Refining

4%   Mining

3%   Iron and Steel

3%   House Furnishings and Appliances

2%   Agriculture

2%   Paper and Containers

0.2% Sporting and Military Powders

9.8% Other Industries

1   2   3   4

288

extremely resistant to all acids, and could withstand heat above 700° F. Classified secret during World War II, the substance found limited use in the storage of corrosive compounds, and not until the 1960s did *Teflon* become commercially significant in an ever expanding variety of uses.[7]

After World War II du Pont, the old powder manufacturer, exploded into the production and marketing of a vast array of consumer goods, ranging from synthetic fibers and paint to plastics, photographic film, and insecticides. In 1975 du Pont sales reached $7.2 billion and the company ranked seventeenth in sales volume among all the industrials.

A restructuring of du Pont's administrative organization was concurrent with the development of new products and new markets. Du Pont production and sales are managed by ten autonomous operating divisions, such as advertising, purchasing, development, and traffic, and by an investments division that controls foreign operations and manages investments in outside companies. Broad corporate policies are guided by an executive committee and a finance committee, which constitute the board of directors. The president and vice-presidents on the board have no direct control over any of the operating divisions, but evaluate their performance and allocate corporate resources, including capital, plant and equipment, and technological and administrative skills. Fourteen auxiliary departments that coordinate services used by all the operating divisions report to the executive and finance committees. (See Figure 18.2.) This decentralized structure facilitates diversification while efficiently coordinating resource use and marketing. The pattern has become common to most multi-industrial corporations.[8]

Polaroid

The dominance of older, established firms has been challenged by the emergence of new products and processes, which have often forced the older firms to diversify their product line. For instance, Polaroid's new photographic process eroded Eastman Kodak's long-held leadership in the film and camera industry.

FIGURE 18.2. Du Pont organizational structure.

(1) All departments but two report to the Executive Committee, which is the active manager of the business. The Treasurer's and Secretary's departments report to the Finance Committee. Two smaller committees (not shown) administer bonuses and salaries and direct the audit.

(2) The fourteen auxiliary departments service all operating departments.

(3) The ten industrial operating departments are essentially independent units, but transfer approximately 15 percent of their business and skills from one department to another.

(4) The last stage indicates into what major industries the products of du Pont industrial departments flow.

Source: W. H. Allner for Fortune Magazine, October 1950.

Polaroid was organized in 1937, and became a Kodak competitor only in 1947 with the development of a revolutionary one-step dry photographic process. In twenty years Polaroid leaped from obscurity to become the twenty-first largest industrial corporation in volume of sales.[9] Polaroid was the work of Herbert Edwin Land, born in 1909 in Bridgeport, Connecticut. Land attended Harvard University and became interested in the polarization of light. In 1932 he developed an antiglare sheet plastic that he called Polaroid. Land left school and established the Land-Wheelwright Laboratory in a Boston basement. In 1935 he began manufacturing antiglare sheet plastic and camera filters. In 1936 American Optical Company began to manufacture Polaroid sunglasses, using Land's plastic. The next year, Land organized the Polaroid Company and obtained patents on the polarized sheet and his manufacturing process.[10]

In 1941 Land developed a film for three-dimensional pictures. The ''3-D'' movie became popular, and was a limited financial success in the 1950s. More important, by 1950 six million pairs of Polaroid sunglasses were being manufactured each week. During World War II Polaroid received defense contracts for infrared optical lenses, gun sights, periscopes, range finders, aerial cameras, and bombsights. These contracts added to both the financial resources of the firm and its technological expertise. On February 21, 1947 Land demonstrated his revolutionary one-step photographic process. Commercial production of the Polaroid Land Camera and film began in 1949. In 1969 Polaroid introduced six new color cameras, headed by the SX-70, and poured $2.2 million into a twelve-day advertising blitz. In all, Polaroid spent $22 million on advertising for the year. By 1973 Polaroid was producing 25,000 cameras a day and enjoying annual sales of $685 million, but technical problems had developed in the color-film batteries, and Kodak had broken the Polaroid monopoly on the new film processes. Meanwhile, Land retired from active management of the company, leaving it to a team of careful, systematic planners. Land's genius manifested itself not only in the area of scientific research but in the selection of talented managers.[11] Polaroid demonstrated that monopoly and oligarchy were impermanent features of the modern industrial system.

Texas Instruments

Another postwar newcomer to the lists of giant enterprise was Texas Instruments, founded in 1951. Texas Instruments is perhaps the archetypical ''research and development'' firm, which stresses innovation and institutionalized market development. Texas Instruments grew out of Geophysical Services Incorporated, a firm founded by John Knowles and Eugene McDermott about 1930 and concerned with seismographic oil exploration. In 1939 GSI separated from the oil-exploration division, and in 1941 it was reorganized. During the war GSI received numerous defense contracts, many of them involving sound-wave reflection. Continued geophysical work became increasingly unprofitable, however, and after the war GSI concentrated on military research projects and under the direction of Patrick Haggerty developed and expanded its electronic facilities. In 1951 Texas Instruments was incorporated, with GSI becoming a wholly owned subsidiary, and the following year Texas Instruments merged with International Rubber Company. Under arrangements with Bell Laboratories, TI began to manufacture transistors. In 1948 Dr. William Shockley and his associates at Bell Laboratories had developed the solid-state transistor, which replaced the cumbersome vacuum tube. This invention made possible "miniaturization," which in turn stimulated tremendous development in computers, missiles, and electronic components of every kind. In 1954 Gordon Teal of TI developed the silicone transistor, which was far superior to existing transistors. Between 1954 and 1960, as transistors came into widespread use in electronic equipment, TI sales rose an average of 40 percent a year. Between 1954 and 1974 they rose an average of 30 percent each year. TI broadened its line to include semiconductors, calculators, integrated circuits, electronic data-processing equipment, and aircraft-control and -guidance systems.[12]

As TI sales soared, the administrative organization of the company followed the pattern of decentralized operating divisions acting independently under a general policy board. A Semi-Conductor Group is responsible for the manufacture of silicone transistors and integrated circuits; the Chemical Division produces silicone; the Supply Division distributes electronic components; the Equipment Group handles most of the defense (radar and anti-submarine devices) and air-traffic-control contracts. The Service Group sponsors geophysical oil exploration, and the Materials and Electrical Products Division was organized in response to a government contract to "clad" coins. Texas Instrument sales rose from $230 million in 1960 to $1.6 billion in 1975.[13]

Employee relations are perhaps more "advanced" in this space-age firm than in any other firm. The company stresses youth, innovation, and individualism. Employees are encouraged to set their own production goals. Retirement is mandatory at the age of fifty-five. Employees participate in psychoanalysis in order to become more productive. Basic employee goals are to achieve and to be loved and appreciated. Workers are members of the company-sponsored Texan Association, which provides attractive recreational and leisure opportunities for employees and their families. Texas Instruments' employee morale, production, profits, and growth are among the highest of the major corporations. Few of the product lines represented by TI existed before World War II. Like Polaroid, it is essentially an all-new industry.

Xerox

For all practical purposes Xerox Corporation has post–World War II origins. The firm was founded upon a revolutionary innovation, the electrographic copying process, or Carlson process, developed in 1946 at the Battelle Memorial Institute in Columbus, Ohio. Its parent company was Haloid, a relatively small family-owned photographic-paper manufacturer begun by Haloid Wilson in Rochester, New York in 1906. Haloid obtained the rights to the Carlson process in 1946 in exchange for royalties, and between 1947 and 1960 it poured $75 million into development. In 1955 the company obtained full patent rights and termed its process xerography, from the Greek for "dry writing." The company changed its name to Haloid Xerox in 1958, and its first commercial automatic copying machine, the 914, was marketed in 1959. Company sales rose from $33 million in 1959 to $66 million in 1961, at which time the Xerox name was adopted and the company still was not ranked among *Fortune*'s 500 leading industrials.[14]

Xerox reproduction processes emerged at a time that mass-media communications were coming of age. Xerography's closest competition consisted of the mimeograph machine, invented by Thomas A. Edison; photostatic-copy processes, which were slower, cumbersome, and more expensive; and microfilm processes, which served a specialized function more than a mass-circulation medium. Xerography was something unique that enjoyed a tremendous demand. Xerox became the "Cinderella corporation" of the 1960s. Its sales, earnings, stock values, and dividends climbed steadily (Table 18.1).

TABLE 18.1

Xerox Revenues

YEAR ENDED	OPERATING REVENUES ($MILL.)	EARNINGS PER SHARE	DIVS. DECLARED	PRICE RANGE HIGH-LOW
1962	$ 104.5	$ .24	$ .04	11–5
1963	176.0	.38	.07	29–9
1964	268.0	.63	.13	44–23
1965	392.6	.93	.18	71–31
1966	528.3	1.24	.28	89–41
1967	701.4	1.48	.37	104–65
1968	896.4	1.73	.48	109–76
1968a	1,224.4	1.68	—	
1969a	1,482.9	2.07	.57	115–80
1970	1,718.6	2.39	0.60	115–65

Note: Adj. for stk. splits: 5-for-1, 1/64; 3-for-1, 5/69. a-Incl. Scientific Data Systems and reflects consolidation of Rank Xerox Ltd., 1968 pro-forma.

Source: *Moody's Handbook of Common Stocks* (New York: Moody's Investors Service, Inc., October 1971), p. 1007.

Xerox's essential dependence on a single product made it vulnerable, despite its marketing successes. By the close of the 1960s numerous competitors had appeared, not the least of them International Business Machines (IBM).

Xerox constantly fought legal battles over both its patent monopoly on xerography and the infringement by users of copyright laws. In 1973 Xerox was accused by the Federal Trade Commission of operating a monopoly, and it began to lose its exclusive control over xerography. By this time, Xerox's marketing techniques, such as lease-rental arrangements, its continued development of improved copiers (such as the 2400), and its established reputation had assured the company a majority position in the copy industry. But increased competition also brought increased costs of production and lower per-unit profits. Xerox sought to sustain its growth potential through the classic strategy of diversification accompanied by decentralization.

Under the leadership of C. Peter McColough, Xerox expanded through acquisitions and mergers into computers, education, medicines, and communications. The company acquired Electro Optical System of Pasadena, University Microfilm of Ann Arbor, Scientific Data Corporation, Basic Systems, and American Education Publications. Although Xerox's primary business is the copy machine, it offers a diverse product line ranging from computers (in competition with IBM and others) to information-retrieval systems, publishing, microfilm services, and telecopies. Xerox has consistently stressed innovation, service, and quality in its product lines. Its extensive advertising campaigns stress that Xerox seeks to do good things for people while making money. The company seems to have done both.[15] In 1975 Xerox, which had not been listed among *Fortune*'s 500 leading industrial corporations until 1962, ranked thirty-ninth among the 500.

Of the largest 500 corporations in 1975, 203 reported sales in excess of $1 billion annually. Twenty-seven reported sales in excess of $5 billion. Over the years, smaller firms have generally reflected a faster rate of growth in sales and in profits. The ten companies demonstrating the largest percentage of gain in sales between 1954 and 1974 were not among the top 500 in 1954. One of them, Occidental Petroleum, earned only $3,000 that year; most of them came into existence only after World War II. Twenty-two companies on the list were absorbed by mergers between 1954 and 1974. *Fortune* editors observed "a lot of coming and going among the 500 largest industrials." Although large corporations seem to be getting bigger, newcomers are constantly joining the ranks.[16]

In the long run, the business and industrial firm often changes its form, its function, and its internal structure. One of the great advantages of the American economy, and of the business units within that economy, is its considerable fluidity and formlessness. Stratification and rigidity, imposed externally or internally, contribute to stagnation and "no-growth." There is little evidence of such ridigity developing over the past three decades. Undoubtedly, government antitrust vigilance has helped maintain flexibility, but government bureaucracy and regulatory legislation often offset this by creating rigidity in situations that should be less structured. Furthermore, although there is presently a distinct trend toward decentralization and diversification by industry, the organizational structure

TABLE 18.2

Fortune's twenty largest industrial corporations (ranked by sales), 1975.

RANK 1975 1974	COMPANY	SALES ($000)	ASSETS ($000)	Rank	NET INCOME ($000)	Rank
1 1	Exxon (New York)	44,864,824	32,839,398	1	2,503,013	1
2 2	General Motors (Detroit)	35,724,911	21,664,885	2	1,253,092	3
3 4	Texaco (New York)	24,507,454	17,262,448	3	830,583	4
4 3	Ford Motor (Dearborn, Mich.)	24,009,100	14,020,200	6	322,700	23
5 5	Mobil Oil (New York)	20,620,392	15,050,287	5	809,877	5
6 6	Standard Oil of California (San Francisco)	16,822,077	12,898,150	7	772,509	7
7 9	International Business Machines (Armonk, N.Y.)	14,436,541	15,530,476	4	1,989,877	2
8 7	Gulf Oil (Pittsburgh)	14,268,000	12,425,000	8	700,000	8
9 8	General Electric (Fairfield, Conn.)	13,399,100	9,763,500	11	580,800	11
10 11	Chrysler (Highland Park, Mich.)	11,699,305	6,266,728	17	−(259,535)	492
11 10	International Tel. & Tel. (New York)	11,367,647	10,407,941	9	398,171	15
12 13	Standard Oil (Ind.) (Chicago)	9,955,248	9,854,099	10	786,987	6
13 12	U.S. Steel (Pittsburgh)	8,167,269	8,148,174	12	559,614	12
14 14	Shell Oil (Houston)	8,143,445	7,010,753	14	514,827	13
15 18	Atlantic Richfield (Los Angeles)	7,307,854	7,364,787	13	350,395	17
16 16	Continental Oil (Stanford, Conn.)	7,253,801	5,184,581	20	330,854	22
17 17	E.I. du Pont de Nemours (Wilmington, Del.)	7,221,500	6,425,000	16	271,800	25
18 15	Western Electric (New York)	6,590,116	4,999,944	22	107,308	81
19 28	Procter & Gamble (Cincinnati)	6,081,675	3,652,673	32	333,862	21
20 19	Westinghouse Electric (Pittsburgh)	5,862,747	4,866,286	23	165,224	45

Source: From "The Fortune Directory of the 500 Largest Industrial Corporations," *Fortune*, May, 1976, p. 318.

of big business is highly volatile and flexible. Whereas decentralization is the trend of today, centralization may be the trend of tomorrow.

BUSINESS AND GOVERNMENT

The flexibility of the corporate structure has allowed it to organize a strong research and development component. Much of the money for research and development has been provided by government. Indeed, many industries, such as the aircraft, shipbuilding, space, and satellite-communications industries, have virtually delegated the research and development function to government. This has created a liaison, if not an alliance, between government and business. This relationship is often one of partners rather than one of control by one party or the other. Such a relationship is by no means new; it has extended into the agricultural realm at least since the organization of the Agricultural Experiment Station program in 1887. The Agricultural Experiment Station is the federally subsidized research and development component of the privately owned and operated American farm. Since World War II this relationship has been extended to industry. Oak Ridge, White Sands and the National Aeronautics and Space Administration were laboratories for Raytheon, American Telephone and Telegraph, the Radio Corporation of America, Remington Rand, and Boeing, among others. "Funding," largely by federal grants, is a contemporary form of underwriting private research and development on an enormous scale.

Government-business accord is also growing within the regulatory agencies. Over the long run these agencies begin to identify with the systems they propose to regulate, and they are strongly influenced, both directly and indirectly, by the regulated industry groups. Railroad commissions on the state level and the Interstate Commerce Commission on the federal level must be somewhat

FIGURE 18.3. Environmental Protection Agency Laboratory for studying ways to control air pollution by automobiles.

Source: Environmental Protection Agency.

responsive to the interests of the railroads they regulate. They are as interested as the railroads themselves in the preservation of the business. The Civil Aeronautics Board, the National Labor Relations Board, the Food and Drug Administration, and the Federal Reserve Board, to mention only a few, have a vested interest in the preservation and extension of the systems they propose to regulate. Some would say that the regulatory body becomes a lobbying device of the private firm. On the local level, for example, a zoning and planning commission might be dominated by local realtor and banking interests. The product of this government-business liaison is that the business unit seeks preferential treatment and government itself becomes a decentralized, often conflicting amalgam of competing interest groups. Government, like the economy and the firm, is a constantly changing form, but one, like the firm, that can centralize or decentralize its functions.

To beg the question, the relationship that has developed between government and business is all that economists, social critics, political scientists, and businessmen say that it is. It is at once a hostile relationship, a familial relationship, a relationship in which private business directs public interests, and a relationship in which private enterprise benefits at one moment and loses at another. Whatever that relationship is, it is impermanent, as it has always been. Whatever that relationship is, it has generally been profitable over the past three decades, not only for the business firms but for the American people. Although the form and structure of both government and business have changed, they have displayed a strong continuity with the past. There is, moreover, little evidence that the preference of the American people for "free enterprise," however it is defined, has changed. Nonetheless, there is no guarantee that a free-enterprise system will endure. It cannot endure when the aspirations, the incentives, and opportunities for profit, private ownership of property, and a free market cease to exist or to be the dominant influence in American economic life.

Notes

[1] Testimony of Willard P. Mueller, *Economic Concentration, Overall and Conglomerate Aspects,* Hearings before the Subcommittee on Antitrust and Monopoly of the Committee of the Judiciary, U.S. Senate, 88th Cong., 2nd sess. (Washington, D.C.: Government Printing Office, 1964), p. 115.

[2] *Ibid.*, p. 115.

[3] Linda Grant Martin, "The 500: A Report on Two Decades" *Fortune,* May 1975, pp. 238–41.

[4] See Alfred D. Chandler, Jr., "The Structure of American Industry in the Twentieth Century: A Historical Overview," *Business History Review*, 43 (Autumn, 1969), 255–97.

[5] See Chandler, "The Structure of American Industry," pp. 274–81.

[6]See Lawrence P. Lessing, "Du Pont," *Fortune* (October 1950), p. 86–180.

[7]See Lessing, "Du Pont," pp. 130–32.

[8]See Linda Grant Martin, "The 500: A Report on Two Decades," pp. 238–241, and Chandler, "The Structure of American Industry," pp. 255–297.

[9]"Polaroid" *Forbes*, June 15, 1969, pp. 34–44.

[10]See "Polaroid" *Forbes*, June 15, 1969, pp. 34–44, and *Current Biography*, 1953, pp. 339–41.

[11]See "Polaroid" *Forbes*, June 15, 1969, pp. 34–44; "Polaroid's Big Blitz," *Business Week*, March 1, 1969, p. 54; and "Dr. Land Redesigns His Camera Company," *Business Week*, April 15, 1972, pp, 70–73.

[12]See J. M. McDonald, "The Men Who Made T.I.," *Fortune*, November, 1961, pp. 116–226; John McDonald, "Where Texas Instruments Goes From Here," *Fortune*, December, 1961, pp. 110–238; J. B. Weiner, "Texas Instruments," *Duns Review*, January, 1967, pp. 28–31; "Texas Instruments," *Business Week*, June 27, 1970, p. 102.

[13]See John McDonald, "Where Texas Instruments Goes From Here," pp. 160–238; McDonald, "The Men Who Made T.I.," pp. 116–226; and "The Fortune Directory of the 500 Largest Industrial Corporations," *Fortune*, May, 1976, pp. 316–43.

[14]See "Copy Machine Boom-and Xerox Boom," *Newsweek*, November 8, 1965, p. 84–90; John Brooks, "Profile: Xerox," *New Yorker*, April 1, 1967, pp. 46–50; and "Xerox: The McColough Era," *Forbes*, July 1, 1969, pp. 24–26.

[15]See "The Copy War," *Time*, May 4, 1970, p. 92; "Monopolist Xerox," *Time*, December 25, 1972, pp. 68–69; and "C. Peter McColough of Xerox Corp.," *Nation's Business*, September, 1972, p. 446.

[16]See Linda Grant Martin, "The 500: A Report on Two Decades," pp. 238–41.

SUGGESTED READING

BAUGHMAN, JAMES P., ed., *The History of American Management*. Englewood Cliffs, N.J.: Prentice-Hall, 1969.

CHANDLER, ALFRED D., JR., *Strategy and Structure: Chapters in the History of the Industrial Enterprise*. Cambridge, Mass.: M.I.T. Press, 1962.

GALBRAITH, JOHN KENNETH, *The New Industrial State*. Boston: Houghton Mifflin, 1967.

GILLAM, RICHARD, ed., *Power in Postwar America: Interdisciplinary Perspectives on a Historical Problem*. Boston: Little, Brown, 1971.

HANSEN, ALVIN H., *The Postwar American Economy: Performance and Problems*. New York: Norton, 1964.

HEILBRONER, ROBERT L., *The Limits of American Capitalism*. New York: Harper & Row, 1965.

MACRAE, NORMAN, *America's Third Century*. New York: Harcourt, Brace & Jovanovich, 1976.

MILLS, C. WRIGHT, *The Power Elite*. New York: Oxford University Press, 1956.

PERROW, CHARLES, *The Radical Attack on Business: A Critical Analysis*. New York: Harcourt, Brace & Jovanovich, 1972.

THE GENERAL WELFARE

We the People of the United States, in Order to form a more perfect Union, establish Justice, insure domestic Tranquility, *provide for the common defense*, *promote the general Welfare*, and secure the Blessings of Liberty to ourselves and our Posterity, do ordain and establish this Constitution for the United States of America.

Welfare economics has to do with the distribution of scarce resources according to social goals or values. The enlargement of government's role in economic activity derives largely from two sources—war and welfare. War and national defense have historically accounted for the major portion of federal spending. Since 1940 the volume of defense spending has soared, but there has been relatively little opposition to the basic idea of defense spending since World War II ended. There has been conflict over the volume of spending and over the direction such spending should take—that is, whether it should be for ships, submarines, aircraft, missiles, or tanks—but in the broad perspective total expenditures have been little affected. Welfare spending constituted a small portion of federal spending until the 1930s, but since World War II it has grown to equal, and even surpass, defense spending.

WELFARE

What does government welfare spending propose to do that the free-market economy has not done, or cannot do? One goal of welfare economics is to alleviate or end the cyclical swings, the recessions and depressions, following each period of expansion that have been characteristic of the economy. The formula for such a curative generally follows the guidelines established by John Maynard Keynes, but the tax-spend recipe has never been literally applied, and if applied there is considerable doubt that it would provide a satisfactory solution.

Nevertheless, welfare economics proposes to end this ancient nemesis of capitalist economies, and our government does to a greater or lesser degree spend, or curb spending, in order to maintain stable economic growth.

Other problems in our society that the free-enterprise system seemingly cannot solve, or indeed may foster, are poverty, unemployment, accidents, sickness, birth defects, aging, pollution, and depletion of natural resources. At various times past, farmers, industrial laborers, migrant workers, Chinese, Irish, Chicanos, slum dwellers, and the illiterate or uneducated have been identified as underprivileged segments of the society. Women and blacks have been identified as groups which fail to share equitably in the general welfare. Most of these social conditions are not peculiar to the American socioeconomic order. These conditions, or parallel ones, exist in all human societies, but in relatively few nations are they recognized as *problems*—that is, as conditions that are undesirable and that can be solved.

The recognition of social problems most often occurs concurrently with the availability of the resources to solve the problem. The development of welfare policies usually follows a distinct pattern: (1) the recognition of the problem; (2) the review of resources and methods for the solution of that problem—often involving journalistic, literary, and legislative debate; (3) the inception and application of a plan or technique (a piece of legislation or a program). A fourth and final step is to review the program to see if it is accomplishing its purposes and to determine its costs. Years may pass between the recognition of a problem and an attempt to solve it. The social costs of a solution may be great; many hidden costs or benefits may emerge generations later.

Social problems are measured relative to actual or assumed social values. As the value system or mores of a society change, the characteristics and dimensions of its problems will vary, and as its structural or technological capacities alter, so will the character of its problems. The automobile, for example, was once hailed as the answer to urban pollution because there would be no more horse manure on the streets. Poverty was once believed to be a natural, if not divinely ordained, state in human society that was beyond the means or purposes of society to eradicate. Poverty was not a problem then; our society now believes that it is a problem. It took generations to reach this conclusion, and admittedly there are those who do not agree, but the consensus is that poverty is a socially undesirable condition that can and should be eliminated. Similar attitudes are expressed about pollution, depletion of natural resources, disabilities and insecurity caused by aging, race, or sex, epidemics, and other problems. Our society has chosen to attack these ills through welfare programs administered by the federal, state, and local governments. These programs require the allocation of resources through nonmarket decisions, or welfare economics.

Inasmuch as the ultimate goal of our welfare programs appears to be to guarantee to every American "equal opportunity" or a "fair" standard of living now and in the future regardless of age, sex, or race, it is appropriate to consider public welfare spending and poverty in the broad context rather than in the guise

FIGURE 19.1. VISTA nurses visiting elderly man.

Source: ACTION/Vista

of specific programs that can be little more than identified in the space available. How do we measure the general welfare? What do Americans believe is a fair or minimum standard of living? What is the "poverty line?" What groups or segments of society appear to fall below the minimum income level? How much of our resources should we allocate to welfare programs? How effective or efficient are welfare programs? What are the short- and long-run benefits and costs? The answers are both quantitative and qualitative, and on both counts incomplete, but the contemporary student of economic history has the great advantage of a mass of statistical data that derives from the quantitative revolution of the past three decades. There is at least the opportunity for far more precise measurement than was previously possible.

The initial measurement of the general welfare is the Gross National Product (GNP). GNP is the total market value of the goods and services produced by the nation's economy. It comprises the purchases of goods and services by consumers and government, private investment, and net exports. National income, or net national product, consists of the aggregate earnings of labor and property arising from the current production of goods and services. Personal income represents current income received by persons (excluding corporations but including unincorporated enterprises, nonprofit institutions, and private funds), inclusive of transfers from government and business but excluding transfers among persons. Disposable personal income is that remaining to the individual after payments of taxes or other funds to the government. Per-capita data divides the various indexes by total population to provide an average or median base. As we noted earlier, a rising GNP does not invariably mean rising per-capita real income.

Table 19.1 presents annual GNP and per-capita income between 1941 and 1970. Note that real per-capita income declined in 1970 despite an increased GNP; this reflects inflation costs. But real per-capita income has risen 80 percent since 1941.

There is no question that the general welfare has improved tremendously since 1941. There are other supporting indexes for this conclusion. The nutritive value of urban diets, for example, has risen from a daily average of 2,840

TABLE 19.1

Gross National Product, Total and Per Capita, in Current and 1958 Prices, 1941–1970.

YEAR	CURRENT PRICES		1958 PRICES		IMPLICIT PRICE INDEX (1958 = 100)
	Total (Billions of Dollars)	*Per capita (Dollars)*	*Total (Billions of Dollars)*	*Per capita (Dollars)*	
1941	124.5	934	263.7	1,977	47.2
1942	157.9	1,171	297.8	2,208	53.0
1943	191.6	1,401	337.1	2,465	56.8
1944	210.1	1,518	361.3	2,611	58.2
1945	211.9	1,515	355.2	2,538	59.7
1946	208.5	1,475	312.6	2.211	66.7
1947	231.3	1,605	309.9	2,150	74.6
1948	257.6	1,757	323.7	2,208	79.6
1949	256.5	1,719	324.1	2,172	79.1
1950	284.8	1,877	355.3	2,342	80.2
1951	328.4	2,129	383.4	2,485	85.6
1952	345.5	2,201	395.1	2,517	87.5
1953	364.6	2,285	412.8	2,587	88.3
1954	364.8	2,247	407.0	2,506	89.6
1955	398.0	2,408	438.0	2,650	90.9

TABLE 19.1 (cont.)

YEAR	CURRENT PRICES		1958 PRICES		IMPLICIT PRICE INDEX (1958 = 100)
	Total (Billions of Dollars)	Per capita (Dollars)	Total (Billions of Dollars)	Per capita (Dollars)	
1956	419.2	2,492	446.1	2,652	94.0
1957	441.1	2,576	452.5	2,642	97.5
1958	447.3	2,569	447.3	2,569	100.0
1959	483.7	2,731	475.9	2,688	101.6
1960*	503.7	2,788	487.7	2,699	103.3
1961	520.1	2,831	497.2	2,706	104.6
1962	560.3	3,004	529.8	2,840	105.8
1963	590.5	3,120	551.0	2,912	107.2
1964	632.4	3,296	581.1	3,028	108.8
1965	684.9	3,525	617.8	3,180	110.9
1966	749.9	3,815	658.1	3,348	113.9
1967	793.9	3,995	675.2	3,398	117.6
1968	864.2	4,306	706.6	3,521	122.3
1969	930.3	4,590	725.6	3,580	128.2
1970	977.1	4,808	722.5	3,555	135.2

*Denotes first year for which figures include Alaska and Hawaii.

Source: *Historical Statistics of the United States Colonial Times to 1970,* Series F 1–5, p. 224.

calories in 1942 to 3,110 calories in 1965. The daily caloric intake of the lowest third of urban households in the same period rose from 2,670 calories to 2,960 calories; the nutrients available per capita per day have risen from 90.9 in 1940 to 102.5 in 1970 (index: 1967 = 100). Average personal income rose from $3,566 in 1947 to $11,106 in 1970. The average annual growth rate of the GNP since 1929 has been 3 percent, and from 1960 to 1970 the average rate was 4.5 percent. Despite a genuinely remarkable record of postwar expansion, however, the United States' performance has been exceeded by other countries (Table 19.2).

In almost any selected year since 1941, the United States, with approximately 5 percent of the world's population, has accounted for more than one third of the world's income. Most of the available data support the proposition that abundance and a very high standard of living distinguish Americans from most other peoples of the world. What, then, is poverty in America, and who are the impoverished?

POVERTY

The first step in evaluating the incidence of poverty is to see how the national income is distributed. Tables 19.3 and 19.4 show average income levels and distribution patterns by income groups for the period 1947–1970.

TABLE 19.2

Growth Rates (Percentage) of GNP and Output per Employee for the United
States and Six Countries, 1929–1969.

PERIOD	UNITED STATES	JAPAN	GERMANY	UNITED KINGDOM	FRANCE	ITALY	CANADA
	Annual Growth Rates of Gross National Product						
1929–1969	3.3	4.9	4.2	2.2	2.5	3.2	3.8
1929–1950	2.9	.6	1.9	1.6	—	1.0	3.2
1950–1969	3.9	9.7	6.8	2.7	5.3	5.6	4.5
1950–1960	3.2	8.2	8.6	2.7	4.9	5.6	4.0
1960–1969	4.5	11.1	4.7	2.8	5.8	5.6	5.2
	Annual Growth Rates of Output per Employee						
1929–1969	2.0	—	3.1	1.6	2.5	3.1	2.1
1929–1950	1.7	—	1.2	1.1	.3	1.0	2.0
1950–1969	2.3	8.3	5.3	2.2	5.2	5.6	2.2
1950–1960	2.1	6.7	6.0	1.9	5.4	4.5	2.1
1960–1969	2.6	9.5	4.6	2.5	5.0	6.4	2.2

Source: *Historical Statistics of the United States Colonial Times to 1970,* Series F 10–16, p. 225.

Tables 19.1–19.4 not only portray the general welfare but illustrate the
proportions in which different segments of society share in the national income.
Those in the lowest-income groups are clearly less well off than those in the
upper categories. But our definition of poverty is more sophisticated. The poor
are those who earn insufficient annual income to afford the necessities judged
basic by dominant middle-class opinion. This "market basket" approach to
poverty means that the poverty level varies annually with price indexes. Thus,
for example, the poverty level for an urban family of four was about $3,500 in
1968 and $4,300 in 1973. For a rural family the range was from $2,500 to $3,600
for the same period. Generally, over the past decade 15 to 20 percent of American families have subsisted at or below the poverty level. The incidence of
poverty is higher among blacks, although in total numbers there are far more
poor among whites. The incidence of poverty among whites tends to be higher
among the elderly. Poverty in the South is most often rural; poverty in the North
and West is most often urban. Overall, the poor in America are mostly the
uneducated, the unskilled, the insecure, and the aged. Although the problem of
evaluating the causes of poverty and its impact on society at large are beyond the
scope of this study, such inquiry is necessary to an understanding of poverty, and
of the goals of social welfare. Suffice it to say here that our society believes that
poverty can be eradicated, or at least its symptoms alleviated, and that to do so
would be beneficial to the general welfare.

TABLE 19.3

Distribution of Money Income Among Families, 1947–1970 (in 1967 dollars).

YEAR	NUMBER OF FAMILIES (THOUSANDS)	DISTRIBUTION BY INCOME LEVEL (PERCENTAGE)						
		Under $3,000	$3,000 to $4,999	$5,000 to $6,999	$7,000 to $9,999	$10,000 to $11,999	$12,000 to $14,999	$15,000 or more
1947	37,237	49.4	31.3	11.7	4.9		2.7	
1948	38,624	45.7	33.6	12.5	5.4		2.9	
1949	39,303	47.6	32.0	12.6	5.0		2.6	
1950	39,929	42.5	34.3	14.2	5.8		3.3	
1951	40,578	35.9	35.3	17.6	7.6	1.5	.9	1.2
1952	40,832	33.4	33.9	19.4	9.0	1.7	1.2	1.3
1953	41.202	30.2	31.7	21.3	11.6	2.5	1.6	1.3
1954	41,951	31.7	31.0	20.4	11.1	2.7	1.6	1.4
1955	42,889	28.5	30.1	22.2	13.0	3.0	1.8	1.4
1956	43,497	25.6	27.4	23.5	15.6	3.5	2.5	2.0
1957	43,696	24.5	25.9	24.8	16.4	4.0	2.5	1.9
1958	44,232	24.1	24.6	24.4	16.8	4.7	2.9	2.4
1959	45,111	22.7	21.8	24.2	18.9	5.4	3.7	3.1
1960	45,456	21.7	20.3	23.7	20.0	6.2	4.4	3.7
1961	46,341	21.4	19.9	21.9	20.7	6.6	4.6	4.6
1962	46,998	19.9	19.1	22.4	21.0	7.6	5.3	4.9
1963	47,436	18.5	17.7	21.3	22.5	8.3	6.2	5.4
1964	47,835	17.6	17.0	19.8	23.2	9.5	6.9	6.3
1965	48,279	16.1	15.6	18.8	24.2	10.1	7.6	7.6
1966	49,065	14.1	13.7	17.7	24.6	11.5	9.3	9.3
1967	49,834	12.6	12.9	16.2	24.4	11.9	10.7	11.4
1968	50,510	10.3	12.1	14.5	23.4	12.5	12.4	14.7
1969	51,237	9.3	10.7	12.3	21.7	13.0	13.7	19.3
1970	51,948	8.9	10.3	11.8	19.9	12.7	14.1	22.3

Source: *Historical Statistics of the United States Colonial Times to 1970*, Series G 1–15, p. 289.

PUBLIC SPENDING

How much of our resources do we choose to allocate through government welfare programs? Since 1930 the proportion of the GNP dedicated to welfare spending has risen from about 4 percent to 16 percent. Welfare spending has more than doubled since 1947. Major categories of government aid include social insurance, public aid, medical care, education, housing, and veterans programs. (See Table 19.5).

Public welfare derives its economic justification from the fact that the underutilization of national resources on the one hand and the waste and exploita-

TABLE 19.4

Average Money Income of Families, 1947–1970.

							AVERAGE (MEAN) MONEY INCOME								
	1970	1969	1968	1967	1966	1965	1964	1963	1962	1961	1960	1959	1955	1950	1947
ALL RACES															
Total	*$11,106*	*$10,577*	*$9,670*	*$8,801*	*$8,395*	*$7,704*	*$7,336*	*$6,998*	*$6,670*	*$6,471*	*$6,227*	*$5,976*	*$5,010*	*$3,832*	*$3,566*
Lowest fifth	3,021	2,951	2,722	2,411	2,330	2,011	1,882	1,763	1,674	1,505	1,479	1,473	1,202	862	892
Second fifth	6,775	6,552	6,000	5,461	5,205	4,699	4,409	4,230	4,042	3,844	3,798	3,663	3,056	2,280	2,104
Third fifth	9,795	9,377	8,572	7,855	7,451	6,860	6,489	6,176	5,880	5,659	5,536	5,334	4,434	3,334	3,031
Fourth fifth	13,216	12,550	11,464	10,504	9,973	9,214	8,807	8,391	7,997	7,707	7,457	7,117	5,862	4,483	4,119
Highest fifth	22,723	21,461	19,587	17,769	17,017	15,739	15,094	14,426	13,757	13,644	12,868	12,293	10,471	8,200	7,703
Top 5 percent	34,584	32,894	30,190	26,773	26,125	23,929	23,372	22,156	20,917	21,497	19,789	19,040	16,834	13,259	12,481
WHITE															
Total	*11,495*	*10,953*	*10,002*	*9,116*	*8,726*	*8,021*	*7,625*	*7,306*	*6,962*	*6,741*	*6,483*	*6,235*	*5,228*	*3,991*	*3,717*
Lowest fifth	3,311	3,220	2,986	2,653	2,570	2,230	2,082	1,987	1,883	1,699	1,686	1,690	1,333	958	1,004
Second fifth	7,196	6,955	6,361	5,821	5,567	5,061	4,743	4,577	4,369	4,152	4,100	3,962	3,294	2,454	2,267
Third fifth	10,150	9,721	8,877	8,141	7,749	7,155	6,775	6,477	6,165	5,912	5,757	5,559	4,679	3,472	3,159
Fourth fifth	13,558	12,892	11,747	10,784	10,262	9,497	9,066	8,676	8,274	7,938	7,682	7,342	6,091	4,630	4,237
Highest fifth	23,266	21,977	20,039	18,182	17,478	16,162	15,456	14,813	14,119	14,004	13,190	12,620	10,744	8,441	7,917
Top 5 percent	35,520	33,823	31,046	27,439	26,928	24,641	23,958	22,809	21,499	22,124	20,370	19,628	17,462	13,729	12,935
NEGRO AND OTHER RACES															
Total	*7,759*	*7,255*	*6,689*	*5,985*	*5,450*	*4,827*	*4,726*	*4,259*	*3,948*	*3,937*	*3,873*	*3,463*	*2,890*	*2,128*	*2,015*
Lowest fifth	1,754	1,748	1,599	1,439	1,346	1,127	1,042	950	835	780	711	691	578	372	433
Second fifth	4,093	3,939	3,569	3,160	2,959	2,602	2,488	2,215	2,085	1,943	1,882	1,676	1,488	1,085	1,038
Third fifth	6,498	6,138	5,549	5,024	4,611	4,014	3,816	3,463	3,306	3,167	3,201	2,867	2,572	1,873	1,612
Fourth fifth	9,621	8,971	8,281	7,371	6,807	5,959	5,723	5,239	4,842	4,819	4,876	4,384	3,685	2,681	2,398
Highest fifth	16,829	15,482	14,448	12,934	11,527	10,434	10,560	9,432	8,670	8,974	8,695	7,695	6,127	4,639	4,594
Top 5 percent	23,913	22,012	20,602	18,530	15,925	14,597	15,955	14,055	12,484	13,276	12,533	10,825	8,265	7,065	6,932

Source: *Historical Statistics of the United States Colonial Times to 1970*, Series G 31–138, p. 292.

TABLE 19.5
Social Welfare Expenditures Under Public Programs, 1890–1970 (Millions of Dollars).

YEAR	Total	% of gross national product	Percentage of all government expenditures[1]	Per capita (actual prices)	Social Insurance Total	Old-age, survivors, disability, and health insurance	Railroad retirement	Public-employee retirement	Unemployment insurance and employment services	Railroad unemployment insurance	Railroad temporary disability insurance	State temporary disability insurance	Workmen's compensation	Public Aid Total	Public assistance	Health and Medical Programs
1890	318	2.4	38.0	—	—	—	—	—	—	—	—	—	—	a	—	18
1913	1,000	2.5	34.0	—	15	—	—	113	—	—	—	—	—	a	—	150
1929	3,921	3.9	36.3	32	342	—	—	113	—	—	—	—	229	60	60	351
1930	4,085	4.2	a	33	361	—	—	122	—	—	—	—	239	78	78	378
1931	4,201	5.1	a	33	368	—	—	136	—	—	—	—	233	164	145	406
1932	4,303	6.4	a	34	355	—	—	146	—	—	—	—	209	256	190	435
1933	4,462	7.9	a	35	344	—	—	164	—	—	—	—	180	689	344	418
1934	5,832	9.7	a	46	362	—	—	186	3	—	—	—	173	2,531	436	400
1935	6,548	9.5	48.6	51	406	—	—	209	9	—	—	—	188	2,998	624	427
1936	10,184	13.2	a	79	456	—	1	233	18	—	—	—	204	3,079	656	454
1937	7,858	9.1	a	60	545	20	6	244	45	—	—	—	231	3,436	780	500
1938	7,924	9.0	a	60	849	26	86	257	236	—	—	—	244	3,233	991	540
1939	9,213	10.5	a	70	1,181	37	110	270	517	2	—	—	247	4,230	1,102	575
1940	8,795	9.2	49.0	66	1,272	40	117	283	553	19	—	—	259	3,597	1,124	616
1941	8,953	8.0	a	66	1,330	91	125	298	507	21	—	—	288	3,524	1,108	724
1942	8,609	6.1	a	63	1,376	137	130	322	452	11	—	—	324	2,777	1,062	949
1943	8,283	4.7	a	60	1,259	177	134	305	281	4	—	1	357	1,550	1,012	1,886
1944	8,228	4.1	8.4	59	1,256	217	138	332	174	4	—	5	387	1,032	1,015	2,225
1945	9,205	4.4	a	65	1,409	267	145	355	217	4	—	5	417	1,031	1,029	2,354
1946	12,798	6.1	a	90	3,652	358	157	413	2,256	24	—	5	440	1,151	1,148	1,904
1947	17,337	7.8	a	119	4,160	466	178	510	2,454	51	—	16	485	1,442	1,442	1,367
1948	18,652	7.6	a	126	3,603	559	230	580	1,601	36	29	33	536	1,702	1,702	1,416
1949	21,165	8.1	a	140	4,186	661	288	649	1,876	51	32	50	580	2,089	2,089	1,753
1950	23,508	8.9	37.6	153	4,947	784	306	818	2,190	120	31	72	625	2,496	2,490	2,064

Year															
1951	24,055	7.7	*	154	4,772	1,569	322	920	1,063	28	29	143	699	2,592	2,585	2,783
1952	25,576	7.6	*	160	5,671	2,067	400	999	1,189	26	28	175	787	2,585	2,584	3,331
1953	27,045	7.5	*	167	6,607	2,717	467	1,124	1,143	58	45	198	856	2,728	2,728	3,190
1954	29,547	8.2	*	179	8,265	3,364	518	1,251	1,872	100	47	211	903	2,788	2,776	3,099
1955	32,640	8.6	32.7	195	9,835	4,436	556	1,389	2,081	159	54	218	943	3,003	2,941	3,103
1956	35,131	8.6	*	206	10,646	5,485	608	1,577	1,624	60	52	233	1,008	3,115	3,024	3,307
1957	39,350	9.1	*	227	12,472	6,666	686	1,785	1,842	88	52	270	1,084	3,309	3,231	3,776
1958	45,457	10.3	*	258	15,957	8,221	730	2,026	3,303	176	55	304	1,142	3,615	3,540	4,091
1959	49,821	10.6	*	278	18,287	9,616	790	2,343	3,731	200	57	327	1,223	3,998	3,891	4,401
1960	52,293	10.6	38.0	286	19,307	11,032	935	2,570	2,830	215	69	348	1,309	4,101	4,042	4,464
1961	58,236	11.5	39.3	314	22,365	12,161	996	2,870	4,280	213	58	385	1,401	4,444	4,301	4,927
1962	62,659	11.6	39.4	332	24,194	13,985	1,037	3,190	3,854	163	57	407	1,501	4,945	4,675	5,230
1963	66,766	11.6	39.5	349	25,614	15,345	1,077	3,569	3,391	123	53	444	1,612	5,296	5,029	5,594
1964	71,491	11.7	40.0	368	26,971	16,201	1,107	4,057	3,274	93	50	468	1,722	5,642	5,381	6,004
1965	77,175	11.8	42.4	391	28,123	16,998	1,128	4,529	3,003	77	46	484	1,859	6,283	5,875	6,246
1966	88,000	12.2	43.4	441	31,934	20,295	1,212	5,145	2,662	52	43	508	2,017	7,301	6,497	6,938
1967	99,710	12.9	42.4	494	37,339	24,581	1,278	5,904	2,752	38	38	530	2,217	8,811	7,832	7,628
1968	113,840	13.8	43.2	558	42,740	28,748	1,417	6,582	2,929	46	36	574	2,409	11,092	9,887	8,459
1969	127,149	14.1	44.7	617	48,772	33,389	1,551	7,494	2,947	44	58	648	2,641	13,439	11,926	9,006
1970	145,893	15.3	47.8	701	54,676	36,835	1,610	8,659	3,819	38	61	718	2,936	16,488	14,434	9,753

[1] Government expenditures exclude workmen's compensation and temporary disability insurance payments made through private insurance carriers and self-insurers, although these (payable under statutory provisions) are included as social welfare expenditures, series H 1.

[2] Not computed.

[3] "Public aid" included with "Other social welfare."

TABLE 19.5 (cont.)

YEAR	EDUCATION Total[a]	Elementary secondary	Higher education	Vocational and adult	VETERANS PROGRAMS Total	Pensions and compensation	Health and medical programs	Education	Life insurance	Welfare and other	HOUSING	OTHER SOCIAL WELFARE Total[b]	Vocational rehabilitation	Institutional care	Child nutrition
1890	**146**	—	—	—	**113**	—	—	—	—	—	—	**41**[3]	—	—	—
1913	**525**	—	—	—	**196**	—	—	—	—	—	—	**114**[3]	—	—	—
1929	**2,434**	2,216	182	35	**658**	435	51	—	136	36	—	**76**	2	75	—
1930	**2,523**	2,288	196	38	**668**	433	59	—	140	35	—	**78**	2	76	—
1931	**2,440**	2,218	180	41	**744**	504	68	—	138	34	—	**79**	2	77	—
1932	**2,352**	2,144	164	42	**825**	562	78	—	146	39	—	**81**	2	79	—
1933	**2,104**	1,911	153	39	**819**	565	70	—	145	39	—	**89**	2	87	—
1934	**1,914**	1,733	143	37	**530**	333	42	—	125	30	(Z)	**96**	2	94	—
1935	**2,008**	1,820	148	39	**597**	387	51	—	123	38	13	**99**	3	71	—
1936	**2,228**	2,021	155	51	**3,826**	411	55	—	118	3,241	42	**101**	3	72	(Z)
1937	**2,376**	2,144	178	54	**893**	409	62	—	113	308	3	**105**	4	66	(Z)
1938	**2,563**	2,297	199	67	**627**	415	65	—	108	40	4	**108**	4	56	1
1939	**2,504**	2,221	209	73	**606**	430	69	—	76	31	3	**114**	4	62	1
1940	**2,561**	2,267	218	75	**629**	443	76	—	77	33	4	**116**	4	62	4
1941	**2,617**	2,255	226	135	**613**	448	70	—	69	26	9	**136**	5	72	14
1942	**2,694**	2,263	251	179	**645**	446	72	—	60	67	14	**154**	5	78	23
1943	**2,793**	2,324	269	198	**623**	458	75	—	67	23	14	**159**	6	79	23
1944	**2,800**	2,392	262	144	**720**	513	87	—	94	26	13	**182**	7	86	34
1945	**3,076**	2,621	314	139	**1,126**	767	102	10	201	46	11	**198**	10	83	47
1946	**3,297**	2,834	364	98	**2,403**	1,280	244	369	376	135	159	**233**	14	98	57
1947	**4,089**	3,479	497	111	**5,683**	1,834	578	2,273	441	556	281	**316**	20	114	100
1948	**4,897**	4,130	634	132	**6,638**	1,911	564	2,630	433	1,101	27	**369**	25	126	117
1949	**5,807**	4,890	769	146	**6,927**	1,980	718	2,818	452	958	8	**396**	27	131	132
1950	**6,674**	5,596	915	161	**6,866**	2,092	748	2,692	476	858	15	**448**	30	146	160

1951	7,415	6,330	912	170	2,114	5,996	696	2,019	515	652	35	462	31	150	166
1952	8,246	7,115	948	179	2,184	5,256	767	1,381	555	370	37	451	33	144	154
1953	9,231	8,034	1,013	179	2,449	4,735	739	707	539	301	51	503	35	149	192
1954	10,084	8,816	1,082	184	2,507	4,631	740	596	538	249	67	612	37	203	240
1955	11,157	9,734	1,214	205	2,690	4,834	761	706	490	187	89	619	42	195	240
1956	12,154	10,579	1,350	222	2,805	5,061	760	810	476	210	112	735	56	232	294
1957	13,732	11,857	1,629	241	2,886	5,119	787	816	477	153	120	823	67	225	364
1958	15,313	13,151	1,893	261	3,127	5,427	844	737	490	229	134	920	78	332	325
1959	16,498	14,139	2,063	283	3,304	5,472	905	609	486	170	156	1,010	87	359	368
1960	17,626	15,109	2,191	298	3,403	5,479	954	410	494	219	177	1,139	96	421	399
1961	19,337	16,448	2,546	317	3,665	5,624	1,020	258	493	189	196	1,343	109	590	406
1962	21,005	17,744	2,878	354	3,749	5,654	1,041	157	499	207	217	1,415	129	550	464
1963	22,671	18,916	3,300	421	3,913	5,751	1,113	101	489	136	248	1,593	149	669	480
1964	24,989	20,688	3,740	513	4,002	5,862	1,173	70	472	146	278	1,746	182	693	522
1965	28,108	22,358	4,826	854	4,141	6,031	1,229	41	434	186	318	2,066	211	790	617
1966	32,825	25,566	6,023	1,108	4,409	6,358	1,285	34	442	187	335	2,309	299	737	537
1967	35,808	27,742	6,629	1,296	4,499	6,898	1,359	297	548	195	378	2,848	410	860	589
1968	40,590	31,675	7,328	1,435	4,644	7,247	1,439	466	504	194	428	3,285	466	888	706
1969	43,673	33,705	8,174	1,648	4,987	7,934	1,531	679	493	243	532	3,792	583	1,115	743
1970	50,848	38,632	9,914	2,146	5,394	9,018	1,784	1,019	502	320	701	4,409	704	1,307	896

Z Less than $500,000.

3 "Public aid" included with "Other social welfare."

3 Includes administrative costs and research, not shown separately.

4 Includes child welfare, anti-poverty programs, and miscellaneous social welfare expenditures, not shown separately.

9 Source: *Historical Statistics of the United States, Colonial Times to 1970*, Series H 1–31, p. 340.

tion of national resources on the other are inherently inefficient and retard national productivity and economic expansion. Full employment, for example, is regarded as an indicator of a healthy economy and a concomitant of maximum economic growth because it means that one of the basic economic resources—labor—is being fully utilized. Employment or unemployment indicators, however, lack sophistication because they do not reflect the quality or kind of labor quantified. Is it skilled or unskilled labor? Is the "contrived" employment of labor by government or the subsidization of the unemployed or aged a cost-efficient system? It could be, or it may not be. A common estimate is that less than one third of all welfare payments actually go to the poor. Indeed, social goals may be such that the cost-benefit computation does not matter. The point is that the goals of welfare economics are at least in part consistent with the idea of economic efficiency, collective security, and national economic growth.

Welfare economics, to a greater or lesser degree, have been a part of the American free-enterprise system from the beginning. It was early assumed that certain social activities could be administered better by the government than by private interests, the post office and education being the best examples. This idea has been enlarged upon in the twentieth century to the extent that government has been given a strong subordinate, and sometimes primary, position in research, transportation, energy, insurance, and health. Significantly, in no area of economic activity does government have exclusive jurisdiction. We need good quantitative and qualitative studies of the parallels in the growth of the public and private sectors of the economy relating to each of the above areas.

The vast expansion of public-welfare programs emerged from the social unrest of the 1960s, an unrest created by prosperity. Broad segments of the society experienced considerable improvement in personal well-being, but prosperity, or even comfort, seemed elusive for many. Social discontent also grew out of change itself—increasing mobility, depersonalization, and changing moral standards. The "hippie" movement attacked the "materialism" and conformity of the middle class while creating a "counter-culture" that stressed conforming to a "nonconformist" mold and seeking a new kind of leisure. The quality of life was everywhere being brought into question. It was a time when most Americans were under the age of twenty-five and when older Americans were living longer but potentially less secure lives. It seemed to be a time of almost unlimited opportunity, yet the opportunity somehow was never fully realized. It was the time for a "New Frontier" and a "Great Society."

THE NEW FRONTIER

Senator John F. Kennedy of Massachusetts won a closely contested race for the presidential nomination against Senator Lyndon B. Johnson of Texas before the Democratic National Convention in Chicago in 1960. Johnson accepted the

JOHN FITZGERALD KENNEDY *(1917–1963)*
President of the United States, 1961–1963.
Courtesy The White House.

Democratic vice-presidential nomination, and the Democrats won the November elections over Republican nominee Richard M. Nixon, who had completed two terms as Dwight Eisenhower's vice-president. Kennedy, the son of a Boston millionaire, was America's first Catholic president. He was a graduate of Harvard, had a distinguished naval record, and served in Congress from 1947 until his election. Lyndon B. Johnson was a self-made millionaire from the rural, agricultural Southwest. He attended a small college and taught school for a short time. He began his political career in the House of Representatives under the New Deal in 1937, and achieved a distinguished career in the Senate between 1949 and 1961. Despite their different backgrounds, Johnson and Kennedy shared similar political ideas.

The New Frontier must be viewed in the social and diplomatic context of the early 1960s. When Kennedy came to office, the nation was beset with sit-ins and marches as blacks protested discrimination in jobs, education, and services. Cuba was in the throes of revolution. The Soviet Union achieved humanity's first orbital flight, and East Germany began building the Berlin Wall. There were signs of a recession, and there was a national housing shortage. Kennedy wanted to improve the quality of life in America. He asked for and obtained from Congress extended minimum-wage and hour laws, broader Social Security coverage, and new public-housing assistance. He also sought federal aid for education, a federal medical-care program for the aged, tax reforms, more foreign aid (particularly for his Latin America Alliance for Progress program), higher farm prices supports, and an end to racial discrimination in employment.

But Kennedy had won the presidency by the smallest possible margin, and he failed to win congressional approval of his programs. Civil rights was nonetheless extended through the use of executive and judicial powers.

Kennedy forbade discrimination in the sale of housing financed or insured by federal agencies such as the Federal Housing Administration. He required equal employment opportunities in all offices of the federal government, and appointed members of many different minority groups to federal positions. Arthur Goldberg, of Jewish descent, was appointed secretary of labor, and later associate justice of the Supreme Court. John Gronowski, of Polish descent, became postmaster general. Robert Weaver, who became administrator of the Federal Housing and Home Finance Agency, was one of many black Americans appointed to high positions. Others included Thurgood Marshall (to the Circuit Court of Appeals) and Howard Jenkins, Jr. (to the National Labor Relations Board). Mexican-Americans and representatives of almost every other ethnic and minority group in America found at least a symbolic expression of new opportunity in the constitution of the New Frontier. But for most of the disadvantaged Americans the opportunities remained little more than symbolic. Discontent and even violent confrontation became more common.

In 1962 James Meredith was denied admission to the University of Mississippi. A federal court order required the university to admit him. The governor of Mississippi personally intervened to block Meredith's registration. Federal troops were sent in to force his admission. In Alabama federal power was also used to gain the admission of blacks to the state university. Over ten thousand civil rights demonstrations occurred in 1963 alone. Violence erupted in Birmingham, Savannah, Cambridge, Jackson, Detroit, Boston, and Chicago, among other places. Problems at home, however, were almost overshadowed by international confrontations.

Following the abortive Bay of Pigs invasion of Cuba by American-supported Cuban exiles, President Kennedy declared a blockade on Russian ships carrying missiles to Cuba and demanded the removal of Russian missiles and launching pads, threatening an immediate military attack by American forces. Russia withdrew in return for an American promise not to invade. Meanwhile, the Berlin Wall grew higher. France under Charles de Gualle withdrew from NATO, and President Kennedy increased American support for the government of South Vietnam, authorizing American bombing missions against targets inside that country.

At home, economic indicators began to improve as unemployment declined to 5.7 percent from the 1961 high of 6.7 percent, and President Kennedy began making plans for his reelection bid in 1964. He was assassinated in Dallas on November 22, 1963, before his New Frontier goals were achieved. Both foreign and domestic problems were as unresolved as they had been in 1960, but a new commitment to end poverty and improve the quality of life had gained popular credence.

THE GREAT SOCIETY

Elected President for a full term in 1964, Lyndon Johnson declared a "war on poverty." Congress approved an $11-billion tax cut to stimulate the economy. Aid to higher education was increased. Federal assistance was approved for mass transit in urban areas and for conservation of wilderness areas. The Elementary and Secondary Education Act of 1965 channeled new federal funds into public schools on the basis of the number of children from poor families in each school district. Another bill provided government rent subsidies to low-income families. Social Security benefits were raised, and Medicare became law. Federal expenditures rose sharply in the areas of defense, space research and technology, health, social security, housing, education, and interest on the public debt (Table 19.6).

TABLE 19.6

Selected Outlays of the Federal Government, 1961–1970 (Millions of Dollars).

YEAR	DEFENSE	SPACE	HEALTH	INCOME SECURITY	EDUCATION	COMMUNITY DEVELOPMENT AND HOUSING	INTEREST
1961	43,381	744	873	21,227	1,227	191	8,108
1962	51,097	1,257	1,130	22,530	1,406	589	8,321
1963	52,257	2,552	1,379	24,084	1,502	−880	9,215
1964	53,591	4,170	1,716	25,110	1,751	−185	9,810
1965	49,578	5,091	1,704	25,702	2,284	288	10,357
1966	56,785	5,933	2,509	29,016	4,258	2,644	11,285
1967	70,081	5,423	6,667	31,164	5,853	2,616	12,588
1968	80,517	4,721	9,608	34,108	6,739	4,076	13,744
1969	81,232	4,247	11,611	37,699	6,525	1,961	15,791
1970	80,295	3,749	12,907	43,790	7,289	2,965	18,312

Source: *Historical Statistics of the United States Colonial Times to 1970*, Series Y 472–87, p. 1116.

Despite a 100-percent increase in federal expenditures between 1961 and 1970 (see Table 19.7), economic expansion provided the revenues needed without any significant upward revision of tax rates. Furthermore, federal spending as a proportion of GNP rose only from 18.8 percent in 1961 to 20.7 percent in 1968. This suggests that the essential balance between private productivity and government spending had been preserved by growth in the economy. But because of the nature of the welfare programs and the political processes that implemented them, high-level government spending could not easily be reduced; indeed, it had built-in accelerators. Thus, continued economic growth became increasingly important to the sustenance of welfare spending. The alternatives would have been to reduce defense expenditures or to erode the savings and investment capacity of the economy by higher taxation or inflation.

TABLE 19.7

Federal Finances, 1961–1970 (Billions of Dollars).

YEAR	RECEIPTS	OUTLAYS	SURPLUS OR DEFICIT	TOTAL GROSS FEDERAL DEBT
1961	94.4	97.8	− 3.4	292.9
1962	99.7	106.8	− 7.1	303.3
1963	106.6	111.3	− 4.8	310.8
1964	112.7	118.6	− 5.9	316.8
1965	116.8	118.4	− 1.6	323.2
1966	130.9	134.7	− 3.8	329.5
1967	149.6	158.3	− 8.7	341.3
1968	153.7	178.8	−25.2	369.8
1969	187.8	184.5	3.2	367.1
1970	193.7	196.6	−2.8	382.6

Source: *Historical Statistics of the United States Colonial Times to 1970,* Series Y 339–42, p. 1105.

There is as yet no real measure to determine how much government welfare spending the economy can sustain without impairing autonomous investment and the ability of the economy to grow. It is likely that as government spending becomes a larger percentage of national productivity, the economy loses its resiliency and growth potential. The course of Great Britain in the postwar era would appear to be a case in point. It is also clear that some government spending has become a necessary adjunct of the free-enterprise system in order to promote its basic goals. What is perhaps more critical is that massive increases in military expenditures that might be occasioned by war, of which the Vietnam experience was a foretaste, must be superimposed on the welfare budget.

The Vietnam War was President Johnson's albatross, not only because it could not be brought to a successful conclusion but also because it forced the withdrawal of money from welfare on the one hand and from business on the other. The war was unpopular with both the business community and the economically disadvantaged, as well as with those who decried war on moral and philosophical grounds. Despite the considerable domestic accomplishments of Johnson, the war in Vietnam cost the Democratic Party the election of 1968. Whatever business advantages might have accrued from war contracts and higher employment (unemployment averaged 3.7 percent from 1966 to 1969) were eroded by rising inflation. Wholesale prices rose an average of 6 percent, with no regression in sight.

RICHARD NIXON AND THE ECONOMY

When Richard M. Nixon began his first term as president in 1969, the situation in Vietnam and the state of the domestic economy were deteriorating. Nixon had promised a disengagement in Vietnam, but new offensives staged to lay a foundation for American military withdrawal created fresh opposition to the war while failing to accomplish long-term military objectives. Inflation remained the most vexing domestic problem. Wholesale prices rose from an average base of 100 in 1967 to 119 in 1972, 135 in 1973, and 150 in 1974. The United States experienced a growing foreign-trade deficit. Monetary instability created confusion in world trade and banking as the dollar lost value in comparison with gold. Gold prices began to fluctuate widely in international markets, which further undermined dollar stability. Unemployment rolls jumped from less than three million in 1969 to almost five million in 1971. In August, 1971 President Nixon announced a ninety-day wage, price and rent freeze in an unprecedented effort to halt inflation. He also freed the dollar from its gold valuation and halted the conversion of foreign-held dollars into gold. In "Phase II" of the freeze, federal boards were appointed to monitor wage and price increases, and prices were to be gradually decontrolled. Inflation was in fact slowed, but unemployment remained high and American trade deficits continued to rise.

In December 1971 the president announced an 8.57-percent devaluation of the dollar, which raised the price of gold to $38 per ounce. By taking this step Nixon hoped to make the United States more competitive in world markets. At the same time, the president spearheaded a new diplomacy that sought "détente" with traditional cold-war antagonists in an effort to prevent the localized fighting in such areas as Vietnam, Pakistan, and the Middle East from spreading into global confrontations. Nixon visited Peking in February, 1972 and Moscow in May of that year. A direct result of the new détente policies seems to have been the conclusion of grain-sales agreements with Russia and Nixon's reelection to the presidency in 1972. American trade balances began to show signs of improvement, and in January, 1973 all mandatory wage and price controls were lifted. In February the United States announced a further 10-percent devaluation of the dollar and subsequently allowed the dollar to "float free" in international markets. Massive foreign grain sales triggered soaring domestic grain- and meat-price increases in early 1973. New ceilings were imposed on wholesale and retail meat prices in late March, and in June the administration imposed a new freeze on retail prices (excluding rent, interest, dividends, and raw agricultural products). As almost every business index began to show improvement in mid 1973, a total ban on oil exports to the United States by the OPEC (Arab oil-producing) nations created severe energy and monetary crises. On top of this, the Watergate investigations resulted in a severe lack of confidence in government and produced political crises that ended with the resignations of the vice-president and, on August 9, 1974, the president of the United States.

The administrations of Gerald R. Ford (1974–1976) and Jimmy Carter, who assumed office in 1976, inherited the now traditional problems of poverty, defense, and inflation coupled with the complex and critical energy crisis. The responses of Republican and Democratic administrations to these problems indicate the continuing growth in the responsibility and authority of government over economic affairs. The new phenomena of "stagflation"—rising unemployment coupled with inflation—seems to defy techniques of both the traditional and the "new" economics. Federal spending, it has become clear, does not assure economic growth or invariably rectify social problems. Quality, rather than quantity, is becoming a new guideline for government as well as for economic life. Despite very real economic problems, the American economy is intrinsically sound, and by virtue of its enormous capacities and technological expertise it retains an unprecedented opportunity for new growth and development. Because of the increasingly delicate balance between the public and private sectors of the political economy, the good management of the one and the sound growth of the other have an immediate reciprocal impact on the quality of life in America.

SUGGESTED READING

FUSFELD, DANIEL R., *The Age of the Economist,* 2nd ed. Glenview, Ill.: Scott, Foresman, 1972.

HEILBRONER, ROBERT L., *Business Civilization in Decline.* New York: Norton, 1976.

HUGHES, JONATHAN R., *The Government Habit: Economic Controls from Colonial Times to the Present.* New York: Basic Books, 1977.

HUGHES, JONATHAN R., *The Vital Few: American Economic Progress and Its Protagonists.* Boston: Houghton Mifflin, 1965.

MCCLELLAND, DAVID C., *The Achieving Society.* Princeton, N.J.: Van Nostrand, 1961.

NELSON, KEITH L., ed., *The Impact of War on American Life; The Twentieth Century Experience.* New York: Holt, Rinehart & Winston, 1971.

NORTH, DOUGLASS C., *Growth and Welfare in the American Past,* 2nd ed. Englewood Cliffs, N.J.: Prentice-Hall, 1974.

ROWEN, H., *The Free Enterprisers: Kennedy, Johnson and the Business Establishment.* New York: Putnam's, 1964.

SCHLESINGER, ARTHUR M., Jr., *A Thousand Days.* Boston: Houghton Mifflin, 1965.

ULMER, MELVILLE J., *The Welfare State, U.S.A.* Boston: Houghton Mifflin, 1969.

THE PRESENT
IN PERSPECTIVE

_____ chapter XX __

A NEW MIX OF PROBLEMS

There are problems with the American free-enterprise system. This is nothing new. The era of constitution making, the "Jeffersonian Revolution of 1800," the time of Jackson and the Bank War, the Civil War, the Populist era, and the Great Depression were all periods in which the future of the free-enterprise system rested upon a resolution of the problems of the day. What is new about the present crises are the kinds and peculiar mix of problems—poverty, war, inflation, equal rights, human rights, energy, ecology, environment, quality of life, welfare, emerging nations, black awareness, women's liberation, unemployment, taxation, urban blight, and regimentation.

The quest for economic growth, for more goods and services, has impelled the growth of both government and business. The size and collective authority of the government and business, which have become necessary for the sustenance of _people,_ simultaneously threaten the integrity, individuality, and liberty of the _person._ Growth has occurred at the expense of natural resources and has contributed to increasing pollution of the environment. Growth has brought social change and new social tensions and has sometimes aggravated social inequities. Expansion, the rise of a sophisticated business-industrial society, and welfare have in turn created a governmental authority and a public expense that erode private rights in property.

FREE ENTERPRISE: THE LONG RUN

The resolution of our immediate problems affects the course of free enterprise in the long term. Prognostications about the future of the system as we know it today range from bleak to despairing; few are optimistic. The Cassandras are evident on the left, on the right, and in the center of the philosophical spectrum. One extreme holds basically that we are destroying our free-enterprise system, and the other that we should do this. Robert Heilbroner's little fable of "Conservative Smith" and "Radical Smith" illustrates the concern.

In Washington, D.C., businessman Conservative Smith learns that a proposed merger of his company with another will be forbidden by government ruling. He telephones the news to his home office at rates set by a government agency and returns home in an airplane whose route, maintenance, and equipment, operating procedures, and fares have all been government-determined.

> Home again, he relaxes in his apartment whose construction was partly subsidized by Government, and idly watches a Government-licensed television station dutifully complying with a Government regulation to devote a portion of prime time to public-interest broadcasting. His son, who attends a Government-supported university, comes in to borrow the family's car, which has been designed to meet certain government specifications. Before retiring, Smith looks over his mail, which includes a bill from the Government for Social Security payments he must make for his maid. Switching off the lights, for which he has been paying at Government-established rates, he settles into his bed, from whose mattress dangles the Government-decreed tag ("Do Not Remove Under Penalty of Law"), and as he finally dozes off, he asks himself: "Is this still capitalism? God, no!"[1]

Wage earner Radical Smith, on the other hand, has just arrived in Washington aboard Amtrack, a railroad that government has taken over in an attempt to shore up a sagging industry. He is unimpressed, and perhaps surprised, when he hears that Conservative Smith is unable to effect a merger, knowing that the top 100 corporations own a larger percentage of total corporate assets than the top 200 industrial firms only twenty years before. As he travels home aboard the airline that is subject to government regulations concerning competition, he reflects that his low-income housing is terribly inadequate and expensive and that he pays a far larger proportion of his income in taxes than do the wealthiest one percent of taxpayers. Moreover, his maid earns less than enough to live on, and the government assures the utility company a ten-percent profit margin. As Radical Smith dozes off he asks: "Is this capitalism? Of course, what else?"[2]

The radical view holds essentially that capitalist achievement has been at the "cost of terrible distortions to the human spirit and to nature, and its products are as unevenly distributed as its freedoms." The future of America lies in the achievement of a domestic socialist society. The past has been a "twisted dream."[3] The conservative position holds that freedom and free enterprise, which includes the right of the individual to own property and the exclusive right to manage that property, are inseparable. "Never was there a place where free enterprise was destroyed and human freedom was not destroyed also."[4]

JOSEPH SCHUMPETER

Paradoxically, according to Joseph Schumpeter, the crisis of the free-enterprise system is attributable to its successes rather than its failures. The economic and social foundations of capitalism are beginning to crumble for three reasons: first, the obsolescence of the entrepreneurial function; second, the destruction of protecting political strata; and third, the destruction of the institutional framework of capitalist society.

The entrepreneurial function, that of innovation, has been reduced to routine. Technological progress, says Schumpeter, is the business of teams of specialists who turn out what is required and make it work in predictable ways. Economic progress tends to become depersonalized and automatized. Walter W. Rostow's "take-off" theory, for example, envisions a self-sustained and institutionalized economic growth that is inherently beneficial.[5] But Schumpeter suspects that "capitalist enterprise, by its very achievements, tends to automatize progress . . . " and so "make itself superfluous." He suspects that the "true pacemakers of socialism were not the intellectuals and agitators who preached it but the Vanderbilts, Carnegies and Rockefellers." Schumpeter believes that the consolidation of business, and even the corporate shareholding system, which exemplifies dematerialized, "defunctionalized," and absentee ownership, undermine the moral allegiance to private property. Moreover, high taxation, farm and labor legislation, and government regulation destroy the vital institutions of capitalism—the free market and private control over private property. The result, Schumpeter concludes, is capitalism kept alive in an oxygen tent.[6]

ROBERT HEILBRONER

Robert L. Heilbroner views the future of capitalism in much the same context as Schumpeter, but attributes the crisis to a weakening of the spirit and values of capitalist society rather than to structural or institutional changes. Given the rate of expansion of industrial growth, he believes that modern industrial societies will deplete available resources and pollute the environment (within one century) to the extent that growth can no longer be sustained. The cessation of growth will be accompanied by a diminution or halt in the "consuming passion of a business civilization for private expansion." The cessation of growth will place rights in property in a less defensible position as the claims of the poor concentrate more heavily on the existing wealth and fail to be placated by projections of future wealth. The threatened exhaustion of resources necessitates planning for resource allocation and utilization, and the "plannification of capitalism" is a source of its extinction. Planning by central authority is incompatible with the prerogatives of private property and the mechanics of the marketplace. Moreover, "the defense of capitalism has always rested on the social contentment that was presumed to result from the release of mankind from its historic condition of material insufficiency."[7] When capitalism can no longer presume to fulfill this obligation it can no longer sustain respect or allegiance. Where the human appetite for material growth is suppressed the individual must turn to other value systems for satisfaction.[8]

Heilbroner's projections invite one quick afterthought. There is no more certainty that the prospect of resource exhaustion would turn allegiance away from the business interests that no longer seem able to deliver the "goods," than it might undermine allegiance to the welfare state, whether of communist, socialist, or capitalist origins, which has made an even greater commitment and promise to raise the standard of living and improve social welfare. Might society be persuaded that government has adversely interfered with the "normal" processes of technological development and economic growth? And might not government itself, urged by popular sanction, the need for self-preservation, and some acknowledged inability by the "planners" to satisfy human needs, be willing, if not eager, to delegate greater rather than less authority over resource allocation to private enterprise and the free market? President Carter's idle comment that democracies should not demonstrate too often their own ineffectualness deserves notice. It is feasible to imagine that the next century will experience a rededication to the institutions and values of free enterprise because of the inability of governments of all ideologies to satisfy human needs.

JOHN K. GALBRAITH

Most projections presume that government and business conjoined are incompatible with free enterprise. But over the long run public goals and human aspirations have not been incompatible with government or with the industrial system. The state and business are part of a much larger complex, both have changed, and the relationships between them have changed to accord with human aspirations, values, and necessities. The mature corporation, for example, has within the lifetime of most Americans now living become a part of the larger administrative complex associated with the state: "The control by the mature corporation over its prices, its influence on consumer behavior, the euthanasia of stockholders' power, the regulation by the state of aggregate demand, the effort to stabilize prices and wages, the role of publicly supported research and development, the role of military, space and related procurement, the influence of the firm on these government activities and the modern role of education are, more or less, accepted facts of life."[9] "If economic goals," writes Galbraith, "are the only goals of society, it is natural that the industrial system should dominate the state and the state should serve its end."[10] The problem that Galbraith perceives is not that government and business are in mortal conflict, but rather that they are partners. As long as this partnership is dedicated exclusively to economic, welfare, and growth goals, other human goals and values, such as personal liberty, will be subordinated. The salvation of the system lies, however, in the creation of a community that is sufficiently affluent to no longer have to equate human progress with economic survival and growth. The industrial system has created a society that can reject the traditional view of social purpose to the end that that industrial system may be acknowledged as a technical adjunct of society whose role is simply to provide "convenient goods and services in adequate volume."[11] Free enterprise, in other words, requires not only production but liberty and freedom of choice. The industrial system has made this more attainable, not less.

THE MULTINATIONAL CORPORATION

A futuristic projection, if not an aberration of Galbraith's new industrial state, envisions a world in which the role of the state has been subordinated, if not displaced, by the multinational corporation (MNC). Science fiction writers, such as George Orwell in *1984*, and some serious economists consider the development of MNC as variously a threat to or a promise for free enterprise. The MNC could become so big and powerful that it no longer needs the state and is indeed hampered by the state. It may cut the national governments loose, or subordinate them as well as its employees and customers to its own goals. It may become the exclusive organizing structure of human society. It is not too difficult to imagine, as Orwell did, that such an arrangement would mean the obliteration of freedom.

Most economists doubt that the MNC could become a viable means of organizing society. There is little evidence that the MNC has displaced the authority of government. There is more evidence that government has responded to the needs of the MNC by enlarging its protective umbrella. Thus, colonialism, "dollar diplomacy," and more recently "collective government" through organizations such as the Common Market and even OPEC provided a political framework for international business interests. Rather than displacing the nation-state, the MNC may provide the incentive to international political collaboration, if not federal regional or world government.

The futuristic implications of the MNC aside, it does exist and it exerts a strong influence on human life-styles in every part of the world, especially our own. The simple truth is that the American economy is no longer a detached national economy but a vital part of an adolescent world economy. American business has indeed become the world's business. The world views American values largely through the image of the MNC. That view portrays a part, but not the whole, of what the free-enterprise system is all about.

Whatever their size and dimensions, and whatever their relationships, government and business are social institutions formulated to best serve the needs of people. People, as we in America understand them, require sustenance and liberty. The historic role of the American political economy is to provide both, as far as is humanly possible.

Notes

[1]Robert L. Heilbroner, *Business Civilization in Decline* (New York: Norton, 1976), p. 19.

[2]*Ibid.*, p. 21.

[3]Douglas F. Dowd, *The Twisted Dream: Capitalist Development in the United States Since 1776* (Cambridge, Mass.: Winthrop, 1974), xiv.

[4]Milton Friedman, "The Future of Capitalism," Address at Texas A&M University, February 13, 1975.

[5]See Walter W. Rostow, "The Take-Off into Self-Sustained Economic Growth," *Economic Journal,* 66 (March 1956), 25–48.

[6]Joseph Schumpeter, *Capitalism, Socialism and Democracy,* 2nd ed. (New York: Harper & Row, 1947), 59–142.

[7]Heilbroner, *Business Civilization in Decline,* p. 112.

[8]See Heilbroner, *Business Civilization in Decline,* pp. 101–24.

[9]John Kenneth Galbraith, *The New Industrial State* (Boston: Houghton Mifflin, 1967), pp. 394–95.

[10]*Ibid.*, p. 399.

[11]See Galbraith, *The New Industrial State,* pp. 388–99.

SUGGESTED READING

DOWD, DOUGLAS F., *The Twisted Dream: Capitalist Development in the United States Since 1776*. Cambridge, Mass.: Winthrop, 1974.

GALBRAITH, JOHN KENNETH, *Economic Development*. Boston: Houghton Mifflin, 1964.

GALBRAITH, JOHN KENNETH, *The Affluent Society*. Boston: Houghton Mifflin, 1958.

GALBRAITH, JOHN KENNETH, *The New Industrial State*. Boston: Houghton Mifflin, 1967.

HEILBRONER, ROBERT L. *Business Civilization in Decline*. New York: Norton, 1976.

MACRAE, NORMAN, *America's Third Century*. New York: Harcourt, Brace & Jovanovich, 1976.

PEJOVICH, SVETOZAR, ed. *Governmental Controls and the Free Market: The U.S. Economy in the 1970's*. College Station, Texas: Texas A&M University Press, 1976.

RIESMAN, DAVID, *The Lonely Crowd.* New Haven: Yale University Press, 1961.

SCHUMPETER, JOSEPH, *Capitalism, Socialism and Democracy,* 2nd ed. New York: Harper & Row, 1947.

TOFFLER, ALVIN, *Future Shock.* New York: Random House, 1970.

INDEX

Missouri Compromise (1850), 111
Mitchell, Charles, 240
Mitchell, John, 216
Mobile, Alabama, 48
Molasses Act (1733), 44, 46
Molly Maguires, 176
Money:
    bimetallism, 130-2
    bullion, 130-2
    currency in circulation, 1863-76, *table* 130
    discussed, 130-2
    monopoly, 219
    (*See also* Greenbacks, Banking)
Monopoly, 284-5
Monroe, James, 73
Montgomery Ward, 153
Morgan, Edmund S., *n* 68
Morgan, John Pierpont, 149, 160-1, 216
Morison, Samuel Eliot, *n* 18
Morrill Land-Grant College Act, 92, 191
Morris, Robert, 55
Mowry, George E., *n* 228, *n* 229
Mueller, Charles F., 283-4
Mueller, Willard P., *n* 296
Multinational corporation (MNC), 321-2
Mumford, Lewis, 194-5, *n* 211, *n* 212
Munn v. *Illinois* (1877), 189

Namier, Sir Lewis, 46
Nash, Gerald D., *n* 262
Nashville, Tennessee, 59
Natchez, Mississippi, 48
National Association of Manufacturers, 185
National Bank Act:
    1863, 85, 128
    1865, 128
National Farmers' Alliance (See Farmers' Alliance)
National Forest Service, 218
National Grange of the Patrons of Husbandry
    (See Grange)
National Industrial Recovery Act (NIRA, 1933),
    254-5
National Labor Relations Act (NLRA, 1935),
    257
National Labor Union, 181-2
    universal strike, 183
Nationalism:
    and capitalism, 13-14
Navigation Acts, 42-5
Negro Alliance, 190
Nelson, Keith L., *n* 316
Nettels, Curtis, *n* 211
Neutrality Act (1937), 264
Nevins, Allan, 156, *n* 162
New Deal, 247-62
    agricultural agencies, 1933-39, 253-4

New Deal *(cont'd.)*
    banking, 248-9
    labor, 258-9
    legislation, 249-57
New England system, 31
Newfoundland, 21, 48
New Freedom, 219-221
New Frontier, 16, 310-12
New Hampshire, 21
"New immigration," 196
New Nationalism, 217-18
New Orleans, Louisiana, 21
    early settlement, 207-8
    immigration, 208-9
    port, 209
"New South," 122, 134
New York City, 21
    ethnic groups, 206
    manufacturing, 205
    trade, 204-5
New York Stock Exchange, 132, 204, 236-41
Nixon, Richard M., 311, 314-16
NLRB v. *Jones & Laughlin Steel Corporation*
    (1937), 258
Norris-LaGuardia Act (1932), 258
North American Kerosene Gas Light Company,
    156
North Atlantic Treaty Organization (NATO),
    272
North Carolina, 21
North, Douglass C., *n* 19, 99, *n* 104, 141, *n* 316
North, Simeon, 80
Northern Securities Company, 216
Northwest Ordinance (1787), 60-1, 91
Northwest territory, 60
Nova Scotia, 48
Nugent, Walter T. K., *n* 137
Nullification Ordinance (1832), 106

Ocala demands, 190-1
Occidental Petroleum, 293
O'Connor, Thomas, H., *n* 120
Office of Price Administration (OPA), 265-7
Office of War Mobilization, 265
Ohio Company, 48, 59-60
Ohio valley, 48, 58-9
Olds, Ransom, 222-3
O'Neill, William L., *n* 229
Organization of Petroleum Exporting Countries
    (OPEC), 282, 315
Orwell, George, 321
Ostend Manifesto (1854), 110
Osterweis, Rollin G., *n* 119, *n* 120
Ousley, Frank Lawrence, *n* 119, *n* 120

Pacific coast, 24
Packing industry, 207